Readings from LEFT to RIGHT

Readings from

Victor E. Amend /

New York

LEFT to RIGHT

Leo T. Hendrick, eds.

[FP] The Free Press

Collier-Macmillan Canada, Ltd., Toronto, Ontario

Library of Congress Catalog Card Number: 77–93111

printing number
1   2   3   4   5   6   7   8   9   10

Contents

Contents by Rhetorical Topics

Preface

Upon reflection, one realizes that the brilliant aphorism of Santayana can be accepted only with reservations: that the *Left* is the side of the heart; the *Right* is the side of the liver. In carefully selected contexts—and those selected from the distant past (say, the death of Socrates, the Scopes "Monkey Trial," or child labor in the coal mines)—the identification of *Left* and *Right* seems clear and valid. However, other contexts (and especially current ones) do not lend themselves to so sharp a perspective. Moreover, the two terms do not properly characterize whole movements (for example, the French Revolution developed from Left to Right), complex institutions (for example, the British government supports both socialized medicine and the monarchy), nor even persons (many college teachers are political liberals, but educational conservatives).

Notwithstanding these reservations, the concepts *Left* and *Right* are invaluable tools of thought; it is useful, sometimes even necessary, to see in terms of contrarieties, to define ideas by their opposites. Academic experience inevitably supplies these contrarieties; and classroom discussion, almost by definition, thrives on them. But there is, too, a *Middle* ground, where some minds rest or find virtue—a position as old as Aristotle. And the thinkers of the middle ground find neither Left nor Right congenial. They often contradict both extremes and thus serve to define them more sharply by asserting how these go too far. In short, then, the Left, the Middle, and the Right—when examined concomitantly—help to illumine one another, to set one another in relief.

It is the aim of the following groups of readings to present, as it were, three minds in collision. It is by no means the intention that readers should marshal themselves consistently either Left, or Right, or Middle, though such, no doubt, will occasionally happen.

[xi]

Instead, it is an end in itself that educated students should entertain contradictory ideas at the same time. These ideas, however,
ought to be focused on explicit issues; and they ought to be
presented by thoughtful and capable writers. Without, therefore,
going beyond compatible depths into ultimate definitions of *Left,
Middle,* and *Right,* the editors present simply a series of confronta-
tions of first-rate thinkers (attacking, explaining, defending—
orthodoxy, convention, tradition, and the past, or whatever) on
certain important questions in the spheres of politics, religion,
philosophy, education, literature, and science.

The main purpose of the book, of course, is to stimulate
discussion; and this discussion, in turn, should provide topics for
composition: The editors include, after each essay, what they
hope are provocative questions on the content and fruitful subjects
for student writing. In addition, since all of the essays are by
writers of established reputation, they may serve as models of
stylistic and rhetorical excellence. And to this end, the editors
also include questions bearing on analysis of style and rhetoric.

The editors wish to thank their respective institutions, Butler
University and Olivet College, for released time in which to work
on this book. Finally, the editors would be less than grateful not
to mention their indebtedness to Professors Richard Cauger and
Lewis Rosenthal, whose casual remarks and wit sparked the
inspiration for this book.

V. E. A.

L. T. H.

1 Civil Rights

History will no doubt record "Civil Rights" as one of the great problems confronted by civilization in the twentieth century. Men of both good and ill will throughout the world are engaged in advancing or preserving what they conceive to be their "rights." Though the problem emerges on all continents and involves all races, the United States may be considered the forcing ground, while the rights of black and white provide the dominant collision. Historically, the United States has identified with "freedom," "equality," "opportunity," "representative government," and like abstract values. Yet clearly these values have never been equitably interpreted nor universally applied. No man of sense will argue that the ideal has been achieved; few men will argue that it ought not to be achieved.

The question seems largely one of strategy for attaining the just society: Specifically, when and how shall Negroes, as well as whites, share what we say belongs to all men? Representative answers (that is, Left, Middle, and Right) to the questions when and how appear in the three following selections. Stokely Carmichael, a young and vigorous Negro radical, says: now, by means of black power; the Reverend Martin Luther King, a recent martyr for his cause, says: eventually, through faith in the Christian imperatives of brotherhood and nonviolence; and William F. Buckley, a recurring voice for conservatism in all areas, says: gradually, as the present trend continues, but without federal intervention.

STOKELY CARMICHAEL

Power and Racism

One of the tragedies of the struggle against racism is that up to now there has been no national organization which could speak to the growing militancy of young black people in the urban ghetto. There has been only a civil rights movement, whose tone of voice was adapted to an audience of liberal whites. It served as a sort of buffer zone between them and angry young blacks. None of its so-called leaders could go into a rioting community and be listened to. In a sense, I blame ourselves—together with the mass media—for what has happened in Watts, Harlem, Chicago, Cleveland, Omaha. Each time the people in those cities saw Martin Luther King get slapped, they became angry; when they saw four little black girls bombed to death, they were angrier; and when nothing happened, they were steaming. We had nothing to offer that they could see, except to go out and be beaten again. We helped to build their frustration.

For too many years, black Americans marched and had their heads broken and got shot. They were saying to the country, "Look, you guys are supposed to be nice guys and we are only going to do what we are supposed to do—why do you beat us up, why don't you give us what we ask, why don't you straighten yourselves out?" After years of this, we are at almost the same point—because we demonstrated from a position of weakness. We cannot be expected any longer to march and have our heads broken in order to say to whites: come on, you're nice guys. For you are not nice guys. We have found you out.

An organization which claims to speak for the needs of a community—as does that Student Nonviolent Coordinating Com-

From The New York Review, *Vol. 7 (September 22, 1966).* *Reprinted by permission of the Student Nonviolent Coordinating Committee.*

mittee—must speak in the tone of that community, not as somebody else's buffer zone. This is the significance of black power as
a slogan. For once, black people are going to use the words they
want to use—not just the words whites want to hear. And they
will do this no matter how often the press tries to stop the use
of the slogan by equating it with racism or separatism.

An organization which claims to be working for the needs of
a community—as SNCC does—must work to provide that community with a position of strength from which to make its voice
heard. This is the significance of black power beyond the slogan.

Black power can be clearly defined for those who do not attach
the fears of white America to their questions about it. We should
begin with the basic fact that black Americans have two problems: they are poor and they are black. All other problems arise
from this two-sided reality: lack of education, the so-called
apathy of black men. Any program to end racism must address
itself to that double reality.

Almost from its beginning, SNCC sought to address itself to
both conditions with a program aimed at winning political
power for impoverished Southern blacks. We had to begin with
politics because black Americans are a propertyless people in a
country where property is valued above all. We had to work for
power, because this country does not function by morality, love,
and nonviolence, but by power. Thus we determined to win
political power, with the idea of moving on from there into
activity that would have economic effects. With power, the
masses could *make or participate in making* the decisions which
govern their destinies, and thus create basic change in their day-
to-day lives.

But if political power seemed to be the key to self-determination, it was also obvious that the key had been thrown down a
deep well many years earlier. Disenfranchisement, maintained
by racist terror, made it impossible to talk about organizing for
political power in 1960. The right to vote had to be won, and

SNCC workers devoted their energies to this from 1961 to 1965. They set up voter registration drives in the Deep South. They created pressure for the vote by holding mock elections in Mississippi in 1963 and by helping to establish the Mississippi Freedom Democratic Party (MFDP) in 1964. That struggle was eased, though not won, with the passage of the 1965 Voting Rights Act. SNCC workers could then address themselves to the question: "Who can we vote for, to have our needs met—how do we make our vote meaningful?"

SNCC had already gone to Atlantic City for recognition of the Mississippi Freedom Democratic Party by the Democratic convention and been rejected; it had gone with the MFDP to Washington for recognition by Congress and been rejected. In Arkansas, SNCC helped thirty Negroes to run for School Board elections; all but one were defeated, and there was evidence of fraud and intimidation sufficient to cause their defeat. In Atlanta, Julian Bond ran for the state legislature and was elected—twice—and unseated—twice. In several states, black farmers ran in elections for agricultural committees which make crucial decisions concerning land use, loans, etc. Although they won places on a number of committees, they never gained the majorities needed to control them.

All of the efforts were attempts to win black power. Then, in Alabama, the opportunity came to see how blacks could be organized on an independent party basis. An unusual Alabama law provides that any group of citizens can nominate candidates for county office and, if they win 20 per cent of the vote, may be recognized as a county political party. The same then applies on a state level. SNCC went to organize in several counties such as Lowndes, where black people—who form 80 per cent of the population and have an average annual income of $943—felt they could accomplish nothing within the framework of the Alabama Democratic Party because of its racism and because the qualifying fee for this year's elections was raised from $50 to $500 in order to prevent most Negroes from becoming candidates. On May 3, five new county "freedom organizations" convened and nominated candidates for the offices of sheriff, tax assessor, members of the school boards. These men and women are up for election in November—if they live until then. Their ballot symbol is the black panther: a bold, beautiful animal, representing the strength and dignity of black demands today. A man needs a black panther on his side when he and his family must endure—as hundreds of Alabamians have endured—loss of job, eviction, starvation, and sometimes death, for political activity. He may also need a gun and SNCC reaffirms the right of black men everywhere to defend themselves when threatened or attacked. As for initiating the use of violence, we hope that such programs as ours will make that unnecessary; but it is not for us to tell black communities whether they can or cannot use any particular form of action to resolve their problems. Responsibility for the use of violence by black men, whether in self-defense or initiated by them, lies with the white community.

This is the specific historical experience from which SNCC's call for "black power" emerged on the Mississippi march last July. But the concept of "black power" is not a recent or isolated phenomenon: It has grown out of the ferment of agitation and activity by different people and organizations in many black communities over the years. Our last year of work in Alabama added a new concrete possibility. In Lowndes County, for example, black power will mean that if a Negro is elected sheriff, he can end police brutality. If a black man is elected tax assessor, he can collect and channel funds for the building of better roads and schools serving black people—thus advancing the move from political power into the economic arena. In such areas as Lowndes, where black men have a majority, they will attempt to use it to exercise control. This is what they seek: control. Where Negroes lack a majority, black power means proper representation and sharing of control. It means the creation of power bases from which black people can work to change statewide or nationwide patterns of oppression through pressure from strength—instead of weakness. Politically, black power means what it has always meant to SNCC: the coming-together of black people to elect representatives and *to force those representatives to speak to their needs.* It does not mean merely putting black faces into office. A man or woman who is black and from the slums cannot be automatically expected to speak to the needs of black people. Most of the black politicians we see around the country today are not what SNCC means by black power. The power must be that of a community, and emanate from there.

SNCC today is working in both North and South on programs of voter registration and independent political organizing. In some places, such as Alabama, Los Angeles, New York, Philadelphia, and New Jersey, independent organizing under the black panther symbol is in progress. The creation of a national "black panther party" must come about; it will take time to build, and it is much too early to predict its success. We have no infallible master plan and we make no claim to exclusive knowledge of how to end racism; different groups will work in their own different ways. SNCC cannot spell out the full logistics of self-determination but it can address itself to the problem by helping black communities define their needs, realize their strength, and go into action along a variety of lines which they must choose for themselves. Without knowing all the answers, it can address itself to the basic problem of poverty, to the fact that in Lowndes County, 86 white families own 90 per cent of the land. What are black people in that county going to do for jobs, where are they going to get money? There must be reallocation of land, of money.

Ultimately, the economic foundations of this country must be shaken if black people are to control their lives. The colonies of the United States—and this includes the black ghettoes within its borders, north and south—must be liberated. For a century, this nation has been like an octopus of exploitation, its tentacles stretching from Mississippi and Harlem to South America, the Middle East, southern Africa, and Vietnam; the form of exploitation varies from area to area but the essential result has been the same—a powerful few have been maintained and enriched at the expense of the poor and voiceless colored masses. This pattern must be broken. As its grip loosens here and there around the world, the hopes of black Americans become more realistic. For racism to die, a totally different America must be born.

This is what the white society does not wish to face; this is why that society prefers to talk about integration. But integration speaks not at all to the problem of poverty, only to the problem of blackness. Integration today means the man who "makes it," leaving his black brothers behind in the ghetto as fast as his new sports car will take him. It has no relevance to the Harlem wino or to the cottonpicker making three dollars a day. As a lady I know in Alabama once said, "The food that Ralph Bunche eats doesn't fill my stomach."

Integration, moreover, speaks to the problem of blackness in a despicable way. As a goal, it has been based on complete acceptance of the fact that *in order to have* a decent house or education, blacks must move into a white neighborhood or send their children to a white school. This reinforces, among both black and white, the idea that "white" is automatically better and "black" is by definition inferior. This is why integration is a subterfuge for the maintenance of white supremacy. It allows the nation to focus on a handful of Southern children who get into white schools, at great price, and to ignore the 94 per cent who are left behind in unimproved all-black schools. Such situations will not change until black people have power—to control their own school boards, in this case. Then Negroes become equal in a way that means something, and integration ceases to be a one-way street. Then integration doesn't mean draining skills and energies from the ghetto into white neighborhoods;

then it can mean white people moving from Beverly Hills into Watts, white people joining the Lowndes County Freedom Organization. Then integration becomes relevant.

Last April, before the furor over black power, Christopher Jencks wrote in a *New Republic* article on white Mississippi's manipulation of the anti-poverty program:

The war on poverty has been predicated on the notion that there is such a thing as *a community* which can be defined geographically and mobilized for a collective effort to help the poor. This theory has no relationship to reality in the Deep South. In every Mississippi county there are *two* communities. Despite all the pious platitudes of the moderates on both sides, these two communities habitually see their interests in terms of conflict rather than cooperation. Only when the Negro community can muster enough political, economic and professional strength to compete on somewhat equal terms, will Negroes believe in the possibility of true cooperation and whites accept its necessity. En route to integration, the Negro community needs to develop greater independence—a chance to run its own affairs and not cave in whenever "the man" barks . . . Or so it seems to me, and to most of the knowledgeable people with whom I talked in Mississippi. To OEO, this judgment may sound like black nationalism . . .

Mr. Jencks, a white reporter, perceived the reason why America's anti-poverty program has been a sick farce in both North and South. In the South, it is clearly racism which prevents the poor from running their own programs; in the North, it more often seems to be politicking and bureaucracy. But the results are not so different: In the North, non-whites make up 42 per cent of all families in metropolitan "poverty areas" and only 6 per cent of families in areas classified as not poor. SNCC has been working with local residents in Arkansas, Alabama, and Mississippi to achieve control by the poor of the program and its funds; it has also been working with groups in the North, and the struggle is no less difficult. Behind it all is a federal government which cares far more about winning the war on the Vietnamese than the war on poverty; which has put the poverty program in the hands of self-serving politicians and bureaucrats rather than the poor themselves; which is unwilling to curb the misuse of white power but quick to condemn black power.

To most whites, black power seems to mean that the Mau Mau are coming to the suburbs at night. The Mau Mau are coming, and whites must stop them. Articles appear about plots to "get Whitey," creating an atmosphere in which "law and order must be maintained." Once again, responsibility is shifted from the oppressor to the oppressed. Other whites chide, "Don't forget— you're only 10 per cent of the population; if you get too smart, we'll wipe you out." If they are liberals, they complain, "What about me?—don't you want my help any more?" These are people supposedly concerned about black Americans, but today they think first of themselves, of their feelings of rejection. Or they admonish, "you can't get anywhere without coalitions," without considering the problems of coalition with whom?; on what terms? (coalescing from weakness can mean absorption, betrayal); when? Or they accuse us of "polarizing the races" by our calls for black unity, when the true responsibility for polarization lies with whites who will not accept their responsibility as the majority power for making the democratic process work.

White America will not face the problem of color, the reality of it. The well-intended say: "We're all human, everybody is really decent, we must forget color." But color cannot be "forgotten" until its weight is recognized and dealt with. White America will not acknowledge that the ways in which this country sees itself are contradicted by being black—and always have been. Whereas most of the people who settled this country came here for freedom or for economic opportunity, blacks were brought here to be slaves. When the Lowndes County Freedom Organization chose the black panther as its symbol, it was christened by the press "the Black Panther Party"—but the Alabama Democratic Party, whose symbol is a rooster, has never been called the White Cock Party. No one ever talked about "white power" because power in this country *is* white. All this adds up to more than merely identifying a group phenomenon by some catchy name or adjective. The furor over that black panther reveals the problems that white America has with color and sex; the furor over "black power" reveals how deep racism runs and the great fear which is attached to it.

Whites will not see that I, for example, as a person oppressed because of my blackness, have common cause with other blacks who are oppressed because of blackness. This is not to say that there are no white people who see things as I do, but that it is black people I must speak to first. It must be the oppressed to whom SNCC addresses itself primarily, not to friends from the oppressing group.

From birth, black people are told a set of lies about themselves. We are told that we are lazy—yet I drive through the Delta area of Mississippi and watch black people picking cotton in the hot sun for fourteen hours. We are told, "If you work hard, you'll succeed"—but if that were true, black people would own this country. We are oppressed because we are black—not because we are ignorant, not because we are lazy, not because we're stupid (and got good rhythm), but because we're black.

I remember that when I was a boy, I used to go to see Tarzan movies on Saturday. White Tarzan used to beat up the black natives. I would sit there yelling, "Kill the beasts, kill the savages, kill 'em!" I was saying: Kill *me*. It was as if a Jewish boy watched Nazis taking Jews off to concentration camps and cheered them on. Today, I want the chief to beat hell out of Tarzan and send him back to Europe. But it takes time to become free of the lies and their shaming effect on black minds. It takes time to reject the most important lie: that black people inherently can't do the same things white people can do, unless white people help them.

The need for psychological equality is the reason why SNCC today believes that blacks must organize in the black community. Only black people can convey the revolutionary idea that black people are able to do things themselves. Only they can help create in the community an aroused and continuing black consciousness that will provide the basis for political strength. In the past, white allies have furthered white supremacy without the whites involved realizing it—or wanting it, I think. Black people must do things for themselves; they must get poverty money they will control and spend themselves, they must conduct tutorial programs themselves so that black children can identify with black people. This is one reason Africa has such importance: The reality of black men ruling their own nations gives blacks elsewhere a sense of possibility, of power, which they do not now have.

This does not mean we don't welcome help, or friends. But we want the right to decide whether anyone is, in fact, our friend. In the past, black Americans have been almost the only people whom everybody and his momma could jump up and call their friends. We have been tokens, symbols, objects—as I was in high school to many young whites, who liked having "a Negro friend." We want to decide who is our friend, and we will not accept someone who comes to us and says: "If you do X, Y, and Z, then I'll help you." We will not be told whom we should choose as allies. We will not be isolated from any group or nation except by our own choice. We cannot have the oppressors telling the oppressed how to rid themselves of the oppressor.

I have said that most liberal whites react to "black power" with the question, What about me?, rather than saying: Tell me what you want me to do and I'll see if I can do it. There are answers to the right question. One of the most disturbing things about almost all white supporters of the movement has been that they are afraid to go into their own communities—which is where the racism exists—and work to get rid of it. They want to run from Berkeley to tell us what to do in Mississippi; let them look instead at Berkeley. They admonish blacks to be nonviolent; let them preach nonviolence in the white community. They come

to teach me Negro history; let them go to the suburbs and open
up freedom schools for whites. Let them work to stop America's
racist foreign policy; let them press this government to cease
supporting the economy of South Africa.

There is a vital job to be done among poor whites. We hope to
see, eventually, a coalition between poor blacks and poor whites.
That is the only coalition which seems acceptable to us, and we
see such a coalition as the major internal instrument of change
in American society. SNCC has tried several times to organize
poor whites; we are trying again now, with an initial training
program in Tennessee. It is purely academic today to talk about
bringing poor blacks and whites together, but the job of creating
a poor-white power bloc must be attempted. The main responsibility for it falls upon whites. Black and white can work together
in the white community where possible; it is not possible, however, to go into a poor Southern town and talk about integration.
Poor whites everywhere are becoming more hostile—not less—
partly because they see the nation's attention focused on black
poverty and nobody coming to them. Too many young middle-
class Americans, like some sort of Pepsi generation, have wanted
to come alive through the black community; they've wanted to
be where the action is—and the action has been in the black
community.

Black people do not want to "take over" this country. They
don't want to "get whitey"; they just want to get him off their
backs, as the saying goes. It was for example the exploitation by
Jewish landlords and merchants which first created black resentment toward Jews—not Judaism. The white man is irrelevant to blacks, except as an oppressive force. Blacks want to be
in his place, yes, but not in order to terrorize and lynch and
starve him. They want to be in his place because that is where
a decent life can be had.

But our vision is not merely of a society in which all black
men have enough to buy the good things of life. When we urge
that black money go into black pockets, we mean the communal

pocket. We want to see money go back into the community and used to benefit it. We want to see the cooperative concept applied in business and banking. We want to see black ghetto residents demand that an exploiting landlord or storekeeper sell them, at minimal cost, a building or a shop that they will own and improve cooperatively; they can back their demand with a rent strike, or a boycott, and a community so unified behind them that no one else will move into the building or buy at the store. The society we seek to build among black people, then, is not a capitalist one. It is a society in which the spirit of community and humanistic love prevail. The word love is suspect; black expectations of what it might produce have been betrayed too often. But those were expectations of a response from the white community, which failed us. The love we seek to encourage is within the black community, the only American community where men call each other "brother" when they meet. We can build a community of love only where we have the ability and power to do so: among blacks.

As for white America, perhaps it can stop crying out against "black supremacy," "black nationalism," "racism in reverse," and begin facing reality. The reality is that this nation, from top to bottom, is racist; that racism is not primarily a problem of "human relations" but of an exploitation maintained—either actively or through silence—by the society as a whole. Camus and Sartre have asked, can a man condemn himself? Can whites, particularly liberal whites, condemn themselves? Can they stop blaming us, and blame their own system? Are they capable of the shame which might become a revolutionary emotion?

We have found that they usually cannot condemn themselves, and so we have done it. But the rebuilding of this society, if at all possible, is basically the responsibility of whites—not blacks. We won't fight to save the present society, in Vietnam or anywhere else. We are just going to work, in the way *we* see fit, and on goals *we* define, not for civil rights but for all our human rights.

FOR THE STUDENT

Rhetoric

1. *Is it the "blackness" or the "power" that causes apprehension in white conservative circles?*
2. *Try to* visualize *the black panther symbol: what panther-like qualities do you see?*
3. *This essay combines two styles: an academic, formal style and a colloquial, informal style. Find passages representative of both.*

Discussion

1. *Is Carmichael's definition of integration as "a subterfuge for the maintenance of white supremacy" a fair appraisal of the situation?*
2. *What could any white person find offensive about "black power" as Carmichael defines it?*
3. *Would any organization on your campus be likely to invite Carmichael as a lecturer? Why?*

Writing

1. *Carmichael refers to a "set of lies about themselves" that black people are told from birth, that is, having good rhythm, Tarzan movies, etc. Write a paper discussing these and other popular lies about the Negro.*
2. *Theme topic: "My Grandmother's Reaction (or My Own) to Carmichael's Essay."*

Martin Luther King

We last saw the Reverend Dr. Martin Luther King early last August, at the Ebenezer Baptist Church in Atlanta—a red brick building on the corner of Jackson Street and Auburn Avenue. His office, in the Sunday-school annex, to the left of the church, smelled of paraffin and linoleum glue. On the bulletin board, children's prayer cards of Jesus pointing at his heart were pinned above Southern Christian Leadership Conference posters proclaiming the summer's theme: "Black Is Beautiful." A broken Crayola popped underfoot. In the course of our conversation, Dr. King told of a recent threat against his life, in Cleveland. "It has been given to me to die when the Lord calls me," he said, digressing from his narrative. "The Lord called me into life and He will call me into death. I've known the fear of dying. Yes, I lived with that fear in Montgomery and in Birmingham, down in the State of Alabama, when brother fell upon brother in 1963." His voice was rich as his sentences rolled inexorably toward their conclusions. It had a kind of patience that was hard to distinguish from fatigue. "Since then, I've stood on the banks of the Jordan and I've looked into the promised land," he went on. "Maybe I won't make the journey, but I know that my *people* are going to make the journey, because I've stood and looked. So it doesn't *particularly* matter anymore. I've conquered the fear of dying, and a man that's conquered the fear of dying has conquered everything. I don't have to fear *any* man." He reached for a leather-bound Bible, worn to a dull shine, like an old watch, and turned to the fourth chapter of II Timothy. " 'I have fought a good fight,' " he read. " 'I have finished my course, I have kept the faith.' " He paused, and closed the book. (When we returned to the passage later, we noticed that

From The New Yorker, *Vol. 44 (April 13, 1968). Reprinted by permission;* © *1968 The New Yorker Magazine, Inc.*

it continued, "Henceforth, there is laid up for me the crown of righteousness.") Dr. King seemed embarrassed at ending the conversation there, but he had to catch a plane. As we stood with him on Auburn Avenue while he waited for his car, he mentioned that he was born "down the block." Along the avenue, modern cinder-block offices, their windows smeared with palm prints, stood beside clapboard houses. Cast-iron washtubs and rusting automobile parts lay scattered in yards. We remember that a young black girl in a stiff organdie dress was spinning a hubcap on the hot pavement.

We find ourselves now, as after any disaster, investing small things with an urgent, outsize relevance. The girl in the organdie dress keeps returning to our mind; somehow she must bear for us the meaning of Dr. King's death. We haven't looked to our memory of her for meaning; her picture simply appears to us, as if through some short circuit of our intelligence. One can no longer clearly grasp the relevance of new events. They involve us all, we talk about them all day, soon we find them squeezing everything else out of our lives, but we're not sure how to weight them. This is not because one can't foresee in detail where they're leading; one never could. The frightening thing is that one can no longer *imagine* what forms the solutions to our problems will assume. One isn't even sure what a solution would look like. Ordinarily, the news media might gives us clues. But the relevances we seek now aren't buried in news stories. Friday, the *Times* ran an eight-column headline on Dr. King's death. It ran eight-column headlines Monday, Tuesday, Thursday, and Saturday, too. Tucked inside Friday's paper were many stories about Dr. King's career. Their assumption seemed to be that by reëntering his past we might get a running start into our future without him.

The pell-mell events of the previous weeks no doubt undermined our response to Dr. King's death. Over the past several years, we have learned to accept the fact that our destiny is not entirely what we make of ourselves. But in these last weeks, perhaps for the first time since the Second World War, we've had a sense of being submerged in history, and of becoming inured to its stupefactions. About the time of the Tet offensive, one was close to despair. Then, with Eugene McCarthy's victory in New Hampshire and Robert Kennedy's announcement that he would run for the Presidency, with President Johnson's announcement of a bombing halt and then his announcement that he would not run again, followed by a direct peace overture from North Vietnam, one began to feel that suddenly, just when things were darkest, America had found her way back to the path. Now Dr. King's death comes to us as a reproach. We had let ourselves drift away from the reality of our trouble. Finding the path will not be so easy.

Word of the assassination reached us while we were working late at our office, and we immediately switched on a television-network special report. Perhaps because we received each piece of news minutes after it happened, we came to feel that we were at the eye of a historical hurricane. Our national leaders appeared before us to guide our responses. "America is shocked and saddened by the brutal slaying tonight of Dr. Martin Luther King," the President said, in measured tones. "I know that every American of good will joins me in mourning the death of this outstanding leader and in praying for peace and understanding throughout this land." We sat, it seemed dumbly, in the gray haze of our television screen. Other notables—we can't remember which—expressed dismay. Several, staring sternly into the camera, urged viewers to "keep their cool." The argot, unfamiliar to their mouths, made it plain to whom the admonitions were addressed. Curiously, what gave us a stronger sense of tragedy than anything our leaders said was the disorder on the networks: the missed cues and fades, the A.B.C. technician who walked behind Bob Young reading a sheet of teletype paper, Keith McBee stuttering when he suddenly realized he was on camera. When our leaders did appear, their eyes glassy and focused above the camera, we felt a strange sense of identification with the poverty of their response, and with the way they underscored one another. Too much had happened in the

had fostered and unified was now polycentric. Yet large
...ers of even the most militant Negroes continued to revere
...ing. People knew that he could not be bought. Even if they
...selves saw a different reality, they knew that he was true to
...wn vision. They knew that his caution was also tranquillity,
...his arrogance came from deep within him, and that its source
...the source of his humility as well. In a struggle in which
...d is often met with hatred, they knew he was genuine in lov-
...he human being, however he deplored the deed. To the last,
...King assumed that when the legal and extralegal barriers to
...munication between races were hewn down, people would be-
...o see their brotherhood beneath the skin and begin to know
...majestic heights of being obedient to the unenforceable." In
...nt years, many blacks came to lose faith in this theory alto-
...er. Others simply grew impatient waiting for it to come true
...heir own lives. But even Stokely Carmichael, who on the night
...he assassination urged "retaliation by the black community,"
...he kind of rhetoric that Dr. King most deplored, called him
...only member of the older generation whom young blacks still
...rd.

...When Dr. King was scheduled to take part in a conference or a
..., black people of every persuasion knew it would be honest.
...y knew he wouldn't try to trick them. White people believed in
...honesty, too. He never "told it like it is," the way Malcolm X
..., later, Stokely Carmichael did—he was perhaps the most
...rteous revolutionary who has ever lived—but neither did he
...srepresent situations by telling audiences what they wanted to
...r. Radicals sometimes tried, without success, to lump Dr. King
...h the placators among his colleagues. A refined civility ran
...ough him to the core; he didn't need to dissemble, to conceal
...reds, for none smoldered within him—except the hatred of evil.
...is is why Dr. King never frightened whites; however radical his
...marks have seemed ideologically, they were never venomous. It
...s a failure that cost him admiration within his own flock, per-
...ps, but never among those who understood that he confronted

last week. They had been called upon too often. They could, with
honor, fail to help us.

After watching the news for more than an hour, we walked out
into the office corridor. The cleaning woman, an elderly Negro
woman in a green shift and stretch socks, was sitting in the broom
closet weeping and muttering to herself, "They're going to get
him, and they're going to get everybody." We had nothing we
could say to her, and, to judge by her reluctance to notice us,
there was nothing she wanted to hear. When we returned to our
office, Vice-President Humphrey was in the midst of dismissing
predictions of violence, because, he said, no one could respond
with anything but grief on this sad occasion. Even as he spoke, we
could hear the wail of sirens rising through the long canyon of
Sixth Avenue. Shortly afterward, we heard loud shouts and the
splintering of glass. We walked onto a balcony outside our office,
on the nineteenth floor, and, below, on Forty-fourth Street, saw a
crowd of black youths ambling toward Times Square. One, holding
a flap of his torn shirt, skipped ahead of the others and, from time
to time, spun around to yell at them. We stared (we hadn't yet
heard reports of trouble in New York), and said to ourself, "Now
it has happened." We shut off the television set and sat in silence.
The dreamy ululation of police cars racing toward Harlem continued into the night. After a while, we called a friend. If we could
not define our feelings, we could at least share them, undefined. As
we talked with our friend, we discovered that although in 1963 the
mystery of who assassinated President Kennedy had fascinated us,
there was nothing we cared to learn about the man who shot Dr.
King. We knew who he was.

John Kennedy's death came like lightning from a clear sky.
Dr. King's was something that for a long time we'd been hoping
wouldn't happen. We would have been alarmed if Kennedy, or any
President, had prophesied his own murder, yet we have grown
accustomed to such predictions from civil-rights leaders. Dr. King
spoke reluctantly of what he suspected would be his destiny, and
most often at the prompting of journalists. Dark premonitions can

easily become obsessive, as they did for Malcolm X; they never preoccupied Dr. King. Yet he was the most important example of a new kind of political leader in America—one who cannot exercise leadership without first coming to terms with the probability of his own violent death. A speech that Dr. King delivered on Wednesday evening, scarcely twenty hours before his assassination, and that the networks televised on Thursday night was notable, then, but not surprising. He spoke of having (like Moses) "been to the mountaintop" and there become reconciled. "And then I got into Memphis, and some began to talk about the threats that were out," Dr. King said. "Like anybody, I would like to live a long life. Longevity has its place. But I'm not concerned about that now. I just want to do God's will. And He's allowed me to go up to the mountain. And I've looked over, and I've seen the promised land. I may not get there with you, but I want you to know tonight that we as a people will get to the promised land." Dr. King's prophetic speech was striking only in retrospect, perhaps because we had not been duly conscious of one of his most urgent tasks: *preparing* his apostles, and his public, for their loss of him. On Tuesday night, his flight from Atlanta to Memphis was delayed by a baggage search that airline officials said resulted from threats on his life. But, as most of us have no room in our lives for much else, so Dr. King had no room for worry about himself.

Many of Dr. King's people had lately grown discontented with him. They saw him standing in the doorway he had opened, an old champion become an obstruction. He wished to solidify old gains, they imagined, while they wanted to push through the doorway. Some ridiculed the basis of his work because it was ethical and religious rather than strategic. They referred to him as "De Lawd" and spoke mockingly of his "meetin' body force with *soul* force." Some others derided what they took for rigid, irrelevant platitudes and florid plagiarisms. The week after we saw Dr. King in his office, he returned to Atlanta to address a convention of the National Association of Radio Announcers at the Regency Hyatt

House. Nearly every sentence of his conv[...] somewhere in that speech. Like the polit[...] death, Dr. King often gave the impressi[...] fixed inventory of responses. His speeche[...] seemed repetitive; they drew their resona[...] that prompted them. But the inventory wa[...] him of the distracting obligation of respo[...] to every new situation. It was also a sour[...] straint, shielding him from the temptation t[...] thought—unconsidered feelings that were [...] whites' most dramatic outrages, such as the [...] of 1963. Dr. King did not have to change [...] from the Montgomery boycott of 1956 to [...] problems remained the same: hatred and [...] perhaps too abstractly, "sin." The problems [...] the White Citizens Councils or the Ku Klu[...] famous letter from the Birmingham prison; t[...] white moderate who is more devoted to orde[...] prefers a negative peace, which is the absence[...] tive peace, which is the presence of justice." [...] of Dr. King's life was that although his simpl[...] very depth at which he confronted the proble[...] from many of his brothers, black and white.

The broad "coalition of conscience" wi[...] hoped to work was too broad, in the end, to [...] who rejected the goal of "working into" a whi[...] sidered malignant. A coalition that included [...] unions, the N.A.A.C.P., and the Liberal Den[...] gradual reforms, they conceded, but they, or [...] grown indifferent to any kind of "progress" sho[...] upheaval. Reforms did not come thick and fa[...] black leadership in line behind him. During the [...] which culminated, at the Democratic National [...] Atlantic City compromise over the Mississipp[...] crats—it became clear that the movement th[...]

problems head on, in their total enormity, without wasting an ounce of energy on blame or vengeance. Whites could listen to him because he managed to attack evil without attacking *them*—because he always made evil seem something they could separate themselves from and join with him against.

Dr. King was a radical in the truest sense: he insisted at the same time upon the terrible reality of our problems and upon their solubility, and he rejected everything that was irrelevant to their solution. Could his death be a radicalizing event, in this same sense, for both races? Perhaps no one was completely happy with him—what he finally did was always a little different from what anyone wanted him to do—but he came closer to being a national hero for both blacks and whites than any other figure in history. Last April, when Dr. King became the first prominent American to oppose the war in Vietnam publicly, he became more than a "black leader." He made himself a leader of all men who care for peace and justice, and reluctantly estranged those of his colleagues who had focused single-mindedly on the issue of civil rights. He served a complicated cause in a complicated time. In his life, no faction could ever fully claim him as an ally. But with his death every faction—from ghetto blacks tossing brickbats to the Administration of the United States government—loses an ally. His death is difficult for us because it deprives us of the embodiment of the cause he represented for all Americans—the more difficult because of the threat inherent in that deprivation. Incidents of arson and other violence were reported from over forty cities within twenty-four hours of his murder, and on Friday lootings occurred two blocks from the White House. Before the weekend was over, twenty-eight were dead and more than six thousand arrested across the country. But his death also forces upon us the possibility that our common need to avoid the danger of losing touch with his ideals can bring us together in a kind of desperate symbiosis. Perhaps that desperation might even draw us close enough together to see that, as one of Dr. King's annoying plagiarisms insisted, the same things make us laugh and cry and bleed.

One tends to forget, under the pressure of events and of the fashions of political vocabulary, that most men, black or white, are essentially non-violent, and that Dr. King was trying to marshal this non-violence—to inspire and direct it, and make it count for something in the affairs of men. He brought about a sense of a black-and-white community of decent men, and until the Mississippi march of 1966 he shakily maintained it. On the day after Dr. King's death, we went to a small, dispiriting rally for him on the Mall in Central Park. As the ideologues dwelled too long and too stridently on the irony of his murder, it began to seem that the course of events would again be determined by that diffuse community of the deranged—black and white, Right and Left and apolitical—which Dr. King, at the time of his death, was again forming a community to overcome. But by Sunday—Palm Sunday —things had changed. As marchers gathered, twenty abreast and eventually seven dense blocks long, at 145th Street and Seventh Avenue, and as they marched—with few signs, and, for the most part, silently—black and white, arms linked, down Seventh Avenue, there was a sense that the non-violent, freed ever so slightly by the President's speech of last week from the dividing pressure of Vietnam, were returning in force to civil rights. It seemed that Dr. King's people, of both races, were assembling again from everywhere, to resume where they left off after Mississippi. They marched past cars whose headlights were on out of respect for Dr. King. They marched over the splinters of broken glass lining the streets of Harlem, past the churches, the abandoned houses, the stores, and the funeral homes. Some carried palm fronds; others wore armbands that read "Our King will never die." A group of the ultra-militant young Five Percenters took their places at the front of the march. No one questioned them. They were as quiet as the rest. The march was informal—no marshals and no leaders. Bystanders on Seventh Avenue joined at the front or the sides or the rear, or did not choose to join. It was completely reflective and completely orderly. At 110th Street, the march paused, and a siren was audible in the distance. A jet passed overhead. Little boys standing at the entrance to the Park put their feet in the line of march, as though testing the water, and then joined in. Photographers were scattered on overhanging rocks. Reporters for various radio news services spoke very quietly, in their several languages, into microphones. Children gathered around them. The march entered the Park, and walked past cyclists, past very good-natured police, past players on a baseball diamond (an integrated game) near Ninety-sixth Street. Mayor Lindsay and Governor Rockefeller joined it there, and people from all over the Park, some with dogs or balloons, began to drift toward the march, inquire what it was, and then join it. The Mall, by the time the marchers got to it, was filled with a crowd several times the size of the march itself. There were hippies, two Great Danes, and several hot-dog stands, but mainly the crowd looked citywide, very mixed. We stood on the hill in back of the Mall and watched the two crowds merge. They did so almost silently, and totally, in great waves, so there was no way of knowing, from that distance, who had marched and who had been standing on the Mall waiting, and it was hard to tell who was black and who was white.

FOR THE STUDENT

Rhetoric

1. *Do not try to outline this essay. There are four main parts to it: state the central sense of each part.*
2. *Contrast the quotations from King with those of three or four other people quoted.*

Discussion

1. *Judging from the Carmichael essay and the evaluation of King in the third part of the article, what would be the major points of disagreement between the two men?*

2. *What kind of punishment would you expect King to give to his own assassin? What kind would you give?*

3. *The author says, at the beginning of the fourth part, that "most men, black or white, are essentially non-violent." How does he know?*

Writing

1. *Using the second section as a model, write an impressionistic account of some disaster (real or imagined) which you have experienced.*

2. *Compose a short speech—as King might have said it—to the court which will try his murderer.*

WILLIAM F. BUCKLEY, JR.

Desegregation—Will It Work? No

What, I am asked, is the conservatives' solution to the race problem in the South? I answer: there is no present solution to it. Such an answer appalls. It brings to mind, to move from tragedy to flippancy, the cartoon of the farmer leaning on his pitchfork and replying to the motorist: "Come to think of it, Mister, I don't think you can *get* to Glens Falls from here." There are those who approach all problems as though they involved merely getting an automobile from here to there: there is always a road. There are others who know that some problems are insoluble. These last are for the most part conservatives; and I am here to defend them.

Let us begin by stressing that no matter how convinced a people may be of the wrongness of an existing situation, it does not follow that the people should be prepared to resort to whatever means may be necessary to attempt to make that situation right. That may sound obvious—the end does not justify any means; but when we examine some of the drastic proposals that are being put forward with the end of securing the rights of the Negro (e.g., a constitutional amendment depriving the individual states of their right to set up voting qualifications), the time has come to reiterate the obvious. We acknowledge, for instance, that it is wrong to drive at excessive speeds; but no state in the union seems prepared to impose a heavier penalty on the speeder than the automatic suspension of his license for thirty days. There would be less speeding, and hence less violent slaughter—the two figures, the experts inform us, are inextricably related—if speeders were packed off to jail for a week. Even so, notwithstanding the established correlation between fast driving and aborted lives, we shrink from so drastic a penalty; and the speeding, and the deaths, go on.

From Saturday Review, *November 11, 1961. Copyright 1961 Saturday Review, Inc. Reprinted by permission.*

[27]

Let us take the word of the predominating school of social scientists and stipulate that segregation is the cause of personality disturbances. And—mark this—not only against the Negro, but also against the white. The argument is not new; it has often been used against corporal punishment. It is not only the victim who is damaged, psychiatrists report, but also the executioner, in whom sadistic impulses are dangerously encouraged. No one who has contemplated a man brandishing a fiery cross and preaching hatred needs help from social science to know that the race problem has debasing effects on black and white alike.

Assume all this to be true. Assume, also, that the legal and political power is wholly at the disposal of the society to effect its point of view in the South. Assume, in other words, that *Brown* vs. *Board of Education* and the supporting decisions of the Supreme Court deconstitutionalized segregated public schooling beyond the point of argument. Then assume that the raw power necessary to enforce that decision is available to the present Administration, and that the will of the nation is such as to insure that Congress will supply power where power is lacking. Should the Federal Government then proceed?

The list of sanctions available to the government is endless. The economic power of the Federal Government has in our time reached the point where it cannot be denied; cannot, in fact, be defied. If Congress can seriously entertain the question whether to spend money to aid public schooling in any state whose public schools are segregated, why can't Congress debate the question whether it is prepared to spend money for road-building in a segregated state? Or for unemployment? Or for farmers' subsidies? Already the Attorney General has hinted he is considering (for purely punitive reasons) recommending to his old friend the Commander-in-Chief the removal of our large military installations from segregated areas.

In a word, the Federal Government is in a position to visit intolerable economic sanctions against the defiant state. Not to mention the government's arsenal of legal weapons. Why cannot the Congress (assuming always a purposive mood on the subject of segregation) pass laws increasing the penalties for those held guilty of contempt of court in a certain category of cases? And why can't the courts rule—as Professor Auerbach of the University of Wisconsin has recommended—that any state which, having fought to the end of the legal road, sets out to close down its public schools rather than integrate them, be forbidden to do so on the grounds that such action, under such circumstances, becomes not the free exercise of the state's power, but an act of defiance of a federal court? By such reasoning the Federal Government could take over the operation of the schools.

The crucial question arises: Will the government of the United States move in such a fashion? The answer is: probably not; for the reason that, along the way, the ideological stamina would very likely give out, as the public contemplated the consequences of an assault of such magnitude on a whole region. Another question is: *should* the government of the United States take that kind of action to end segregation? The answer to that is, in my judgment: no, most definitely not.

"You know, the world is hard enough and people is evil enough without all the time looking for it and stirring it up and making it worse," says Leona, in a novel by the eloquent, tormented Negro writer James Baldwin, who celebrates his bitterness against the white community mostly in journals of the far political left. What would be accomplished by turning the legislative, judicial, and executive resources of this country over to a crash program of integration? Let us suppose the program were so successful as to make South Carolina like New York City. This spring [1961] a distinguished New York Negro told the audience of the television program "Open End" that he did not know three white people in all of New York with whom he felt genuinely comfortable, such is the prevalence of prejudice even in this cosmopolitan center. Louis Lomax may be more sensitive, and hence more bit-

ter, than the average New York Negro, and so unrepresentative of
the state of Negro serenity in the North; but then, too, Dr. Martin
Luther King is more sensitive, and so more bitter, than the average
Southern Negro, and hence unqualified as a litmus of the Southern
Negro's discontent. But only one of the other Negro guests on the
program challenged as extreme that remarkable testament to race
relations in the city under which the fires of the melting pot burn
hottest.

   The deep disturbances isolated by the social scientists are not,
I think, of the kind that are removed by integrating the waiting
rooms and the schools. It has even been revealed (*Villanova Law
Review,* Fall, 1960) that the very tests cited by the Supreme Court
in *Brown* as evidence that Southern Negro children were suffering
personality damage, when administered in the North yielded not
merely similar results, but results that seemed to indicate a greater
psychic disturbance in integrated Northern Negroes than in segregated Southern Negroes! I believe that the forms of segregation,
which so much engross us at the moment and which alone are
within the reach of the law to alter, are of tertiary importance, and
of transitory nature; and under the circumstances the question
arises even more urgently: *Should* we resort to convulsive measures that do violence to the traditions of our system in order to
remove the forms of segregation in the South? If the results were
predictably and unambiguously successful, the case might be made
persuasively. If a clean stroke through the tissue of American
mores could reach through to the cancer, forever to extirpate it,
then one might say, in due gravity: let us operate. But when the
results are thus ambiguous? Use the federal power to slash through
the warp and woof of society in pursuit of a social ideal which was
never realized even under the clement circumstances of a Chicago
or a New York or a Philadelphia?

   I say no. A conservative is seldom disposed to use the Federal
Government as the sword of social justice, for the sword is generally two-edged ("The Government can only do something for the

people in proportion as it can do something to the people," Jefferson said). If it is doubtful just what enduring benefits the Southern Negro would receive from the intervention of government on the scale needed to, say, integrate the schools in South Carolina, it is less doubtful what the consequences of interposition would be to the ideal of local government and the sense of community, ideals which I am not ready to abandon, not even to kill Jim Crow.

What, meanwhile, are the Negroes actually losing that they would not lose if the government took over in the South? One thing alone, I think, and that is the institutional face of segregation. That is important; but it is in the last analysis only a form. What matters is the substance of segregation. The kind of familiarity that might lessen racial consciousness is outside the power of the government to effect. I would even argue that it is outside the power of the government to accelerate. J. Kenneth Galbraith tells us that the ultimate enemy of myth is circumstance, and I think he is correct. If it is true that the separation of the races on account of color is nonrational, then circumstance will in due course break down segregation. When it becomes self-evident that biological, intellectual, cultural, and psychic similarities among the races render social separation capricious and atavistic, then the myths will begin to fade, as they have done in respect of the Irish, the Italian, the Jew; then integration will come—the right kind of integration. But meanwhile there *are* differences between the races which surely will not be denied by an organization explicitly devoted to the advancement of colored people. The Negro community must advance, and is advancing. The Reverend William Sloane Coffin of Yale University, returning from his whirl with the Freedom Riders, rejected the request of Mr. Robert Kennedy that the Riders withdraw to let the situation cool off with the words: "The Negroes have been waiting for ninety years." Mr. Coffin spoke nonsense, and showed scant respect for the productive labors, material and spiritual, of three generations of Negroes. A sociologist at Brooklyn College only a few weeks before had observed that never in the history of nations has a racial minority advanced so fast as the Negroes have done in America. How far will they go on to advance? To the point where social separation will vanish?

I do not know, but I hope that circumstance will usher in that day, and that when the Negroes have finally realized their long dream of attaining to the status of the white man, the white man will still be free; and that depends, in part, on the moderation of those whose inclination it is to build a superstate that will give them Instant Integration.

FOR THE STUDENT

Rhetoric

1. *Part of Buckley's point is that, in some ways, the Negro is worse off in the North than in the South. What is the rest of his point?*
2. *What is the source and meaning of the "litmus" metaphor applied to Martin Luther King?*
3. *Jefferson was considered a violent liberal in his day. How does it come about that Buckley cites him in support of his conservative position?*

Discussion

1. *Buckley mentions two "drastic proposals" in paragraph two —a constitutional amendment on voting and jail sentences for speeding. What makes them so drastic?*
2. *Notice that Stokely Carmichael, as well as Buckley, is concerned with "the ideals of local government and the sense of community" (paragraph ten). What divergent meanings do the two men attach to these ideals?*

3. *Is this Buckley's argument: that the present "rapid advance" of the Negro has resulted in New York and Chicago ghettoes and that federal intervention will result in New York and Chicago ghettoes in the South?*

Writing

1. *Write a paper describing the consequences if the federal government—for any reason—were to impose on your state or city the "sanctions" mentioned in paragraphs five and six.*
2. *Theme topic: "Carmichael, King, Buckley: Whose Vision Will Prevail Ten Years from Now?"*

2 The Individual in Modern Society

One of the enduring problems of modern Western civilization (we need go back here only as far as Tocqueville and Jefferson) is how to reconcile the values of individualism with the values of society: simply stated, both the individual and society have "rights," and these rights are in constant, if not inevitable, conflict. The one extreme (as advocated and for a time practiced by Thoreau) leads to anarchy; the other (which might be illustrated by Mussolini's "everything for the state" philosophy) leads to totalitarianism. But this polarity of individual versus state is perhaps too simple for our present time. Recent history has added a new dimension to the problem: vast industrial and economic organizations within the state have posed new threats to various individualistic values. In brief, the question confronting us today seems to be this: how can we contrive to protect privacy, integrity, freedom of expression, and the like in a crowded, complex, highly organized, industrialized society?

Aldous Huxley, the British novelist, in one of the ensuing essays, presents his answer to this question and at the same time underlines the conventional range of approaches used throughout this book: "As usual," says Huxley, "the only safe course is in the middle, between the extremes of laissez-faire at one end of the scale and of total control at the other." John Kenneth Galbraith, distinguished American economist, proposes state planning to "reject the monopoly of social purpose by the industrial system." Throughout his essay he wishes to foster beauty, order, and artistic expression over industrial efficiency. This position we will call the "Left." The "Right" position is represented by Leonard R. Sayles, a professor in *the Graduate School of Business at Columbia University, who finds the concept of the organization man an over-simplification with little validity in fact. The effective organization of tens of thousands of people in a modern business, he argues, is a towering achievement of our time and need not interfere with the pattern of the individual's family and community life.*

JOHN KENNETH GALBRAITH

The Future of the
Industrial System

In the latter part of the last century and the early decades of this, no subject was more discussed than the future of capitalism. Economists, men of unspecific wisdom, political philosophers, knowledgeable ecclesiastics, and George Bernard Shaw all contributed their personal revelation. All agreed that the economic system was in a state of development and in time would transform itself into something hopefully better but certainly different. Socialists drew strength from the belief that theirs was the plausible next step in the natural process of change.

Now the future of the modern industrial economy is not much discussed. The prospect for agriculture is still subject to debate; it is assumed to be in a process of transition. So are the chances for the small businessman. But General Motors is an ultimate achievement. One does not wonder where he is going if he has already arrived. That there will be no further change in institutions that are themselves a result of such vast change is highly implausible. The future of the modern industrial system is not discussed, partly because of the influence it exercises over our belief. We agree that unions, the churches, airplanes, and the Congress lack absolute perfection. The modern corporation, however, is a perfected structure. So it has won exemption from speculation as to how it might be improved.

Additionally, to consider its future is to fix attention on where it already is. Among the least attractive phrases in the American business lexicon are planning, government control, and socialism.

[38]

To consider the chance for these in the future is to bring home the extent to which they are already a fact. The government influences industrial prices and wages, regulates demand, supplies the decisive factor of production, which is trained manpower, underwrites much technology, and provides the market for products of highest technical sophistication. In the formally planned economies of Eastern Europe, the role of the state is not startlingly different. And these things have arrived, at a minimum with the acquiescence, and at a maximum at the demand, of private enterprise itself.

The next step will be a general recognition of the convergent tendencies of modern industrial systems, even though differently billed as socialism or capitalism. And we must also assume that this is a good thing. In time it will dispose of the notion of inevitable conflict based on irreconcilable difference. This difference is still cherished by the ideologists on both sides. To Marxists, the evolution here described, and most notably the replacement of capitalist power by that of technical organization, is unacceptable. Marx did not foresee it, and Marx has always been required by his disciples to have had the supernatural power of foreseeing everything for all time—although some alterations are allowed on occasion in what he is thought to have seen. And ideologists in the West who speak for the unbridgeable gulf that divides the free from the Communist world are protected by a similar theology, supported in many cases by a rather proud immunity to intellectual influences. But these positions can survive the evidence only for a time. Men lose their resistance when they realize that they are coming to look retarded or old-fashioned. Vanity is a great force for intellectual modernization.

The modern planned economy requires that the state underwrite its more sophisticated and risky technology. The weapons competition provides the rationale for much of this underwriting at the present time. This competition depends, in its turn, on the notion of irreconcilable hostility based on irreconcilable difference between economic systems. But the fact is convergence. The conclusion follows and by no especially elaborate chain of reasoning. The difference between economic systems, from which the assumption of hostility and conflict derives, does not exist. What exists is an image adhered to on both sides that serves the underwriting of technology. And very obviously, there are other ways of underwriting technology.

To bring the weapons competition to an end will not be easy. But it contributes to this goal, one trusts, to realize that the economic premises on which it rests are not real. None of this disposes of different attitudes on intellectual and cultural freedom and the First Amendment. I set rather high store by these. But these have been thought to be partially derivative of the economic systems.

Private enterprise has anciently been so described because it was subordinate to the market and those in command derived their power from the ownership of private property. The modern corporation is no longer subordinate to the market; those who guide it no longer depend on ownership for their authority. They must have autonomy within a framework of goals. But this allows them to work intimately with the public bureaucracy and, indeed, to perform tasks for the bureaucracy that it cannot do, or cannot do as well, for itself. In consequence, for tasks of technical sophistication, there is a close fusion, as we have seen, of the modern industrial system with the state. As I have earlier observed, the line that now divides public from so-called private organization in military procurement, space exploration, and atomic energy is so indistinct as to be nearly imperceptible. Men move easily across the line. Technicians from government and corporations work constantly together. On retirement, admirals and generals and high civil servants go more or less automatically to government-related industries. One close and experienced observer, Professor Murray L. Weidenbaum, a former employee of Boeing, has called this the "seminationalized" branch of the economy.

He is speaking of firms which do all or a large share of their business with the government. But most large firms do a substantial share of their business with the state. And they are as dependent on the state as the weapons firms for the other supports to their planning. It requires no great exercise of imagination to suppose that the mature corporation, as it develops, will eventually become a part of the larger administrative complex with the state. In time the line between the two will largely disappear. Men will marvel at the thin line that once caused people to refer to General Electric, Westinghouse, or Boeing as *private* business.

Although this recognition will not be universally welcomed, it will be healthy. And if the mature corporation is recognized to be part of the state or some penumbra of the state, it cannot plead its inherently private character, or its subordination to the market, as cover for the pursuit of goals of primary interest to its own guiding organization. It can be expected to accept public goals in matters of aesthetics, health and safety, and general social tranquillity that are not inconsistent with its survival. The public bureaucracy has an unquestioned tendency to pursue its own goals and reflect its own interest and convenience. But it cannot plead this as a right. So with the corporation as its essentially public character comes to be accepted.

Other changes can be imagined. As the public character of the mature corporation comes to be recognized, attention will doubtless focus on the position of the shareholder. This is already anomalous. A shareholder is a passive and functionless figure, remarkable only in his capacity to participate, without effort or even, given the planning, without risk, in the gains of the growth by which the directing organization now measures its success. No grant of feudal privilege in history ever equaled, for effortless return, that of the American grandparent who thoughtfully endowed his descendants with a thousand shares each of General Motors and IBM. But I do not need to pursue these matters here. Questions of equity as between the accidentally rich have their own special expertise.

Some will insist that the world of the modern large firm is not the whole economy. At the opposite pole from General Motors and Standard Oil is the world of the independent shopkeeper, farmer, shoe repairman, bookmaker, narcotics peddler, pizza merchant, streetwalker, and owner of the car and dog laundry. Here prices are not controlled. Here the consumer is sovereign. Here pecuniary motivation is unimpaired. Here technology is simple, and there is no research or development to make it otherwise. Here there are no government contracts; independence from the state, the narcotics trade and prostitution possibly apart, is a reality. But one should cherish his critics and protect them where possible from foolish error. The tendency of the great corporation in the modern industrial system to become part of the administrative complex of the state cannot be refuted by appeal to the contrary tendencies of the miniscule enterprise.

The two questions most asked about an economic system are whether it serves man's physical needs and whether it is consistent with his liberty and general happiness. There is little doubt as to the ability of the modern industrial system to supply man with goods—it is able to manage consumer demand only because it supplies it so abundantly. Wants would not be subject to management or manipulation had they not been first dulled by sufficiency. In the United States, as in other advanced countries, there are many poor people. But they are not to be found within the part of the economy with which we are here concerned. That these articles do not deal with poverty does not mean, incidentally, that I am unaware of its existence.

The prospect for liberty is far more interesting. It has always been imagined, especially by conservatives, that to associate all, or a large part, of economic activity with the state is to endanger freedom. The individual in one way or another will be sacrificed to the convenience of the political and economic power so conjoined. As the modern industrial system evolves into a penumbra of the state, the question of its relation to liberty thus arises in urgent form. In recent years in the Soviet Union and in the Soviet-type economies, there has been a poorly concealed conflict between the state and the intellectuals. It has been between those who speak for the needs of the state and its disciplines, as economic planner and producer of goods, and those who assert the higher claims of intellectual and artistic expression. Is this a warning to us?

The instinct which warns of dangers in this association of economic and public power is quite sound. Unhappily, those who warn look in the wrong place. They have feared that the state might reach out and destroy the vigorous moneymaking entrepreneur. They have not noticed that, all the while, the successors to this vintage hero have been uniting themselves ever more closely with the state and rejoicing in the result. With equal enthusiasm, they have been accepting drastic abridgement of their own freedom. This is partly the price of organized activity. But they were also losing freedom in the precise pattern of classical expectation. The officers of Republic Aviation, which does all of its business with the United States government, are no more likely in public to speak critically of some nonsense perpetrated by the Air Force than is the head of a Soviet *combinat* of the ministry to which he reports. No Ford executive will ever fight Washington as did Henry I. No head of Montgomery Ward will ever again breathe defiance of a President as did Sewell Avery in the age of Roosevelt. Manners may be involved here. But most would state the truth: "Too much is now at stake!"

But the problem is not the freedom of the businessman. It can be laid down as a general rule that those who speak most of liberty least use what they have. The businessman who praises it most is a disciplined organization man. The retired general who now lectures on the threat of Communist regimentation was invariably a martinet who relished an existence in accordance with military regulations. The Secretary of State who speaks most feelingly of the free world most admires the fine conformity of his own thought.

The greater danger is in the subordination of belief to the needs of the modern industrial system. As this persuades us on the

goods we buy, and as it persuades us on the public policies that
are necessary for its planning, so it also accommodates us to its
goals and values. These are that technology is always good; that
economic growth is always good; that firms must always expand;
that consumption of goods is the principal source of happiness;
that idleness is wicked; and that nothing should interfere with the
priority we accord to technology, growth, and increased consumption.

If we continue to believe that the goals of the modern industrial system and the public policies that serve these goals are co-
ordinate with all of life, then all of our lives will be in the service
of these goals. What is consistent with these ends we shall have or
be allowed; all else will be off limits. Our wants will be managed
in accordance with the needs of the industrial system; the state in
civilian and military policy will be heavily influenced by industrial
need; education will be adapted to similar need; the discipline required by the industrial system will be the conventional morality of
the community. All other goals will be made to seem precious, un-
important, or antisocial. We will be the mentally indentured servants of the industrial system. This will be the benign servitude of
the household retainer who is taught to love her master and mistress and believe that their interests are her own. But it is not
exactly freedom.

If, on the other hand, the industrial system is seen to be only a
part, and as we grow wealthier, a diminishing part, of life, there
is much less occasion for concern. Aesthetic goals will have pride
of place; those who serve them will not be subject to the goals of
the industrial system; the industrial system itself will be subordinate to the claims of larger dimensions of life. Intellectual preparation will be for its own sake and not merely for the better service
to the industrial system. Men will not be entrapped by the belief
that apart from the production of goods and income by progressively more advanced technical methods there is nothing much in
life. Then, over time, we may come to see industrial society as a

technical arrangement for providing convenient goods and services in adequate volume. Those who rise through its hierarchy will so see themselves. And the public consequences will be in keeping. For if economic goals are the only goals of the society, the goals of the industrial system will dominate the state. If industrial goals are not the only goals, other purposes will be pursued.

Central among these other purposes is the aesthetic dimension of life. It is outside the scope of the modern industrial system. And that is why the industrial system tends to dismiss aesthetic considerations as precious and impractical and to condemn their proponents as "aesthetes."

The conflict arises in three forms. First and simply, there is the conflict between beauty and industrial efficiency. It is cheaper to have power lines march across the fields; to have highways take the most direct route through countryside or villages or towns or cities; or to allow jet aircraft to ignore the tranquillity of those below; or to pour industrial refuse into the air or into the water.

Next, there is a conflict between the artist and organization. Scientists and engineers can specialize; artists cannot. Accordingly, the organization which accommodates the specialist, though right for the engineer or scientist, is wrong for the artist. The artist does badly as an organization man; the organization does badly by the artist. So the artist tends to stand outside the modern industrial system; and it responds, naturally enough, by minimizing the importance of the aesthetic concerns it cannot easily embrace.

Finally, some important forms of artistic expression require a framework of order. This is notably true of structural and landscape architecture and urban design. It is order rather than the intrinsic merit of their buildings which accounts for the charm of Georgetown or Bloomsbury or Haussman's boulevards. Not even the Taj Mahal would be terribly attractive between two gasoline stations and surrounded by neon signs. Individuals, nevertheless, have served better their economic interest by rejecting Haussman's designs or by getting a Shell franchise adjacent to the Taj.

The need is to subordinate economic to aesthetic goals—to sacrifice efficiency, including the efficiency of organization, to beauty. Nor must there be any nonsense about beauty paying in the long run. It need not pay. The requisite order will also require strong action by the state. Because of the abdication of this function in the interest of economic goals, no city, some noncommercial capitals apart, built since the Industrial Revolution attracts any particular admiration. And millions flock to admire ancient and medieval cities where, as a matter of course, such order was provided. The liberalism which allowed every individual and every entrepreneur to build as he wished was faster, more adaptable, and more efficient, and accommodated site better to need, than anything that could be provided under a "controlled" environment. But the aesthetic effect was at best undistinguished, and more often it was ghastly.

The change in goals and values which is here required is aided by the fact that the modern industrial system is intellectually demanding. It brings into existence, to serve its technical and scientific and other intellectual needs, a very large community of educated men and women. Hopefully this community will, in turn, reject the monopoly of social purpose by the industrial system.

But the rewards of time and understanding can also be hastened and enlarged by energetic political action. It is through the state that the society must assert the superior claims of aesthetic over economic goals and particularly of environment over cost. It is to the state that we must look for freedom of individual choice as to toil; for a balance between liberal education and the technical training that primarily serves the industrial system; and it is for the state to reject images of international politics that underwrite technology but at the price of unacceptable danger. If the state is to serve these ends, the scientific and educational estate and the larger intellectual community must be aware of their power and their opportunity and they must use them. There is no one else.

FOR THE STUDENT

Rhetoric

1. *The essay is organized into three parts. Construct a sentence outline of any one or a topic outline of all three.*
2. *Note the metaphor "penumbra" (third part, paragraph two). Explain it.*

Discussion

1. *In the last few paragraphs Galbraith refers to the "liberalism" which built our ghastly cities and the "liberal education" which will hopefully improve our environment. Is there any sense in which these terms are related? In which they conflict?*
2. *Is Galbraith too optimistic about state and industry cooperating in aesthetic purpose? What evidence is there of similar cooperation in the architecture of your own campus?*
3. *President Eisenhower's farewell address warned against the threat of a "military-industrial complex" which would increasingly control society. How can this be prevented?*

Writing

1. *Reread carefully the first and last sentences of each paragraph. See if you can work out from this an exact, one-paragraph summary of the essay.*
2. *Attack or defend the following thesis in a paper of three hundred words: "Capitalism in America is exclusively (or primarily) interested in money, not beauty."*

ALDOUS HUXLEY

Over-Organization

The shortest and broadest road to the nightmare of Brave New World leads, as I have pointed out, through over-population and the accelerating increase of human numbers—twenty-eight hundred millions today, fifty-five hundred millions by the turn of the century, with most of humanity facing the choice between anarchy and totalitarian control. But the increasing pressure of numbers upon available resources is not the only force propelling us in the direction of totalitarianism. This blind biological enemy of freedom is allied with immensely powerful forces generated by the very advances in technology of which we are most proud. Justifiably proud, it may be added; for these advances are the fruits of genius and persistent hard work, of logic, imagination and self-denial—in a word, of moral and intellectual virtues for which one can feel nothing but admiration. But the Nature of Things is such that nobody in this world ever gets anything for nothing. These amazing and admirable advances have had to be paid for. Indeed, like last year's washing machine, they are still being paid for—and each installment is higher than the last. Many historians, many sociologists and psychologists have written at length, and with a deep concern, about the price that Western man has had to pay and will go on paying for technological progress. They point out, for example, that democracy can hardly be expected to flourish in societies where political and economic power is being progressively concentrated and centralized. But the progress of technology has led and is still leading to just such a concentration and centralization of power. As the machinery of mass production is made more efficient it tends to become more complex and more expensive—and so less available to the enterpriser of limited means. Moreover, mass production cannot work without mass distribution; but mass distribution raises problems which only the largest producers can satisfactorily solve. In a world of mass production and mass distribution the Little Man, with his inadequate stock of working capital, is at a grave disadvantage. In competition with the Big Man, he loses his money and finally his very existence as an independent producer; the Big Man has gobbled him up. As the Little Men disappear, more and more economic power comes to be wielded by fewer and fewer people. Under a dictatorship the Big Business, made possible by advancing technology and the consequent ruin of Little Business, is controlled by the State—that is to say, by a small group of party leaders and the soldiers, policemen and civil servants who carry out their orders. In a capitalist democracy, such as the United States, it is controlled by what Professor C. Wright Mills has called the Power Elite. This Power Elite directly employs several millions of the country's working force in its factories, offices and stores, controls many millions more by lending them the money to buy its products, and, through its ownership of the media of mass communication, influences the thoughts, the feelings and the actions of virtually everybody. To parody the words of Winston Churchill, never have so many been manipulated so much by so few. We are far indeed from Jefferson's ideal of a genuinely free society composed of a hierarchy of self-governing units—"the elementary republics of the wards, the county republics, the State republics and the Republic of the Union, forming a gradation of authorities."

We see, then, that modern technology has led to the concentration of economic and political power, and to the development of a society controlled (ruthlessly in the totalitarian states, politely and inconspicuously in the democracies) by Big Business and Big Government. But societies are composed of individuals and are good only insofar as they help individuals to realize their potentialities and to lead a happy and creative life. How have individuals been affected by the technological advances of recent years? Here is the answer to this question given by a philosopher-psychiatrist, Dr. Erich Fromm:

Our contemporary Western society, in spite of its material, intellectual and political progress, is increasingly less conducive to mental health, and tends to undermine the inner security, happiness, reason and the capacity for love in the individual; it tends to turn him into an automaton who pays for his human failure with increasing mental sickness, and with despair hidden under a frantic drive for work and so-called pleasure.

Our "increasing mental sickness" may find expression in neurotic symptoms. These symptoms are conspicuous and extremely distressing. But "let us beware," says Dr. Fromm, "of defining mental hygiene as the prevention of symptoms. Symptoms as such are not our enemy, but our friend; where there are symptoms there is conflict, and conflict always indicates that the forces of life which strive for integration and happiness are still fighting." The really hopeless victims of mental illness are to be found among those who appear to be most normal. "Many of them are normal because they are so well adjusted to our mode of existence, because their human voice has been silenced so early in their lives, that they do not even struggle or suffer or develop symptoms as the neurotic does." They are normal not in what may be called the absolute sense of the word; they are normal only in relation to a profoundly abnormal society. Their perfect adjustment to that abnormal society is a measure of their mental sickness. These millions of abnormally normal people, living without fuss in a society to which, if they were fully human beings, they ought not to be adjusted, still cherish "the illusion of individuality," but in fact they have been to a great extent deindividualized. Their conformity is developing into something like uniformity. But "uniformity and freedom are incompatible. Uniformity and mental health are incompatible too. . . . Man is not made to be an automaton, and if he becomes one, the basis for mental health is destroyed."

In the course of evolution nature has gone to endless trouble to see that every individual is unlike every other individual. We reproduce our kind by bringing the father's genes into contact with the mother's. These hereditary factors may be combined in an almost infinite number of ways. Physically and mentally, each one of us is unique. Any culture which, in the interests of efficiency or in the name of some political or religious dogma, seeks to standardize the human individual, commits an outrage against man's biological nature.

Science may be defined as the reduction of multiplicity to unity. It seeks to explain the endlessly diverse phenomena of nature by ignoring the uniqueness of particular events, concentrating on what they have in common and finally abstracting some kind of "law," in terms of which they make sense and can be effectively dealt with. For examples, apples fall from the tree and the moon moves across the sky. People had been observing these facts from time immemorial. With Gertrude Stein they were convinced that an apple is an apple is an apple, whereas the moon is the moon is the moon. It remained for Isaac Newton to perceive what these very dissimilar phenomena had in common, and to formulate a theory of gravitation in terms of which certain aspects of the behavior of apples, of the heavenly bodies and indeed of everything else in the physical universe could be explained and dealt with in terms of a single system of ideas. In the same spirit the artist takes the innumerable diversities and uniquenesses of the outer world and his own imagination and gives them meaning within an orderly system of plastic, literary or musical patterns. The wish to impose order upon confusion, to bring harmony out of dissonance and unity out of multiplicity is a kind of intellectual instinct, a primary and fundamental urge of the mind. Within the realms of science, art and philosophy the workings of what I may call this "Will to Order" are mainly beneficent. True, the Will to Order has produced many premature syntheses based upon insufficient evidence, many absurd systems of metaphysics and theology, much pedantic mistaking of notions for realities, of symbols and abstractions for the data of immediate experience.

But these errors, however regrettable, do not do much harm, at any rate directly—though it sometimes happens that a bad philosophical system may do harm indirectly, by being used as a justification for senseless and inhuman actions. It is in the social sphere, in the realm of politics and economics, that the Will to Order becomes really dangerous.

Here the theoretical reduction of unmanageable multiplicity to comprehensible unity becomes the practical reduction of human diversity to subhuman uniformity, of freedom to servitude. In politics the equivalent of a fully developed scientific theory or philosophical system is a totalitarian dictatorship. In economics, the equivalent of a beautifully composed work of art is the smoothly running factory in which the workers are perfectly adjusted to the machines. The Will to Order can make tyrants out of those who merely aspire to clear up a mess. The beauty of tidiness is used as a justification for despotism.

Organization is indispensable; for liberty arises and has meaning only within a self-regulating community of freely co-operating individuals. But, though indispensable, organization can also be fatal. Too much organization transforms men and women into automata, suffocates the creative spirit and abolishes the very possibility of freedom. As usual, the only safe course is in the middle, between the extremes of *laissez-faire* at one end of the scale and of total control at the other.

During the past century the successive advances in technology have been accompanied by corresponding advances in organization. Complicated machinery has had to be matched by complicated social arrangements, designed to work as smoothly and efficiently as the new instruments of production. In order to fit into these organizations, individuals have had to deindividualize themselves, have had to deny their native diversity and conform to a standard pattern, have had to do their best to become automata.

The dehumanizing effects of over-organization are reinforced by the dehumanizing effects of over-population. Industry, as it expands, draws an ever greater proportion of humanity's increasing

the Social Ethic, "must not demand too much of her husband's time and interest. Because of his single-minded concentration on his job, even his sexual activity must be relegated to a secondary place." The monk makes vows of poverty, obedience and chastity. The organization man is allowed to be rich, but promises obedience ("he accepts authority without resentment, he looks up to his superiors"—*Mussolini ha sempre ragione*) and he must be prepared, for the greater glory of the organization that employs him, to forswear even conjugal love.

It is worth remarking that, in *1984,* the members of the Party are compelled to conform to a sexual ethic of more than Puritan severity. In *Brave New World,* on the other hand, all are permitted to indulge their sexual impulses without let or hindrance. The society described in Orwell's fable is a society permanently at war, and the aim of its rulers is first, of course, to exercise power for its own delightful sake and, second, to keep their subjects in that state of constant tension which a state of constant war demands of those who wage it. By crusading against sexuality the bosses are able to maintain the required tension in their followers and at the same time can satisfy their lust for power in a most gratifying way. The society described in *Brave New World* is a world-state, in which war has been eliminated and where the first aim of the rulers is at all costs to keep their subjects from making trouble. This they achieve by (among other methods) legalizing a degree of sexual freedom (made possible by the abolition of the family) that practically guarantees the Brave New Worlders against any form of destructive (or creative) emotional tension. In *1984* the lust for power is satisfied by inflicting pain; in *Brave New World,* by inflicting a hardly less humiliating pleasure.

The current Social Ethic, it is obvious, is merely a justification after the fact of the less desirable consequences of over-organization. It represents a pathetic attempt to make a virtue of necessity, to extract a positive value from an unpleasant datum. It is a very unrealistic, and therefore very dangerous, system of morality. The social whole, whose value is assumed to be greater than that of its component parts, is not an organism in the sense that a hive or a termitary may be thought of as an organism. It is merely an organization, a piece of social machinery. There can be no value except in relation to life and awareness. An organization is neither conscious nor alive. Its value is instrumental and derivative. It is not good in itself; it is good only to the extent that it promotes the good of the individuals who are the parts of the collective whole. To give organizations precedence over persons is to subordinate ends to means. What happens when ends are subordinated to means was clearly demonstrated by Hitler and Stalin. Under their hideous rule personal ends were subordinated to organizational means by a mixture of violence and propaganda, systematic terror and the systematic manipulation of minds. In the more efficient dictatorships of tomorrow there will probably be much less violence than under Hitler and Stalin. The future dictator's subjects will be painlessly regimented by a corps of highly trained social engineers. "The challenge of social engineering in our time," writes an enthusiastic advocate of this new science, "is like the challenge of technical engineering fifty years ago. If the first half of the twentieth century was the era of the technical engineers, the second half may well be the era of the social engineers"—and the twenty-first century, I suppose, will be the era of World Controllers, the scientific caste system and Brave New World. To the question *quis custodiet custodes?*—Who will mount guard over our guardians, who will engineer the engineers?—the answer is a bland denial that they need any supervision. There seems to be a touching belief among certain Ph.D.'s in sociology that Ph.D.'s in sociology will never be corrupted by power. Like Sir Galahad's, their strength is as the strength of ten because their heart is pure—and their heart is pure because they are scientists and have taken six thousand hours of social studies.

Alas, higher education is not necessarily a guarantee of higher virtue, or higher political wisdom. And to these misgivings on ethical and psychological grounds must be added misgivings of a purely scientific character. Can we accept the theories on which the social engineers base their practice, and in terms of which they justify their manipulations of human beings? For example, Professor Elton Mayo tells us categorically that "man's desire to be continuously associated in work with his fellows is a strong, if not the strongest human characteristic." This, I would say, is manifestly untrue. Some people have the kind of desire described by Mayo; others do not. It is a matter of temperament and inherited constitution. Any social organization based upon the assumption that "man" (whoever "man" may be) desires to be continuously associated with his fellows would be, for many individual men and women, a bed of Procrustes. Only by being amputated or stretched upon the rack could they be adjusted to it.

Again, how romantically misleading are the lyrical accounts of the Middle Ages with which many contemporary theorists of social relations adorn their works! "Membership in a guild, manorial estate or village protected medieval man throughout his life and gave him peace and serenity." Protected him from what, we may ask. Certainly not from remorseless bullying at the hands of his superiors. And along with all that "peace and serenity" there was, throughout the Middle Ages, an enormous amount of chronic frustration, acute unhappiness and a passionate resentment against the rigid, hierarchical system that permitted no vertical movement up the social ladder and, for those who were bound to the land, very little horizontal movement in space. The impersonal forces of over-population and over-organization, and the social engineers who are trying to direct these forces, are pushing us in the direction of a new medieval system. This revival will be made more acceptable than the original by such Brave-New-Worldian amenities as infant conditioning, sleep-teaching and drug-induced euphoria; but for the majority of men and women, it will still be a kind of servitude.

FOR THE STUDENT

Rhetoric

1. *What is Huxley's purpose in introducing Milton's Adam and Eve into a discussion of the Organization Man?*
2. *There are a half-dozen sentences in this essay which might serve as its thesis. Pick out two or three.*

Discussion

1. *Huxley shows apprehension about "social engineering." Would he think of Galbraith as a "social engineer"?*
2. *Does the sexual ethic of* Brave New World *or of* 1984 *correspond more closely to that of today's society?*
3. *Comment on: "Alas, higher education is not necessarily a guarantee of higher virtue, or higher political wisdom."*

Writing

1. *Expand and explain, in a four-hundred-word paper, Huxley's brief remarks about the "Will to Order." Supply illustrative examples where appropriate.*
2. *Write an imaginative essay describing a society of "Ant Men."*

LEONARD R. SAYLES

The Organization Man:
How Real a Problem?

Recently we have witnessed a new variation on the old theme that business destroys (or at least eats away) the souls of those who come within its grasp. The eating-away process used to refer to ethics and morality. Caught up in the profit-making system, men who otherwise might dedicate themselves to a life of unselfish service sought instead a far tinnier Holy Grail—the almighty dollar. Although as generalizations about an entire system these condemnations embodied exaggerations, they had the virtue of sensitizing the community to excesses. A growing sense of business responsibility and protection against willful discharge and sweatshop servitude may to some extent be due to their harsh repetition. If this is true, then there may be a virtue in what is otherwise a somewhat puzzling new accusation: Life in the business organization induces excessive conformity and dependence.[1]

The critics do not mean that people caught up in the soulless web of the corporation are converted into money-grubbing robots or ever-fearful wage slaves. They say, rather, that contemporary organizations are a threat to the psyche. Employees and managers

This material was presented at the Arden House conference and later published in Eliot D. Chapple and Leonard R. Sayles, The Measure of Management, *The Macmillan Company, New York, 1961. Copyright by The Macmillan Company, 1961.*

1. Two of the most extensive nonfiction works representing this new critique of business are: William H. Whyte, Jr., *The Organization Man,* Simon and Schuster, Inc., New York, 1956; and (with a very different point of view) Chris Argyris, *Personality and Organization,* Harper & Row, Publishers, Incorporated, New York, 1957. A recent fictionalized account of the debilitations induced by the large corporation is Alan Harrington's *Life in the Crystal Palace,* Alfred A. Knopf, Inc., New York, 1959. [Author's note]

in our large companies lose their sense of independence, their pluck, and their daring. Instead of devoting themselves to highly individualistic programs of self-improvement (money-grubbing?), they become dedicated to the seductive goals of being accepted and even being liked by boss and colleague. These are the organization men.

The highly negative fear of losing acceptance becomes the dominating motive, to replace the more positive goal of conquering new frontiers. The critics argue that conforming to the group and kowtowing to the boss absorb all the energies which might be more healthily devoted to constructive development of personality and the corporate and community balance sheet. The result must be slow but sure destruction of national character.

Perhaps the generous reception given to the organization-man image is a hallmark of our steady progress in humanizing the conditions of work and the position of the subordinate. Rather than the callous, over-demanding boss who gets what he wants regardless of the human cost, we are apparently now concerned with his diametric opposite—the group thinker who is more concerned with social cohesion than he is with profit. Surely we have now come around the full circle. Less than two decades ago Elton Mayo's fear about the lack of administrators who could banish the sense of individual isolation (or "anomie," the concept he drew from Durkheim) was the accepted tenet of faith.

As more adherents join a bandwagon that has the additional lure of playing a quasipsychiatric theme, one is reminded of the extremes of "progressive" education and child rearing. Not long ago, the home and the school were the villains. Both at the hearth and at the blackboard our young were being repressed, their individualism squashed long before it could flower. The reasoning was much the same—humans flourish best in an unfettered, unrestricted, free-to-do-as-they-please environment. Fixity of structure, it was insisted, must produce rigidity of mind. The extremists felt, as does the organization-is-an-inhibitor school of thought, that discipline and controls, externally imposed goals, hurt the individual who both desired and needed complete freedom.

Parenthetically, we might ask why the concept of an "organization man" has had such wide and immediate appeal. Is it not the perfect self-rationalization for those individuals whose success has not measured up to their ambitions? They are reassured by the belief that group thinking and conformity have so won over the decision makers in our large corporations that the individual who stands out from the crowd cannot get ahead. Some who use this ready-made excuse confuse the lip service given by companies to presently popular clichés like "teamwork" and "participation" with an actual description of what management expects. Platitudinous statements concerning objectives, values, or goals may bear little resemblance to the types of activities in which a company engages. The organization, as we shall be observing, both needs and rewards distinctive and unique personality characteristics such as high energy, initiative, and the ability to tolerate unfriendly responses. They may talk about a good "team man," but the uncommon men are the ones who will get ahead and eventually reach the top-level positions.

Opposite Findings from Research

Students of man cannot help but be amused by this whole surprising trend in the critique of business. There are no studies that show man in some Eden-like status of complete independence. In the most primitive state and in all the records of history, man has sought and flourished in tribes and clans, communities, and associations. If half a dozen people are placed in a room with a common task, we can predict they will quickly evolve common routines of behavior and even a self-imposed organizational structure. The latter will include leadership to initiate instructions, and the group will penalize deviations from approved standards of behavior. Conformity will be expected, and dependence will be readily forthcoming. The street-corner gang, like the office clique, makes such excessive demands for conformity in thought and action with an impunity that makes the routines of the organization and the demands of its authority pale by comparison.

Man apparently neither wants nor has experienced this postulated state of complete autonomy. People have always demanded structure in their lives. With few exceptions, men depend on human relationships, some fixity of structure, routine, and habit to survive psychologically. Although we do not like to admit it, most of us flee from a vacuumlike absence of structured relationship. Students of business organization know well that one of management's basic problems is to find enough people with characteristics of leadership who will take initiative and who can operate in a relatively unstructured situation. The demand of subordinates for situations in which they can be dependent, not the supply of overbearing authority, is frequently the problem. Companies seeking to make decentralization operative discover, to their sorrow, that unwillingness to accept responsibility or to take initiative, and the desire to have each decision sanctified by the boss's OK are everpresent blocks to successful delegation.

What about the emotional needs of the man on the work level? Is it not true that extremes of the division of labor and autocratic, dominating supervisors rob the individual of any real sense of accomplishment and satisfaction in his job?

Put in these terms, this concern might also be shown to be misplaced. Many workers voluntarily choose the simplest, most routine, most subdivided task. While job enlargement must appeal to some, for many it is a threat to the more idyllic assurance of untroubled working hours, free for daydreaming, social chatter, and strategic planning to "beat the rate." Employees certainly do not always seek additional responsibility and decreased dependence.

The Nature of Organization

Contemporary fiction, sermons, and social science have become enamored of their moans over the fate of the individual in the large organization. Unfortunately, the eagerness with which the term "organization man" has been adopted has resulted in substantial confusion, a good portion of which stems from its original promulgation. The essence of organization, of organizational behavior, involves learning to follow routine procedures. Of necessity the organization must be a predictable system of human relationships, where rhythm and repetition are the vital components. This may come as a rude shock to those who think of managers as constantly improvising new activities. Chester Barnard once commented candidly that during a year as president of the New Jersey Bell Telephone Company he had to make only *one* decision that was, in fact, a real choice between alternatives. The preponderant elements of organizational behavior consist of matters such as Joe's knowing that he must check Bill's activities two or three times a week, must be available when Al gets into trouble, and must sit with his boss at least an hour a day to work through plans for the following day. The combination of work-flow imperatives and personality needs provides the raw material for these predictable and rhythmical patterns of interaction.

It must be remembered that in speaking of an organization we imply some degree of permanence—the need for predictable repetition, self-maintenance, assured continuity, and regulated activity. Only when the regular business of an organization is functioning properly—following the *routines* of acquisition, processing, and distribution (of ideas, materials, or paper)—can individuals apply, or are they likely to be permitted to apply, their rational, creative talents to the challenge of new, unsolved problems. Imagination, innovation, and intellectual vigor cannot prosper where individual energies are fully utilized in handling recurring crises.

In this regard, the president of the Brookings Institution recently observed:

If administrators are asked to nominate the aspects of the task that are most time-consuming and frustrating to the exercise of their responsibilities, they will agree that they are preoccupied with distractions; with inconsequential little things that push themselves ahead of important issues; with the tyranny of the telephone; with the relentless flitting from one issue to another; with the ceaseless procession of interviews and ceremonials; with the pressure of circumstance and deadlines; and with the absence of time to collect one's wits, much less to think or reflect. Only a superb or a hard-boiled administrator can cut through this daily morass to concentrate on the important responsibilities that he cannot shirk.[2]

Although Barnard's statement may well be something of an exaggeration, among the most crucial problems of any organization are those concerned with the development of predictable routines. Frayed tempers, suppressed and not so suppressed, hostility, and individual frustration resulting from ineffective organization destroy individual competence.

In other fields in which organization plays a part we are not so shocked by this. The most dramatic and best known is sport. Baseball and football teams are the most common examples of organizations where the interrelation of the work routines (the plays) is dependent upon the careful adjustment of players to one another and to the coaches. Here complicated plays and split-second coordination cannot be executed unless the organization is made up of individuals well adjusted to one another. The job of the coach is to see that this is accomplished, to select a series of plays best fitted to the capacities of his materials, and to fit together players who can supplement each other's abilities. To develop a smooth-working organization, he must handle personalities so skillfully that good teamwork becomes almost second nature. As a result, the experts and the fans discuss learnedly whether coach A is getting the most out of his material, whether catcher B can handle his pitchers, whether star C is wrecking the morale of the team.

2. Robert D. Calkins, "The Decision Process in Administration," *Business Horizons,* vol. 2, no. 3, p. 20, Fall, 1952. [Author's note]

Business organizations are like teams, but vastly more complicated. The same factors of plays and personalities combine to make an organization, and the adjustment that goes on from day to day determines whether the company is to have effective coordination or will constantly suffer from personnel dissatisfaction, labor disputes, and inefficiency.[3]

Does this necessity create "organization men"? Members of outstanding instrumental groups like the Budapest String Quartet have developed almost perfect coordination; they can count on each other for completely predictable behavior. It is doubtful that this coordination has destroyed their individuality. Off the job, in the full development of their personalities and interests, they live very different lives. Great athletic teams have consisted of people who had little liking for one another—e.g., "Tinker to Evers to Chance"—amply demonstrating their uncongeniality in their personal lives. Nevertheless, they learned the skills and routines essential for the successful conduct of their organizational affairs.

One would hazard a guess that a great deal of the excitement about conformity is due to the *absence* of knowledge concerning what is required for effective organizational activity, like the primitive tribe that does not understand the movements of the heavenly bodies and the occurrence of thunderstorms. Not knowing how to assess Jones's contribution to effective management, we evolve irrational fetishes and taboos. The striped tie, the ivy-league suit, the sheepskin, the appropriate tone of voice, automobile, wife, and home location, even the testing programs designed to exclude all but the "safe" pedestrian types: these are all manifestations of imperfect knowledge about how to evaluate an executive or a new employee. They are not the inevitable products of life in a large organization.

As we develop more understanding about methods of improv-

3. We hope the reader will not think we are indulging in the old stereotype of the company president in exhorting his coworkers, "We're all on the same team, boys." We are not talking about "togetherness," but the development and synchronization of a complex set of plays (organization) by which the company operates. [Author's note]

ing the mastery of organizational behavior, we can believe that the nonsensical elements will disappear just as rain dances have fallen into disrepute in most civilized locations. Fitting personalities together to evolve coordination and sound structure does not require fixed patterns of thought and of family and community life.

We must be careful to urge businessmen to deal with real problem areas, not those that may be the easiest to sell during a period when terms like *conformity* are so popular. The human relations problems of business will not be solved by extreme, sweeping assertions and accusations, any more than the field of mental health will be improved by arguments that neuroses are enveloping us all. It has always been good sport to beat at our sources of institutional power, including business, and one of the strengths of Western democracy has been this permissive climate. But we must not confuse sermons with science. We readily concede that there are problems of large scale in contemporary life. Mass communications, for example, in our type of society raise serious questions concerning opportunities for individual expression, privilege in democracy that we rightfully cherish. Further, living with authority, of course, has never been easy. Philosophers undoubtedly will continue to struggle with one of the persistent problems of life: freedom versus authority. The balance is always a tenuous one. Life in the presence of other human beings involves cooperative endeavors and government, and consequently necessitates authority. We must always live with an uneasy balance between the inevitable personal restrictions and our ambivalent needs for both dependence and freedom. The problem neither began nor will it end with the corporation.

The Modern Manager versus
The Business Buccaneer

As an alternative to this straw man, the organization man, the old-style business buccaneer is having a renaissance. In the current swing to idolize the swashbuckler, even the robber baron

has had a resurrection. After all, weren't these the true believers—
the nonconformists who allowed neither codes nor public disapproval nor built-in inhibition to stand in the way of their single-
minded objectives? By contrast, the contemporary manager,
concerned with public and industrial relations and with an organizational structure to maximize human effectiveness, at best casts
only a faint shadow. Or so the critics would have us believe.

It is strange indeed that the contemporary manager is now
being maligned for what is his greatest challenge and potential
accomplishment. The maintenance of effective human relationships
in large-scale organizations is one of the marvels of our age. The
skills of administration required to direct and control tens of
thousands of people with differing backgrounds and interests, in
order to produce coordinated effort directed toward predetermined
objectives, tower above the achievements of the business bucca-
neers of an earlier age. They dealt with a few, simple variables
primarily in the market place. Their apparent bravery and daring
were more a product of the simplicity of their problem than of
extraordinary skills or brute native courage. The diverse and complex responsibilities of the modern business offer a challenge many
times more exciting to human abilities than an uncomplicated
"inner-directed" objective of maximum personal profits.

FOR THE STUDENT

Rhetoric

1. *After you have read the entire essay, re-read the first paragraph and formulate a thesis sentence from it.*
2. *How valid do you find the analogies of business organizations to the baseball team and the string quartet? Early in
   the essay Sayles speaks of "the lip service given by companies to presently popular clichés like 'teamwork' and*

'*participation.*' " *After his analogy to the baseball team, he says, "Business organizations are like teams. . . ." Is this lip service?*

3. *Explain the implications of the statement near the end of this essay: "But we must not confuse sermons with science."*

Discussion

1. *How does Sayles attempt to make a virtue out of the concept of the organization man?*
2. *Does Sayles imply that "complete independence" or "complete autonomy" is what the critics of the organization, man consider the alternative to organization? Examine Sayles's discussion closely on this point.*
3. *Huxley in "Over-Organization" states: "It is in the social sphere, in the realm of politics and economics, that the Will to Order becomes really dangerous." How would Sayles answer this statement?*

Writing

1. *Write a paper of five hundred words on the topic, "Freedom versus Authority," using an extended illustration to develop your thesis.*
2. *Write an imaginary dialogue between Huxley and Sayles on the organization man.*

3 Civil Disobedience

While the subject of civil disobedience probably has greater currency today than at any other time in our history, it is in no way a recent phenomenon. More than two thousand years ago, Socrates discussed disobedience to the laws and the state. In the United States, Thoreau's "Civil Disobedience" is the almost definitive statement on the problem. His views have ranged far. Gandhi stated explicitly that Thoreau's essay provided the philosophical basis for his acts of civil disobedience against British rule in India. While the problem today frequently concerns the legal and moral limits of civil disobedience, no one expresses a rational opposition. As Joseph L. Sax states in his essay, people simply want those laws they like enforced and those they do not like ignored.

The three writers whose essays follow explore various facets of the problem. While the range of views from Left to Right may not appear very great, there exist important differences in points of view. Joseph L. Sax, a professor of law at the University of Michigan, opposes the "mystique" of "the law"; he is concerned with "humane judgments" and extralegal considerations in dealing with civil disobedience; in brief, he advocates justice over mere legality. Salvador de Madariaga, a Spanish diplomat and a teacher at some of the great European universities, counsels prudence, caution, and scrupulous moral analysis, but his ultimate concern is with the free individual and the individual's responsibility. Abe Fortas, former Justice of the Supreme Court, while not actually a conservative, gives the main thrust of his argument a conservative direction. His constant theme is the rule of law; his point of view is that of society and the dangers which massive civil disobedience might bring to the state.

JOSEPH L. SAX

Civil Disobedience:
The Law Is Never Blind

Nobody is opposed to civil disobedience; people simply want the laws that they deem important to be vigorously enforced and those they consider unfair to be ignored. Most motorists consider the idea of a speed trap outrageous, but rarely complain when policemen conceal themselves in public washrooms to ferret out homosexuals. The annual antics of American Legion conventioneers are viewed as harmless enough fun, but let political protestors go out in the streets and all the rigors of the law relating to trespass, obstruction of traffic, and disturbing the peace are suddenly remembered, whereupon we are solemnly told that acquiescence in illegality is the first step on the road to anarchy.

Through the miracle of prosecutorial discretion—a device central to the operation of the legal system, but widely ignored in discussions of civil disobedience—criminality can be, and is, produced or ignored virtually at will by law enforcement officials. Businessmen know that if the building and fire laws were fully implemented they could be in court virtually every day, a fact which is allegedly brought home to them when they are so unwise as to refrain from buying tickets to the annual policemen's ball.

Justice Jackson once said that "a prosecutor has more control over life, liberty, and reputation than any other person in America . . . he can choose his defendant . . . a prosecutor stands a fair chance of finding at least a technical violation of some act on the part of almost anyone." No more profound statement was ever made about the legal system.

From Saturday Review, *September 28, 1968. Copyright 1968 Saturday Review, Inc. Reprinted by permission.*

[71]

The law is so vast in its technical coverage and so open-ended in its possibilities for interpretation by police officers, prosecutors, and judges that it becomes almost meaningless to talk about civil disobedience as if there were conduct which "the law"—as some external force—declared illegal.

In fact, no society could operate if it did not tolerate a great deal of technically or arguably illegal conduct on the ground that certain laws were obsolescent and others unwise as written or as applied to particular situations. A few weeks ago, newspapers carried the story of a man who had lured several boys to a mountain cabin, bound and then sexually abused them. One of the boys worked himself free, seized a rifle, and killed his abductor. The local prosecutor announced that no proceedings against the boy were contemplated, a result undoubtedly approved by every reader. Because the law of self-defense is so restrictive in permitting the use of deadly force, a technical case of murder might have been made out against the boy; the circumstances, however, made clear that it would have been unjust to prosecute. It is not strict obedience to the law, but the sense of justice, which we require in the administration of the legal system.

The same breadth of discretion which produced justice in the case of the abducted boy can be turned toward less attractive ends, depending on the inclinations of those who are charged with administering the law. To be sure, such discretion is not generally exercised arbitrarily. It is used to "fill the interstices," as lawyers sometimes put it—that is, to act in accordance with what it is thought the legislature would have done if it had considered the particular circumstances of the pending case. It is only a special class of cases which ordinarily raise the danger of unjust manipulation—those where political considerations make prosecution indiscreet or, conversely, where there are special incentives to go forward.

In the former category are cases where the rich and the powerful find themselves able to "settle" potential criminal prosecutions.

Thus, the Southern oligarchs were not indicted for criminal conspiracy when they produced their massive resistance campaign against the school integration decision, or led the fight to stand in the schoolhouse door, while Dr. Spock and other war resisters were readily brought to trial under the umbrella of the vague and amorphous conspiracy doctrine.

No one who sat through the four weeks of trial in which Benjamin Spock, William Sloane Coffin, Mitchell Goodman, and Michael Ferber were convicted of conspiracy to abet violation of the draft law could have doubted that Judge Francis Ford was persuaded of the rightness of the Government's case against them, or that the trial reflected his persuasion. The fact that one of the five defendants was ultimately acquitted is not a tribute to the fairness of the trial, but is, rather, a measure of the sloppiness with which the Government put its case together.

The possibilities for judicial management were most clearly illuminated by the way in which Judge Ford handled the question of the Vietnam war. A principal issue which the defense wished to raise was that the conduct of the Vietnam war violated international treaties governing such questions as the treatment of civilians and devastation of cities and towns. If the conduct of the war was illegal, the defendants argued, then to advocate refusal to participate in the war would be lawful, for it is not a crime to counsel one to refuse to do an illegal act. Moreover, even if the defendants were wrong about the legality of the war, they might have been found to have had a reasonable and good-faith belief in its illegality. Such a belief might itself have been sufficient to produce an acquittal under the legal precedents governing their case.

For each of these reasons it was tactically essential to the defendants that they be permitted to introduce evidence about the conduct of the war; not only would such evidence lend support to the foregoing claims, but it would have converted the trial from a turgid reiteration of the defendants' speeches to a dramatic inquiry into the justification for the radical political posture in which they found themselves.

Had the judge permitted such evidence to be introduced, and had the jury been told that they might have acquitted upon finding the defendants' beliefs to be reasonable and held in good faith, the chances for acquittal would obviously have been vastly increased. A sympathetic, or less hostile, judge might very well, and rationally, have taken such a course. And had there been an acquittal, the case would have been at an end; Dr. Spock and his co-defendants would walk the streets today as fully free men, and there would be no issue of civil disobedience to talk about in their case.

To anyone who appreciated the freedom of choice available to Judge Ford during the trial, and his ample use of it, it was particularly ironic to hear the prosecuting attorney's closing argument on civil disobedience:

They feel something is wrong or right. They feel it and they act on that feeling on their conscience.

Is this country going to be tied to a string that is tied to Mr. Coffin's conscience? Is it going to be tied to a string, even to the conscience of a man as sincere and as dedicated and as great as Dr. Spock?

It can't be.

The prosecutor failed to remind the jury of the extent to which their decision had been tied to a string that was tied to Francis Ford's inclinations, or that they wouldn't have been there at all had not some prosecutor decided that these five people, out of the thousands who had acted similarly, ought to be tried.

There is no answer to the question of whether Dr. Spock and his co-defendants violated "the law." It is not that law imposes no constraints upon a judge; it is simply that there is so much room for maneuver within those constraints that either of two conflicting results can frequently be produced. Francis Ford presided over their conviction; another judge could have found a dozen cogent reasons, all supported by precedent and good legal logic, to have dismissed the indictment before the trial ever began. Nor is the opportunity for appeal necessarily any solution, for the process of choice continues right up the judicial ladder. A dozen wrong men —all part of the same legalistic tradition—produce as little justice as one.

Since the law could have been used either to acquit or convict, the only truly relevant question is whether it was just that the law be used to convict. It is no easy task to make lawyers peek out from behind that supposedly value-free façade, "the law," and to talk about unjust laws and unjust administration of the law; but out they must come and face the reality of prosecutorial and judicial discretion.

There are a series of quite concrete considerations which can be applied to resolve the issue of the Spock-Coffin case and other similar prosecutions. Of course, they have no scientific certainty, and many may disagree as to the answers. But such uncertainty is the essence of the problem, and one deceives himself if he thinks he can avoid such individualization by recourse to the law—he is only tying himself to a string which is tied to some Francis Ford.

The first question is what social good is to be achieved by incarcerating men like Spock, Coffin, Goodman, and Ferber. They do not present the immediate danger to others of those who commit violent acts. Indeed, by advocating a form of passive resistance to governmental fiat, they operate at one of the least abrasive levels of conduct respecting an impact on the rights or property of others.

Moreover, the nature of their resistance is such that a layer of governmental decision is always imposed between their action and the prospect of harm to others. For example, it is clearly less intrusive for one opposed to school integration to boycott the schools than it is to stand in the doorway and prevent others from entering. And the boycott is very far removed from the acts of those who express their dissent by throwing a stone or a bomb. This is not to suggest that passive resistance should always be in-

sulated from legal sanctions, but merely that the society's willingness to tolerate such conduct should be much greater than for
direct action.

Another conventional rationale for incarceration is the desire
to deter others similarly inclined. Where dissenting political activity
is involved, history strongly suggests the inefficacy of such a response. One is hard-pressed to cite a political movement which
has been suppressed through the jailing of its leaders. While it was
said in the Spock-Coffin case that the prosecution was not directed
at ideology, but rather at particular conduct, the record suggests
the dubiousness of the distinction made by the Government between thought and action.

The defendants were charged only with talking and publishing,
collecting and returning some draft cards, and engaging in peaceful
demonstrations. Even the Government did not urge that any of its
conduct in itself put a significant burden on the prosecution of its
policies. The essence of the Government's case was that the defendants' persuasiveness and prestige were an incitement to young
men to resist the draft—not that their touching of draft cards, or
any such formal acts, were at the heart of the danger which they
supposedly posed to the state. Yet it was the formal act of participating in a draft card return which made the Government's technical legal case against them. Upon such sands is the difference between criminality and innocence built in "the law." A commonsense inquiry into the justice of their prosecution makes it easy to
see that it was their respectablity, ideology, and forcefulness which
were really at stake. Those elements are not likely to be amenable
to incarceration.

It is also important to ask whether the society is likely to be
affirmatively benefited by the defendants' acts. Here two considerations apply. Are they raising an important issue which ought to be
confronted by the public, and are they raising it in as minimally
abrasive a way as circumstances and the limitations of legal institutions permit? Certainly the former question can be answered

affirmatively; the attempt to promote an investigation of the conduct of the Vietnam war in light of American treaty obligations is decidedly a matter of great public importance. And the inability to get that issue raised in any conventional proceeding, such as the formal committee of inquiry which defendant Marcus Raskin had been urging, invites some degree of tolerance for their unconventional conduct. This element of a constructive goal in their acts ought to weigh heavily in vindication of their conduct and distinguish it from activity which is limited to active obstruction of a matter adequately settled through some political or legal institution.

As one turns away from legalistic thinking about the problems of protest, it becomes apparent that no large, general formulae are going to resolve the infinitely varied issues which arise. In the common situation where a group of housewives block a bulldozer's path to protect the destruction of a park, for example, there are at least two good reasons to refrain from prosecution at the outset, though technically a conviction might easily be obtained for trespassing or the obstruction of traffic. Often such a maneuver is designed to inform the general public of an unknown situation and to promote more serious consideration by the appropriate public officials.

Certainly these are acceptable goals, and as a practical matter only newspaper publicity is likely to be an effective prod. Considering the tendency of the papers to ignore less dramatic moves and the generally minimal adverse impact on the project by a few days' obstruction, the ladies' tactic would seem an appropriate and tolerable means of promoting the political process. We ought not to balk at taking into account the reality that a neighborhood group is unlikely to be very effective in going through the more conventional channels used by established lobbies or that they are unlikely to have the means to produce a substantial paid advertising campaign.

Once having achieved appropriate attention, however, the social benefit of their protest is generally exhausted; having been prodded, the political process in an area such as this tends to be viable, and the public need not accommodate itself to perpetual obstruction. In fact, this is precisely the way such matters are usually resolved; prosecutorial discretion is exercised to refrain from initiating a criminal prosecution at the early publicity stage of protest. We accommodate to a degree of civil disobedience whose social usefulness outweighs its detriments, and hang "the law" which says obstructing traffic is a crime.

Refusal to pay income taxes for reasons of political protest presents another variant of the problem. The device is a useful one, for the refusal to pay taxes is a serious act and the degree to which it is adopted on a particular issue can be a significant measure of the breadth and depth of public feeling on that issue. While a government cannot be expected simply to ignore the nonpayment of taxes, it has at its command an intermediate device whereby it can accommodate to both the positive and negative aspects of refusals.

Where political protest is involved in the refusal, the Government can refrain from criminal prosecution, while going forward to recover the money due by attaching other assets of the taxpayer. This process involves some cost and inconvenience to the taxpayer, as it does to the Government; yet from the point of view of both, the price thus paid is small considering the benefits of promoting vigorous interchange between them. Again, this is a device which the Government seems to use with many tax protests; and again the rigors of the civil disobedience dilemma are resolved at the low visibility level of a discretionary decision.

As one moves on toward more overt direct action, such as the recent situation in which the Reverend Philip Berrigan poured blood over some draft board records in protest against the Vietnam war, the problem obviously becomes more difficult. Nonetheless, certain guidelines can be used to ask how accommodating we ought to be. Certainly it is relevant to weigh the symbolic content of the act against its adverse impact on the state.

Where only a few records are defaced, and they are easily re-placed or duplicated, and where the protest involves an issue as imminent in its impact on human life as war, it is reasonable to ask for a substantial degree of tolerance. Whatever the statute re-lating to the destruction of government records might say, or however the free speech provision might be read by lawyers, it is the essence of a justly administered system that it be able to dis-tinguish between an act with so little destructive impact and one in which whole sets of files were systematically destroyed. And even in such a case, consideration ought at least to be given to the moral differential between property destruction and the effort to pre-serve life from the ravages of war.

It is precisely these distinctions which the formal legal system seems to be so unwilling to consider, as evidenced by the Supreme Court decision this year upholding the conviction of a draft-card burner; that, surely, was an act overwhelmingly of protest content, with only the most trivial justification of need for possession of selective service documents by individual registrants.

Both the draft-card burning case and that of Father Berrigan—in which sentences of six years were imposed—are illustrative of another element in the formal legal system produced by its unwill-ingness to recognize a certain tolerant flexibility as an essential of justice. This is the general refusal to review sentences.

It is fruitless to argue abstractly, as the debates over civil dis-obedience usually do, about whether Father Berrigan should have been convicted. The real issue is whether we ought to be willing in substantial measure to accommodate ourselves to such protests as his in recognition of their social value. There would be little to debate if Berrigan had been sentenced to a symbolic thirty days in jail; the injustice of his case is the extraordinarily vindictive nature of the sentence, by which he is classed with those who commit the most vicious crimes against the personal liberty of others.

Similarly irrelevant is the fear that every man will become a law unto himself. That is not the issue at all; no one in his right mind would suggest that a man should be exculpated from criminal responsibility simply because he thinks he ought to be. Rather, the issue is whether the public will be willing to tolerate some conduct that policemen, prosecutors, and judges think ought not to be tolerated.

The principal weapon available to implement a counterforce to such officials is an independent public unwilling to abdicate consideration of the justice with which the law is enforced. Where the criminal law is employed against political opponents of government, such independence is most urgently needed, lest self-interest affect the usual restraint through which justice and the law are harmonized. A public less bedazzled by the mystique of "the law" and more willing to look through to the question of justness will inevitably be strengthened in its ability to impose upon public officials pressure to be less (or, as the case may be, more) vigorous in seeking to attribute criminality to particular kinds of conduct.

A substantial outcry by the press and general public against the Spock trial would have gone far to stifle the prospect of other such prosecution; instead, we got the widespread response that "the law" left the Government little choice but to proceed as it did. Sometimes more direct action may be required. Jurors may simply have to refuse to convict, or grand jurors to indict. An independent citizenry has ways.

Finally, it should be noted that at no point is it suggested that weight ought to be given to the fact that the actor is sincerely and conscientiously committed to his point of view. That issue is one of the typical red herrings thrust into ordinary civil disobedience debates. As is often and correctly pointed out, one can be as sincere and conscientious about exterminating the Jews as about ending the war in Vietnam. It is not sincerity that counts, but the justness of one's goals and the appropriateness of the means employed to reach them. The greatest danger of all is that an excessive focusing upon the legality of situations tends to blind one to the obligation to make humane judgments, a responsibility that cannot be obscured by the observation that no scientific consensus can be reached. A society which cares about itself requires a citizenry that is ready to see a moral difference between one who protests against the killing in a place such as Vietnam and one who protests to prevent black children from getting a decent education. To abdicate that responsibility is only to begin the march in law-abiding lockstep toward moral oblivion.

FOR THE STUDENT

Rhetoric

1. *State Sax's thesis in one sentence.*
2. *Comment on the use of the word* abrasive *in paragraph seventeen.*
3. *Make a list of ten "learned" words from this essay. Does this list lead to any conclusions about Sax's style?*

Discussion

1. *How do Sax's comments on the prosecuting attorney's closing argument in the Spock-Coffin case illustrate what he has earlier called the open-ended possibilities for interpretation of the law?*
2. *How would Sax respond to this statement: "Ours is a government of laws, not of men"?*
3. *How do Sax's arguments uphold the view that legality is not necessarily morality?*
4. *Suppose Sax were the public prosecutor at the appropriate time: how would he rule on the "civil disobedience" of Socrates? Of Jesus Christ?*

Writing

1. *Consult the* Readers' Guide *in your library for articles about the Spock-Coffin case. Compile arguments pro and con.*
2. *Make up three examples of illegality (for example, traffic and parking violations) which ought to go unprosecuted. Write a paper explaining why and defending your decisions.*

SALVADOR DE MADARIAGA

Civil Disobedience

There is no other objective way of understanding political progress than as an evolution from government by force to government by consent. A country is the more advanced the less violence it needs for the ordinary running of its collective affairs and even for its critical periods, when a phase of its life gives way to another phase. A typical example is Great Britain, where not only the normal change over from Labour to Tory government or vice versa is effected without a single pane being as much as scratched in the country, but where as profound a sociological revolution as that which began in 1914 and is still going on is taking place in perfect internal peace.

Since this way of understanding progress is grounded on the rule of law, the issue of disobedience to the law as a moral issue would at first seem idle. Disobedience to the law is a form of violence. It is therefore regressive. This conclusion, however, must be carefully qualified.

It is all very well to assert that we must obey the law. But whose law? What if the law itself is a form of violence? As a first approximation to a solution of this thorny problem, a distinction might be suggested between legitimate law and illegitimate law. Legitimate law must be obeyed. Illegitimate law need not be obeyed, and might even have to be disobeyed.

Our problem now has shifted to one of discovering a criterion to tell legitimate from illegitimate law. Here again we may seek a first approximation: legitimate can only be a law freely accepted by the freely organized institutions of the community to which it applies. This means that the community in question is governed by its own public opinion.

From A Matter of Life *edited by Clara Urquhart, 1963. Reprinted by permission of Jonathan Cape, Ltd., London, England.*

[83]

It follows that, provided a community is ruled by its public opinion, civil disobedience amounts to violence, and is therefore regressive.

Yet, even now we find on reflection that our conclusion stands in need of both clarification and qualification. Clarification, first. The statement that the rule by public opinion is the basis of a true democracy presupposes that this public opinion is free, spontaneous and well informed. Were this not so, the legitimacy of the law would evidently not be established. It seems plain, therefore, that it is open to any citizen to raise the question of the legitimacy of the law on this particular, purely institutional ground.

Does this justify civil disobedience? There is no prefabricated answer to this question. It seems that, within the four corners of a hypothetical situation such as that described here, there is room for seeking to improve matters by discussion; and that, if such is the case, civil disobedience would not be justified. If, however, the situation gave rise to no hope of betterment by discussion, or in cases of urgency, the dissentient citizen would find himself before a moral problem. He would have to decide whether his unfavourable judgment on the working of public opinion in his country was to prevail over that of the vast majority of his countrymen. I do not say it shouldn't. I say that it takes a tremendous faith in one's own judgment to believe that it must, and that there is here a risk of arrogance and therefore of error. This, however, is a caution, not a bar to action. It merely appeals to the free responsibility of the free citizen. That is all.

Once he has decided that he is right and the majority wrong, the dissident citizen has still to examine whether civil disobedience is the best or the only way to mend matters. He must be fully conscious of a number of reasons which would counsel prudence; for instance: that, in its very core, civil disobedience is regressive, even if in the case in question its immediate effects might in fact be progressive; or that what he does today, with his first-rate intellect and his pure heart, may be imitated tomorrow by duller brains and darker hearts. If he can pass over all these hurdles unfettered by his conscience, let him disobey.

So much for the clarification. Now, the qualification. A public opinion may be free, spontaneous and well informed and yet hopelessly wrong. It is a sad, disquieting, but indisputable fact that public opinion may go astray, indeed berserk. The ways it can err are so varied, the form and the gravity of the errors may differ so much, that, here again, the citizen is left to his own resources (subject to what I may have to say later on this precise point). There are cases too obvious to doubt. The world is unfortunately familiar with many, owing to relatively recent Nazi and communist abominations, events which if any ought to have given forth abundant crops of civic disobedience. But in probably the majority of cases the issue will raise every one of the points outlined above under 'clarification'. Am I sure my judgment is right? Is it not arrogant of me to be so sure of being right when so many people, many of them able, dissent from me? Even if I am right, is civil disobedience the best way out? But it does not follow that the citizen who ends this examination by going boldly for disobedience is necessarily wrong.

It would nevertheless seem advisable in any case for any citizen of a free country not to plunge into civil disobedience without an exhaustive inquiry, a widespread seeking of advice, and a persistent and patient recourse to the usual ways a true liberal democracy leaves open for a change of heart. The advice of other men recognized as disinterested and wise might be perhaps the most important step in this procedure. The sharpest intellect may be induced into error by a passionately held conviction whose very heat would deflect the otherwise straight rays of his vision. A strongly held view may lead to narrowing the field of vision and to twisting the object seen. Minority views are often the heralds of progress. This they achieve when they are not merely freaks but precursors. In such a case they are sure to appeal to at least a good number of wise and disinterested observers. To solicit the advice of such men would be prudent in any case; it becomes indispensable if a step as grave as civil disobedience is contemplated.

So, in the last analysis, the issue remains undecided; and the individual citizen cannot seek refuge in a hard-and-fast rule of behaviour. This is as it should be. The nobility of man's life is in his liberty and that of his liberty in his responsibility; and that of his responsibility in the originality of his every deed. Thus every minute of a free man's life is endowed with creative energy; and that is why freedom is to history what air is to life.

FOR THE STUDENT

Rhetoric

1. *English is not Madariaga's first language: rewrite sentence seven in paragraph nine for clarity.*
2. *Look up the following words in your dictionary and define them in the context of paragraph seven where they are used: prefabricated, dissentient, bar.*

Discussion

1. *Madariaga says, "Minority views are often the heralds of progress." Give three examples from American or European history.*
2. *In paragraph nine Madariaga uses the phrase "civic disobedience." What is the distinction between that and "civil disobedience"?*
3. *Can you understand, from the final paragraph, why some people prefer* not *to be free?*

Writing

1. *The dissentient, Madariaga maintains, must be convinced his disobedience will achieve the greater good and not be imitated "by duller brains and darker hearts." Write a paper in which you apply this statement to some of Sax's examples.*
2. *Theme topics: "The law as a form of violence"; "Civil disobedience amounts to violence in a community ruled by its public opinion." (Develop this topic by use of illustration.)*

ABE FORTAS

Civil Disobedience

"A fanatic is one who redoubles his efforts when he has forgotten his ends."

—George Santayana

"To break the law of the land is always serious, but it is not always wrong."

—Robert Bolt

"Is nonviolence, from your point of view, a form of direct action?" inquired Dr. Thurman. "It is not one form, it is the only form," said Gandhi.

. . . If I had been a Negro in the South, I hope I would have disobeyed the state and local laws denying to Negroes equal access to schools, to voting rights, and to public facilities. If I had disobeyed those laws, I would have been arrested and tried and convicted. Until the Supreme Court ruled that these laws were unconstitutional, I would have been a law violator.

As it turned out, my refusal to obey those laws would have been justified by the courts. But suppose I had been wrong. Suppose the Supreme Court had decided that the laws were constitutional. Despite the deep moral conviction that motivated me—despite the fact that my violation of the discriminatory racial laws would have been in a great cause—I would have been consigned to jail, with no possible remedy except the remote prospect of a pardon.

This may seem harsh. It may seem especially harsh if we assume that I profoundly believe that the law I am violating is immoral and unconstitutional, or if we assume that the question of its constitutionality is close. *But this is what we mean by the rule*

From Concerning Dissent and Civil Disobedience *by Abe Fortas. Copyright © 1968 by Abe Fortas. Reprinted by permission of The New American Library, Inc., New York.*

of law: both the government and the individual must accept the result of procedures by which the courts, and ultimately the Supreme Court, decide that the law is such and such, and not so and so; that the law has or has not been violated in a particular situation, and that it is or is not constitutional; and that the individual defendant has or has not been properly convicted and sentenced.

This is the rule of law. The state, the courts, and the individual citizen are bound by a set of laws which have been adopted in a prescribed manner, and the state and the individual must accept the courts' determinations of what those rules are and mean in specific instances. *This is the rule of law,* even if the ultimate judicial decision is by the narrow margin of five to four!

The term "civil disobedience" has been used to apply to a person's refusal to obey a law which the person believes to be immoral or unconstitutional. John Milton's famous defiance of England's law requiring licensing of books by official censors is in this category. He openly announced that he would not comply with it. He assailed the censorship law as an intolerable restriction of freedom, contrary to the basic rights of Englishmen.

The phrase "civil disobedience" has been grossly misapplied in recent years. Civil disobedience, even in its broadest sense, does not apply to efforts to overthrow the government or to seize control of areas or parts of it by force, or by the use of violence to compel the government to grant a measure of autonomy to part of its population. These are programs of revolution. They are not in the same category as the program of reformers who—like Martin Luther King—seek changes within the established order.

Revolutionists are entitled, of course, to the full benefit of constitutional protections for the *advocacy* of their program. They are even protected in the many types of *action* to bring about a fundamental change, such as the organization of associations and the solicitation of members and support at the polls. But they are not protected in the use of violence. Programs of this sort, if they are pursued, call for law enforcement by police action. They are not likely to raise issues of the subtlety of those with which I am here concerned.

This kind of violent action is in sharp contrast with the theory of civil disobedience which, even where it involves a total or partial repudiation of the principle that the individual should obey the law, does not tolerate violent methods. Thoreau presents an example of a general refusal to accept the authority of the state. Thoreau said he would pay certain taxes—for example, for roads —but not a general tax to a government which tolerated slavery. He rejected the proposition that the individual must support all governmental activities, even those which he vigorously opposes. Thoreau asserted the right to choose which taxes he would pay; to decide for himself that this was a morally justified tax and that certain others were not. Government, he said, "can have no pure right over my person and property but what I concede to it." Thoreau's position was not far from that asserted by Joan Baez and others who refused to pay federal taxes which were used to finance the war in Vietnam. But Thoreau's position was less selective. His principle would apply to all acts of government except those which he approved.

The term "civil disobedience" has not been limited to protests in the form of refusal to obey a law because of disapproval of that particular law. It has been applied to another kind of civil disobedience. This is the violation of laws which the protester does not challenge because of their own terms or effect. The laws themselves are not the subject of attack or protest. They are violated only as a means of protest, like carrying a picket sign. They are violated in order to publicize a protest and to bring pressure on the public or the government to accomplish purposes which have nothing to do with the law that is breached. The great exponent of this type of civil disobedience was Gandhi. He protested the British rule in India by a general program of disobedience to the laws governing ordinary civil life.

The first type, as in Milton's case—the direct refusal to obey the specific law that is the subject of protest—may sometimes be a means, even an essential means, of testing the constitutionality of the law. For example, a young man may be advised by counsel that he must refuse to report for induction in order to challenge the constitutionality of the Selective Service Act. This is very different from the kind of civil disobedience which is *not* engaged in for the purpose of testing the legality of an order within our system of government and laws, but which is practiced as a technique of warfare in a social and political conflict over other issues.

Frequently, of course, civil disobedience is prompted by both motives—by both a desire to make propaganda and to challenge the law. This is true in many instances of refusal to submit to induction. It was true in the case of Mrs. Vivian Kellems, who refused to pay withholding taxes because she thought they were unlawful and she wanted to protest the invasion of her freedom as a capitalist and citizen.

Let me first be clear about a fundamental proposition. The motive of civil disobedience, whatever its type, does not confer immunity for law violation. Especially if the civil disobedience involves violence or a breach of public order prohibited by statute or ordinance, it is the state's duty to arrest the dissident. If he is properly arrested, charged, and convicted, he should be punished by fine or imprisonment, or both, in accordance with the provisions of law, unless the law is invalid in general or as applied.

He may be motivated by the highest moral principles. He may be passionately inspired. He may, indeed, be right in the eyes of history or morality or philosophy. These are not controlling. It is the state's duty to arrest and punish those who violate the laws designed to protect private safety and public order.

The Negroes in Detroit and Newark and Washington and Chicago who rioted, pillaged, and burned may have generations of provocation. They may have incontestable justification. They may have been pushed beyond endurance. In the riots following the assassination of Martin Luther King, Jr., the Negroes may have been understandably inflamed by the murder of their leading advocate of nonviolence. But that provides no escape from the consequences of their conduct. Rioters should be arrested, tried, and convicted. If the state does not do so, it is either because of a tactical judgment that arrest and prosecution would cause more harm than good, or because the state is incompetent.

The same principles apply to the police and officers of the law. They, too, are liable for their acts. The fact that they represent the state does not give them immunity from the consequences of brutality or lawlessness. They, like the rioters, may be motivated by long and acute provocation. It may be that their lawlessness was the direct product of fear, or of righteous anger. They may have been moved to violence by more pressure than they could endure. But they, too, are subject to the rule of law, and if they exceed the authorized bounds of firmness and self-protection and needlessly assault the people whom they encounter, they should be disciplined, tried, and convicted. It is a deplorable truth that because they are officers of the state they frequently escape the penalty for their lawlessness.

We are a government and a people under law. It is not merely *government* that must live under law. Each of us must live under law. Just as our form of life depends upon the government's subordination to law under the Constitution, so it also depends upon the individual's subservience to the laws duly prescribed. Both of these are essential.

Just as we expect the government to be bound by all laws, so each individual is bound by all of the laws under the Constitution. He cannot pick and choose. He cannot substitute his own judgment or passion, however noble, for the rules of law. Thoreau was an inspiring figure and a great writer; but his essay should not be read as a handbook on political science.

A citizen cannot demand of his government or of other people obedience to the law, and at the same time claim a right in himself to break it by lawless conduct, free of punishment or penalty.

Some propagandists seem to think that people who violate the laws of public order ought not to be arrested and punished if their violation has protest as its purpose. By calling the criminal acts "civil disobedience," they seek to persuade us that offenses against public and private security should be immune from punishment and even commended. They seek to excuse physical attacks upon police; assaults upon recruiters for munitions firms and for the armed services; breaking windows in the Pentagon and in private stores and homes; robbing stores; trespassing on private and official premises; occupying academic offices; and even pillaging, looting, burning, and promiscuous violence.

We are urged to accept these as part of the First Amendment freedoms. We are asked to agree that freedom to speak and write, to protest and persuade, and to assemble provides a sanctuary for this sort of conduct. But that is nonsense.

The Supreme Court of the United States has said, over and over, that the words of the First Amendment mean what they say. But they mean what they say and not something else. They guarantee freedom to speak and freedom of the press—not freedom to club people or to destroy property. The First Amendment protects the right to assemble and to petition, but it requires—in plain words—that the right be peaceably exercised.

The use of force or violence in the course of social protest is a far cry from civil disobedience as practiced by Gandhi. Gandhi's concept insists upon peaceful, nonviolent refusal to comply with a law. It assumes that the protester will be punished, and it requires peaceful submission to punishment.

Let me elaborate this by reference to an article written by Dr. Martin Luther King, Jr., and published in September of 1961. In this article, Dr. King set forth the guiding principles of his approach to effective protest by civil disobedience. He said that many Negroes would disobey "unjust laws." These he defined as laws which a minority is compelled to observe but which are not binding on the majority. He said that this must be done openly and peacefully, and that those who do it must accept the penalty imposed by law for their conduct.

This is civil disobedience in a great tradition. It is peaceful, nonviolent disobedience of laws which are themselves unjust and which the protester challenges as invalid and unconstitutional.

Dr. King was involved in a case which illustrated this conception. He led a mass demonstration to protest segregation and discrimination in Birmingham. An injunction had been issued by a state court against the demonstration. But Dr. King disregarded the injunction and proceeded with the march as planned. He was arrested. He was prosecuted in the state court, convicted of contempt, and sentenced to serve five days in jail. He appealed, claiming that the First Amendment protected his violation of the injunction.

I have no doubt that Dr. King violated the injunction in the belief that it was invalid and his conduct was legally as well as morally justified. But the Supreme Court held that he was bound to obey the injunction unless and until it was set aside on appeal; and that he could not disregard the injunction even if he was right that the injunction was invalid. Dr. King went to jail and served his time.

I have no moral criticism to make of Dr. King's action in this incident, even though it turned out to be legally unjustified. He led a peaceable demonstration. He acted in good faith. There was good, solid basis for his belief that he did not have to obey the injunction—until the Supreme Court ruled the other way. The Court disagreed with him by a vote of five to four. I was one of the dissenters. Then Dr. King, without complaint or histrionics, accepted the penalty of misjudgment. This, I submit, is action in the great tradition of social protest in a democratic society where all citizens, including protesters, are subject to the rule of law.

But since those relatively early days of the protest movement, discontent has greatly increased in volume and depth of feeling, and the tactics of the discontented—both of the Negroes and the antiwar and antidraft groups—have become more forceful and less restrained. We confront instances of riots, sporadic violence, and trespass. These call for police and law enforcement and do not present the problem with which we are concerned. But we are also faced with the prospect of mass civil disobedience. Unless the greatest care is exercised, programs of this sort can disrupt the life and work of major cities. Mass demonstrations like the March on Washington in 1963 can be staged with good effect, by careful preparation and discipline, on the basis of cooperative planning between the leaders of the demonstration and the city officials. They can take place without appreciable law violation, under absolute constitutional protection. But when they are characterized by action deliberately designed to paralyze the life of a city by disrupting traffic and the work of government and its citizens— they carry with them extreme danger.

The danger of serious national consequences from massive civil disobedience may easily be exaggerated. Our nation is huge and relatively dispersed. It is highly unlikely that protesters can stage a nationwide disruption of our life, comparable to the effects of a general strike such as France and other nations have witnessed. But a program of widespread mass civil disobedience, involving the disruption of traffic, movement of persons and supplies, and conduct of government business within any of our great cities, would put severe strains on our constitutional system.

These mass demonstrations, however peacefully intended by their organizers, always involve the danger that they may erupt into violence. But despite this, our Constitution and our traditions, as well as practical wisdom, teach us that city officials, police, and citizens must be tolerant of mass demonstrations, however large and inconvenient. No city should be expected to submit to paralysis or to widespread injury to persons and property brought on by violation of law. It must be prepared to prevent this by the use of planning, persuasion, and restrained law enforcement. But at the same time, it is the city's duty under law, and as a matter of good sense, to make every effort to provide adequate facilities so that the demonstration can be effectively staged, so that it can be conducted without paralyzing the city's life, and to provide protection for the demonstrators. The city must perform this duty.

An enormous degree of self-control and discipline are required on both sides. Police must be trained in tact as well as tactics. Demonstrators must be organized, ordered, and controlled. Agitators and *provocateurs,* whatever their object, must be identified, and any move that they may make toward violence must be quickly countered.

However careful both sides may be, there is always danger that individual, isolated acts of a few persons will overwhelm the restraint of thousands. Law violation or intemperate behavior by one demonstrator may provoke police action. Intemperate or hasty retaliation by a single policeman may provoke disorder, and civil disobedience may turn into riot. This is the dangerous potential of mass demonstrations. When we add to it the possibility that extremists on either side are likely to be at work to bring about the cycle of disorder, arrest, resistance, and riot, the danger assumes formidable proportions.

FOR THE STUDENT

Rhetoric

1. *Study paragraphs five and six, in which Fortas distinguishes between civil disobedience and revolution. Note the distinctions he makes and the pattern of development.*
2. *What rhetorical device does Fortas frequently use to help clarify his idea? Point out several instances of his use of this device. Should Madariaga have used it more often than he did?*
3. *Does Fortas rely too much upon italics for emphasis? Can you rephrase sentences in which he uses italics in such a way that you obtain the proper emphasis through words alone?*

Discussion

1. *What is the basic distinction between acceptable and unacceptable "civil disobedience"?*
2. *Over four hundred years ago, Thomas More, in his* Utopia, *raised the question of how a just man can serve an unjust government. He gave no satisfactory answer. Can you?*
3. *In a conflict between national law and international law, which should prevail? Why?*

Writing

1. *Use any one of the quotations at the beginning of the essay as a thesis and develop it into a paper of three hundred words.*
2. *Write a research paper on the civil disobedience of Gandhi, Thoreau, or Martin Luther King.*

4 The Revolt of Youth

After the passive fifties came the active and often turbulent sixties. The generation of the sixties has been analyzed ad infinitum by this time. The revolt of youth is by no means a national but a worldwide phenomenon, although the reasons for the revolt may and do vary from country to country. If any one generalization can come nearer to explaining the cause than another, it must be that youth are disillusioned with the world created by their elders. Hence, the oft-discussed generation gap. While some commenting on the current scene find a few parallels between the generations of the sixties and of the twenties, they also point out striking differences. Many representatives of the sixties are serious-minded, intelligent young people who earnestly desire to improve their society. Others, of course, are merely rebels without a cause.

The three writers here chosen to discuss the revolt of youth represent the Left-to-Right view only in a relative sense. Lawrence Lipton, poet and novelist, spokesman for the disaffiliate, sympathizes with the young rebel who is disillusioned by various American middle-class values. The disaffiliate knows what he is rebelling against—and his rebellion often commands sympathy—but he lacks a positive cause or solution. Kenneth Rexroth, writer and critic, emphasizes the moral basis of the revolt among college students as well as the desire to correct flagrant wrongs and injustices in contemporary society. Joseph Wood Krutch, a man of many distinctions in the areas of literature, philosophy, and social commentary—and hardly to be considered a conservative in views—sympathizes with the spirit but not with certain actions of the alienated. He calls for retention of the traditions of private morality, integrity, and honor. The three writers present a cross-sectional view of alienated youth and suggest the complexity of the problem.

LAWRENCE LIPTON

Down with the Rat Race:
The New Poverty

Those who see the American businessman as the fount from
whence all blessings flow, enterpriser *par excellence,* organizer of
Progress, job-maker, charity-giver, endower of churches and universities and patron of the arts, who has given us the highest
standard of living in the world, have never been able to understand
why the figure of the businessman has fared so badly at the hands
of the intellectuals. As for the businessmen themselves, the early
industrialists were never worried about their reputation with the
intellectuals. Many of them were only semiliterate, and while they
were quick to retaliate against sticks and stones, whether thrown
by labor or by their competitors, they were merely contemptuous
of words. But the growth of advertising as a formidable weapon
opened the businessman's eyes to the possibility that while he was
watching out for sticks and stones, words might break his bones.

It was not until after the Depression, the New Deal and World
War II, though, that the public relations men and the advertising
men were able to arouse the businessman to active retaliation
against the treatment he was receiving in novels, plays, radio and
films, and even in the churches and classrooms. During the Depression he had to lick his wounds in bitter silence while he heard
himself called a "malefactor of great wealth" by that "traitor to his
class" Franklin D. Roosevelt. He had to suffer in silence while de-
tractors were being entertained in the White House and providing
verbal ammunition for a New Deal that looked to him like nothing more than a "hate business" conspiracy which his political
spokesmen have since rephrased as "twenty years of treason."

Reprinted from The Holy Barbarians, *by Lawrence Lipton, by permission of Julian Messner, a Division of Simon & Schuster, Inc.
Copyright © 1959 by Lawrence Lipton.*

[101]

It is little wonder that his pent-up resentments should have taken the form of a vengeful "housecleaning" after the war, not only of political officeholders but of the New Deal's intellectual and literary friends as well.

Hand in hand with the loyalty oaths and investigations has gone a widespread propaganda campaign on the platform and in the press against all intellectuals, a campaign in which friendly highbrows are regarded as only a little less dangerous than unfriendly ones and potentially treasonous. The halfhearted and timorous "wooing back" of the egghead that began with the successful Soviet orbiting of Sputnik I is confined to scientists and technicians, and is concerned, characteristically, with *buying brains* rather than encouraging the intellectual to think straight and speak out plainly.

The word intellectual has never been altogether free from suspicion in the United States; calling a man a brain has been fightin' words for a hundred years. Intellectualism is, needless to say, equated with leftism, a proposition that has at least the merit of being half true, but not in the way *they* mean it. It is even equated with modernism in art—unless it can be turned into window displays, high fashion fabrics, liquor ads and clever television commercials.

But the businessman had a bad conscience long before he ever became a target of the intellectual. Profit, which is the basis of business, has been under a cloud for centuries, certainly since the time of the prophet Hosea and probably long before him. Among the Church Fathers there were not a few who echoed the words of the Hebrew prophets against malefactors of great wealth, well before "That Man" in the White House blasted them on the radio.

And when Dave Gelden speaks of writing poetry in the lavatory of the airplane plant on the boss' time and on the boss' toilet paper and says, "It wasn't stealing, I was just getting my own," he speaks out of an old and honored tradition. He speaks for the few who *can* reject the rewards that a business civilization offers those who are willing to help it sell its ideology.

Moneytheism is everywhere, in everything we see and read and hear. The child is indoctrinated with it from birth, not in the schools, which try to counter it with the humanities—as much as they dare—but in the large school of experience where most of our education is received. It is only after a long process of dis-education and re-education that one sees it clearly and sees it whole—the price-wage shell game, the speed-up treadmill, the Save!-Spend! contradictions dinned into our ears night and day, the heartbreaking brutalities of class-made law, lawyer-made law, judge-made law, money-made law, and the unspeakable vulgarities of hypocritical religion, the nerve-shattering Stop! and Go! Hurry! and Go Slow! Step Lively! and Relax! warnings flashing before our eyes and bombarding our ears without letup, making the soul a squirrel cage whirligig from the first stimulant in the morning till the last sedative at night. The rat race. A rat race that offers only two alternatives: to run with the hare or hunt with the hounds.

Disaffiliation: The Way of the Beat Generation

Disaffiliation is a voluntary self-alienation from the family cult, from Moneytheism and all its works and ways.

The disaffiliate has no blueprint for the future. He joins no political parties. He is free to make his own inner-directed decisions. If he fails to vote altogether, that, too, is a form of political action; half the eligible voters of the United States normally fail to do so. In his case it is a no-confidence vote.

The disaffiliate doesn't like the smell of burning human flesh, whether it come from the lynching tree, the witness chair or the electric chair.

Having read history from the bottom up as well as from the top down, he knows that culture moves both ways, interactively, and there are times—the present is one of them—when the cultural top is at the economic bottom.

He is not against industrialization. He is not against "things," material things as opposed to spiritual things.

Why, then, disaffiliation in an era when *Time-Life-Fortune* pages are documenting an American Way of Life that is filled with color-matched stainless steel kitchens, bigger and faster cars, electronic wonders, and a future of unlimited luxuries like television-telephones and rocket trips to the moon? Because it is all being corrupted by the cult of Moneytheism. In the eyes of a Nelson Algren it is all a "neon wilderness." In the eyes of a Henry Miller it is all an "air-conditioned nightmare." Because, as Kenneth Rexroth has put it, you can't fill the heads of young lovers with "buy me the new five-hundred-dollar deep-freeze and I'll love you" advertising propaganda without poisoning the very act of love itself; you can't hop up your young people with sadism in the movies and television and train them to commando tactics in the army camps, to say nothing of brutalizing them in wars, and then expect to "untense" them with Coca-Cola and Y.M.C.A. hymn sings. Because underneath Henry Luce's "permanent revolution" —the New Capitalism, the People's Capitalism and Prosperity Unlimited—lies the ugly fact of an economy geared to war production, a design, not for living, but for death.

If the disaffiliate is on the side of the accused instead of on the side of the accusers, it is because the accuser *has* his spokesmen, a host of them, well paid, with all the mass media at their command and all the laws and police on their side.

Where the choice is between two rival tyrannies, however pious their pretensions, the disaffiliate says, not a plague but a pity on both your houses.

The Art of Poverty

The New Poverty is the disaffiliate's answer to the New Prosperity.

It is important to make a living, but it is even more important to make a life.

Poverty. The very word is taboo in a society where success is equated with virtue and poverty is a sin. Yet it has an honorable ancestry. St. Francis of Assisi revered Poverty as his bride, with holy fervor and pious rapture.

The poverty of the disaffiliate is not to be confused with the poverty of indigence, intemperance, improvidence or failure. It is simply that the goods and services he has to offer are not valued at a high price in our society. As one beat generation writer said to the square who offered him an advertising job: "I'll scrub your floors and carry out your slops to make a living, but I will not lie for you, pimp for you, stool for you, or rat for you."

It is not the poverty of the ill-tempered and embittered, those who wooed the bitch goddess Success with panting breath and came away rebuffed.

It is an independent, voluntary poverty.

It is an art, and like all arts it has to be learned. It has its techniques, its tricks and short cuts, its know-how.

What is poverty for one may be extravagance for another. The writer must have his basic library, the composer his piano, the painter his canvases and tools, and everyone must have at least a few of the books he wants, if only in paperback editions, a few good recordings and some objects of art, if only in prints and cheap imitations.

It all depends on what the disaffiliate values most. Kenneth Rexroth, for instance, has a scholar's library that may be worth ten thousand dollars—all of it shelved in packing cases set up one above the other to serve as bookshelves—in a fifty dollar slum apartment. A composer I know has a microfilm library of the world's best music that is matched only by that of the Library of Congress and perhaps a few private collections, and stints on food and clothing almost to the point of beggary. Each must work out the logistics of the problem to fit his own case.

The writer as disaffiliate has a special problem of his own. He may not have much control over the size of his income—a book may flop or it may be a runaway best seller—but he does have some measure of control over how much he spends. And how he spends it. And where he lives. For, as Nelson Algren has expressed it, "Scarcely any way now remains of reporting the American Century except from behind the tote-board. From behind the TV commercials and the Hearst headlines, the car ads and the subtitles, the editorials and the conventions. For it is only there that the people of Dickens and Dostoevski may be found any more."

Behind the billboards lie the slums. Here one may hold his standard of living down to the level of a dedicated independent poverty with some measure of ease and self-respect. It is a way of life that is obligatory only on the truth-telling artist but it is a good way of life for him; it helps him keep the long, lean view. He will go farther on less if he learns how to travel light. In the slum he will learn that the health of a civilization should be judged by the maxim laid down by one of humanity's greatest physicians: "Inasmuch as ye did it not unto one of these least, ye did it not unto me." He will learn what Diane Lattimer (in George Mandel's novel, *Flee the Angry Strangers*) meant when, at the last, out of the depths of her agony and pain, she said: "Come, sit in the Cosmopole. You don't need anything in this world; only poverty is holy."

The Logistics of Poverty

The dedicated independent poverty is an art, but it is also a science of survival. It has its strategies and logistics.

Those who choose manual labor soon find out that, so far as the trades are concerned, breaking into the ranks of labor is neither easy nor cheap. Joining the proletariat is like trying to join an exclusive club and often quite as expensive, what with trade union initiation fees and numerous qualifications and restrictions. For the most part the beat generation disaffiliate is confined to the fringe jobs in the labor market, like small house painting jobs if he is an artist trying to find part-time work to pay for his colors and canvases and keep some canned goods in the larder. Some

painters in the Los Angeles area have occasionally found cartoon-
ing jobs and sculpting on a part-time basis in the studios, particularly at the Walt Disney Studio. Ceramics has provided some
income for artists, as well as costume jewelry designing, free lance
or in the employ of some small businessman. Frame making can
be a source of income. And some artists do not mind teaching a
few hours a week at some art school or as private tutors.

In Venice West some have made it for a while as typewriter re-
pairmen, postal employees and arts and crafts teachers—"occupational therapy"—in mental hospitals, or attendants in the mental
wards, or psychology assistants giving Rorschach tests. In San
Francisco they sometimes ship out with a crew for a few months
and come home with a bank roll, or join a road construction gang
in Canada or Alaska. Allen Ginsberg financed a trip to North
Africa and Europe that way. The lumber camps of the Northwest
sometimes serve the same purpose for a while. Some part-time
jobs are to be found as laboratory technicians, X-ray technicians
and the like, if one is willing to spend a few months preparing
himself for the job.

In New York there are jobs that offer an opportunity to work
in odd-hour shifts, much desired by the beat, as art gallery guards,
deck hands on ferryboats, and for those who seek solitude and
plenty of time to think, goof or write, the job of barge captain is
the answer. Those who are polylingual or have traveled abroad
can find part-of-the-year employment as travel guides, either self-
employed if they have a little organizing ability or in the employ
of travel agencies.

In Greenwich Village there are some who make it by doing
hauling in small trucks, and some by delivering packages and
messages. New Yorkers also find good pickings at the many open-
ings and *premières* in art galleries and other places—to say nothing of pickups, but for this racket you have to own at least one
good party suit, unless you can pass for a painter or an interesting "character." New York is also good for free-lance manuscript
reading jobs for publishers and part-time jobs reading proof for

publishers or printers. Musicians who are making the beat scene do copy work for composers and music publishers, or compile "fake books" containing melodies and chord symbols, with or without words, and peddle them to commercial musicians in a kind of under-the-counter deal, sometimes on the union hall floor and other hangouts for musicians in New York and Hollywood.

In Venice West and elsewhere there is always the possibility of an occasional hitch with the gas and electric company as a meter reader. There is clerking in bookstores and now there are a few jobs in espresso coffeehouses. For those who live near a university there is library work on an hourly basis. Landscape gardening is a year-round possibility for West Coast beatniks. Some of them have made it as counselors for juvenile delinquents, in the employ of the city or county. The job of shipping clerk is a popular one. When you have saved all the money you think you are going to need for a while, you quit and pass the word around to your friends to go there and apply. In this way a job is "kept in the family," just as the pads are kept in the family by being passed on from one tenant to the next, with the landlord often none the wiser—or richer.

Job opportunities are always more numerous for the girls, of course. They can always find work in dress shops and department stores, with the telephone company and the telephone answering services, as doctors' reception clerks and dental assistants. If they have had some dancing school they can find part-time jobs as dancing teachers in private schools and summer jobs in girls' camps. There are any number of office jobs a girl can fill. There is manuscript typing and other free-lance typing work. In Los Angeles some find jobs as script girls in the TV and movie studios. Comparison shopping and the *sub rosa* job of starting whispering campaigns in the subways for commercial products is strictly for the "angle-shooters" among the Village chicks in New York. Modeling is open to those who have the face and the figure for it. The job of B-girl in the taverns is very much sought after because it pays well and the hours are desirable, but rarely do the chicks of beatland double as call girls or do a week-end stint in the whore-houses. That is a monopoly of respectable working girls and house-wives in need of extra money to support their families or expensive tastes in clothes and cars. It is no part of the beat scene.

The musically inclined among the girls seek jobs in record shops and with music and record publishers. The artistically talented among the chicks sometimes make it as dress designers, window dressers and interior decorators, but here they run into competition with the beat homosexuals. Homosexual writers and artists are the most hard put to it to find—and hold onto—employment of any kind.

If all else fails there are always the foundations, the Huntington Hartford Foundation near Venice West, where one can find food and shelter for three months (renewable for three months longer) if he is judged eligible and comes properly recommended, and, on the East Coast, Yaddo and the McDowell colony. Some have been the recipients of Guggenheim fellowships or other grants.

There are windfalls now and then. An industrial firm or a university will let it be known that it needs guinea pigs for some research test, like the sleep tests at the U. of C., or some other research problem. One beatnik I know made it for some months as a sweater. He sweated so many hours a day for a cosmetics firm testing a new product.

And there are the standard jobs for itinerants and occasional workers—cab driving, dish washing, bus boy work, filling station work, and, for the girls, jobs as car-hops in drive-in restaurants or waitresses. In Venice West there are jobs for girls on the Pacific Ocean Park Amusement Pier. Some of the younger chicks who are still going to college—or can keep up a reasonable appearance of doing so—get money from home. If you are older and have children to support and no visible means of support, the county will come to your aid.

With all that, there are still many problems. Poverty is not easy to manage. It requires some planning and some conniving.

The pressure is toward conformity, with regular working hours and consumer spending in ways and in quantities that will make the American Way of Life look good in the Labor Department reports and the Department of Commerce statistics. Buying a secondhand suit for five or ten dollars at a Windward Avenue uncalled-for clothing store or a three-dollar secondhand dress at an East Side rummage shop does nothing for the statisticians or the Chamber of Commerce.

Sponging, scrounging, borrowing and angle-shooting are too undependable as a regular source of income, and street begging takes too much time, as Henry Miller has shown, with inspired documentation, in *Tropic of Cancer*. Pushing pot is too hazardous and peddling heroin is a one-way ticket to the penitentiary, if not to the grave. Shoplifting is only a stopgap measure at best. It is an art that takes long practice to master if one is to make a living at it, and is better left to those who have a talent for it. One amateur I know found herself confronted one day with an ideological, if not a moral, problem. The supermarket where she sometimes shoplifted a quarter of a pound of butter—more as social protest when butter prices took a sudden jump than from any actual necessity—was being picketed by strikers. Out of sympathy with the striking union she went across the street to the little independent grocer and did her shoplifting there till the strike was over.

Inheritances sometimes provide a few valuables to be divided among the needy in true communal fashion. Somebody who has wigged out and been committed to a mental institution for a while, or been busted for pot for the third or fourth time and sent up for a long stretch, will leave behind a pad with household effects, furniture, clothes, books, phonograph records, pictures and hi-fi equipment. The accepted practice is that such stuff becomes community property. If a cat moves out of town he sometimes wills such things to his friends quite informally rather than try to tote them with him or go to the expense of having them shipped. When he comes back he will find any pad open to him, or can divide his guesting between several of his choosing. It is the traditional hospitality of the poor, one of the few traditions of the square that the beat honor scrupulously.

"Why don't more of them simply marry rich women?" I heard a square ask one evening at a party in one of the Venice West pads. Chuck Bennison took it upon himself to answer.

"It's a full-time job," he said.

FOR THE STUDENT

Rhetoric

1. *Study the long sentence in the paragraph beginning "Moneytheism is everywhere. . . ." Analyze its rhetorical structure. How does Lipton sum up all his examples in the concluding phrases of the sentence?*
2. *How effective do you find Lipton's example of the* Time-Life-Fortune *documentation of the American Way of Life? What others could you add?*
3. *Make a list of the slang words and expressions in this essay. Can you justify their use?*
4. *Is Lipton justified in devoting between one-third and one-half of his essay to a discussion and listing of kinds of jobs open to the disaffiliate? Frame your answer in the light of the abstract ideas discussed earlier in the essay.*

Discussion

1. *Summarize Lipton's view of the conflict between the businessman and the intellectual as presented in the first section of his essay.*
2. *In what respects does Lipton consider the new poverty an art?*

3. *Give some examples of Lipton (or at least the disaffiliate) flying in the face of conventional moral and ethical conduct.*

4. *Do you think that Lipton likes or admires the people he describes? Give supporting evidence for your answer. Would these people find acceptance in your group?*

5. *Lipton was sixty-one at the time he wrote this essay. As you read it, were you aware of a two-generation gap between writer and reader?*

Writing

1. *Write a descriptive paper on the rat race, or the American Way of Life, adopting Lipton's tone and manner.*

2. *Write a paper using "The Neon Wilderness" or "The Air-Conditioned Nightmare" as your title. Be certain that your paper is unified around your symbol and that you provide sufficient concrete detail to support your abstract statements about modern civilization.*

it is far more sensitive than ever before. Individual action does tell. Give a tiny poke at one of the insignificant gears down in its bowels and slowly it begins to shudder all over and suddenly belches out hot rivets. It is a question of qualitative change. Thousands of men built the pyramids. One punched card fed into a mechanical brain decides the gravest questions. A few punched cards operate whole factories. Modern society has passed the stage when it was a blind, mechanical monster. It is on the verge of becoming an infinitely responsive instrument.

So the first blows struck back were tiny, insignificant things. Not long after the last war Bayard Rustin got on a bus in Chicago and headed south. When they crossed the Mason-Dixon Line, he stayed where he was. The cops took him off. He "went limp." They beat him into unconsciousness. They took him to jail and finally to a hospital. When he got out, he got on another bus and continued south. So it went, for months—sometimes jail, sometimes the hospital, sometimes they just kicked him into the ditch. Eventually he got to New Orleans. Eventually Jim Crow was abolished on interstate carriers. Individual nonviolent direct action had invaded the South and won. The Southern Negro had been shown the only technique that had any possibility of winning.

Things simmered for a while and then, spontaneously, out of nowhere, the Montgomery bus boycott materialized. Every moment of the birth and growth of this historic action has been elaborately documented. Hour by hour we can study "the masses" acting by themselves. It is my modest, well-considered opinion that Martin Luther King, Jr., is the most remarkable man the South has produced since Thomas Jefferson—since, in other words, it became "the South." Now the most remarkable thing about Martin Luther King is that he is not remarkable at all. He is just an ordinary minister of a middle-class Negro church (or what Negroes call "middle class," which is pretty poor by white standards). There are thousands of men like him all over Negro America. When the voice called, he was ready. He was ready because he was himself part of that voice. Professional, white-baiting

Negroes who thrill millionairesses in night clubs in the North would call him a square. He was a brave square. He is the best possible demonstration of the tremendous untapped potential of humanity that the white South has thrown away all these years. He helped to focus that potential and exert it. It won.

No outside organizers formed the Montgomery Improvement Association. They came around later, but they could never quite catch up with it. It is pretty hard to "catch up with," to institutionalize, a movement which is simply the form that a whole community has assumed in action. Although the force of such action is shaped by group loyalty, in the final analysis it must always be individual and direct. You can't delegate either boycott or nonviolence. A committee can't act for you, you have to act yourself.

The Montgomery bus boycott not only won where Negro Zealotism, as well as Uncle Tomism, had always failed, but it demonstrated something that had always sounded like sheer sentimentality. It is better, braver, far more effective and far more pleasurable to act with love than with hate. When you have won, you have gained an unimpeachable victory. The material ends pass or are passed beyond. "Desegregated" buses seem natural in many Southern cities today. The guiltless moral victory remains, always as powerful as the day it was gained. Furthermore, each moral victory converts or neutralizes another block of the opponents' forces.

Before the Montgomery episode was over, Bayard Rustin and Martin Luther King had joined forces. Today they are world statesmen in a "shadow cabinet" that is slowly forming behind the wielders of power, and the advisers and auxiliary leaders in the councils of Negro Africa. At home in America the Montgomery achievement has become the source from which has flowed the moral awakening, first, of Negro, and following them, of white youth.

Everything seemed to be going along nicely. According to the papers and most of their professors, 99 and $^{44}/_{100}$ per cent of the nation's youth were cautiously preparing for the day when they could offer their young split-level brains to GM, IBM, Oak Ridge or the Voice of America. Madison Avenue has discovered its own pet minority of revolt and tamed it into an obedient mascot. According to *Time, Life,* MGM and the editors and publishers of a new, pseudo avant-garde, all the dear little rebels wanted to do was grow beards, dig jazz, take heroin and wreck other people's Cadillacs. While the exurbanite children sat with the baby sitter and thrilled to Wyatt Earp, their parents swooned in the aisles at *The Connection* or sat up past bedtime reading switch-blade novelists. The psychological mechanisms were the same in both cases —sure-fire, time-tested and shopworn.

But as a matter of fact, anyone with any sense traveling about the country lecturing on college campuses during the past five years could tell that something very, very different was cooking. Time and again, hundreds of times, I have been asked, by some well-dressed, unassuming, beardless student, "I agree with you completely, but what shall we, my generation, *do?*" To this question I have been able to give only one answer: "I am fifty. You are twenty. It is for you to tell me what to do. The only thing I can say is, don't do the things my generation did. They didn't work." A head of steam was building up, the waters were rising behind the dam; the dam itself, the block to action, was the patent exhaustion of the old forms. What was accumulating was not any kind of programmatic "radicalization," it was a moral demand.

Parenthetically, I might say that a legend of the Red Thirties was growing up too. Let me say (and I was there): As far as practically every campus except CCNY and NYU was concerned, the Red Thirties are pure myth. At the height of the great upsurge in California labor, led in its own imagination by the Communist Party, neither the Young Communist League nor the Youth Peoples Socialist League was able to keep a functioning student cadre in continuous operation on the University of California campus. At least every four years they had to start over again. And the leadership, the real bosses, were middle-aged party functionaries sent in from "The Center." One of them, bellowing with early senility, was to show up at the recent Un-American Activities Committee riot in San Francisco and scandalize the students.

The plain fact is that today students are incomparably better educated and more concerned than their elders. As the young do, they still tend to believe things written on paper. For the past five years, bull sessions have been discussing Kropotkin, Daniel De Leon, Trotsky, Gandhi, St. Simon, Plato—an incongruous mixture of the world's cat bellers—looking for the answer. The gap between the generations has been closing up. Teaching them is a new group of young professors, too young to have been compromised by their actual role in the splendid Thirties, themselves realistic-minded products of the GI Bill; and neither ex-dupes nor ex-fellow travelers, but serious scholars of the radical past. It is only just recently that they have come up, only just recently that the creative minority of students has stopped assuming that just because a man stood at a podium he was *ipso facto* a fraud. So the head of steam built up, the waters mounted behind the dike.

And then one day four children walked into a dime store in a small Southern city and pulled out the plug. Four children picked up the massive chain of the Social Lie and snapped it at its weakest link. Everything broke loose.

Children had won at Little Rock, but they had not initiated the action, they had been caught in the middle in a conflict of equally dishonest political forces, and they had won only a token victory. All the world had marveled at those brave young faces, beautiful under the taunts and spittle. If they had not stood fast, the battle would have been lost; it was their bravery alone that won it. But it was a battle officered by their elders, and like all the quarrels among their elders nowadays, it ended in a morally meaningless compromise.

From the first sit-ins the young have kept the command in their own hands. No "regularly constituted outside authority" has been able to catch up with them. The sit-ins swept the South so rapidly that it was impossible to catch up with them physically,

but it was even harder for routinized bureaucrats with vested interests in race relations and civil liberties to catch up with them
ideologically. The whole spring went by before the professional
leaders began to get even a glimmering of what was happening. In
the meantime the old leadership was being pushed aside. Young
ministers just out of the seminary, maverick young teachers in
Jim Crow colleges, choir mistresses and schoolmarms and Sunday-
school teachers in all the small cities of the South pitched in and
helped—and let the students lead *them,* without bothering to
"clear it with Roy." In a couple of months the NAACP found
itself with a whole new cadre sprung up from the grass roots.

The only organization which understood what was going on
was CORE, the Committee on Racial Equality, organized years
ago in an evacuated Japanese flat, "Sakai House" in San Francisco, by Bayard Rustin, Caleb Foote and a few others, as a di-
rect-action, race-relations offshoot of the Fellowship of Reconciliation (the FOR) and the Friends Service Committee. CORE was
still a small group of intellectual enthusiasts and there simply
weren't enough people to go around. To this day most Negroes
know little more of CORE than its name, which they have seen
in the Negro press, and the bare fact that its program is direct,
nonviolent action. This didn't deter the high-school and college
students in the Jim Crow high schools and colleges in Raleigh and
Durham. They set up their own direct nonviolent-action organization and in imitation of CORE gave it a name whose initials
spelled a word, COST. Soon there were COST "cells" in remote
hill-country high schools, complete with codes, hand signals, cour-
iers, all the apparatus of youthful enthusiasm. Needless to say, the
very words frightened the older Negro leadership out of its wits.

The police hosed and clubbed the sit-inners, the Uncle Tom
presidents of the captive Jim Crow colleges expelled them in
droves, white students came South and insisted on being arrested
along with the Negroes, sympathy picket lines were thrown in
front of almost every chain variety store in almost every college
town in the North. Even some stores with no branches in the

South and no lunch counters anywhere found themselves picketed until they cleared themselves of any implication of Jim Crow.

The effect on the civilized white minority in the South was extraordinary. All but a few had gone on accepting the old stereotypes. There were good Negroes, to be sure, but they didn't want to mix. The majority were ignorant, violent, bitter, half-civilized, incapable of planned, organized action, happy in Jim Crow. "It would take another two hundred years." In a matter of weeks, in thousands of white brains, the old stereotypes exploded. Here were the Negro children of servants, sharecroppers and garbagemen—"their" servants and sharecroppers and garbagemen, who had always been content with their place—directly engaged in the greatest controlled moral action the South had ever seen. They were quiet, courteous, full of good will to those who abused them; and they sang, softly, all together, under the clubs and firehoses. "We will not be moved." Long protest walks of silent Negroes, two abreast, filed through the provincial capitals. A major historical moral issue looked into the eyes of thousands of white spectators in Southern towns which were so locked in "our way of life" that they were unaware they lived in a great world. The end of Jim Crow suddenly seemed both near and inevitable. It is a profoundly disturbing thing to find yourself suddenly thrust upon the stage of history.

I was at the first Louisiana sit-in with a girl from the local paper who had interviewed me that morning. She was typical, full of dying prejudices, misinformation and superstitious fears. But she knew it. She was trying to change. Well, the sit-in did a good job of changing her. It was terrific. A group of well-bred, sweet-faced kids from Southern University filed into the dime store, hand in hand, fellows and girls in couples, and sat down quietly. Their faces were transfused with quiet, innocent dedication. They looked like the choir coming into a fine Negro church. They weren't served. They sat quietly, talking together. Nobody, spectators or participants, raised his voice. In fact, most of the bystanders didn't even stare rudely. When the police came, the youngsters spoke softly and politely, and once again, fellows and girls hand in hand, they filed out, singing a hymn, and got in the paddy wagon.

The newspaper girl was shaken to her shoes. Possibly it was the first time in her life she had ever faced what it meant to be a human being. She came to the faculty party for me at Louisiana State that night. Her flesh was still shaking and she couldn't stop talking. She had come up against one of the big things of life and she was going to be always a little different afterward.

The response on the campuses of the white colleges of the South was immediate. There had always been interracial committees and clubs around, but they had been limited to a handful of eccentrics. These increased tremendously and involved large numbers of quite normal students. Manifestations of sympathy with the sit-ins and joint activities with nearby Negro schools even came to involve student-government and student-union bodies. Editorials in college papers, with almost no exceptions, gave enthusiastic support. Believe me, it is quite an experience to eat dinner with a fraternity at a fashionable Southern school and see a can to collect money for CORE at the end of the table.

More important than sympathy actions for and with the Negroes, the sit-ins stimulated a similar burst, a runaway brush fire, of activity for all sorts of other aims. They not only stimulated the activity, they provided the form and in a sense the ideology. Nonviolent direct action popped up everywhere—so fast that even the press wire services could no longer keep track of it, although they certainly played it up as the hottest domestic news of the day. The actions dealt with a few things: compulsory ROTC, peace, race relations, civil liberties, capital punishment—all, in the final analysis, moral issues. In no case were they concerned with politics in the ordinary sense of the word.

Here the ROTC marched out to troop the colors and found a line of students sitting down across the parade ground. In another school a protest march paraded around and through and between the ranks of the marching ROTC, apparently to everybody's amusement. In other schools the faculty and even the administration and, in one place, the governor joined in protest rallies against ROTC. There were so many peace and disarmament meetings and marches it is impossible to form a clear picture—they seem to have taken place everywhere and, for the first time, to have brought out large numbers. Off campus, as it were, the lonely pacifists who had been sitting out the civil-defense propaganda stunt in New York called their annual "sit out" and were dumbfounded at the turnout. For the first time, too, the courts and even the police weakened. Few were arrested, and fewer sentenced.

The Chessman execution provoked demonstrations, meetings, telegrams, on campuses all over the country. In Northern California the "mass base" of all forms of protest was among the students and the younger teachers. They provided the cadre, circulated petitions, sent wires, interviewed the Governor, and kept up a continuous vigil at the gates of San Quentin. All this activity was unquestionably spontaneous. At no time did the American Civil Liberties Union or the regular anti-capital-punishment organizations initiate, or even take part in, any mass action, whatever else they may have done. Chessman, of course, had a tremendous appeal to youth; he was young, he was an intellectual, even an artist of sorts; before his arrest he had been the kind of person they could recognize, if not approve of, among themselves. He was not very different from the hero of *On the Road,* who happened to be locked up in San Quentin along with him. As his life drew to a close, he showed a beautiful magnanimity in all he did or said. On all the campuses of the country—of the world, for that matter—he seemed an almost typical example of the alienated and outraged youthful "delinquent" of the post-World War II era—the product of a delinquent society. To the young who refused to be demoralized by society, it appeared that that society was killing him only to sweep its own guilt under the rug. I think almost everyone (Chessman's supporters included) over thirty-five seriously underestimates the psychological effect of the Chess-man case on the young.

At all points the brutal reactionary tendencies in American life were being challenged, not on a political basis, Left versus Right, but because of their patent dishonesty and moral violence. The most spectacular challenge was the riot at the hearing of the Un-American Activities Committee in San Francisco. There is no question but that this was a completely spontaneous demonstration. The idea that Communist agitators provoked it is ludicrous. True, all that were left of the local Bolsheviks turned out, some thirty of them—Stalinists and the two groups of Trotskyites. Even the "youth leader" who, twenty-eight years before, at the age of thirty, had been assigned to lead the YCL, showed up and roared and stomped incoherently, and provided comic relief. Certainly no one took him seriously. There was one aspect about the whole thing that was not spontaneous. That was the work of the committee. They planned it that way. Over the protests and warnings of the city administration they deliberately framed up a riot. When the riot came, it was the cops who lost their nerve and rioted, if rioting means uncontrolled mob violence. The kids sat on the floor with their hands in their pockets and sang, "We shall not be moved."

Spectacular as it was, there are actions more important than the San Francisco riot. Here and there about the country, lonely, single individuals have popped up out of nowhere and struck their blows. It is almost impossible to get information about draft re-sisters, non-registrants, conscientious objectors, but here and there one pops up in the local press or, more likely, in the student press.

Even more important are the individual actions of high-school students whom only a hopeless paranoiac could believe anybody had organized. A sixteen-year-old boy in Queens, and then three in the Bronx, refused to sign loyalty oaths to get their diplomas. As kudos are distributed in a New York suburban high school, a boy gets up and rejects an award from the American Legion.

Everybody is horrified at his bad manners. A couple of days later two of his prizes are offered to the two runners-up, who reject them in turn. This is spontaneous direct action if ever there was. And the important thing about it is that in all these cases, these high-school kids have made it clear that they do not object to either loyalty oaths or the American Legion because they are "reactionary," but because they are morally contemptible.

The Negro faculties and presidents of the Jim Crow colleges, who not only opposed the sit-ins but expelled dozens of the sit-inners, now found themselves faced with deserted campuses. They were overtaken by a tremendous ground-swell of approval of their youngsters' actions from Negro parents, and were dumbfounded by the sympathy shown by a broad stratum of the white South. One by one they swung around, until Uncle Toms who had expelled students taking part in sit-ins during their Easter vacations in other states, went on public record as saying, "If your son or daughter telephones you and says he or she has been arrested in a sit-in, get down on your knees and thank God."

Not only did the New Revolt of Youth become the hottest domestic copy in years, but it reached the ears of all the retired and semiretired and comfortably fixed pie-card artists of every lost and every long-since-won cause of the labor and radical movements. Everybody shouted, "Myself when young!" and pitched in with application blanks. The AFL-CIO sent out a well-known leader of the Esperanto movement who reported that the kids were muddled and confused and little interested in the trade-union movement which they, mistakenly in his opinion, thought of as morally compromised. YPSL chapters of the Thomasite Socialists rose from the graves of twenty years. Youth experts with theories about what their grandchildren were talking about went on cross-country tours. *Dissent* had a subscription drive. The Trotskyites came up with programs. Everybody got in the act—except, curiously, the Communists. As a matter of fact, back in a dusty office in New York, they were grimly deadlocked in their last factional fight. Although the movement was a spontaneous outburst of direct nonviolent action, it didn't quite please the libertarians and pacifists. They went about straightening everybody out, and *Liberation* came out with an article defining the correct Line and pointing out the errors of the ideologically immature.

As the kids go back to school this fall, this is going to be the greatest danger they will face—all these eager helpers from the other side of the age barrier, all these cooks, each with a time-tested recipe for the broth. All over the world this kind of ferment is stewing on college campuses. In Korea and Japan and Turkey the students have marched and brought down governments, and they have humbled the President of the greatest power in history. So far the movement is still formless, a world-wide upheaval of disgust. Even in Japan the Zengakuren, which does have a sort of ideology—the Left communism against which Lenin wrote his famous pamphlet—has only been able to act as a cheerleader. It has failed to impose its leadership, its organization or its principles on the still chaotic upsurge. In France the official Neo-Gandhian Movement, in alliance with certain sections of the Catholic Left, does seem to have given some sort of shape and leadership. I am inclined to think that this is due to the almost total ignorance of French youth of this generation—they had to go to the official sources for information and guidance, they just didn't have enough, themselves, to get started.

Is this in fact a "political" upsurge? It isn't now—it is a great moral rejection, a kind of mass vomit. Everybody in the world knows that we are on the verge of extinction and nobody does anything about it. The kids are fed up. The great problems of the world today are immediate world-wide peace, immediate race equality and immediate massive assistance to the former colonial peoples. All of them could be started toward solution by a few decisive acts of moral courage among the boys at the top of the heap. Instead, the leaders of the two ruling nations abuse each other like little boys caught out behind the barn. Their apologists stage elaborate military and ideological defenses of Marxian socialism and laissez-faire capitalism, neither of which has ever

existed on the earth or ever will exist. While the Zengakuren
howls in the streets, Khrushchev delivers a speech on the anni-
versary of Lenin's "Leftism, an Infantile Disorder" and uses it to
attack—Mao! Meanwhile a boy gets up in a New York suburban
school and contemptuously hands back his "patriotic" prize. He
is fed up.

FOR THE STUDENT

Rhetoric

1. *Rexroth suggests the nature of conformity expected of the
   young by a few well-chosen examples. What is the implication of these examples?*
2. *Compare Rexroth's diction and style with Lipton's. What
   important differences do you note? Does Rexroth use
   slang? as much as Lipton? Does Rexroth use colloquialisms
   where Lipton would use slang?*
3. *Evaluate the following phrases in their contexts and point
   out their effectiveness: "their young split-level brains,"
   "switch-blade novelists," "the world's cat-bellers," "a kind
   of mass vomit."*

Discussion

1. *Identify as many examples of the "steadily growing im-
   moralism" as you can. How effectively do they illustrate
   Rexroth's implied and stated criticism of the times?*
2. *Do you agree that the Revolt of Youth described in this
   essay is a new concept?*
3. *Attack or defend Rexroth's statement that the student take-
   over is not a "political" upsurge but a moral rejection. Has
   he effectively supported this position?*

Writing

1. *Much of Rexroth's essay is devoted to extended illustrations. Write a paper in which you use one or more such illustrations. Be sure to state or clearly imply your abstract meaning.*
2. *Theme topic: My campus needs "a few decisive acts of moral courage."*

JOSEPH WOOD KRUTCH
Honor and Morality

Some years ago a distinguished playwright told me how he had taken his East Side mother-in-law to see Maurice Evans in *Richard III*. The old lady—whose experience with both literature and the theatre was extremely limited—listened intently in silence for half an hour, then waved a derisive thumb in the direction of the mellifluously complaining Richard and announced firmly: "I don't sympathize."

Now this was, of course, a fine tribute to the purely dramatic skill of Shakespeare. He had provoked the reaction he aimed at without any direct indication of what his own attitude was. I remember the anecdote at the moment for a simple reason. "I don't sympathize" vigorously sums up my own response to certain modern Richards, namely those who enlarge with too much self-pity upon their "alienation" from modern society, modern man and, indeed, from the universe as a whole. On the one hand I find myself ready to agree with a good deal of their criticism; on the other I am irritated by their chronic reaction to the things we both abhor.

To take the most obvious and least significant case, consider the beatniks. I dislike—almost if not quite as much as they do—the dominant middle-class and organization-man concept of the Good Life. Although we can't all be philosophers, scholars, artists or monks, I agree that too many moderns aspire to nothing more than the "status symbols" that money can buy, and far too few to what George N. Shuster recently defined as the ultimate

aim of education: "sharing the life of the scholar, poet and saint."
But to respond to this situation by taking a shot of heroin and
driving a car at ninety miles an hour seems unlikely either to improve society or, what is more relevant, lead to a Good Life.

Sympathetic interpreters of the beatniks have described them
as "taking a revenge on society." For example, the hero of a recent novel is described by a reviewer thus: "Seeing too well in a
world dazed by the bomb, Renaud undertakes an alcoholic strike
against humanity." But the phrase "an alcoholic strike," like "a
revenge on society," seems to me merely comic. It suggests the
popular saying about "biting off your nose to spite your face,"
that being precisely what some intellectuals (including many
somewhat above the beatnik level) are doing—as though turning
into a dope addict does not hurt oneself even more than it hurts
anyone else. It seems only slightly less obvious that the more
respectable intellectuals who devote themselves exclusively to exploring and exploiting their "alienation" are doing much the same
thing. Surely it is more productive of personal happiness and even
"more useful to society" to be a candle throwing its beams into
a naughty world than a beatnik crying "revenge, revenge" from
the gutter. We hear a great deal about the responsibility of society toward the individual. The individual also has a responsibility
toward society. And if things are as bad as the alienated say, the
only way one can discharge that responsibility is by being an
honorable man.

I presume that this thesis hardly needs elaboration and is not
likely to be contested outside beatnik circles. But a considerable
number of the most talented novelists, poets, painters and composers of the present day reveal, even if they do not proclaim,
their alienation; and it seems to me that their most frequent response is only less grotesque, not more fruitful, than that of the
beatniks. Even granted, as most of them proclaim in some version of Yeats's often quoted words that "Things fall apart; the
center cannot hold," is there still nothing for a wise man to do
except take heroin with the beatniks or, as is usual among the

alienated squares, elaborate in more and more complicated phrases their dark convictions?

To this question the hearty do-gooder will of course reply: "Why obviously the thing to do is to work for social improvement. Join the party of your choice and the church of your choice; be sure to register for all elections and attend the meetings of your local P.T.A." Without entering into any question concerning the ultimate effectiveness of such a method of employing one's time, it must be admitted that your alienated artist or philosopher is no more likely than a beatnik to undertake it. Let us suppose, therefore, that he has, like Thoreau, both "signed off" from the church and wished that he could as easily sign off from society as a whole. Of course he will be thoroughly disapproved of almost everywhere outside the circle of the completely alienated; but he might, like a few others besides Thoreau, find in this determination to stand alone the possibility of making for himself a private world from which he was *not* alienated, instead of devoting himself exclusively to the task of saying just how alienated he is. He could even find a few justifications formulated in the past for doing just what he has done.

I seem to remember somewhere in Plato the opinion that when times are thoroughly bad a wise man will merely stand by the wall. Similarly, it would appear from the *Meditations* of Marcus Aurelius that although the Emperor was no less aware than Yeats of a world in which "things fall apart," he spent relatively little time in either elaborating or bemoaning the lack of wisdom or virtue in society. He determined instead to cultivate them in himself. Then there is even a wholehearted defense of the mere slacker, which is quoted by Montaigne from one Theodorus who held that "It is not just that a wise man should risk his life for the good of his country and imperil wisdom for fools."

As I see it, the question is not so much whether the alienated would do better to imitate Marcus Aurelius rather than Baudelaire and Apollinaire, for it is a larger and, so many will think, an outrageous question. Is it possible that present-day civilization would be in some important respects better than it is if more people had thought less about how to improve society and more about how to improve themselves?

No doubt the medieval monk was too exclusively concerned with his private salvation. But we have gone to the other extreme and are so obsessed with the idea of society as a whole that it no longer seems quite respectable to seek even intellectual or spiritual self-improvement. I am not saying that we are, in actual fact, excessively unselfish. But the cant of the time requires that we should always be asking of any proposed good, "Can everybody have it?" or "Is it an answer to the general problem?" With astonishing regularity I get letters from people who comment on something I have written with a "Well, that's the answer so far as you are concerned; I guess it could be the answer so far as I am concerned. But only the privileged, or the lucky, or the well educated, or the intelligent, or the whatnot, can do what you and I can. So what is the answer for society as a whole?"

No doubt it would be fine if we could find a universal formula for salvation. I would welcome a convincing one if I ever heard it. But I never have, and I see no reason why, this being true, the individual should not save himself so long as he is not doing so at somebody else's expense. After all, society is composed of individuals. It cannot be "saved" except insofar as the individuals who compose it are.

I am not preaching universal indifference to society and social action as the highest wisdom. I am saying simply that if and when one individual feels (as so many articulate people do seem to feel) that the world is hopeless, then it is wiser to see what one can do about oneself than to give up all hope of that also. "I came into this world," said Thoreau, "not primarily to make it better but to live in it be it good or bad." If you insist, you may soften that a little by substituting "exclusively" for "primarily," but the meaning will still point in the same direction. Or as the same argument was recently discussed in that excellent "little magazine" called *Manas:* "If an artist can find nothing but bad brushes to paint with, he will not dissipate all his energies leading a revolution against bad brushes—but will develop techniques which make it possible for him to paint with bad brushes. He may even discover things that bad brushes do better than good brushes. It is one thing to fight the good fight for good brushes, and another to start to paint."

During the thirties, when most intellectuals moved leftward, quite a number of those who confessed (at least to their friends) that they had embraced communism were nevertheless engaged in writing movies for Hollywood or advertisements for Madison Avenue, while at the same time professing to regard both the movies and advertising as poisonous exhalations from a deliquescent society. Often (and I report from my own experience) they justified themselves by saying that there was no use trying to be anything but rotten in a rotten society. Comes the revolution and we will all be decent. Meanwhile, since we live in an evil society, we submit to it without any bourgeois nonsense about merely personal decency.

Such an attitude is only a logical extreme of the one taken by those who may not completely renounce either personal integrity or personal happiness, but insist upon our duty to think primarily in terms of what can be done for "society," and who sink into despair if we do not know an answer. I will even go so far as to suggest the possibility that society may be in a bad way partly because we have laid so much stress on public education—to take one example—and so little upon self-education. (Perhaps it also has something to do with the fact that I have met "educators" who were not and made no effort to be educated themselves.)

"Philanthropy," so Thoreau wrote, "is almost the only virtue which is sufficiently appreciated by mankind. . . . The kind uncles and aunts of the race are more esteemed than its true spiritual fathers and mothers. I once heard a reverend lecturer on England, a man of learning and intelligence, after enumerating her scientific, literary and political worthies, Shakespeare, Bacon, Cromwell, Milton, Newton and others, speak next of her Christian heroes, whom, as if his profession required it of him, he elevated to a place far above all the rest, as the greatest of the great. They were Penn, Howard and Mrs. Fry. Everyone must feel the falsehood and cant of this. The last were not England's best men and women; only, perhaps, her best philanthropists." This is a tough-minded opinion. It is stated with characteristic exaggeration. But at least there is something to be said for those who do their best even though they do not see at the moment just what practical good it is going to do "for the common man."

After all, the medieval monk did perform a service. Neither the God he served nor the learning he preserved counted for much in the world from which he had retired. But he did exemplify in himself virtues that might otherwise have ceased to exist entirely, and he did preserve learning that without him would have been lost.

What it all comes down to in practice is simply this: if you despair of the world, don't despair of yourself. And it is because so many of the alienated critics of our society with whose criticisms I agree seem unable to do anything of the sort that I find myself alienated from them also.

Thirty years ago when I published a book much more pessimistic than I could possibly write now, I received a good many letters that might have been boiled down to a sentence in one of them: "If these are your convictions why don't you go hang yourself?" The answer was, and has continued to be through all such changes of opinion as I have undergone, that there is a private world of thought and endeavor which society has never been able to take away from me.

Perhaps the most curious and shocking result of the exclusive stress upon social rather than upon private ethics is the disappearance of the concept of honor as distinct from that of morality. One of the differences between the two is simply that honor is relevant to the individual only. True, society may be more affected than some social scientists seem to think by the prevalence or scarcity of honor in the code of the individuals who make it up. But the man of honor always asks first whether or not an action would dishonor him personally, and he is not influenced by an argument that his dishonorable act would have no bad (perhaps even some good) effect upon society and is therefore "moral" even if dishonorable.

The world would not now be as profoundly shocked as it was a generation ago by the phrase "a scrap of paper." We are used to having promises so treated. But the Junkers were merely a little ahead of us in their willingness to believe that since the triumph of Germany would promote the advent of the superman, there was nothing immoral in a broken oath.

Many college students, so the pollsters tell us, see nothing wrong about cheating on examinations. "Everybody does it and it doesn't really *hurt* anyone."

In such statements it is easy to see a reasonable application of the two leading principles of ethics-without-absolutes-and-without-honor, which is sometimes called "socialized morality." These two leading principles are: (1) What everybody does must be permissible since the *mores* determine morality; and (2) "Wrong" can mean only "socially harmful."

If you believe all this and also that the only difference between, let us say, an honest man and a thief is the difference between a man who has been "conditioned" to act honestly and one who has not, then there isn't much basis for argument with the student opinion.

When some scandal breaks in government or journalism or business or broadcasting, the usual reaction of even that part of the public which is shocked by it is to say that it could not have happened if there had been adequate laws supervising this or that activity. But, usually, is it not equally true that it could not have happened if a whole group of men, often including the supposed guardians of public morality, had not been devoid of any sense of the meaning and importance of individual integrity? May one not go further and ask whether any amount of "social consciousness" and government control can make decent a society composed of people who have no conception of personal dignity and honor? It was a favorite and no doubt sound argument among early twentieth-century reformers that "playing the game" as the gentleman was supposed to play it was not enough. But has the time not come to add that it is, nevertheless, indispensable?

If the relevance of all this to the first part of the present discussion is not obvious, please allow me to dot the *i*'s. To those who believe that society is corrupt beyond redemption I propose the ancient but neglected concept of personal integrity, virtue and honor accompanied, if they feel it necessary, with the contempt and scorn recently advocated in a telling article in the [*American*] *Scholar* itself.

Those who hold that "social morality" is the only kind worth considering tend to assume that the end justifies the means. If a broken promise or a cynical invasion of a private right promotes "the greatest good of the greatest number" then it is an act of "higher morality." That seems to me a curiously inverted, soft-hearted and soft-headed Machiavellianism. The man of honor is reluctant to use dishonorable means no matter what ends seem to justify them. And he seems to me to be a safer member of society.

FOR THE STUDENT

Rhetoric

1. *Point out examples of Krutch's diction, phrasing, and sentence patterns that give his style a conversational tone.*
2. *State in your own words the abstract concept illustrated by the quotation from* Manas.
3. *Study the style and tone of the three essays in this group. What do you find distinctive in each? Could you identify a passage from any one of the essays by its style and tone?*

Discussion

1. *At the end of paragraph two, Krutch makes clear that he sympathizes with the spirit but not with the actions of the alienated. Evaluate the examples of his ambivalent attitude that follow in the next two paragraphs.*
2. *Explain fully the distinction Krutch makes between social and private morality. Does this distinction help to explain his attitude toward the alienated?*
3. *What would you imagine Krutch's reaction would be to various examples of youthful revolt discussed by Rexroth?*
4. *Do you believe it possible to despair of the world without despairing of yourself?*
5. *The quotation from Yeats appears in "The Second Coming." Explain how Yeats's vision in the first eight lines of this poem illustrates what the three writers in this section have said about modern society.*

Writing

1. *Write a paper in which Lipton and Krutch debate the problem of the disaffiliated or the alienated. Perhaps you may wish to let Rexroth act as moderator.*
2. *Theme topic: "Cheating on examinations really does not hurt anyone."*

5 Equality

The concept "equality" has perhaps been more politically fruitful than any other concept in modern Western thought: it underlay the French and American Revolutions, it has been basic in the spread of democratic institutions throughout the world, and it provides the rationale for civil rights today. And yet, though equality may seem a common and simple enough value, its interpretation has troubled some of the best minds of the past several centuries: Rousseau, Locke, and Abraham Lincoln, to mention only a few.

Philosophically, the problem seems to be one of epistemology: is equality a "natural" attribute, inborn in all men? Or is it a fiction created by men in a specific time and place? With this approach, two of the following selections—those by Huxley and Rossiter—belong on the "Left," for they question the existence of equality in nature. And Laski, who calls equality "one of the most permanent passions of mankind" would rank on the "Right." But if one considers solely the political thrust of these writers' opinions, that is, if one sees them in a political climate of applied egalitarianism, then surely their order must be different. Harold Laski, a British statesman and a political scientist of international reputation from the University of London, insists that only when equality pervades all spheres of life can man achieve "the natural expansion of the human spirit." This thesis and his concomitant attack on inequality rank Laski on the political "Left." Clinton Rossiter, a contemporary American political scientist, insofar as he can be identified with the conservative view he describes, stands on the Middle ground: he is pessimistic about man's capabilities for self-improvement and self-government *and warns against the "rage for equality." Aldous Huxley, one of the great novelists and social critics of the century, holds here that "equality" is a concept invented by man to mask and justify his natural self-interest. His position may be identified with the political "Right."*

HAROLD J. LASKI

A Plea for Equality

At no period since the French Revolution has there been a skepticism of democracy so profound as at the present time. Its unquestioned supremacy as an ideal is gone, and there are few now so poor as to do it reverence. Some speak with contempt of the bourgeois notions it embodies; others insist upon its futile inefficiency; to others, again, democracy has broken upon the impregnable rock of scientific analysis. It is based, we are told, upon the exploded myth of equality. It is the unnatural offspring of Romanticism, the fruit of a dubious marriage between Envy and Rousseau. Its principles, it is insisted, do not survive examination. Liberty is meaningless save in terms of law; and law demands authority and subordination as conditions of its life. Equality, could it be realized, would merely level the claims of the best to the plane of mediocrity; and it would compel the able and the energetic to fit a Procrustes' bed of identity for which Nature did not create them. Fraternity, moreover, is simple folly in a world where ruthless struggle is the law of life; we cannot love our fellow men until we have won security, and in the uneasy pyramid of society there is no security save as we trample upon our neighbors. All over the world the institutional system, which to the nineteenth century was the pattern laid up in Heaven for emulation, has been challenged; and there is no way to gain a reputation so easily as by insisting that the age of enthusiasm for democratic institutions is now drawing to its close.

Yet a shrewd observer would be a little skeptical of this temper. The democratic movement is not an historic accident. It arose from intelligible causes, and it is still referable to intelligible

From The Dangers of Obedience *by Harold J. Laski. Copyright 1930 by Harold J. Laski; renewed 1958 by Frida Laski. Reprinted by permission of Harper & Row, Publishers.*

principle. It arose as a protest against the possession of privilege
by men whose supremacy was not found to be intimately connected with the well-being of society. Men discovered at long last
that exclusion from privilege is exclusion from benefit. They
learned that if, over any considerable period, they are governed by
a section of themselves, it is in the interest of that section that they
will be governed. Grim experience taught them that power is
poisonous to its possessors; that no dynasty and no class can exclusively control the engines of power without ultimately confusing
their private interest with the public well-being. They learned that
interest elevates prejudice to the level of principle, and that reason
is then used, not to satisfy objective need, but to justify postponement of desirable change. They found, in a word, that if popular
well-being is to be the purpose of government, popular control is
the essential condition of its fulfillment.

Almost a century and a half has passed since 1789, and we
can begin to assess the results of that gigantic upheaval. Broadly, it
may be said to have brought the middle class business man to
power; and its chief consequence has been the abolition of that
political privilege which was the chief obstacle to his ascent. In
the Western world, at least, men can now enjoy the major political
freedoms. There is universal suffrage; there is a relatively wide
liberty of speech and association; there is opportunity for the humble to elevate themselves to a part in the governance of the state.
The old view of government as the natural field of an hereditary
aristocracy has been definitely relegated to the museum of historic
antiquities; and it is certainly difficult not to feel that the scale of
life today is for the average man ampler than at any previous time.
Given political-mindedness, he can hope to play his little part
upon the national stage. Given the sense of organization, and any
will widely representative of popular desire can expect to find its
place, after due effort, in the statute book. The political state is a
democratic state in the important sense that it is no longer built
upon a system of deliberate exclusions.

But if the political state is democratic, it cannot be said that

we are members of a democratic society. The outstanding fact in
the political sphere is equality. Bismarck's insistence that the best
form of government is a benevolent and rational absolutism no
longer commands general assent because historic experience has
shown that no absolutism is ever capable of continuing either
benevolent or rational. Any form of government other than the
democratic suffers from the fatal defect of preventing the natural
expansion of the human spirit. It thwarts the progress of civilization because it belittles men. It elevates the few at the expense of
the many in terms which reason cannot justify. When the monarchy
governed France, when the aristocracy governed England, those
who obtained the fruits of the adventure were rarely those who
toiled for its enlargement. The democratic principle had at least
this major advantage: that it offered a plane where the claims of
men to a share in the common good could be admitted as equal.
Personality as such was dignified by its recognition as citizenship.
To open to ordinary men new avenues of creative effort was not
merely to raise their moral stature; it enlarged also the quality of
the political state by enabling it to base its experiments on a far
wider induction than at any previous time. Political democracy, as
Tocqueville regretfully admitted, more securely civilized the masses
than has ever been the case under alternative systems.

II

But political democracy implies only political equality; and
though it is not necessary to minimize the significance of political
equality, neither is it necessary to magnify it. In most states of the
modern world it has not been followed by equality either in the
social or in the economic spheres. And since politics, after all, is
relatively a small part of life, the ambit of territory within which
the continuous expansion of personality is permitted, in which,
that is to say, the spirit of the individual has genuine elbowroom,
remains notably small. The distribution of wealth is notoriously
unequal; the distribution of educational opportunities hardly less

so. The degree to which occupations in the modern world are, America apart, stereotyped from father to son is astonishing to the observer. The democratic political state has, so far, been curiously unable to alter the inequalities of the social fabric. The result everywhere is grave dissatisfaction, a sense that political institutions are less capable of themselves effecting basic social change than merely of recording in legislation changes that have been effected by revolutionary means. The nineteenth century preached the doctrine that the ballot box was the highroad to the realization of social good. The twentieth century seems not unlikely to urge that violence is the true midwife of radical betterment. That difference in outlook—with all the dangers it implies—is born of nothing so much as our failure to apply the idea of equality outside the merely political sphere. For without equality there cannot be liberty, and without liberty there cannot be the humanization of mankind.

Without equality, I say, there cannot be liberty. All history goes to show that interdependence. For if liberty means the continuous power of expansion in the human spirit, it is rarely present save in a society of equals. Where there are rich and poor, educated and uneducated, we find always masters and servants. To be rich is to be powerful; to be educated is to have authority. To live in subordination by reason of poverty or ignorance is to be like a tree in the shade which perishes because it cannot reach the light. Poverty and ignorance benumb the faculties and depress the energies of men. It is, of course, true that there are those who by the very strength of the conditions which suppress them are goaded to conquest of their environment. But with ordinary men this is not the case. On the contrary, the sense of inferiority which an unequal society inflicts upon them deprives them of that hope which is the spur of effort. They remain contented with a condition in which they cannot make the best of themselves. The distance which separates them from the wealthy and the cultured is so vast that they are never stimulated to make the effort to overpass it. They remain uncivilized because power and consideration are objects too refined for their understanding. They are satisfied with the crude in arts and letters, the brutal in sensual pleasures, the material and the vulgar in objects of desire. And because of their inferiority, they are judged incapable of advancement. Aristocracies, whether of wealth or birth, have never understood the secret of this degradation. In part, they have accepted it as proof of their own superiority; and in part they have welcomed it as a safeguard of their security. They take the deference they are accorded as the proof of their inherent worth; and they do not examine into the causes of its reception.

Aristocracies, historically, have always suffered from an incapacity for ideas. They cannot share the wants or the instincts of the rest of the society of which they are a part. And they always fail, accordingly, to realize that the desire of equality is one of the most permanent passions of mankind. At the very birth of political science, Aristotle had already seen that a failure to satisfy it is one of the major causes of revolutions; it is not less so today. For where there are wide differences in the habits of men, there are wide differences in their thoughts. To think differently is to lose hold of a basis of social unity. A house divided against itself, the Bible says, cannot stand; a nation divided into rich and poor is a house divided against itself. It is only where men have an equal interest in the result of the common effort that there is a bond of genuine fellowship between them. A realization of unequal interest means, inevitably, the growth of a sense of injustice. That sense fastens itself upon the perception of an unequal return to effort; and an abyss is precipitated between classes of which, in the end, revolution is always the outcome.

It appears, therefore, that the less obvious the differences between men in the gain of living, the greater the bond of fellowship between them. And in a society like our own the differences between men are intensified by the fact that they are rarely referable to rational principle. We have wealthy men and women who have never contributed a day's effort to the sum of productivity; and we have poor men and women who have never known relaxation from unremitting toil. Wealth, with us, is so often the result of accident, of corruption, of a power to satisfy demand not inherently social in character, that there is little relation between its possession and a criterion of social benefit. The economic inequalities of society, that is to say, do not so explain themselves that men can regard them as just. Those who support them as necessary are always on the defensive; and they are always occupied in searching for possible concessions to the poor whereby they can be the better preserved. Philanthropy and social legislation are the taxes the rich must pay to keep the poor in order; and instead of a stimulus to cease from poverty they act as an incentive to remain in a routine where the service performed prevents by its character the emergence of a civilized quality in the performer. Our inegalitarian system corrodes the conscience of the rich by extracting ransom from them; and it destroys the creativeness of the poor by emphasizing their inferiority in the very conference of benefit. The rich hate the process of giving, and the poor hate them because they are compelled to receive.

The system, moreover, weakens from decade to decade. It weakens because in the first place it is no longer supported by the authority of religion, and, in the second, because the growth of education is increasingly destructive of the habit of deference. Where poverty was accompanied by deep religious feeling it rarely awoke envy, either because the poor man felt in duty bound to accept the will of God, or because he had an intimate assurance of a due reward in the after life. But he has no longer the sense of being selected for salvation; and despite the development of an increasingly Corybantic Christianity, he insists more and more that his Heaven must be realized in the present life. It is necessary, moreover, continually to raise the standard of education, in part, because an intelligent worker is a condition of our scale of productive effort, and in part because an educated democracy is a primary condition of social peace. Yet the first result of education among the masses is the perception that whatever inequalities may be justified by social needs, the present inequalities are incapable of justification. The more we educate, in short, the more we reveal to

the multitude the inadequacy of the moral principle upon which
our civilization is based. Since we have given political power to
that multitude, either it will use the institutions of democracy to
rectify the inadequacy or it will search for some other institutional
principle whereby the rectification can be made.

III

"Our inequality," said Matthew Arnold, "materializes our
upper class, vulgarizes our middle class, brutalizes our lower." It
does this, moreover, in proportion to the degree of inequality that
exists among us. Anyone who considers the habits of our plutoc-
racy will see how the crass stupidity of their standards is reflected
in every nook and cranny of society. The fact that they govern because they are rich means that wealth is the mark of consideration.
What is held out to other classes for admiration is not elevation of
mind, dignity of character, or beauty of life, but position, show,
luxury, or any other mark by which riches may be displayed.
There is absent, that is to say, from an admiration for this plutoc-
racy any quality that is likely to ennoble the mind. Those who
feed it merely develop in themselves the zest for ostentation, crude
as it is, that they admire. By maintaining inequality, in fact, we
maintain the conditions which inhibit the process of civilizing men.
For where those who are held up to us for emulation are those
whose only qualities are either a genius for acquisition or a capacity to preserve what someone else had acquired, there cannot be
growth of spiritual stature. The religion of inequality, indeed, has
not even the advantage of mysticism; it is too solid, crude, brutal
for that. And, like all religions void of graciousness, it fashions its
acolytes in its own image.

There is, moreover, another aspect from which our religion of
inequality must be regarded. One of the first considerations in any
society is the need for the equal protection of the laws. What is
certain in our society is that an unequal distribution of wealth
means unequal protection in the courts. The rich man can almost

always secure bail; not so the poor. A fine means nothing to the rich; but it may well destroy the poor man's home, or, in default, send him to prison. The rich man has at his disposal all the resources of legal technic; the poor man, for the most part, must either take what lawyer he can get, or rely on the power of the judge to penetrate through his own stumbling inarticulateness. Nor does the difference end here. What we call embezzlement in a junior clerk becomes high finance in a millionaire. What is disorderly conduct in the East End of London becomes high spirits west of Temple Bar. What is theft in Poplar is kleptomania in Kensington. We have no conscience about the fate of Sacco and Vanzetti; but Mr. Thaw's millions enable him to escape their fate. There is, in fact, equality before the law only when there is equal wealth in the parties; and the measure of justice they will obtain is very largely a function of their balance at the bank.

Or consider, from the same angle, the consequence of inequality in the sphere of education. Even where we have conquered illiteracy, education, for the overwhelming majority, ends at fourteen years of age; which means, for most, that the necessary tools of intellectual analysis are incapable of being used. Knowledge and the power to make experience articulate become the monopoly of the few. An inability in the uneducated to state their wants leads, at its lower levels, to a wantlessness which utterly degrades the human spirit. Most men and women go through life completely ignorant of the intellectual heritage of civilization. Yet, personal relations apart, no one who has been vouchsafed companionship in the investigation of that heritage but knows it as the source of the main joy life can offer. To deprive men of access to it does not destroy the impulse of curiosity; it merely deflects into it channels from which no social good can emerge. Education is the great civilizer; and it is, above all, absence of education which provokes the brute in man. The price we pay for that absence anyone can see in Manchester or the underworld of Chicago. Above all, an inequality in this sphere is paid for by the inability of the ignorant to realize the fragility of civilization. They have a sense of angry despair or sodden disillusion; they do not know how to formulate the source either of their anger or their hopelessness. We leave them to destroy because we have not taught them how to fulfill.

There is, moreover, a psychological result of inequality upon which too much stress can hardly be laid. Inequality divides our society into men who give and men who receive orders. The second class, being deprived of initiative, is robbed of the possibility of freedom. Its members spend their lives as prisoners of an inescapable routine they have had no part in making. When their life is compared with that of their governors, whose power of self-controlled initiative is continuous and unbroken, it is obvious enough that distinctiveness of personality has there little chance of survival. And the orders received are irresponsible since, in general, they are born, not of function, but of the possession of wealth. The farm laborer, the domestic servant, the factory worker realize in a high degree that definition of an animate tool which Aristotle insisted was the quintessence of slavery. In the psychological sphere their experience means a continuous inhibition of natural impulse, a want of room to experiment with themselves, which is disastrous to the expansion of personality. Economic equality, for them, would mean the end of government by a narrow oligarchy of wealth whose sole purpose in life is personal pleasure or personal gain. We can understand the need for obedience to a doctor, a tax collector, a policeman. There, as we can realize, the rules they enforce are born of principles of which they, not less than we, are servants; and their relation to the result is a disinterested one. But the orders of the narrow group who own economic power are rarely disinterested and never born of principle unless they choose so to make them. The result is the loss of freedom in those whom they command because they dictate the rules of authority to ends in which their servants cannot share.

It is partly a result of this dictation that it should be incompatible also with freedom in the sphere of the mind. To preserve inequality in social life, the pattern of mental experience must be controlled for the majority. The press, broadly speaking, is a servile instrument of wealthy men. . . . Our governors may well adapt to themselves the aphorism of Fletcher of Saltoun and say that they care not who has the making of the nation's laws so long as they have the making of its news. It is difficult for any observer, however much he strive for impartiality, to see the facts through the clouds of bias, suggestion, and suppression with which he is confronted; and it is the deliberate purpose of those clouds to screen from view the actual workings of a system of which inequality is the basic principle to be defended.

In a less degree, yet still very notably, the same is true of the educational system. It is dangerous in school and university alike to obtain a reputation for political or economic radicalism. The authorities who control appointments are the nominees of the conquerors; and, from dismissal to loss of the chance of promotion, they have at their disposal weapons which effectively prevent any ultimate freedom of thought in their servants. Anyone who scrutinizes the long list of investigations by the American Association of University Professors, or who analyzes the history of those teachers who have affiliated themselves to trade unions, will realize amply enough that liberty of thought in the teaching world is, at the point where the thought touches the existing disposition of social forces, broadly impossible for most. There have not, perhaps, been in England some of the more egregious outrages which have characterized American experience; but that is because there the selection has been more carefully made and dismissal, *a priori,* has been less necessary. For in the theological realm the English record is not an honorable one; and even today, in Oxford and Cambridge, theological teaching is a jealously guarded monopoly of the Church of England. In the result, both in school and university, the picture of the system presented is bound in the overwhelming majority of the cases to be that intellectually necessary for the preservation of the existing order. Exactly as in Soviet Russia where truth means "communist" truth, with a *ne varietur* written over the halls of instruction, so, if more subtly, the actual institutions of an unequal society are presented as though they were the inescapable inevitabilities of the social order. Our educational system is used, not to train the mind as an instrument of critical inquiry, but to bend it to the services of certain presuppositions profitable to the oligarchy which lives by their results.

IV

The price we pay for this inequality is a heavy one. The masses are dehumanized. The middle class is, in general, so wrapped up in its pursuit and worship of property that it has hardly the time, and rarely the inclination, for continuous experience of spiritual values. The wealthy pass their lives in feverish search for aimless pleasures which satiate at the moment of their attainment. Social prestige and conventional respectability are not ideals likely to produce a great civilization when they are regarded as ends in themselves. Yet they are the inevitable outcome of a society which regards inequality as its first and most natural law. For what it must do to maintain them as ideals is to frown upon those who do not follow the beaten track. Our personalities must be cast into molds which satisfy the norms of this pitiful principle. Even our charities are thought of, not in terms of their objects, but of those who support them. An English social worker who desires to raise funds for his organization knows perfectly well that he can double his subscriptions if he can persuade the Prince of Wales to permit the use of his name. A theatrical performance for charity in New York in one of the great houses, with members of the Junior League as its pathetic exponents, would raise far more money than one given by the Theatre Guild. Incredible organizations like the Primrose League in England and the Daughters of the American Revolution in America live by their ministration to the instinct for snobbery in an unequal society. What are so curiously termed the great hostesses entertain Mr. Shaw and Mr. Wells, Professor Einstein, and Mr. Ramsay MacDonald, not out of

interest in, or sympathy for, their ideas, but for the advertising
value of their presence at a social function.

The unequal society demands a standardized and uniform outlook as the condition of its preservation. It is fatal to individuality,
because individuality implies the novel and the unexpected; and
these are dangerous to conventional habits. It has to impose upon
its members beliefs, ideas, habits, rules which prevent that affirmation of self from which the increase of civilization flows. To offer
us the type of life our acquisitive society practices is to offer us a
religion which leaves unsatisfied the claims alike of knowledge, of
beauty, and of manners. The claims of knowledge: for we cannot
afford the truth about social or economic organization. We cannot give more than the smatterings of education to the multitude
if it is to remain properly subservient to its masters. On most of
the vital aspects of sex we maintain a deliberate conspiracy of
silence; and the very implications of the phrase "a good marriage"
are tragi-comic evidence of the way in which the ideal of sexual
comradeship is perverted. The claims, also, of beauty: for these
always make room—as our slums, our factories, and our egregious
villadom proclaim—to the demands of property. Successful art is
either art which meets a vulgar demand or that which receives
temporary canonization because it pleases the powerful; and when
England wants a trustee of the National Gallery, it selects, not
Roger Fry, but Lord Curzon, not Laurence Binyon, but Sir Philip
Sassoon. The claims, finally, of manners: at the base, it is clear
enough that manners will not emerge where overcrowding makes
impossible the observance of the elementary decencies of life. The
middle and the apex of the pyramid have been amply described for
us by Mr. Galsworthy and Proust. Manners do not mean, as our
system makes them mean, the uneasy and apprehensive search to
maintain one's social position which gives to New York and London, to Paris and Rome, their pathetically elaborate code of trivial-
ities, their ludicrous formalism, their contemptible craving for the
publicity of the social column. The Duc de Guermantes, who calls
for his ticket at the theatre and is able to show a greater courtesy

to the attendant than a nobleman of lesser rank because he has a more assured social prestige, is a real symbol of our society.

We live in terror of doing the wrong thing instead of in hope of finding the right. We lack a healthy individualism which might give us the courage to experiment with ourselves. Instead of developing a self-respect born of a satisfied and harmonious personality, we sacrifice ourselves on the Procrustes' bed of traditional conventions, each one of which thwarts impulses that are basic to our character. We are trying to have our cake and eat it—a matter of impossibility in affairs of social logic. We have given the people power in the realm of politics, and we are trying to pretend to ourselves that the equalization of authority therein implied may rightly cease at its boundaries. The pretense is folly. The whole principle of democracy is nothing less than the affirmation by the people of its own essence; and this is incompatible with irrational privilege in any sphere. The law of democracy is the attachment of prestige, not to the accident of birth or wealth, but to the performance of social function. A democracy can understand why the President of the United States is important; but sensibly enough, it resents the attachment of importance and power to a leisured aristocracy with no duties save the pursuit of pleasure. It will give its respect to great artists, poets, scientists, philosophers, but it sees no reason to revere Commodore Vanderbilt or that Duke of Norfolk upon whose marriage the *London Times* of half a century ago bestowed the incredible epithalamium of a leading article.

The democratic demand for social and economic equality is, in fact, built upon the simple insistence that without it first things cannot come first. And that simple insistence is impossible in any community where, because the rights of property are unequally distributed, all other rights are modeled in their image. That is not, it is perhaps worth while to remark, the affirmation of dangerous radicalism. Conservative philosophers like Aristotle, publicists of genius like Harrington in England and Madison in America, critics of society like Matthew Arnold, all alike have insisted that as the rights of property are, so the complexion of society will be.

Make the first unequal, and all else in life for which men strive will adjust itself to those terms. If, doubtless, the distribution of property were built upon a principle of unquestionable justice so that each man received in proportion to his contribution to the common stock, it would not greatly matter that there were differences of position in society. Inequality would be a function of merit, intelligible and defensible. But this is so demonstrably not the case, that inequality everywhere is the nurse of envy and hate and corruption; and of these, everywhere as well, the outcome is revolution. So that states which seek the postponement of equality have always within themselves a festering sore which is bound to break out sooner or later. They lack the essential condition of stable government, which is a widespread sense of allegiance to the constitution as the protector of the equal rights of men.

"The surest way to prevent seditions," said Bacon, "is to take away the matter of them." Where we have a state in which no man is so rich that he can buy his neighbor and none so poor that he must sell himself, we have present the fundamental condition of security. For men who can purchase others are free only at the cost of these; and men who are driven to sell themselves turn naturally to revolution as the alternative to slavery. In an equal state we confer upon all citizens the effective hope of bettering their conditions. We elevate the quality of their effort by giving them the right to aspire. We prevent that persistent frustration of impulse which is the major consequence of inequality. The divisions of society build themselves on the actual service they perform. Upon any other basis this is not the case. Intrust, as we intrust, the governance of the state to an aristocracy, whether of wealth or birth, and it is bound, in the end, to govern badly. For it cannot escape temptation and flattery. It is unacquainted with the realities of life as these are experienced by those over whom it rules. It is driven to elevate its own sense of superiority to the position of a social axiom; and it entirely fails to observe that the axiom is in fact the narrowest of indications from the most partial of evidence, the substance of its own desires. The proof of this is

simple enough. Confront any aristocracy with novelty, and it is
patently incapable of its rational examination. The nobility of the
ancien régime in France, the Romanoff dynasty in Russia, the
English landowner in Ireland, the Austrian conqueror in Italy—
these had before their eyes the evidence of a new and inescapable
temper with which terms had to be made; and they could only
equate it with original sin. Yet great agitations are not marks of
popular crime; popular crime is only a mark of great agitation
born of some suffering too grievous to be endured. And the root
of great passions is the unchanging passion for equality.

The skeptic, of course, is horrified at a panegyric of this sort.
All that we know, he argues, teaches us that men are different in
taste and different in talent; to treat them as equals is to fly in the
face of elementary principles of nature. But this is to mistake
equality with identity. Equality does not mean that the differences
of men are to be neglected; it means only that those differences are
to be selected for emphasis which are deliberately relevant to the
common good. It refuses to recognize the legitimacy of barriers
which are born, not of the nature of things, but of accident illegitimate in its social consequence. It does not mean that the Heaven-
sent painter shall be compelled to the study of advanced mathematics; but merely that the Heaven-sent painter shall not be driven
to waste his talent through the absence of organized opportunity.
It means a shift in the emphasis of social action from the few to
the many. It implies the utilization, of set purpose, of the national
resources to the elevation of quality in the ordinary man. It is built
upon a belief that when the ordinary man is trained to coöperate
in the government of society, his powers are quickened, his self-
respect increased. He is something more than a passive spectator
of the social process. His individuality becomes articulate; he
contributes his little stock of experience and wisdom to the common store. The tradition he inherits is widened and quickened
by his knowledge and opinion. The power of social adaptation
is strengthened by the wider induction that can be made.

We need not doubt, with the skeptic, that a single individual of outstanding ability will often perform better the functions of government than the members of a democratic state. Caesar, Cromwell, Napoleon, Lenin had, doubtless, more energy, more perseverance, more capacity to plan in a wholesale way, and more art to perfect the details of their planning. But the answer to this is at least twofold. The energy, the perseverance, the capacity of the great dictators are almost always from the outset, and in the end invariably, purchased at the expense of the growth of those qualities in those over whom they rule. Democracy is not the most efficient form of government; neither is it the most capable of conceiving the greatest ideas. But a democratic government provokes in its citizens that which no other political system is able to secure. There flows from its equality in citizenship a restless energy, a pervasive vitality, more favorable to individuality than any other qualities. The knowledge there that the road lies open to power is a spur and an incentive which neither the favors of a dictatorship nor the prestige of an aristocracy can evoke. And the equalization of citizenship in the political field is itself a safeguard of the public interest. The political leader in a democratic state may be, often enough, less able or less honorable than the leader of an aristocracy. But his tenure of power is subject always to the condition that he must, in the end, submit himself to the will of the majority. His interest is in the democratic system more securely merged with the interest of the whole than is the case in any alternative scheme. The government of an aristocracy is, at its best, always in some sort a conspiracy against the nation. The very fact that it is protecting the privileged interest of a minority tends to make it shape institutions to its own ends and to protect them against invasion for the benefit of the whole. That has been, of course, unconsciously the history of the interpretation of the American Constitution by the Supreme Court; and, still more notably and again unconsciously, the history of the interpretation of trade-union law by English judges. Minority government always narrows public policy to mean the perpetuation of its own power.

Nor, finally, must we forget the significance of the historical aspect of the problem. Englishmen, to whom equality is still a strange ideal, Americans, who rarely observe the growth of a privileged aristocracy among themselves, too often forget that the history of society is supremely the history of the abolition of differences which reason cannot explain and justice cannot excuse. That has been the case in the sphere of religion; it has been, in Western civilization, predominantly the case in politics. Everyone has read the half-dozen remarkable pages in which Tocqueville explained how the movement of French history has been the evolution of an irresistible tendency to equalization of conditions. "Those who have knowingly labored in its cause," he wrote, "and those who have served it unwittingly; those who have fought for it and those who have announced themselves its opponents; all have been driven along the same track; . . . the gradual development of equal conditions . . . possesses all the characteristics of a divine decree; it is universal; it is desirable; it constantly eludes all human interference; and all events as well as all men contribute to its progress."

Certainly it does not appear likely that a democracy which has established equality in religion and politics, which has overthrown the power of churches and kings and aristocracies, will leave untouched the economic and the social field. Yet nothing is more dangerous in social philosophy than the postulation of inevitable victories. The power of inequality is still immense, the interests it protects gigantic. To be optimistic about the prospect of its abdication is folly; to believe that it is certain of defeat is overconfidence. It is the tragedy of modern society that science has made social conflict the parent of social disaster; for the forces of democracy in this new realm to try their strength with the forces of privilege may well make the second state worse than what they seek to overthrow. We must rather have faith in the power of reason to direct the human spirit to the prospects of concession and sacrifice. We must rather seek to persuade our masters that our equality is their freedom.

FOR THE STUDENT

Rhetoric

1. *Try to state the point of each section of the essay in one sentence. Do the four sections then hang together as one central thesis?*
2. *Laski is not generally admired for clarity and precision of* style: *in short, he is often wordy and awkwardly complex. See if you can rewrite the second paragraph of the fourth part and* simplify *the diction and syntax.*

Discussion

1. *Laski wrote this essay in 1930, warning that inequality would result in a revolution. What revolutions in recent history have arisen from inequality?*
2. *Is the "passion for equality" in fact based in nature? Do all men have it? Do animals?*
3. *In the third part, Laski says: "The press, broadly speaking, is a servile instrument of wealthy men." What evidence of this does he (or can you) give?*
4. *Reread the concluding paragraph of the third section. Does it seem to you a fair description of American education today?*

Writing

1. *Write one paragraph supporting and one paragraph attacking the following proposition: Inequality is immoral.*
2. *Laski discusses political equality, economic equality, social equality, and educational equality. You should discuss only one.*

CLINTON ROSSITER

The Conservative View
of Man and Society

The Conservative holds rather strong opinions about man's nature, his capacity for self-government, his relations with other men, the kind of life he should lead, and the rights he may properly claim. On these opinions, which taken together represent a stiff questioning of the bright promises of Liberalism, rests the whole Conservative tradition.

Man, says the Conservative (who conceals only poorly his distaste for such an abstraction), is a fabulous composite of some good and much evil, a blend of several ennobling excellencies and several more degrading imperfections. "Man is not entirely corrupt and depraved," William McGovern and David Collier have written, "but to state that he is, is to come closer to the truth than to state that he is essentially good." As no man is perfect, so no man is perfectible. If educated properly, placed in a favorable environment, and held in restraint by tradition and authority, he may display innate qualities of rationality, sociability, industry, and decency. Never, no matter how he is educated or situated or restrained, will he throw off completely his other innate qualities of irrationality, selfishness, laziness, depravity, corruptibility, and cruelty. Man's nature is essentially immutable, and the immutable strain is one of deep-seated wickedness. Although some Conservatives find support for their skeptical view of man in recent experiments in psychology, most continue to rely on religious teaching and the study of history. Those who are Christians, and most

Conservatives are, prefer to call the motivation for iniquitous and irrational behavior by its proper name: Original Sin.

The Conservative is often accused of putting too much stress on man's wickedness and irrationality and of overlooking his many good qualities, especially his capacity for reason. The Conservative's answer is candid enough. While he is well aware of man's potentialities, he must counter the optimism of the Liberal with certain cheerless reminders that are no less true for telling not quite all the truth: that evil exists independently of social or economic maladjustments; that we must search for the source of our discontents in defective human nature rather than in a defective social order; and that man, far from being malleable, is subject to cultural alteration only slowly and to a limited degree. The Conservative therefore considers it his stern duty to call attention, as did John Adams, to the "general frailty and depravity of human nature" and to the weakness of reason as a guide to personal conduct or collective endeavor. He is, in his most candid moments, an admirer of instinct, the "innate feeling for the good and the bad," and at least an apologist for prejudice, "the poor man's wisdom."

This view of human nature is saved from churlish cynicism by two beliefs. First, man is touched with eternity. He has a precious soul; he is a religious entity. His urges toward sin are matched, and with God's grace can be overmatched if never finally beaten down, by his aspiration for good. For this reason, the Conservative asserts man is an object of reverence, and a recognition of man's heaven-ordained shortcomings serves only to deepen this reverence. Second, to quote from Burke, the father of all Conservatives, "The nature of man is intricate." The confession of an eminent psychologist, Gardner Murphy, "Not much, I believe, is known about man," is applauded by the Conservative, who then adds, "Not much, I believe, will ever be known about him." Man is a mysterious and complex being, and no amount of psychological research will ever solve the mystery or unravel the complexity.

No truth about human nature and capabilities, the Conservative says, is more important than this: man can govern himself, but there is no certainty that he will; free government is possible but far from inevitable. Man will need all the help he can get from education, religion, tradition, and institutions if he is to enjoy even a limited success in his experiments in self-government. He must be counseled, encouraged, informed, and checked. Above all, he must realize that the collective wisdom of the community, itself the union of countless partial and imperfect wisdoms like his own, is alone equal to this mightiest of social tasks. A clear recognition of man's conditional capacity for ruling himself and others is the first requisite of constitution-making.

The Conservatism that celebrates Burke holds out obstinately against two popular beliefs about human relations in modern society: individualism and equality. Putting off a discussion of individualism for a few pages, let us hear what the Conservative has to say about the explosive question of equality.

Each man is equal to every other man in only one meaningful sense: he is a man, a physical and spiritual entity, and is thus entitled by God and nature to be treated as end rather than means. From the basic fact of moral equality come several secondary equalities that the modern Conservative recognizes, more eloquently in public than in private: equality of opportunity, the right of each individual to exploit his own talents up to their natural limits; equality before the law, the right to justice on the same terms as other men; and political equality, which takes the form —and a rather distressing form it often seems—of universal suffrage. Beyond this the Conservative is unwilling to go. Recognizing the infinite variety among men in talent, taste, appearance, intelligence, and virtue, he is candid enough to assert that this variety extends vertically as well as horizontally. Men are grossly unequal —and, what is more, can never be made equal—in most qualities of mind, body, and spirit.

The good society of Conservatism rests solidly on this great truth. The social order is organized in such a way as to take advantage of ineradicable natural distinctions among men. It exhibits a class structure in which there are several quite distinct levels, most men find their level early and stay in it without rancor, and equality of opportunity keeps the way at least partially open to ascent and decline. At the same time, the social order aims to temper those distinctions that are not natural. While it recognizes the inevitability and indeed the necessity of orders and classes, it insists that all privileges, ranks, and other visible signs of inequality be as natural and functional as possible. The Conservative, of course—and this point is of decisive importance—is much more inclined than other men to consider artificial distinctions as natural. Equity rather than equality is the mark of his society; the reconciliation rather than the abolition of classes is his constant aim. When he is forced to choose between liberty and equality, he throws his support unhesitatingly to liberty. Indeed, the preference for liberty over equality lies at the root of the Conservative tradition, and men who subscribe to this tradition never tire of warning against the "rage for equality."

While Conservatism has retreated some distance from Burke and Adams under the pressures of modern democracy, it has refused to yield one salient: the belief in a ruling, serving, taste-making aristocracy. "If there is any one point," Gertrude Himmelfarb writes, "any single empirical test, by which conservatism can be distinguished from liberalism, it is a respect for aristocracy and aristocratic institutions. Every tenet of liberalism repudiates the idea of a fixed aristocracy; every tenet of conservatism affirms it." If it is no longer good form to use the word "aristocracy" in a political debate, nor good sense to expect that an aristocracy can be "fixed" to the extent that it was one hundred and fifty years ago, the Conservative is still moved powerfully by the urge to seek out the "best men" and place them in positions of authority. Remembering Burke's warning that without the aristocracy "there is no nation," he continues to assert the beneficence of a gentry of talent and virtue, one that is trained for special service and thus entitled to special consideration. He continues to believe that it takes more than one generation to make a genuine aristocrat. His best men are "best" in manners as well as in morals, in birth as well as in talents.

The world being what it is today, the Conservative spends a good deal of his time in the pulpit exhorting his fellow men to live godly, righteous, and sober lives. He does not do this gladly, for he is not by nature a Puritan, but the times seem to have made him our leading "moral athlete."

Man, the Conservative asserts, is stamped with sin and carnality, but he is also blessed with higher aspirations. If human nature in general can never be much improved, each individual may nevertheless bring his own savage and selfish impulses under control. It is his duty to himself, his fellows, and God to do just this—to shun vice, cultivate virtue, and submit to the guidance of what Lincoln called "the better angels of our nature." Only thus, through the moral striving of many men, can free government be secured and society be made stable.

What virtues must the individual cultivate? The Conservative of the tower, the Conservative of the field, the Conservative of the market place, and the Conservative of the assembly each give a somewhat different answer to this question, yet all seem to agree to this catalogue of primary virtues: wisdom, justice, temperance, and courage; industry, frugality, piety, and honesty; contentment, obedience, compassion, and manners. The good man is peaceful but not resigned and is conservative through habit and choice rather than sloth and cowardice. He assumes that duty comes before pleasure, self-sacrifice before self-indulgence. Believing that the test of life is accomplishment rather than enjoyment, he takes pride in doing a good job in the station to which he has been called. He is alert to the identity and malignity of the vices he must shun: ignorance, injustice, intemperance, and cowardice; laziness, luxury, selfishness, and dishonesty; envy, disobedience, violence, and bad manners. And he is aware, too, of the larger implications of his own life of virtue: self-government is for moral men; those who would be free must be virtuous.

At the center of that constellation of virtues which make up the good man (who is also, needless to say, the good Conservative) is prudence. "Prudence," Burke wrote, "is not only first in rank of the virtues political and moral, but she is the director" of all the others. The literature of Conservatism spends a good deal more time celebrating this quality than defining it, yet there is no doubt that it represents a cluster of urges—toward caution, deliberation, and discretion, toward moderation and calculation, toward old ways and good form—which gives every other standard virtue a special look when displayed by a true Conservative.

Education looms importantly in the literature of Conservatism, for it is the road that leads through virtue to freedom. Only through education—in family, church, and school—can children be shaped into civilized men. Only through education can man's vices, which are tough, be brought under control and his virtues, which are frail, be nourished into robust health. The instruments of education should teach a man to think, survive, ply a trade, and enjoy his leisure. Their great mission, however, is to act as a conserving, civilizing force: to convey to each man his share of the inherited wisdom of the race, to train him to lead a moral, self-disciplined life, and to foster a love of order and respect for authority.

The Conservative's understanding of the mission of education explains his profound mistrust of modern theories, most of which, he feels, are grounded in a clear misreading of the nature and needs of children. The school has always been a conservative force in society, and the Conservative means to keep it that way. He admits that there is a stage in the education of some individuals —those who are to go on to leadership—when self-development and self-expression should get prime consideration. First things must come first, however, and before this stage is reached, the individual must be taught his community's values and be integrated into its structure.

Before we can describe the Conservative consensus on freedom and responsibility, we must learn more of the circumstances in which men can enjoy the one because they accept the other.

Some of the Conservative's best thoughts are directed to society and the social process. The key points of his social theory appear to be these:

Society is a living organism with roots deep in the past. The true community, the Conservative likes to say, is a tree, not a machine. It rose to its present strength and glory through centuries of growth, and men must forbear to think of it as a mechanical contrivance that can be dismantled and reassembled in one generation. Not fiat but prescription, not the open hand of experiment but the hidden hand of custom, is the chief creative force in the social process.

Society is cellular. It is not an agglomeration of lonely individuals, but a grand union of functional groups. Man is a social animal whose best interests are served by cooperating with other men. Indeed, he has no real meaning except as contributing member of his family, church, local community, and, at certain stages of historical development, occupational association. The group is important not only because it gives life, work, comfort, and spiritual support to the individual, but because it joins with thousands of other groups to form the one really stubborn roadblock against the march of the all-powerful state. The Conservative is careful not to ride the cellular analogy too hard, for he is aware that it can lead to a social theory in which man loses all dignity and personality.

In addition to intrinsic groups like the family and church, a healthy society will display a balanced combination of "institutions": constitution, common law, monarchy or presidency, legislature, courts, civil service, armed services and subdivisions, colleges, schools, forms of property, corporations, trade unions, guilds, fraternal orders, and dozens of other instrumentalities and understandings that mold the lives of men. Such symbols of tradition, of national unity and continuity, as anthems, flags, rituals, battlefields, monuments, and pantheons of heroes are equally dear to the Conservative heart. All men are staunch defenders of the institutions that meet their practical and spiritual needs, but the Conservative places special trust in them. "Individuals may form communities,"

Disraeli warned, "but it is institutions alone that can create a nation."

Society is structured. The Conservative, as we have learned already, recognizes the existence of classes and orders as a positive good. By no means wedded to the habit of making rigid distinctions, he sees the social structure not as a series of neat strata laid one on top of another, but, in Coleridge's phrase, as "an indissoluble blending and interfusion of persons from top to bottom." There must, in any case, be a top, visible and reasonably durable; and it is not surprising that the self-conscious Conservative is usually to be found in or around it.

Society is a unity. In the healthy community all these groups and institutions and classes fit together into a harmonious whole, and attempts to reshape one part of society must inevitably disturb other parts. The Conservative, though something of a pluralist, never loses sight of the ultimate unity into which all the parts of society must finally merge.

Society cannot be static. Change is the rule of life, for societies as for men. A community cannot stand still; it must develop or decay. And the Conservative must not be afraid to abandon patently outworn institutions and ideals. In the words of Tennyson's *Hands All Round:*

> May Freedom's oak forever live
> With stronger life from day to day;
> That man's the true Conservative,
> Who lops the moulder'd branch away.

"Society must alter," Russell Kirk acknowledges, "for slow change is the means of its conservation, like the human body's perpetual renewal." In recognizing, however grudgingly, this great social truth, the Conservative shows himself to be neither a reactionary nor a standpatter. Yet he is just as emphatically not a liberal or radical, and he therefore sets severe conditions upon social change, especially if it is to be worked by active reform. Change, he insists, must never be taken for its own sake; must have preservation, if possible even restoration, as its central object; must be severely limited in scope and purpose; must be a response to an undoubted social need—for example, the renovation or elimination of an institution that is plainly obsolete; must be worked out by slow and careful stages; must be brought off under Conservative auspices, or with Conservatives intervening at the decisive moment (this is known as "stealing the Whigs' clothes"); and finally, in Disraeli's words, must "be carried out in deference to the manners, the customs, the laws, the traditions of the people." The essence of Conservatism is the feeling for the possibilities and limits of natural, organic change, and the kindred feeling that, in the words of McGovern and Collier, "while change is constant and inevitable, progress is neither constant nor inevitable." In the eloquent phrases of R. J. White of Cambridge:

To discover the order which inheres in things rather than to impose an order upon them; to strengthen and perpetuate that order rather than to dispose things anew according to some formula which may be nothing more than a fashion; to legislate along the grain of human nature rather than against it; to pursue limited objectives with a watchful eye; to amend here, to prune there; in short, to preserve the method of nature in the conduct of the state . . . this is Conservatism.

Society must be stable. Although men can never hope to see their community completely stable, they can create an endurable condition of peace and order. To achieve this great end of order —without which, as Richard Hooker wrote long ago, "there is no living in public society"—they must work unceasingly for a community that has this ideal appearance:

Common agreement on fundamentals exists among men of all ranks and stations. Loyalty, good will, fraternal sympathy, and a feeling for compromise pervade the political and social scene.

Institutions and groups are in functional adjustment; the social order is the outward expression of an inner, largely uncoerced harmony. Political, economic, social, and cultural power is widely diffused among persons, groups, and other instruments; these are held by law, custom, and constitution in a state of operating equilibrium. For every show of power there is a corresponding responsibility. A minimum of friction and maximum of accommodation exist between government and group, government and individual, group and individual.

The authority of each group and instrument, and especially of the government, is legitimate. The laws honor the traditions of the nation, are adjusted to the capacities of the citizenry, meet the requirements of natural justice, and satisfy the needs of society. Men obey the laws cheerfully and readily, and they know why they obey them. They know, too, the difference between authority and authoritarianism, and are thankful that the former helps to govern their lives.

Men are secure; they have a sense of being, belonging, and creating. Their labors are rewarded, their sorrows comforted, their needs satisfied. They have the deep feeling of serenity that arises not merely from material well-being, but from confidence in the future, from daily contact with decent and trustworthy men, and from participation in an even-handed system of justice. Predictability, morality, and equity are important ingredients of this condition of security. Most important, however, is ordered liberty, which makes it possible for men to pursue their talents and tastes within a sheltering framework of rights and duties.

Change and reform are sure-footed, discriminating, and respectful of the past. "Men breathe freely," as F. E. Dessauer puts it, "because change is limited. . . . The changes which are taking place do not frighten the affected."

Unity, harmony, authority, security, continuity—these are the key elements of social stability. In longing for a society in which peace and order reign, the Conservative comes closest to the utopianism that he ridicules in others. . . .

It unsettles the Conservative to see the Liberal flirt with radicalism: it frightens the Liberal to hear the Conservative talk like a reactionary. But both are coming more and more to realize that they are brothers in the struggle against those who would hurry ahead to Utopia or back to Eden. This leaves them more than a

hundred years behind Ralph Waldo Emerson, who said of Liberalism and Conservatism that "each is a good half, but an impossible
whole. . . . In a true society, in a true man, both must combine."

Having said all these kind words about his friend, the Sensible
Liberal, the Conservative, who doesn't think many Liberals are
sensible anyway, takes most of them back and reaffirms his faith
in Conservatism as a unique, superior way of life. When pressed
for a final reckoning of the differences between Conservatism and
Liberalism, he finds at least three worth serious consideration:

First, there is what we have already noted as the difference of
temper, of "mood and bias." The Conservative's stated preferences
for stability over change, experience over experiment, intuition
over reason, tradition over curiosity, and self-control over self-
expression are enough in themselves to set him apart from the
Liberal. His urges are toward aristocracy, the Liberal's toward
democracy. He makes peace, the Liberal disturbs it. He likes to
look back, the Liberal to look ahead. He rallies to Burke, the
Liberal to Tom Paine. Perhaps it is too simple to say that these
differences in temper boil down to the contrast between pessimism
and optimism, but it cannot be denied that the Conservative's
confidence in man, democracy, and progress is far weaker than
the Liberal's, even the Sensible Liberal's. The Conservative finds
this the best of all possible worlds and is generally content to leave
well enough alone. The Liberal thinks the world can stand a lot
of improving and cannot wait to get on the job. (Or, as Ambrose
Bierce put it, the Conservative is "a statesman enamored of existing evils," the Liberal one "who wishes to replace them with
others.")

Next, the Conservative cannot understand how anyone could
mistake his political principles for those of Liberalism. If the
Liberal wants to draw on his stockpile for such ideas as the diffusion of power and the balancing of rights and duties, the Conservative will enter no strong objection; but he wants it clearly
understood that some of his ideas are private property. If the
Liberal wants to share them, he will first have to abandon Liberal-

ism, for the hard core of Conservatism is an austere distrust of the hopes of Jefferson and the promises of Bentham. Certainly the Liberal cannot challenge the Conservative's peculiar claim to the preference for liberty over equality, emphasis on constitutionalism rather than democracy, fear of majority rule, admiration for aristocracy, and devotion to the rights of property. Certainly the Conservative's mission, so different from the Liberal's, gives his political faith a quality all its own.

In the end, the difference between Conservatism and Liberalism seems to be this: both are devoted to liberty as we have known it in the West, but the Conservative thinks of liberty as something to be preserved, the Liberal thinks of it as something to be enlarged. The Conservative suspects that a country like the United States or Britain has got just about as much liberty as it will ever have, that the liberty we enjoy cannot be increased but only redistributed among ourselves, and that persistent efforts either to increase or redistribute it may bring the whole structure of freedom down in ruins. The Liberal, on the other hand, is confident that no country has yet approached the upper limits of liberty, that giving new freedoms to some men does not necessitate taking away old liberties from others, and that the structure of freedom will fall slowly into decay if it is not enlarged by the men of each generation.

FOR THE STUDENT

Rhetoric

1. *Part of Rossiter's technique in defining "conservative" is to play it off against "liberal." Apply this technique in defining some other concept, say "a catholic," or "a high school student."*

2. *Look up* prudence *in a good dictionary. Do any of the definitions fit any American politician?*

Discussion

1. *One frequently hears today about young people "seeking an identity," "trying to understand themselves." Contrast this with the quotation from Gardner Murphy: "Not much, I believe, is known about man."*

2. *Laski says that the desire for equality is "one of the most permanent passions of mankind." Rossiter says that "men are grossly unequal . . . in most qualities of mind, body, and spirit." Can these views be reconciled? Which corresponds most-closely with your own view?*

Writing

1. *Rossiter cites a number of conservative authorities (Burke, Disraeli, Adams, et al.). Consult any standard reference work in your library and write a one-page paper on any two of them, analyzing their conservative policies.*

2. *Paragraph twelve gives a list of conservative virtues and vices. Write a three-page self-portrait, measuring yourself against the list.*

3. *Analyze some Republican speech for references to "unity, harmony, authority, security, continuity."*

ALDOUS HUXLEY

The Idea of Equality

Sunday Faith and Weekday Faith

That all men are created equal is a proposition to which, at ordinary times, no sane human being has ever given his assent. A man who has to undergo a dangerous operation does not act on the assumption that one doctor is just as good as another. Editors do not print every contribution that reaches them. And when they require civil servants, even the most democratic governments make a careful selection among their theoretically equal subjects. At ordinary times, then, we are perfectly certain that men are not equal. But when, in a democratic country, we think or act politically, we are no less certain that men are equal. Or at any rate —which comes to the same thing in practice—we behave as though we were certain of men's equality. Similarly, the pious mediaeval nobleman who, in church, believed in forgiving enemies and turning the other cheek was ready, as soon as he had emerged again into the light of day, to draw his sword at the slightest provocation. The human mind has an almost infinite capacity for being inconsistent.

The amount of time during which men are engaged in thinking or acting politically is very small when compared with the whole period of their lives; but the brief activities of man the politician exercise a disproportionate influence on the daily life of man the worker, man at play, man the father and husband, man the owner of property. Hence the importance of knowing what he thinks in his political capacity and why he thinks it.

The Equalitarian Axiom

Politicians and political philosophers have often talked about the equality of man as though it were a necessary and unavoidable idea, an idea which human beings must believe in, just as they must, from the very nature of their physical and mental constitution, believe in such notions as weight, heat, and light. Man is "by nature free, equal, and independent," says Locke, with the calm assurance of one who knows he is saying something that cannot be contradicted. It would be possible to quote literally thousands of similar pronouncements. One must be mad, says Babeuf, to deny so manifest a truth.

Equality and Christianity

In point of historical fact, however, the notion of human equality is of recent growth, and, so far from being a directly apprehended and necessary truth, is a conclusion logically drawn from preëxisting metaphysical assumptions. In modern times the Christian doctrines of the brotherhood of men and of their equality before God have been invoked in support of political democracy. Quite illogically, however. For the brotherhood of men does not imply their equality. Families have their fools and their men of genius, their black sheep and their saints, their worldly successes and their worldly failures. A man should treat his brothers lovingly and with justice, according to the deserts of each. But the deserts of every brother are not the same. Neither does men's equality before God imply their equality as among themselves. Compared with an infinite quantity, all finite quantities may be regarded as equal. There is no difference, where infinity is concerned, between one and a thousand. But leave infinity out of the quesiton, and a thousand is very different from one. Our world is a series of finite quantities, and where worldly matters are concerned, the fact that all men are equal in relation to the infinite quantity which is God is entirely irrelevant. The church has at all times conducted its worldly policy on the assumption that it was irrelevant. It is only recently that the theorists of democracy have appealed to Christian doctrine for a confirmation of their equalitarian principles. Christian doctrine, as I have shown, gives no such support.

Equality and the Philosopher

The writers who in the course of the eighteenth century supplied our modern political democracy with its philosophical basis did not turn to Christianity to find the doctrine of human equality. They were, to begin with, almost without exception anticlerical writers, to whom the idea of accepting any assistance from the church would have been extremely repugnant. Moreover, the church, as organized for its worldly activities, offered them no assistance, but a frank hostility. It represented, even more clearly than the monarchical and feudal state, that medieval principle of hierarchical, aristocratic government against which, precisely, the equalitarians were protesting.

The origin of our modern idea of human equality is to be found in the philosophy of Aristotle. The tutor of Alexander the Great was not, it is true, a democrat. Living as he did in a slave-holding society, he regarded slavery as a necessary state of affairs. Whatever is, is right; the familiar is the reasonable; and Aristotle was an owner of slaves, not a slave himself; he had no cause to complain. In his political philosophy he rationalized his satisfaction with the existing state of things, and affirmed that some men are born to be masters (himself, it went without saying, among them) and others to be slaves. But in saying this he was committing an inconsistency. For it was a fundamental tenet of his metaphysical system that specific qualities are the same in every member of a species. Individuals of one species are the same in essence or substance. Two human beings differ from one another in matter, but are the same in essence, as being both rational animals. The essential human quality which distinguishes the species Man from all other species is identical in both.

Inconsistencies

How are we to reconcile this doctrine with Aristotle's statement that some men are born to be masters and others slaves? Clearly, no reconciliation is possible; the doctrines are contradictory. Aristotle said one thing when he was discussing the abstract problems of metaphysics and another when, as a slave-owner, he was discussing politics. Such inconsistencies are extremely common, and are generally made in perfectly good faith. In cases where material interests are at stake, where social and religious traditions, inculcated in childhood, and consequently incorporated into the very structure of the mind, can exercise their influence, men will naturally think in one way; in other cases, where their interests and their early-acquired beliefs are not concerned, they will naturally and inevitably think in quite a different way. A man who thinks and behaves as an open-minded, unprejudiced scientist so long as he is repairing his automobile will be outraged if asked to think about the creation of the world or the future life except in terms of the mythology current among the barbarous Semites three thousand years ago; and though quite ready to admit that the present system of wireless telegraphy might be improved, he will regard anyone who desires to alter the existing economic and political system as either a madman or a criminal. The greatest men of genius have not been exempt from these curious inconsistencies. Newton created the science of celestial mechanics; but he was also the author of *Observations on the Prophecies of Daniel and the Apocalypse of Saint John,* of a *Lexicon Propheticum* and a *History of the Creation.* With one part of his mind he believed in the miracles and prophecies about which he had been taught in childhood; with another part he believed that the universe is a scene of order and uniformity. The two parts were impenetrably divided one from the other. The mathematical physicist never interfered with the commentator on the Apocalypse; the believer in miracles had no share in formulating the laws of gravitation.

Similarly, Aristotle the slave-owner believed that some men are born to command and others to serve; Aristotle the metaphysician, thinking in the abstract, and unaffected by the social prejudices which influenced the slave-owner, expounded a doctrine of specific essences, which entailed belief in the real and substantial equality of all human beings. The opinion of the slave-owner was probably nearer the truth than that of the metaphysician. But it is by the metaphysician's doctrine that our lives are influenced today.

Applied Metaphysics

That all members of a species are identical in essence was still, in the Middle Ages, a purely metaphysical doctrine. No attempt was made to apply it practically in politics. So long as the feudal and ecclesiastical hierarchies served their purpose of government, they seemed, to all but a very few, necessary and unquestionable. Whatever is, is right; feudalism and Catholicism *were*. It was only after what we call the Reformation and the Renaissance, when, under the stress of new economic and intellectual forces, the old system had largely broken down, that men began to think of applying the metaphysical doctrine of Aristotle and his mediaeval disciples to politics. Feudalism and ecclesiastical authority lingered on, but as the merest ghosts of themselves. They had, to all intents and purposes, ceased to be, and not being, they were wrong.

It was not necessary, however, for the political thinkers of the eighteenth century to go back directly to Aristotle and the Schoolmen. They had what was for them a better authority nearer home. Descartes, the most influential philosopher of his age, had reaffirmed the Aristotelian and Scholastic doctrine in the most positive terms. At the beginning of his *Discourse on Method* we read that "what is called good sense or reason is equal in all men," and a little later he says, "I am disposed to believe that [reason] is to be found complete in each individual; and on this point to adopt

the opinion of philosophers who say that the difference of greater
or less holds only among the accidents, and not among the forms
or natures of individuals of the same species." Descartes took not
the slightest interest in politics, and was concerned only with
physical science and the theory of knowledge. It remained for
others to draw the obvious political conclusions from what was for
him, as it had been for Aristotle and the Schoolmen, a purely abstract metaphysical principle. These conclusions might have been
drawn at any time during the preceding two thousand years. But
it was only in the two centuries immediately following Descartes's
death that political circumstances in Europe, especially in France,
were favorable to such conclusions being drawn. The forms of government current during classical antiquity and the Middle Ages had
been efficient and well adapted to the circumstances of the times.
They seemed, accordingly, right and reasonable. In the eighteenth
century, on the other hand, particularly on the continent of Europe,
the existing form of government was not adapted to the social
circumstances of the age. At a period when the middle classes were
already rich and well educated, absolute monarchy and the in-
effectual remains of feudalism were unsuitable as forms of government. Being unsuitable, they therefore seemed utterly unreasonable
and wrong. Middle class Frenchmen wanted a share in the government. But men are not content merely to desire; they like to have
a logical or a pseudo-logical justification for their desires; they
like to believe that when they want something, it is not merely
for their own personal advantage, but that their desires are dictated
by pure reason, by nature, by God Himself. The greater part of
the world's philosophy and theology is merely an intellectual justification for the wishes and the daydreams of philosophers and
theologians. And practically all political theories are elaborated,
after the fact, to justify the interests and desires of certain individuals, classes, or nations. In the eighteenth century, middle class
Frenchmen justified their very natural wish to participate in the
government of the country by elaborating a new political philoso-

phy from the metaphysical doctrine of Aristotle, the Schoolmen, and Descartes. These philosophers had taught that the specific essence is the same in all individuals of a species. In the case of *Homo Sapiens* this specific essence is reason. All men are equally reasonable. It follows that all men have an equal capacity, and therefore an equal right, to govern; there are no born slaves nor masters. Hence, monarchy and hereditary aristocracy are inadmissible. Nature herself demands that government shall be organized on democratic principles. Thus middle class Frenchmen had the satisfaction of discovering that their desires were indorsed as right and reasonable, not only by Aristotle, St. Thomas, and Descartes, but also by the Creator of the Universe in person.

Making the Facts Fit

Even metaphysicans cannot entirely ignore the obvious facts of the world in which they live. Having committed themselves to a belief in this fundamental equality of all men, the eighteenth century political philosophers had to invent an explanation for the manifest inequalities which they could not fail to observe on every side. If Jones, they argued, is an imbecile and Smith a man of genius, that is due, not to any inherent and congenital differences between the two men, but to purely external and accidental differences in their upbringing, their education, and the ways in which circumstances have compelled them to use their minds. Give Jones the right sort of training, and you can turn him into a Newton, a St. Francis, or a Caesar according to taste. "The diversity of opinions," says Descartes, "does not arise from some being endowed with a larger share of reason than others, but solely from this, that we conduct our thoughts along different ways, and do not fix our attention on the same objects." "Intelligence, genius, and virtue," says Helvétius, whose work, *De l'Esprit,* was published in 1758, and exercised an enormous contemporary influence, "are the products of education." And again (*De l'Esprit,* Discours III, Ch. 26): "*La grande inégalité d'esprit qu'on aperçoit entre les hommes dépend donc uniquement et de la différente éducation qu'ils reçoivent, et de l'enchaînement inconnu et divers dans lesquels ils se trouvent placés,*"[1] and so on.

The political and philosophical literature of the eighteenth century teems with such notions. It was only to be expected; for such notions, it is obvious, are the necessary corollaries of the Cartesian axiom that reason is the same and entire in all men. They followed no less necessarily from the *tabula rasa* theory of mind elaborated by Locke. Both philosophers regarded men as originally and in essence equal, the one in possessing the same specific faculties and innate ideas, the other in possessing no innate ideas. It followed from either assumption that men are made or marred exclusively by environment and education. Followers whether of Locke or of Descartes, the eighteenth century philosophers were all agreed in attributing the observed inequalities of intelligence and virtue to inequalities of instruction. Men were naturally reasonable and therefore good; but they lived in the midst of vice and abject superstition. Why? Because evil-minded legislators—kings and priests— had created a social environment calculated to warp the native reason and corrupt the morals of the human race. Why priests and kings, who, as human beings, were themselves naturally reasonable and therefore virtuous, should have conspired against their fellows, or why their reasonable fellows should have allowed themselves to be put upon by these crafty corrupters, was never adequately explained. The democratic religion, like all other religions, is founded on faith as much as on reason. The king-priest theory in its wildest and most extravagant form is the inspiration and subject of much of Shelley's finest poetry. Poor Shelley, together with large numbers of his less talented predecessors and contemporaries,

1. "The great inequality of intelligence which one perceives among men results, then, only from the different education which they receive and from the unknown and varied environment in which they are placed." [Author's note]

seems seriously to have believed that by getting rid of priests and kings you could inaugurate the golden age.[2]

The Tests of Experiment

The historical and psychological researches of the past century have rendered the theory which lies behind the practice of modern democracy entirely untenable. Reason is not the same in all men; human beings belong to a variety of psychological types separated one from another by irreducible differences. Men are not the exclusive products of their environments. A century of growing democracy has shown that the reform of institutions and the spread of education are by no means necessarily followed by improvements in individual virtue and intelligence. At the same time biologists have accumulated an enormous mass of evidence tending to show that physical peculiarities are inherited in a perfectly regular and necessary fashion. Body being indissolubly connected with mind, this evidence would almost be enough in itself to prove that mental peculiarities are similarly heritable. Direct observation on the history of families reinforces this evidence, and makes it certain that mental idiosyncrasies are inherited in exactly the same way as physical idiosyncrasies. Indeed, mind being in some sort a function of brain, a mental idiosyncrasy is also a physical one, just as much as red hair or blue eyes. Faculties are heritable: we are born more or less intelligent, more or less musical, mathematical, and so on. From this it follows that men are not essentially equal, and that human beings are at least as much the product of their heredity as of their education.

The Behaviorist Reaction

Recently, it is true, Helvétius's doctrine of the all-effectiveness of nurture and the unimportance of nature and heredity has

2. For a magnificent expression of this idea, read the final speech of the Spirit of the Hour, in Act III of Shelley's *Prometheus Unbound*. [Author's note]

been revived by psychologists of the Behaviorist School. Unlike
the philosophers of the eighteenth century, the Behaviorists have
no political axe to grind and are not metaphysicians. If they agree
with Helvétius, it is not because they want the vote (they have
it), nor, presumably, because they accept the authority of Aristotle, the Schoolmen, and Descartes on the one hand, or of Locke
on the other. They agree with Helvétius on what they affirm to
be scientific grounds. Helvétius's theory, according to the Behaviorists, is in accordance with the observed facts. Before going
further, let us briefly examine their claims.

"The Behaviorist," writes Mr. J. B. Watson, the leader of the
school, "no longer finds support for hereditary patterns of behavior nor for special abilities (musical, art, etc.), which are supposed to run in families. He believes that, given the relatively simple list of embryological responses which are fairly uniform in
infants, he can build (granting that both internal and external environment can be controlled) any infant along any specified line
—into rich man, poor man, beggar man, thief." Taken literally,
this last statement is merely silly. No one was ever such a fool as
to suggest that riches and poverty were heritable in the sense that
a Roman nose or a talent for music may be said to be heritable.
Opulent fathers have long anticipated this great discovery of the
Behaviorists, and have "built their children into rich men" by placing large cheques to their account at the bank. We must presume,
in charity to Mr. Watson, that he does not mean what he says,
and that when he says "rich man, poor man, beggar man, thief,"
he really means something like intelligent man, imbecile, mathematician and non-mathematician, musical person and unmusical
person, etc. Presuming that this is what he does mean, let us examine the Behaviorists' hypothesis, which is identical with that of
the philosophers who, in the eighteenth century, elaborated the
theory of modern democracy. The first thing that strikes one about
the Behaviorists' hypothesis is that the observations on which it
is based are almost exclusively observations on small children, not
on fully grown men and women. It is on the ground that all in-

fants are very much alike that the Behaviorists deny the hereditary transmission of special aptitudes, attributing the enormous
differences of mental capacity observable among grown human
beings exclusively to differences in environment, internal and external. Now it is an obvious and familiar fact that the younger a
child, the less individually differentiated it is. Physically, all newborn children are very much alike: there are few fathers who,
after seeing their newborn infant once, could recognize it again
among a group of other infants. Mr. Watson will not, I suppose,
venture to deny that physical peculiarities may be inherited. Yet
the son who at twenty will have his father's aquiline nose and his
mother's dark, straight hair may be as snubnosed and golden at
two as another child whose father is pugfaced and his mother
blonde, and who will grow up to be like them. If the Behaviorists
had made their observations on children a few months before they
were born, they would have been able to affirm not only the psychological identity of all men and women, but also their physical
identity. Three days after their respective conceptions, Pocahon-
tas, Shakespeare, and a Negro congenital idiot would probably be
indistiguishable from one another, even under the most powerful
microscope. According to Behaviorist notions, this should be regarded as a conclusive proof of the omnipotence of nurture. Since
they are indistinguishable at conception, it must be environment
that turns the fertilized ova into respectively a Red Indian woman,
an English man of genius, and a Negro idiot.

Mind and body are closely interdependent: they come to ma-
turity more or less simultaneously. A mind is not fully grown until the body with which it is connected through the brain has
passed the age of puberty. The mind of a young child is as much
undifferentiated and unindividualized as its body. It does not become completely itself until the body is more or less fully grown.
A child of two has neither his father's nose nor his maternal
grandfather's talent for mathematics. But that is no argument
against his developing both when he is a few years older. A young
child looks and thinks like other children of the same age and not

like his parents. Later on he will certainly look like his parents.
What reason is there to suppose that his mind will not also be
like theirs? If he has his father's nose, why not his father's brain,
and with it his father's mentality? The Behaviorists give us no
answers to these questions. They merely state, what we already
knew, that small children are very much alike. But this is entirely
beside the point. Two fertilized ova may be indistinguishable; but
if one belongs to a Negress and the other to a Japanese, no
amount of nurture will make the Japanese egg develop into a Negro, or vice versa. There is no more valid reason for supposing
the two very similar infants who were to become Shakespeare and
Stratford's village idiot could have been educated into exchanging
their adult parts. To study human psychology exclusively in babies
is like studying the anatomy of frogs exclusively in tadpoles. That
environment may profoundly influence the course of mental development is obvious. But it is no less obvious that there is a heredi-
tarily conditioned development to be modified. Environment no
more creates a mental aptitude in a grown boy than it creates the
shape of his nose.

Equality of Virtue

We have dealt so far with the primary assumption from
which the whole theory and practice of democracy flows: that all
men are substantially equal; and with one of its corollaries: that
the observed differences between human beings are due to environment, and that education, in the widest sense of the term, is
all-powerful. It is now necessary to touch briefly on one or two
other corollaries. Men being in essence equally reasonable, it follows that they are also in essence equally moral. For morality (according to the philosophers who formulated the theory of democracy) is absolute and exists in itself, apart from any actual
society of right- or wrong-doing individuals. The truths of morality
can be apprehended by reason. All men are equally reasonable:
therefore all are equally capable of grasping the absolute truths of

moral science. They are therefore, in essence, equally virtuous, and if, in practice, they behave badly, that is merely an accident, due to corrupting surroundings. Man must be delivered from his corrupting surroundings (and for the most ardent and ruthlessly logical spirits all government, all law, and organized religion are corrupting influences). Finding himself once more in that idyllic "state of nature" from which he should never have tried to rise, man will become, automatically, perfectly virtuous. There are few people now, I suppose, who take the theories of Rousseau very seriously. But though our intellect may reject them, our emotions are still largely influenced by them. Many people still cherish a vague sentimental belief that the poor and uncultivated, who are nearer to the "state of nature" than the cultured and the rich, are for that reason more virtuous.

Democratic Pot and Catholic Kettle

Pots have a diverting way of calling kettles black, and the prophets of the democratic-humanitarian religion have at all times, from the eighteenth century down to the present day, denounced the upholders of Christian orthodoxy as anti-scientific. In certain important respects, however, the dogmas and the practice of orthodox Catholic Christianity were and are more nearly in accordance with the facts than the dogmas and practice of democratic-humanitarianism. The doctrine of original sin is, scientifically, much truer than the doctrine of natural reasonableness and virtue. Original sin, in the shape of antisocial tendencies inherited from our animal ancestors, is a familiar and observable fact. Primitively, and in a state of nature, human beings were not, as the eighteenth century philosophers supposed, wise and virtuous: they were apes.

Practically, the wisdom of the church displays itself in a recognition among human beings of different psychological types. It is not every Tom, Dick, or Harry who is allowed to study the intricacies of theology. What may strengthen the faith of one may bewilder or perhaps even disgust another. Moreover, not all are called upon to rule; there must be discipline, a hierarchy, the subjection of many and the dominion of few. In these matters the theory and practice of the church is based on observation and long experience. The humanitarian democrats who affirm that men are equal, and who on the strength of their belief distribute votes to everybody, can claim no experimental justification for their beliefs and actions. They are men who have a faith, and who act on it, without attempting to discover whether the faith corresponds with objective reality.

The Relation of Theory to Action

It is in the theory of human equality that modern democracy finds its philosophic justification and some part, at any rate, of its motive force. It would not be true to say that the democratic movement took its rise in the theories propounded by Helvétius and his fellows. The origin of any widespread social disturbance is never merely a theory. It is only in pursuit of their interests, or under the influence of powerful emotions, that large masses of men are moved to action. When we analyze any of the historical movements in favor of democracy and self-determination, we find that they derive their original impetus from considerations of self-interest on the part of the whole or a part of the population. Autocracy and the rule of foreigners are often (though by no means invariably) inefficient, cruel, and corrupt. Large masses of the subjects of despots or strangers find their interests adversely affected by the activities of their rulers. They desire to change the form of government, so that it shall be more favorable to their particular national or class interests. But the discontented are never satisfied with mere discontent and desire for change. They like, as I have already pointed out, to justify their discontent, to find exalted and philosophical excuses for their desires, to feel that the state of affairs most agreeable to them is also the state of affairs most agreeable to Pure Reason, Nature, and the Deity. Violent oppression begets violent and desperate reaction.

But if their grievances are only moderate, men will not fight whole-heartedly for their redress, unless they can persuade themselves of the absolute rightness, the essential reasonableness of what they desire. Nor will they be able, without some kind of intellectual rationalization of these desires, to persuade other men, with less immediate cause for discontent, to join them. Emotion cannot be communicated by a direct contagion. It must be passed from man to man by means of a verbal medium. Now words, unless they are mere onomatopoeic exclamations, appeal to the emotions through the understanding. Feelings are communicated by means of ideas, which are their intellectual equivalent; at the sound of the words conveying the ideas the appropriate emotion is evoked. Thus, theory is seen to be doubly important: first, as providing a higher, philosophical justification for feelings and wishes; and second, as making possible the communication of feeling from one man to another. "The equality of all men" and "natural rights" are examples of simple intellectual generalizations which have justified emotions of discontent and hatred, and at the same time have rendered them easily communicable. The rise and progress of any democratic movement may be schematically represented in some such way as this: Power is in the hands of a government that injures the material interests, or in some way outrages the feelings, of all, or at least an influential fraction of its subjects. The subjects are discontented and desire to change the existing government for one which shall be, for their purposes, better. But discontent and desire for change are not in themselves enough to drive men to action. They require a cause which they can believe to be absolutely, and not merely relatively and personally, good. By postulating (quite gratuitously) the congenital equality of all men, by assuming the existence of certain "natural rights" (the term is entirely meaningless), existing absolutely, in themselves and apart from any society in which such rights might be exercised, the discontented are able to justify their discontent, and at the same time to communicate it by means of easily remembered intellectual formulas to their less discontented fellows.

Theory Gets Out of Hand

The invention of transcendental reasons to justify actions dictated by self-interest, instinct, or prejudice would be harmless enough if the justificatory philosophy ceased to exist with the accomplishment of the particular action it was designed to justify. But once it has been called into existence, a metaphysic is difficult to kill. Men will not let it go, but persist in elaborating the system, in drawing with a perfect logic ever fresh conclusions from the original assumptions. These assumptions, which are accepted as axiomatic, may be demonstrably false. But the arguments by which conclusions are reached may be logically flawless. In that case, the conclusions will be what the logicians call "hypothetically necessary." That is to say that, granted the truth of the assumptions, the conclusions are necessarily true. If the assumptions are false, the conclusions are necessarily false. It may be remarked, in passing, that the hypothetical necessity of the conclusions of a logically correct argument has often and quite unjustifiably been regarded as implying the absolute necessity of the assumptions from which the argument starts.

In the case of the theory of democracy the original assumptions are these: that reason is the same and entire in all men, and that all men are naturally equal. To these assumptions are attached several corollaries: that men are naturally good as well as naturally reasonable; that they are the product of their environment; that they are indefinitely educable. The main conclusions derivable from these assumptions are the following: that the state ought to be organized on democratic lines; that the governors should be chosen by universal suffrage; that the opinion of the majority on all subjects is the best opinion; that education should be universal, and the same for all citizens. The primary assumptions, as we have seen, are almost certainly false; but the logic by which the metaphysicians of democracy deduced the conclusions was sound enough. Given the assumptions, the conclusions were necessary.

In the early stages of that great movement which has made the whole of the West democratic, there were only discontent and a desire for such relatively small changes in the mode of government as would increase its efficiency and make it serve the interests of the discontented. A philosophy was invented to justify the malcontents in their demand for change; the philosophy was elaborated; conclusions were relentlessly drawn; and it was found that, granted the assumptions on which the philosophy was based, logic demanded that the changes in the existing institutions should be, not small, but vast, sweeping, and comprehensive. Those who rationalize their desires for the purpose of persuading themselves and others that these desires are in accord with nature and reason find themselves persuading the world of the rightness and reasonableness of many ideas and plans of action of which they had, originally, never dreamed. Whatever is, is right. Becoming familiar, a dogma automatically becomes right. Notions which for one generation are dubious novelties become for the next absolute truths, which it is criminal to deny and a duty to uphold. The malcontents of the first generation invent a justifying philosophy. The philosophy is elaborated, conclusions are logically drawn. Their children are brought up with the whole philosophy (remote conclusion as well as primary assumption), which becomes, by familiarity, not a reasonable hypothesis, but actually a part of the mind, conditioning and, so to speak, canalizing all rational thought. For most people, nothing which is contrary to any system of ideas with which they have been brought up since childhood can possibly be reasonable. New ideas are reasonable if they can be fitted into an already familiar scheme, unreasonable if they cannot be made to fit. Our intellectual prejudices determine the channels along which our reason shall flow.

Of such systems of intellectual prejudices some seem merely reasonable, and some are sacred as well as reasonable. It depends on the kind of entity to which the prejudices refer. In general it may be said that intellectual prejudices about non-human entities appear to the holder of them as merely reasonable, while prejudices about human entities strike him as being sacred as well as reasonable. Thus, we all believe that the earth moves round the sun, and that the sun is at a distance of some ninety million miles from our planet. We believe, even though we may be quite incapable of demonstrating the truth of either of these propositions— and the vast majority of those who believe in the findings of modern astronomy do so as an act of blind faith, and would be completely at a loss if asked to show reasons for their belief. We have a prejudice in favor of modern astronomy. Having been brought up with it, we find it reasonable, and any new idea which contradicts the findings of contemporary astronomy strikes us as absurd. But it does not strike us as morally reprehensible. Our complex of what may be called astronomy-prejudices is only reasonable, not sacred.

The Nearer, the More Sacred

There was a time, however, when men's astronomy-prejudices were bound up with a great human activity—religion. For their contemporaries the ideas of Copernicus and Galileo were not merely absurd, as contradicting the established intellectual prejudices; they were also immoral. The established prejudices were supported by high religious authority. For its devotees, the local and contemporary brand of religion is "good," "sacred," "right," as well as reasonable and true. Anything which contradicts any part of the cult is therefore not only false and unreasonable, but also bad, unholy, and wrong. As the Copernican ideas became more familiar, they seemed less frightful. Brought up in a heliocentric system, the religious folk of ensuing generations accepted without demur the propositions which to their fathers had seemed absurd and wicked. History repeated itself when, in the middle of the nineteenth century, Darwin published his *Origin of Species.* The uproar was enormous. The theory of natural selection seemed much more criminal than the Copernican theory of planetary motion. Wickedness in these matters is proportionate to the distance from ourselves. Copernicus and Galileo had propounded unorthodox views about the stars. It was a crime, but not a very grave one; the stars are very remote. Darwin and the Darwinians propounded unorthodox views about man himself. Their crime was therefore enormous. The dislike of the Darwinian hypothesis is by no means confined to those who believe in the literal truth of the Book of Genesis. One does not have to be an orthodox Christian to object to what seems an assault on human dignity, uniqueness, and superiority.

Democracy as a Religion

The prejudices in favor of democracy belong to the second class; they seem, to those who cherish them, sacred as well as reasonable, morally right as well as true. Democracy is natural, good, just, progressive, and so forth. The opponents of it are reactionary, bad, unjust, antinatural, etc. For vast numbers of people the idea of democracy has become a religious idea, which it is a duty to try to carry into practice in all circumstances, regardless of the practical requirements of each particular case. The metaphysic of democracy which was in origin the rationalization of certain French and English men's desires for the improvement of their governments, has become a universally and absolutely true theology which it is all humanity's highest duty to put into practice. Thus, India must have democracy, not because democratic government would be better than the existing undemocratic government—it would almost certainly be incomparably worse—but because democracy is everywhere and in all circumstances right. The transformation of the theory of democracy into theology has had another curious result: it has created a desire for progress in the direction of more democracy among numbers of people whose material interests are in no way harmed, and are even actively advanced, by the existing form of government which they desire to change. This spread of socialism among the middle classes, the spontaneous granting of humanitarian reforms by power-holders to whose material advantages it would have been to wield their power ruthlessly and give none of it away—these are phenomena which have become so familiar that we have almost ceased to comment on them. They show how great the influence of a theory can be when by familiarity it has become a part of the mind of those who believe in it. In the beginning is desire; desire is rationalized; logic works on the rationalization and draws conclusions; the rationalization, with all these conclusions, undreamed of in many cases by those who first desired and rationalized, becomes one of the prejudices of men in the succeeding generations; the prejudice determines their judgment of what is right and wrong, true and false; it gives direction to their thoughts and desires; it drives them into action. The result is that a man whose interests are bound up with the existing order of things will desire to make changes in that order much more sweeping than those desired by his grandfather, though the latter's material interests were genuinely injured by it. Man shall not live by bread alone. The divine injunction was unnecessary. Man never has lived by bread alone, but by every word that proceeded out of the mouth of every conceivable God. There are occasions when it would be greatly to man's advantage if he did confine himself for a little exclusively to bread.

FOR THE STUDENT

Rhetoric

1. *What aesthetic judgment would you make about the unconventional organization of this essay?*
2. *Look up the word* equal *in a good dictionary. Make a list of those definitions which have a possible political application.*

Discussion

1. *Abraham Lincoln, in his Springfield speech of 1857, saw the significance of the Declaration of Independence ("All men are created equal")* to be prophetic, *not* descriptive: ". . . a standard maxim for a free society . . . constantly labored for, and even though never perfectly attained, constantly approximated . . . and augmenting the happiness and value of life to all people of all colors everywhere." What light does this throw on Huxley's concluding section, "Democracy as a Religion"?*

2. *Aristotle's notion of slaves and masters was accepted in Western thought for some 2,000 years. But Laski speaks of a* natural *passion for equality. How would Huxley reconcile these two ideas?*

3. *Does the fact that Huxley was born a British citizen help explain his views?*

Writing

1. *Write a short paper discussing the consequences of applying* equality *in education or in athletics.*

2. *Create an imaginary dialogue between Laski, Rossiter, and Huxley.*

6 Liberalism Versus Conservatism

The United States achieved nationhood through revolution and an experiment in a liberal form of government. For the next hundred years its citizens settled, developed—and exploited—in a manner that can scarcely be described as conservative, vast territories stretching three thousand miles across the continent. However, once the frontiers had been wiped out, several vast fortunes had been accumulated, the industrial revolution accomplished, and a respectable and comfortable middle class established, many Americans began to seek means to maintain the status quo. At this point the prevailing view toward political and economic activities became conservative. This is not to imply that conservatism had not previously existed in this country nor that it had exercised little power. Rather it is to suggest that the United States became what may be described as a conservative nation.

The split between liberal and conservative is by no means a simple one. (One of the purposes of this book is to demonstrate that premise. See the statements in the Preface.) The line politically dividing the two has become blurred in the past few decades, and even the definitions of the two terms seem not as certain as they once were. Today, we hear as much about the radical Right as about the radical Left. During the presidential campaign of 1964, when Barry Goldwater was supposed to be the conservative's candidate, many maintained that he was not a conservative (though none called him a liberal). Perhaps we are moving toward a new definition of policies that determine one's political and economic stances liberal or conservative.

David Spitz, professor of political science at Ohio State

University, is a self-confessed liberal. In a comparative study of liberalism and conservatism, he emphasizes the liberal position in the political, economic, and intellectual spheres. K. W. Thompson, formerly a professor of political science and now a foundations executive, occupies a Middle position by virtue of his attempt to give an objective definition of the terms and to indicate in part their historical growth. Clinton Rossiter, professor of government at Cornell University, while conservative in his views, argues for moderation in pointing out what he considers the superior attributes of conservatism.

DAVID SPITZ

A Liberal Perspective on Liberalism and Conservatism

Political labels may be employed either as general categories or as ideological weapons. As categories, they are models or ideal types, not descriptions of empirical realities. As ideological weapons, they are slogans or epithets that serve, all too commonly, as pigeonholes into which individuals and groups may be squeezed. That very few people fall completely into a single classification matters little to purveyors of political rhetoric or caricature intent on manipulation.

To the extent that we seek understanding, we need, therefore, to guard against the confusions wrought by political slogans. We need to avoid certain other pitfalls as well. Of these, none is more pernicious than the notion that political labels explain the motives of those who embrace them. Motives, even of a single act, are always complex; and when diverse men unite behind a common label or cause, it is generally for a variety of reasons. Some seek to promote their self-interests; others are driven by blind prejudice or idealistic commitment; and still others are there simply because they are there: Prisoners of inertia or of habit, it would no more occur to them to abandon a traditional allegiance than it would to incite a revolution against themselves. Yet all employ the language of high principle; all appeal to justice, or the national interest, or the common good, or the inherent nature and dignity of man. But since the real grounds on which they hold their beliefs are not always the grounds alleged, a refutation of those avowed grounds will not persuade them to abandon their

From Robert A. Goldwin (editor), Left, Right and Center *(Chicago: Rand McNally & Co., 1964). Copyright © by the Public Affairs Conference Center, Kenyon College.*

cause. Reasoning alone is but a poor instrument of political conversion, as instance any attempt to argue the biological merit of
miscegenation with a Southern racist.

For related reasons, political labels are not to be identified
with a particular man or party or position on a specific issue.
Men hold different positions, and in different degrees of commitment, depending on the issue at stake. One may be mildly or extremely liberal or conservative; one may be conservative in some
things and liberal in others. When Representative Robert Taft,
Jr., was a candidate for the United States Senate in the Ohio
election of 1964, he declared that he was a conservative on fiscal
matters, a middle-of-the-roader on issues of education, health,
and welfare, and a liberal on civil rights. Unkind critics might
conclude that he was a sadly disjointed man. But surely the more
useful and accurate view is to recognize the need to draw distinctions, and that an apparent inconsistency such as Taft's may be
inconsistent in a superficial sense only; for it might reflect significant differences in the character of the consequences of those
diverse positions and thus be in harmony with a larger purpose.
Consistency, moreover, while a necessity in logic, is not a pervasive or characteristic attribute in politics; and it is perhaps as
often the case that men are both liberal and conservative as that
they are either of these alone.

Positions change. Conservatives who defended and liberals
who attacked the Supreme Court in the 1930's have now reversed
their roles; for in the earlier period the Court was identified as
the protector of property rights and now it is regarded as the
protector of human rights.

Political parties change; they also display both internal agreement and diversity on ideological questions. On the issue of national power versus states' rights, both of the major American
parties have historically committed themselves to opposing positions, not once but repeatedly, according to whether or not they
occupied the seats of national power. In Germany, the Social
Democratic party after the First World War was not what it had

been before, and the party today is significantly different again.
In England, both the Conservative and Labour parties have
shifted their positions markedly over time. In Italy, the Communist party after the Second World War even supported the union
of Church and State, and more recently mourned the death of a
pope. In all these and other democratic states, members of the
same political party have often divided on some issues and united
on others, and have crossed party lines accordingly.

Political labels do not have the same meaning across national
boundaries. To be a Liberal in Italy is to be a member of the
Right; in America liberalism is associated with the Left. Conservatives in Britain, while on the Right, are in many respects far
to the left of conservatives in the United States.

In short, political labels, by the very fact that they are verbal
abridgments of political life, are as mischievous as they are useful. Indeed, if they are to be useful, not merely as ideological
weapons but as categories of analysis, they must be employed
with extreme caution, and as guides to rather than as specific descriptions of political realities. All this has to be borne in mind
when one encounters the use of such labels in contemporary
America, nowhere more so than in the case of such terms as
liberalism and conservatism. Are these terms, in fact, of any use
in describing actual political alignments, or do they belong to the
lexicon of political mythology?

.   .   .

If we are to talk sensibly of liberalism and conservatism, we
must probe somehow to a common core of meaning—a core that
transcends though it does not obliterate the many diversities and
transformations of liberal and conservative doctrine. We may
well want to distinguish between, say, classical liberalism and
modern liberalism, or between liberalism as a dogma (e.g., the
doctrines of John Locke or of Herbert Spencer), liberalism as an
ideology (the reflection of a mood or the rationalization of certain economic or political interests), and liberalism as a philosophy (whether skeptical about ultimate values or optimistic about

human progress). But inexorably we return to the crucial question: Is there a constellation of policies and attitudes that tend to correspond to and appear concomitantly with the one or the other label? If there is a recurring convergence of such policies and attitudes, then these labels have a viable and abiding significance, and it is possible to speak of them in terms of a tradition or a unity.

I believe that such a unity does exist, even though it is not always described in precisely the same way. Sometimes it is presented as a cleavage between parties or classes. Here liberalism, or the Left, is identified with that party associated with and representative of the interests of the lower classes, while conservatism, or the Right, is the party associated with and representative of the interests of the upper or dominant class. Sometimes this unity is found at the intellectual or philosophical level. Here liberalism is tied to the principle of experimentalism, to the open-ended negotiation of differences, whether of ideas or of policies, while conservatism bespeaks the cause of absolute truth, of a belief in an objective moral order, of a relatively closed rather than an open society. Both these conceptions of liberalism and conservatism, I think, are broadly correct, but because they do not readily distinguish between or adequately encompass the different spheres of thought and action—the political, the economic, the intellectual or cultural—they need to be incorporated into a larger and multidimensional framework.

In the political sphere, the unity or tradition of liberalism is unambiguous. Its pre-eminent principle is political equality. Whatever the form of state, whatever the historical situation or national character, the liberal has associated himself with the battle against entrenched privilege. Always the liberal has denied that power and station are the appropriate perquisites of lineage, or of the exercise of force, or of something called History or God. Always the liberal has looked to that which is common to men, not to that which divides them. This does not mean that the liberal is oblivious to the fact that men are not identical, that there are indeed differences of religion and race, wealth and power, talent and intelligence. What it does mean is that for the liberal such differences, important though they may be for certain purposes, are politically irrelevant. Each man has a life to live, the poorest as well as the richest man. Each man requires freedom—to exercise his reason, to discover and develop his talents, to achieve his full growth and stature as an individual. And each man suffers the consequences of deprivation and injustice, the oppressor no less than the oppressed. Hence each man has a common stake in the conditions, and in the determination of the conditions, under which he lives.

Liberals have no faith in human infallibility, or in the capacity of an allegedly superior few to respect the principle of equality or to withstand the corrupting temptations of power. Hence, while liberals recognize that political decisions taken by the people may be wrong, decisions taken by a self-proclaimed aristocracy are not necessarily right. Indeed, their wrongs have been far more numerous! What is crucial, then, is a political arrangement that makes possible the peaceful and effective correction of error. This dictates democracy, for only democracy provides a constitutional mechanism for the removal of the rulers by the ruled. Whatever its limitations or defects, democracy commends itself to liberals by this one overriding virtue—the principle of responsibility, by which the governed can protect themselves from misgovernment. This is why liberalism has consistently opposed authoritarianism in politics, why it has fought against all forms of oligarchical rule.

Conservatism, in contrast, has traditionally been identified with the impulse to hierarchy, a hierarchy based on the inequality of men. What is impressive to the conservative is that societies are made up of men, not Man, and that men are different. Some men (it is held) are wiser, more intelligent, more talented, better informed, than others. And if some men are superior and others average or inferior, it is the height of folly, conservatives argue, to let the unwise, through their numerical superiority, govern the

wise or even themselves. For if they are unwise, they will make
wrong decisions and thus defeat the very purposes they seek to
accomplish. Indeed, because they are unwise, they cannot, save by
accident, know what the right purposes are. It is true that conservatives are not always in agreement as to the character of the
superior few. Some believe this superiority derives from race or
blood; others, that it is an attribute of wealth or strength; still
others, that it is associated with intelligence or virtue. But that
there are a superior few, whether determined by nature or nurture, conservatives do not doubt. Hence the right political order
is in the conservative view that which in one way or another in-
stitutionalizes this crucial fact.

Moreover, when the conservative speaks of order, he has in
mind an order that is given, not contrived. Its laws are to be discovered, not created, to be adhered to, not defied. Just as the
heavenly bodies have their accustomed place, just as the waters
fall and the trees rise, so there is pattern and degree in human
communities. Each man, said the ancient philosopher, must be
given his due; but no man must seek more than his due. Hence
those who are qualified to rule must rule; those who are fit but
to obey must obey. And if, at a particular moment, the few who
actually occupy the seats of power are not those fitted by reason
and nature to rule, if, as Santayana and others of this persuasion
sometimes admit, past aristocracies have been artificial rather than
natural and just aristocracies, still it is better to have order than
disorder. This is why conservatives, despite internal disagree-
ments, have throughout history defended the prevailing aristocratic
order, resisted the encroachments of egalitarianism, and associated
themselves with the upper or dominant class.

In the economic sphere, this distinction between liberalism as
representative of the interests of the lower classes and conservatism as spokesman for the interests of the upper classes is even
more clear. There is, however, one crucial exception that must be
noted. This is the disjunction among conservatives on the identification of wealth and virtue. When Socrates asked why it is that

philosophers are to be found at the doors of the rich but the rich do not wait at the doors of the philosophers, he expressed in rhetorical form a contempt—shared by liberals and some conservatives alike—for the notion that money means wisdom. For the philosophers attend the rich only because philosophers know what they need; the rich do not. Consequently wealth, far from constituting proof of one's virtue or superiority—unless perhaps we speak here of superiority in chicanery and greed—establishes the reverse. With respect to the things that matter, the wealthy, precisely because they have spent their lives and their thoughts on the acquisition of money and material goods, are essentially philistines.

Yet it is a peculiar fact that even conservatives of this sort, who like to denote themselves "philosophical" conservatives, or even drop the term conservatism completely, tend in their practical conduct to unite with other conservatives who esteem wealth and account it a mark of virtue. When the lines are drawn, conservatives of all persuasions come together, in greater rather than in lesser degree, to defend the interests of the upper classes. In part, this may be because all conservatives revere "order," not any system of order, to be sure, but that order which reflects the tastes and values of men of quality, men who embody the aristocratic spirit, who understand the dictates of nature or of nature's God. In part, therefore, this joint conservative defense of the upper classes is the product of their conviction that, however we conceive the relation between wealth and virtue, the lower classes are the classes of the common man, who is in this view the vulgar, the mass, the inferior man. As such, he is disrespectful of law and order, he lacks knowledge and understanding of the "right" order, he does not—because he cannot—appreciate the need for standards and quality. In part, however, it is also to be explained by the fact that, whatever the grounds on which conservatives arrive at their position, all tend to share the view, even if only the suspicion, that the men at the top of the economic ladder are there because they really are men of superior ability. They are, on the

whole, educated men. They have nice manners. They exhibit some
at least of the outward trappings of "culture." They are, therefore, in certain visible ways superior to the men at the bottom.
Above all, they think of themselves as superior men, they act like
superior men. By comparison, the poor, the uneducated, the hew-
ers of wood and the drawers of water, are a sad and visibly inferior lot. Economic policies, consequently, should not only be
made by those who are competent, who "know" what is right;
they should be geared, in the first instance, to the advantage of
those superior men, for only that state which uses its political
power to secure and further the interests of those who have economic power can hope to achieve that stability which is necessary
to survival in our troubled world.

The argument, in fact, can be pushed further. As a conservative like Alexander Hamilton fully understood, economic power
divorced from and antagonistic to political power makes for an
unhealthy, perhaps an impossible, situation. For economic power
will not stand idly by and permit itself to be destroyed. On the
contrary, because it perceives its interests, because it has the
knowledge and skills appropriate to the promotion of those interests, and because, above all, it possesses the means and the will
to act in defense of those interests, it will destroy the forces antagonistic to it. If, then, order is to be maintained, it must be an
order which unites economic power with political power. And
this, in the conservative view, inexorably means an attachment of
political power to the interests of the dominant economic class.
This is why conservatives defend not simply wealth, but inherited
wealth. This is why conservatives oppose tax policies and measures that seek to regulate the conduct of businessmen, that is, to
reduce their power and position. This is why conservatives speak
little of human or civil rights, but much of property and vested
rights.

Liberalism, on the other hand, has always been identified with
the interests of the lower classes—not because the lower classes
have by some mystery of incarnation been blessed with a monop-

oly of virtue but because wealth, especially inherited wealth, is not a sufficient test of function or capacity. In the liberal view, all men are equal. Insofar as distinctions of place and power must be admitted, they properly derive only from the freely recorded and continuing consent of the people, not from such arbitrary factors as ancestry or ruthless force. It is hoped, and by some believed, that the people will choose wisely, that they will recognize men on the basis of merit, of demonstrated competence. To discover merit, equality of opportunity is essential. This requires the elimination of hereditary privilege and of unwarranted discriminatory practices, such as those based on race or religion or sex. It requires, even more, the reduction of great inequalities of wealth which make equality of opportunity impossible. It requires, from a positive standpoint, the creation of those conditions which assure access to all positions to those who, whatever their origins, demonstrate by their individual qualities and achievements that they merit them. It is thoroughly false and misleading to assert, as some critics of liberalism do, that liberals seek absolute equality of condition, that liberals recognize and respect no differences. On the contrary, what liberals contend is that equality of opportunity is the necessary condition for the rational determination of those qualities in which men are different and truly unequal, and hence in what respects power and position may properly be apportioned. Anything other than this is a defense of artificial and false inequalities.

Liberalism is concerned not only with equality of this sort in the economic sphere; it is concerned also with liberty. Now what is crucial about private ownership of property in the real world is' that such ownership confers power without responsibility; those who own property have the legal right to use it to promote their own interests, whatever the consequences of their decisions on the welfare of others. Such ownership divides men into independent and dependent men; by denying some men equal access to the use of the earth—though we have not, curiously, sought to deny them equal access to air and to water, perhaps because this presents certain practical difficulties—such ownership forces some men to become the slaves or servants of others. This enables those who possess property to use, to exploit, other men for their advantage. And it is this fact, that some men can use other men, can treat them as a means to their purposes rather than as ends in themselves, that constitutes in the liberal view a debasement of man.

For this reason, liberals have traditionally supported the efforts of the lower classes, through legislation by government and through the countervailing pressures of economic organizations, e.g., the labor unions, to curb the great economic powers of the owners and managers and to give workers a voice in determining the conditions under which they labor. They have sought to restrain and curtail the growth of corporate monopoly, which destroys individual enterprise and penalizes the consumer. They have sought to introduce into the operation of the giant large-scale enterprises that today constitute the economic-technological system a pattern of controls that mitigate the depersonalizing and dehumanizing effects of a master-servant relationship. They have even urged government to move directly into the economic sphere through the public ownership and operation of certain services and industries, where private ownership either has served the public interest inadequately or has diverted natural and social resources away from this public interest to the promotion of private gain. In diverse ways, including schemes that look to the transformation of the entire system of economic power, liberals have sought to lessen the harsh impact of oligarchical rule in economic life, to introduce a measure of democracy within or democratic controls over the industrial-technological process, to assure freedom from arbitrary command within the economic no less than within the political sphere. For how can a man be equal and free when he is a dependent and servile man? Not the rights of property, then, however these may be defined, but the rights of man are for liberalism the guiding principle of economic organization and action.

We come, finally, to the distinction between liberalism and conservatism in the intellectual or cultural sphere. Here the issue that divides these camps, while not unrelated to social classes, turns primarily on their respective attitudes toward freedom of inquiry and expression.

Conservatism, it is claimed, seeks to conserve not everything but only the Good. But the Good is not self-evident; hence conservatism requires a standard or body of principles by which we can distinguish the good from the bad. It requires, even more, a demonstration that this standard or set of principles is both applicable and right. Conservatives agree that there is, indeed there must be, such a standard or body of principles. It exists because it is inherent in the very nature of things. It needs, then, only to be discovered and, when discovered, to be obeyed. What defines and accounts for the present malaise, the malpractices and discontents of our time, is from this standpoint the fact that men no longer seek or abide by these true principles. They look to opinion rather than to knowledge, and opinion, precisely because it is not knowledge, is an uncertain and puny guide. More than that, opinion in democratic states is formed by average, which means inferior, men. Hence policies based upon public opinion are likely to be wrong. Only if we recapture and adhere to the true principles of political life, conservatives argue, can we hope to achieve right and good government.

It is true that conservatives are in no sense agreed as to what these true principles are, or why they are warranted. Some conservatives believe that these principles are revealed by God, or, in some constructions, by His teachings as these are mediated by and through His One True Church, whichever it might be—for not all conservatives agree as to which God is God and what it is that God says. Others derive these correct principles from history or tradition, but since there are, alas, conflicting traditions or at least diverse readings of the same tradition, this leads to multiple and not always consistent principles. Still others look to nature, to the doctrines of natural law or natural right, but here again there seems to be considerable disagreement as to what it is that nature teaches. And some, finally, appeal to intuition, to a subjective but nonetheless (it is said) correct apprehension of what is right as distinct from what is wrong; though here again, since men do not all palpitate in the same way, intuitive judgments do not always coincide. Despite these differences and conflicts, which often divide conservatives into congeries of warring sects, they are all, in one crucial respect at least, still conservatives; for they all believe in the existence of an absolute truth, of an objective moral order, and hence of a political system and body of policies deriving from and corresponding to the principles of this true morality.

This is why Walter Lippmann, for example, seeking to transcend internecine conflicts and to unite conservatives behind a cohesive, if general, body of principles, invokes the Public Philosophy, or the Traditions of Civility, as an appropriate substitute for otherwise diverse conservative labels. This is why, too, he seeks their warrant not in logical or historical demonstration but in need. We must, he says, "repair the capacity to believe"; we must accept as valid those principles on which sincerely and lucidly rational men, when fully informed and motivated by good will, tend to agree. This is why, finally, conservatives are so partial to religion, though it is curious to note that their defense of religion is often couched not in terms of its truth but in terms of its utility. For conservatives generally, as even for men otherwise so diverse in their outlooks as Hobbes and Rousseau, concerned as they are with stability, it is far more important to have a single religion than to have the "right" religion. A universal or general commitment to the same religion—in contemporary America, according to some conservatives, *any* religion—not only precludes religious, i.e., civil, wars; it also makes for piety, which makes for obedience, which makes for stability and peace.

Whatever the specific formulation of the conservative creed, the fact that it does build throughout on a claimed objective truth produces the same practical consequences. Above all, these include the disparagement of freedom of inquiry and a readiness to limit and control freedom of expression. Since the truth is already known, freedom of inquiry rests in the conservative view on a false premise: that it is proper seriously to entertain error. In fact, because error may appear in attractive and plausible guise, unsophisticated minds may well mistake it for truth. To permit the unrestrained expression of such falsehoods may lead to their widespread acceptance. Then error, not truth, will govern mankind. Since it is the business of government, according to conservatives, to apply justice and achieve virtue, not speech but "good" speech, not conflicting ideas but "right" ideas, should alone be tolerated. The idea of an open society, in which men are free to utter and debate diverse opinions, including the wrong opinions, is from this standpoint both evil and absurd. What is vital is the inculcation of right attitudes, right habits, right conduct; and this can only be achieved if men who know what is right teach and control those who would not otherwise understand or do what is right. Thus conservatism moves toward an authoritarian, conformist society, based upon the rule of allegedly aristocratic minds. This has been its traditional pattern. This is, on the whole, its present practice.

Liberalism differs from conservatism most sharply in its insistence on the value of individual liberty, and concomitantly on the value of freedom of inquiry and of expression. It may, though it need not, deny that absolute truths, at least with respect to the "right" political principles, are known; but whether these truths are known or not, liberalism insists nonetheless on the freedom to examine them, to subject them to empirical and logical criticism, and to expose them to the challenge of conflicting ideas. Skepticism about ultimate values, that is to say, is often associated with the liberal creed; but while it is appropriate to that creed it is not necessary to it. Individual liberty, however, with all that this implies in the way of cultural diversity or nonconformity in cultural and intellectual life, is indispensable to the liberal idea.

Insofar as liberalism repudiates the conservative claim to absolute and infallible truth, it rests on the assumption that man is born not stupid but infinitely ignorant, and that however much he may learn in his very short span of life, the things he learns amount to but a small portion of what there is to be known. Always the things he does not know are greater than the things he does know. Consequently, the beliefs he holds to be true may prove, on the basis of later knowledge, to be erroneous or only partially true. Awareness of this fact makes for a certain measure of humility; it also leads to a commitment to the methods of rational inquiry, rather than to the specific results that may at any one time emerge from such inquiry. The basic value of the liberal is, from this standpoint, the value of free inquiry; his basic attitude, the skeptical, or at least the inquiring, mind.

It follows that when two rational and relatively well-informed men disagree, it is less likely that one has complete possession of the truth and the other error, than that each has a partially valid insight. This is why liberals find so persuasive John Stuart Mill's argument for the toleration of dissenting ideas: The heretical view, Mill pointed out, where right, enables us to abandon error and embrace the more valid doctrine; where wrong, it helps us perceive the wholeness of our truth, indeed, it prevents us by its very challenge from clinging to our accepted truth in the manner of a prejudice or a superstition, without an adequate comprehension of its meaning; and where partly right, it reinforces our own partial truth and helps us correct our partial error. This is why a political liberal (but economic conservative) like Mr. Justice Holmes insisted that "To have doubted one's own first principles is the mark of a civilized man." And why a liberal philosopher like Morris Cohen added: "To refuse to do so is the essence of fanaticism."

Liberalism need not, however, be identified only with this skeptical approach to knowledge. It is altogether possible for one to believe that the truth is known and still hold to a liberal defense of toleration. In part, this rests on the very arguments advanced by Mill. One's confidence in the validity of his position, along with a conviction that opinion should be countered only by opinion, not by force, is alone sufficient to sustain his readiness to entertain dissent. In part, however, it rests on the recognition that in a society constituted of diverse men and groups many may claim to know the truth. Though all cannot be right, the political problem is to deal with a situation in which all believe they are right. Authoritarians provide a simple method of resolving this difficulty: The "right," that is, the most powerful, group suppresses the others. But since force is irrelevant to truth, the most powerful group may not in fact be the group that is right. Hence reason dictates a solution other than force. This solution, for the liberal, is twofold. On the one hand, he would have the state leave these different groups alone. Where it is possible for each group to pursue its own truths, its own values, without infringing upon or denying the values of the other, there is a prima facie case for freedom. To this extent, at least, the state is a limited state. On the other hand, where such differences produce conflicts, the liberal would seek to negotiate these conflicts through free debate and free criticism in the marketplace of opinion. This does not, of course, assure the victory of the "right" view, but it gives the "right" view its maximum opportunity to prevail. And unless one is prepared to maintain that evidence and logic generally lead men to the wrong conclusions, it is difficult for the liberal to understand why so rational and peaceful a method of resolving differences is inappropriate, why it is better, say, to resort to mutual slaughter. Even if the "wrong" view should carry the day, there remains, through this method, full opportunity to continue to criticize and to show, with the added knowledge of experience, that it requires correction.

The ultimate argument of the liberal in this context, however, is his belief that individual liberty is a good in itself. What defines a man, according to an ancient teaching, is his reason. Now for reason to be exercised, a choice must exist. There can be no choices without alternatives, and there can be no alternatives without liberty. To deny individual liberty, either in the presentation of alternatives or the making of choices, is to deny an individual that which constitutes his humanity. Instead of his right to exercise his reason, someone else's reason is exercised for him. He is then not a man but a child. If he is to be a man, he must be free—to inquire, to consider diverse possibilities, to choose among them, and to pursue, so far as he can, his own way or style of life. From these conflicting ideas and practices, liberalism believes, men can learn and mutually aid one another to grow. Without these, there can be only a deadening uniformity. Individual liberty, and its consequent diversities, becomes then a cardinal principle of liberalism.

It is not to be denied that equality and liberty, both central tenets of liberalism, stand at times in a state of tension. Equality of opportunity, for example, may well run into conflict with the liberty of a parent to raise his child with the benefit of whatever advantages he may be able to give him. Then men must choose between equally ultimate values, and this is admittedly not an easy choice. But this is not a problem unique to liberals, and what liberals can well argue is that through freedom of inquiry and expression men can more rationally and peacefully negotiate these conflicts.

In sum, then, what distinguishes liberalism from conservatism is that, politically, liberalism stands for democracy and the equality of men, while conservatism inclines toward oligarchy based on certain alleged inequalities of men; economically, liberalism represents the interest of the lower classes and argues for equality of opportunity and the protection of human rights, while conservatism is associated with the interests of the upper classes and defends vested property rights; intellectually, liberalism is committed to individual liberty and the freedoms of inquiry and expression, while conservatism is far more concerned with the applications of an already existing objective Truth and the consequent curbing of erroneous and pernicious doctrines. It would be misleading to imply that all liberals, much less all so-called liberal states, affirm and consistently practice all these aspects of the liberal creed, or that conservatives do so with respect to their doctrines. But as categories of analysis rather than as descriptions of actual men or groups, the elements that make up this multidimensional understanding of liberalism and conservatism may enable us more easily to comprehend and to identify what it is that men and groups actually do.

FOR THE STUDENT

Rhetoric

1. *Paragraphs eleven and twelve are constrasting paragraphs treating the liberal and conservative views in the political sphere. In two parallel columns, jot down the contrasting ideas and note their place in the development of the thought within each paragraph.*
2. *Study the three summary statements in the concluding paragraph. Do they adequately summarize Spitz's main points? Without the development he gave each point in the body of his essay, would these statements be somewhat misleading?*
3. *Spitz's style is, perhaps, somewhat academic. How might he have given it greater vitality?*

Discussion

1. *In what different ways does Spitz point out that liberalism and conservatism are relative terms? And relative to what?*
2. *What relationship, according to the conservative, exists between political power and economic power? How does the liberal answer the conservative on this point?*
3. *Liberals often claim that they gain much more enjoyment from their political and related activities than do conserva-*

tives. Could this claim arise in part from the liberals' approach to matters in the intellectual sphere? Explain.

4. *Examine our two-party system and try to determine, in the light of Spitz's analysis, how far the labels of liberalism and conservatism can be applied to the two parties.*

Writing

1. *The obvious topic here is "Why I Am a _____." Instead, write a paper in all candor discussing why your personal (or selfish?) interests dictate why you have assumed your liberal or conservative stance.*

2. *Answer one of Spitz's arguments with which you violently disagree.*

K. W. THOMPSON

Liberal and Conservative

The political and philosophical molds in which popular approaches to domestic and international politics are cast in most Western countries are neither reform nor realism but liberalism and conservatism. One reason for this is doubtless the instrumental and procedural nature of the former. Realism or reform give appraisals of the nature and dynamics of the political process, its requirements, limits, and laws. Liberalism and conservatism by contrast partake of the character of political ideologies. Quite commonly they provide moral justification for the claims of interest groups and they may also in more general terms constitute a philosophy. In Acton's phrase "Liberalism is not only a principle of government but a philosophy of history." One of the difficulties about liberalism and conservatism results from their alternating meaning as philosophy, political ideology, or public mood. In addition, they plainly lack fixed meanings; consider, for example, that liberalism has meant at various stages Manchester laissez-faire, moderate state-interventionism to safeguard liberty and equality (e.g., the liberalism of the New Deal), and utopianism in world affairs. Nevertheless, public policy, including foreign policy, has been influenced by these living political doctrines and, while recognizing with Erasmus that every definition is dangerous, we may usefully explore their place in Western civilization. . . .

Liberalism and conservatism as they have been used in political debate appear at first glance to be simple and straightforward terms. "What is conservatism?" Abraham Lincoln asked. "Is it not adherence to the old and tried, against the new and untried?"

From "Liberal and Conservative," in Political Realism and the Crisis of World Politics, *by Kenneth W. Thompson (copyright © 1960 by Princeton University Press). Reprinted by permission of Princeton University Press.*

Others tell us that conservatism seeks to defend the status quo while liberalism aspires to leave it behind. Conservatism finds its treasures in tradition, custom, prejudice, and prescription. . . . The English constitution is for the conservative an arch-example of custom and prescription for "its sole authority is that it has existed time out of mind." Conservatism with its abiding veneration of the past need not be aligned irrevocably against change as such although this is its besetting danger. . . . Conservatives oppose too rapid social change because of its consequences. Burke assayed to distinguish profound and natural alterations and the radical infatuations of the day. He preferred a gradual course in order to prevent "unfixing old interests at once: a thing which is apt to breed a black and sullen discontent in those who are at once dispossessed of all their influence and consideration [and at the same time] . . . prevent men, long under depression, from being intoxicated with a large draught of new power. . . ." Insights such as these into issues of interest and power have given conservatism an historic relevance sufficient to evoke Harold Laski's remark: "Burke has endured as the permanent manual of political wisdom without which statesmen are as sailors on an uncharted sea."

Nevertheless, this wisdom has been judged and found wanting in the face of rapidly changing conditions in industrial societies. For conservative movements, the exercise of power easily becomes an end in itself and the exclusive aim of political activity. In Karl Mannheim's words "The Conservative type of knowledge originally is the sort of knowledge giving practical control. It consists of habitual orientations towards those factors which are imminent in the present situation." Thus it makes obsolescent administrative techniques serve as a substitute for policy in a world that is ever changing. The demands of a technical society for new institutions, status and power for rising social groups, and far-reaching national programs have led the most progressive peoples to by-pass the conservative point of view. In modern societies, liberalism, being less disposed uncritically to defend every status quo has enjoyed certain a priori advantages. Moreover, liberalism in its various stages has been linked with industrialization and with democracy. Initially, it rallied its followers, especially in Britain and France, to the goal of overturning feudal aristocratic authority, including the authority of the mercantilist state. As the political ideology of a rising middle class, in Reinhold Niebuhr's words, it sought "to free the individual from the traditional restraints of an organic society, to endow the governed with the power of the franchise, to establish the principle of the 'consent of the governed' as the basis of political society; to challenge all hereditary privileges and traditional restraints upon human initiative, particularly in the economic sphere and to create the mobility and flexibility which are the virtues and achievements of every 'liberal society' as distinguished from feudal ones."

In the same way, however, that conservatism ran afoul of the bewildering pace of events that transformed a feudal order into sprawling industrial societies, liberalism became the victim of its own origins. On the one hand, both liberalism and socialism "tend to imagine that changes are morally or practically desirable simply because they are changes." . . . On the other hand, liberalism was identified too narrowly with the claims and interests of the middle class, first as a fighting creed but subsequently as the justification of a new status quo that was threatened by too much government interference. Liberalism in its historical development takes on a dual meaning. In the beginning, while it came into being as a defense of individual freedom, it was freedom interpreted in behalf of industrial and commercial groups. Consequently, in our own day the original libertarian point of view has become the main bulwark for conserving the power of large enterprises and corporate groups. On the other side, the middle classes, once having unleashed in the world the enduring truth of liberalism that justice depends upon freedom from outside restraint, have witnessed its application by others. As liberalism in the beginning served to justify protests by entrepreneurs against the restraints of government, newly emergent classes like labor seeking security and freedom themselves have called upon the state to redress the balance of power. The source and origin of restraints upon freedom for one segment of American life is the overwhelmingly powerful enterprise, while for the other it continues to be the state. Thus liberalism having had its birth in the demands of society for freedom from restraint by the state now in at least one of its versions witnesses the appeals of society—or at least a part of society— that the state become the protector of liberty, equality, and security against the overwhelming power of large industrial groups. To quote Niebuhr again: "Thus in every modern industrial nation the word 'liberalism' achieved two contradictory definitions. It was on the one hand the philosophy which insisted that economic life was to be free of any restraints. In this form it was identical with the only conservatism which nations, such as our own, who had no feudal past, could understand. . . . On the other hand the word was also used to describe the political strategy of those classes which preferred security to absolute liberty and which sought to bring economic enterprise under political control for the sake of establishing minimal standards of security and welfare." . . .

Liberalism is steeped in the principles of the French Enlightenment and in faith in man's essential goodness and his capacity to subdue nature. The articles of faith of the Enlightenment creed include the beliefs that civilization is becoming more rational and moral, that injustice is caused by ignorance and will yield to education and greater intelligence, that war is stupid and can be overcome through reason, that appeals to brotherhood are bound to be effective in the end and if they fail for the moment we need only more and better appeals, and that conflict is simply a matter of misunderstanding. Liberalism as a total philosophy of life accepted the Enlightenment view of human progress and perfectibility. . . . It failed to take seriously the factors of interest and power, the rudiments of political order, the organic and historic character of political loyalties, and the necessity of coercion in forming the solidarities of a community. Indeed the failures of liberalism have tended to inhere in precisely this blindness to the perennial difference between human actions and aspirations, the perennial source of conflict between life and life, the inevitable tragedy of human existence, the irreducible irrationality of human behavior, and the tortuous character of human history.

The corrective to these liberal illusions in Western civilization has been conservatism. Conservatism speaks for the skeptical and cautious side of human nature, which sees all about it too many examples of man's sinfulness, frailty, and caprice. It is full of grave doubts about the goodness and rationality of man, the sagacity of the majority, and the wisdom of reform. It seeks to put the calipers on the possibilities of human attainment. It tends toward pessimism and displays a natural preference for stability over change, continuity over experiment, the past over the future. Two momentous events sparked its emergence: the French Revolution and the Industrial Revolution. Conservatism appeared as a reaction against the extravagant radicalism and utopianism of the former and the dismayingly rapid pace of social change brought about by the latter.

Moreover, while the conservative tradition is a Western phenomenon, its impact has been greatest in particular countries like Great Britain. In France, the background of the Ancien Régime and an organic feudal order ought to have given conservatives an objective past to which to appeal. It would have done so but for one insoluble problem. French conservatives with their rationalism were never able to agree among themselves as to just what it was they wished to preserve. By contrast, Great Britain was able to absorb both the liberalism of John Locke and the conservatism of Edmund Burke. Its constitutional monarchy provides a fusion of the old and the new political philosophies. The conservative tradition grew up in reaction against the destructive forces released in the process of emancipation from aristocracy and feudalism. It was therefore reasonable that European and in particular British conservatives should sound the tocsin against Jacobinism and industrialization in behalf of the vestigial qualities worth preserving in a decaying feudal order.

For America, conservatism from the outset lacked a context in which it could raise its voice. The boundless opportunities of a new continent, the abundance of natural resources, the spirit of freedom, and the release from the shackles of an established order hardly provided fertile soil for its rapid growth and flowering. The industrialists who carved an empire out of this vast wilderness, such as the railway builders and traders, were scarcely conservatives in the European sense. Their very successes made them easy prey for the liberal illusions of progress and perfectibility. . . .

Liberalism alone cannot save us unless it is freed from its worst illusions about human nature and politics. Conservatism—especially American conservatism—is bedeviled by its passionate attachment to each successive status quo and its tendency to see the advance of mankind through the narrow squint of upper-middle-class American life. England's political advance must be reckoned at least partly due to the creative interplay between its traditions of Lockean liberalism and Burkean conservatism. The one has a keen sense of justice while the other is more aware of all the inescapable aspects of community life that are organic in character. Historic conservatism perceives that acknowledged rights and duties, acceptable standards of justice and mutual interests, are more often the result of slow and unconscious growth than of conscious political intervention. It likewise concedes that every political and social realm has its hierarchies of power and authority, not least on the international scene. Finally, it argues that it will not do to assume that peace and order and a more stable community can be had through an effacing of these arrangements. The source of all conflict in the world is never solely the great powers or political parties. As often as not, the weak tempt others to aggression; powerlessness is hardly an assurance of responsibility (a vivid example may be the conduct of certain smaller states in an international assembly such as the United Nations). One of the creative functions of conservatism is continually to remind liberals that whether in field or factory, school or church, congress or the international society, there are hierarchies of leadership and an almost endless number of organic processes that hold the community together, give it whatever cohesiveness it enjoys, and regulate and integrate its life.

However while conservatism in the West has seen the organic processes of each community in true perspective, American conservatism, which is chiefly the remnant of a once vital laissez-faire liberalism, has been blinded to these realities. On the one hand, it has clung to the errors and illusions of Enlightenment liberalism, which saw an easy harmony of interests emerging from every conflict of interests; on the other, to a narrow conception of the hierarchies of leadership in America's national and international life defending the special privileges of the parochial segments of the business community or internationally of the nation as a law unto itself. Because the wisdom of traditional conservatism has been so imperfectly appropriated by American conservatives, it becomes the common property of all those groups, including liberals, who seek for greater realism in world affairs. . . .

FOR THE STUDENT

Rhetoric

1. *Does Thompson use images and figures of speech? Do you wish he had used more?*
2. *What is Thompson's chief source of particulars to support his generalizations?*

Discussion

1. *Compare Thompson's general statements about liberalism and conservatism in his opening paragraph with Spitz's views.*
2. *In paragraphs three and four, Thompson shows that lib-*

eralism was the political ideology of the rising middle class. What has made the middle class in twentieth-century America largely a conservative group?

3. *Why was early America more liberal than conservative? Why, however, did conservatism ultimately grow out of these forces and tendencies?*

4. *Does Thompson provide any correctives for Spitz's views?*

Writing

1. *In a short paper, review some of the changes that Thompson says have taken place in the liberal and the conservative views.*

2. *Theme topics: "Conservatism is too much opposed to change"; "Liberalism is too receptive to change."*

CLINTON ROSSITER

The Defense of Liberty

The new conservative in America, like good conservatives everywhere in the West, will pledge himself firmly to the defense of liberty. If it is for the liberal to expand liberty, it is for the conservative to defend it, especially against experiments that appear to sacrifice real liberty for specious equality. He can do this by prizing the old freedoms *to* over the new freedoms *from,* by emphasizing the reciprocity of rights and duties, and by reminding his fellow citizens that their liberty will rise and fall with the level of faith, virtue, knowledge, animation, and industry they display in their daily lives. As conservative, he will pay particular attention to three great institutional complexes that he has always counted on to support ordered liberty: the churches, the schools and colleges, and the economic system.

Christianity, the carrier of our precious heritages from Israel, Greece, Rome, and all the West, has been a major support of American liberty and morality. Can we retain the Christian ethic while rejecting or neglecting the Christian religion? I have met no thoughtful conservative who would answer yes to this fateful question. American conservatives may be counted on to support organized religion as "foundation of stability, cement of unity, patron of morality, check upon power, and spur to compassion." Conservative believers will do this with enthusiam and conviction. Conservative skeptics and agnostics—and conservatives who are casually indifferent or determinedly unreligious and are therefore imperfect conservatives—will find it a somewhat more difficult task. Yet as conservatives, men charged specifically with the defense of traditions and institutions, they cannot ignore the great truth that the Christian religion remains the most powerful of our traditions, the Christian churches the most esteemed of our inherited institutions. No man who thinks of himself as a conservative can stand idly by and watch America drift away from Christianity. One may hope earnestly that the churches themselves will refuse to be used for narrowly conservative ends, that they will labor diligently to broaden the outlook of conservative businessmen, and that they will remind conservatives who talk about a "revival of religion" of another great truth: the state of religion is measured finally in the number of those who believe and act on their beliefs, not in the number of church members. The new conservative must be concerned to strengthen as well as to defend American religion. Everything I have said, of course, may also be said, *mutatis mutandis,* of Jewish conservatives and Judaism.

A lively concern for education is already evident among American conservatives. The "solid and respectable" men of the Right sit in control of most of the nation's schoolboards; the angry men of the Right, whose zeal makes them seem more numerous and patriotic than they really are, press upon them relentlessly in the interests of orthodoxy and indoctrination. The first of these Rights, in the person of men like Frank Abrams and Irving Olds, seems genuinely concerned about the colleges and anxious to help them maintain both freedom and solvency; the second, in the person of men like William F. Buckley, Jr., and J. B. Matthews, seems to have declared open war on the methods and traditions of our best colleges. The influence of conservatism on American education is certain to be greater in the years ahead, and again the question comes: what kind of conservatism is it going to be?

The answer depends largely on the wisdom and resolution of the new conservatism. Its leaders must represent the interests of the whole community on controlling boards and refuse to succumb to the pressures of organized minorities. They must guard our schools against extremists of the Right as well as of the Left, shield our colleges against "the revolt of the primitives," and seek earnestly to narrow the distressing rift between the academic and business worlds. They must persuade the nation's teachers that conservatism comes as well-intentioned, respectful friend rather than sneaky, contemptuous foe; and if they are to do this successfully, they must not permit men like Allen Zoll and organizations like his National Council for American Education to demoralize teachers and degrade the noble aims of public education. Here in particular, in the field of education, the new conservatism can steer a steady course down the middle—between Deweyites and anti-Deweyites, vocationalists and generalists, all-out democrats and unrealistic elitists, traditionalists and progressives, sectarians and secularists, advocates of "moral education" and advocates of studied indifference, absolutists of the Right and absolutists of the Left. It must not let the community forget the conservative mission of education; it must not let itself forget the difference beween conservatism in the interest of all and reaction in the interest of a few.

The new conservatism will need no persuasion to take an active interest in the American economy. It may be counted on to defend private property and enterprise against determined innovators, of whom there are now precious few, and careless tinkerers, of whom there are still many. It will do this with best results for itself and the nation if it aims purposefully at two major goals: a great deal more knowledge and understanding of the economic system that it proposes to defend, and a conscious determination to make American capitalism the mighty servant of American democracy.

The first of these goals calls for tireless fact-finding and dauntless fact-facing. Most Americans on the Right are captives of assumptions—"facts," they like to call them—that have little relation to the real world of industrial organization, social structure, and government activity in the 1950's. If they are to take a worthy part in the defense and improvement of our economic system, they must know what the system is and, no less important, what it is not. The new conservatism can lead the way to a sharper understanding of twentieth-century developments that have made this in truth the most efficient and equitable of all economic systems. It has already shown its responsible hand in organizations like the Committee for Economic Development, conferences like those of the American Assembly at Arden House, and studies like that produced for Standard Oil of New Jersey by Stuart Chase, a liberal put to work for conservative ends. In time, perhaps, our conservatives may state the case for the new American capitalism in language the rest of the world can understand.

The second goal calls for painstaking yet imaginative construction of a "welfare community" that will prove less dangerous in power and more benevolent in operation than the "welfare state" proposed by enthusiastic reformers. A sweeping majority of Americans endorses the case for capitalism, even when it is badly put. A no less sweeping majority now endorses, in Dean David's words, the case for "America as a society in which every human being is assured of the minimun necessities of food, clothing, and shelter; in which all the needy are cared for—the aged and infirm, the disabled, the destitute, the delinquent, and of course the young and deserted." The new conservative has the responsibility to prove both cases. He must carry forward a number of trends that are already under way in business and industry: acceptance and integration of unions, application of "the new science of human relations," and extension of the pattern of pensions and benefits that is bringing new security and dignity to American workers. At the same time, he must seek to direct and control these trends, for he is, after all, a conservative and has his delaying, preserving, unifying functions to perform. Although he must often mediate between the outrageous demands of economic progressivism and outraged objections of economic standpattism, his chief duty is to lead rather than to compromise.

The conservative's approach to government intervention must be equally balanced and farsighted. He must not be afraid to say no to reforms that are impractical, ill-digested, or radical—or liberal only in the sense of being "liberal with other people's money." He must warn his fellow citizens, not cynically but sadly, that no amount of reform can do away entirely with the sorrows

and frustrations and insecurities of human existence. He must
warn them, too, of a truth well stated by Henry C. Simons:

> A nation which wishes to preserve democratic institutions cannot
> afford to allow its legislatures to become engaged on a large scale in
> the promiscuous distribution of special subsidies and special favors.
> Once this occurs, there is no protecting the interests of the community
> at large, and, what is more important, there is no protecting the
> political institutions themselves.

Yet he must also take honest stock of conditions in industry or
society that have led to demands for special subsidies and favors
and must be prepared, when such conditions are plainly distressing,
to propose positive remedies of his own. He can do this, too, in
a shrewdly conservative way—countering a proposal for stiffer
regulation of industry with one that would encourage self-regulation, a scheme for increased social-security benefits with one for
increased benefits *and* contributions, a master plan for "socialized
medicine" with one that is voluntary, decentralized, and self-sup-
porting. Whatever his course, his approach to social problems must
be humane and charitable. While he remains more "practical" and
"realistic" than liberals and radicals, he cannot be ignoble or indifferent.

His central mission as economic conservative in a capitalist
system is twofold: to preserve and expand the nation's productive
capacity and to defend the integrity of the dollar. Without production at an ever rising pace, there can be no real advance toward
the ideal of social justice and material dignity for all. Without a
stable dollar, there can be no real security for the millions of citizens whose futures are tied up in savings, insurance policies, and
pensions. In resisting reforms or subsidies that point inevitably
toward inflation, the conservative is fulfilling one of his historic
missions: to serve as special champion of private property. Efficient production and a sound currency are not the solution to all
our economic and social problems, but without them we will run
into problems that dwarf any that plague us now. It is for the

new conservative to remind us of all this in a manner both tough-minded and kindhearted.

There will be room in the camp of the new conservatism for wide differences of economic view. Both Fred I. Raymond, the critic of bigness in business, and A. D. H. Kaplan, the apologist for it, will be made welcome. So, too, will Clark Kerr, the critic of factory sociology, and many of the men he condemns so forcefully. The only tests for admission should be earnest devotion to "private enterprise regulated fairly in the public interest" and willingness to face new facts about the economy and set new social goals for it. If the new conservative's duty is to fight the growth of a monstrous and bankrupt welfare state, he must fight with head up, eyes clear, and brain in creative motion. He cannot bid the mighty quest for security begone by branding it unworkable or un-American, especially when he dedicates so much of his attention and earnings to this very purpose. Rather he must recognize that this quest is itself a deeply conservative urge, which with ingenuity he can harness to his own ends. This, as Russell Davenport suggested in "The Greatest Opportunity on Earth," might well be the historic mandate of the new conservative in business: to prove that non-governmental institutions can satisfy the tremendous human needs that have spurred the rise of the positive state. To those needs he cannot forever say no. His retort must be: "I have a better answer"; for if, as Senator Taft wrote, "free enterprise cannot take any more government," free enterprise must aim at making more government unnecessary.

The defense of liberty summons the leaders of the new conservatism to act creatively in many other areas of American life: in government, where they can reverse the long trend toward Washington by modernizing state and local governments and decentralizing federal services; in society, where they can search for ways to bolster the family as a socially significant institution; in the area of business and political ethics, where Blair Bolles has already counseled a number of practical methods to reduce corruption in the "rich man's division of the welfare state." None of this activity will bear rich fruits, however, unless conservatives face up to a truth they have ignored or distorted for generations: American liberty is made up of many freedoms, and of these the economic freedoms are only one part. "Liberty," Ralph Barton Perry writes, "is morally justified when its exercise is consistent with, or conducive to, the exercise of other liberties. . . . The extent to which a man may be considered a lover of liberty is then to be measured in terms of his passion for the liberty of others."

Our conservatives in business and industry never tire of protesting their love of liberty, but their passion for the liberty of others burns notoriously low. They persist in defining liberty narrowly in terms of their own economic freedom; they persist in asserting, in defiance of overwhelming evidence to the contrary, that government is the one real threat to liberty. As a result, they ignore recent reductions in religious, cultural, and political freedom and condone durable prejudices that deprive millions of Americans of any semblance of equality of opportunity. Their narrow, selfish definition of liberty drives the anti-Communist liberal like Sidney Hook to ask why they are "the largest group in the community yet to be drawn into the continuing struggle to preserve the heritage of freedom all along the line," and why "the fight for civil liberties, for academic freedom, for minority rights is left largely to bishops, lawyers, and professors." It drives the large-minded, courageous conservative like Grenville Clark to lament that "the active defense of civil liberty has been allowed to drift very largely into the hands of elements of 'the Left,'" leaving "the unfortunate impression . . . that American conservatives are more interested in the preservation of vested property rights than in the great rights guaranteed by the First Amendment." Worst of all, it shocks and disheartens friends all over the world, for they know that their future will probably be determined by the condition of freedom— social, cultural, religious, political, educational, and economic— in the United States. If our friends abroad tend to overstate the threats to civil liberty in this country, our conservatives at home tend to overlook them.

It would be more fitting, surely, for a conservative to lecture conservatives on this particular subject. Grenville Clark had this to say about "Conservatism and Civil Liberty" as long ago as 1938:

> I venture to say that there is only one sound attitude for conservatives consistent with a real understanding of the essence of American life, namely, an attitude of firm and impartial defense of the rights of the citizen under the Bill of Rights in *every* case where these rights are threatened, and irrespective of whether we approve or disapprove the sentiments and policies of the persons affected.
>
> In respect to a line of action to give expression to such an attitude, I believe it of vital importance that the true conservatives of the country should actively organize and participate in concrete efforts to protect civil liberty against all abuses of power from whatever source those abuses come, leaving aside all considerations of party and of economic and social prejudices. . . .
>
> I have been speaking in terms of obligation to support the best of our tradition, apart from considerations of self-interest. But these considerations are also involved, for, if the idea once takes general hold that it is tolerable to suppress some opinion and criticism but not some other opinion, the conservatives who are complaisant to any such doctrine will lose their moral standing in the forum of public opinion and will have no ground upon which to stand when their own basic rights are imperiled.

The new conservative must lead his brethren of the Right toward principles and practices that honor this wise and hopeful message. He can do this in many ways: by supporting conservative organizations for the defense of civil liberty like the Fund for the Republic and the Committee on Individual Rights as Affected by National Security of the American Bar Association; entering actively into community programs that work for brotherhood and mutual understanding among men of all races, religions, and opinions; lecturing ultra-conservatives boldly on the indecency and folly of fellow-traveling with peddlers of hate like Joseph Kamp

and Gerald L. K. Smith; exposing or at least shunning those in
his own camp who use the word *liberty* promiscuously to defend
special privileges or excessive power or antisocial behavior; reminding his brother traditionalists that the American tradition has
hitherto smiled on nonconformity; and working in his business,
associations, and party to leaven the spirit of American conservatism with the one ingredient it needs most: tolerance. He can do
all this, as Mr. Clark makes clear, by appealing, not alone to the
magnanimity and patriotism and traditionalism of his fellow conservatives, but to "considerations of self-interest."

We have no right to expect "hardheaded conservatives" to be
as agitated about civil liberty as "softhearted liberals," but we can
hope that more and more leaders of business and industry—and
senators and lawyers, too—will interpret the word *liberty* broadly
and show sympathy for the rights of men with different opinions,
interests, and problems from their own. The leaders of the American Right must learn how thoroughly their own freedom, property,
creativity, and security are wrapped up in the defense of liberty
of all kinds and for all Americans. If our freedoms are a "single
bundle," conservatives must be anxious about every stick of freedom in it.

FOR THE STUDENT

Rhetoric

1. *What distinctions is Rossiter making in his phrases "the
   old freedoms to" and "the new freedoms from"?*
2. *Justify Rossiter's giving seven paragraphs to his third "institutional complex," the economic system, whereas he
   gives only one to the churches and two to the schools and
   colleges.*
3. *This essay lends itself to easy outlining. What would you
   make your four main topics?*

Discussion

1. *How does Rossiter, in paragraph two, illustrate what Spitz said about the conservative's attitude toward religion?*
2. *Rossiter speaks of "the conservative mission of education." How fully has he defined it?*
3. *For preventing further government intervention, Rossiter offers the conservative solution of self-regulation. Can you cite examples that have worked successfully? That have failed?*
4. *Throughout this essay, Rossiter pictures his new conservative as a mediator between the extreme Left and the extreme Right. Could a "new liberal" make a like claim for his position?*

Writing

1. *In 500–600 words compare and contrast Spitz's and Rossiter's views on the rights of man and the ways in which those rights can be protected.*
2. *Theme topic: "New social goals for private enterprise."*

7 Politics and Power

It may well be, as Lord Acton suggests, that power corrupts. Yet, as some will argue, power exists in all collective human activity—and must be reckoned with. Not the least important sphere of collective human activity is politics (indeed Aristotle defines man as "a political animal"), and the conjunction of "politics" and "power" is a commonplace of the thinking of this age. It behooves all rational men, therefore, to understand what they can of political power: its sources, its applications, its limitations, and—where they may —the directions it is taking.

There are, of course, countless thousands of writings dealing with various aspects of political power. We have here selected three and attempted to arrange them in our conventional spectrum: the two extremes, as often tends to be the case, are polemic, subjective; the middle essay is scholarly, detached. Irving Howe, a social historian from Hunter College, identifies himself as "a democratic socialist" and on most political issues ranks on the "Left"; here he analyzes and attacks the political power (in his own words, the "political energy" and "pressure") behind the Goldwater movement in the American presidential campaign of 1964. Franz Neumann, a noted contemporary political scientist, by virtue of his detachment and objectivity, ranks in the middle: he describes, in unemotional language, various approaches to political power in the history of Western man. And finally, Barry Goldwater, avowed conservative Republican politician, represents the "Right"; with his characteristic attack on "big" government and the "corrupting influence of power," he would find any other position incompatible.

IRVING HOWE

The Goldwater Movement

Simply by winning the Republican nomination, Senator Goldwater has left a strong imprint on American politics.

Everything now shifts in his direction. The apparatus of a major party lies in the grip of his friends. The terms of public debate will be determined not by the authentic and pressing needs of the country, but by the ideological fantasias of the right wing. And the most committed and fervent political activity may be expected to come from Goldwater partisans who now can finally feel they have a cause of their own.

This last seems to me especially important. There is a new political energy surging up in this country, it is an energy of hard-bitten resentment, and it is driven by intensity of purpose at the very moment that almost all other political tendencies have become sated, slack or feeble. It provides for many Americans an ideological lure in which the imagery of nostalgia nestles against vicarious brinkmanship.

Whatever else, it ought to be clear how inadequate was the official liberalism of the last few decades. Both the Negro movement, on the one hand, and the new right wing, on the other, refuse to settle into the mild assumptions of a political equilibrium, that moderate balance in which "countervailing powers" are supposed to play off one against the other, reconcilable in their opposition. At times our society may approach this kind of equilibrium, and for certain kinds of short-range analyses, like those of Samuel Lubell, it may be useful to employ such a "model." But the realities of our social life are too rough and intractable for the politics of equilibrium to be able to contain them indefinitely. Rapid technological change, gnawing economic inequalities, a profound moral malaise, the growing discrepancy between a politics geared to diffusion and an economy requiring discipline —these are a few such realities. And they are bound to create, as they already have created, new and desperate conflicts of interest and idea. The intellectual guardians of the Goldwater movement, it is worth noting, seem not to have heard about "the end of ideology": perhaps they read the wrong magazines.

A "law" might here be advanced about recent American politics: the more housebroken the left, the more adventuresome the right. When there is not enough pressure from the liberal-labor movements upon both government and society, the right wing feels free to risk its own political course, breaking off from the moderate center to which it has usually been semiattached. For it can then calculate that even in electoral defeat it will gain power, becoming the dominant pressure upon an administration that lacks firm principles of its own.

I would venture the speculation that what crucially enabled the Goldwater movement to enter its "take-off" phase was the failure of the labor and liberal communities to cement a sufficiently strong alliance with the rising Negro movement. Once the right wing saw that the Negroes would more or less have to go it alone; once it became clear that a large fraction of even enlightened white sentiment consisted of passive sympathy, not active solidarity; once, in brief, there was no great danger that if the right wing detached itself from the political center, a resurgent Negro-labor-liberal alliance would pour into the resulting power vacuum— then the Goldwater movement was able to set out on its present course.

And a second "law": in the politics we now have in the United States, the kind and quantity of the pressure put upon the center largely determines where and what the center will be. *The Wall Street Journal* (July 14, 1964) has noted as much:

With American political thought thus polarized between Johnson and Goldwater, the conclusion seems almost inescapable that the center of political gravity must now move rather sharply to the right. By hauling the Republican party rightward . . . Goldwater may actually have achieved some part of his dream of turning the country towards a significantly more conservative choice. . . .

If Goldwater chooses to regard the Eastern financiers as his enemy, bent on control of the GOP for narrow, self-serving aims, Johnson is just as ready to hail them as new-found friends.

No foreseeable society seems likely to be so finely adjusted to the conflicting needs of its population as to preclude serious conflict and discontent. In regard to the United States today, such an expectation is sheer wishful fantasy. Conflict is inescapable, and the only question is what forms it will take and what value it will have. The tragedy of the moment is that it has been the Goldwater movement which has taken upon itself—with comic inappropriateness, but also frightening earnestness—the role of crusader. In its vocabulary, and at least part of its intent, this movement is not satisfied with a mild defense or a mild improvement of the bureaucratic and militarized welfare state. The right wing has also done something which, thus far, no other political movement in America has managed to do: it has stirred thousands of middle-class people to leave their ranch houses and enter the hustle of politics. It has made them into political activists who learn the art of attending meetings and the craft of outsitting and outvoting their more conventional opponents. It has fired them with the passions of a cause which, in the style of many demagogic movements, brings together the rhetoric of national interest with the urgencies of social selfishness. What a comedy that the notion of a "mass society" in which men flounder in apolitical passivity should be shattered by these crusaders from the barbecue pits!

The Goldwater movement is not yet fully formed: there are conflicting interests at work within it and there will be plenty of splits and transformations. Right now it seems to consist of a loose coalition between a hard reactionary core, providing muscle, ideology, and money, and a larger scatter of traditional conservatives, providing votes, emotion, and precinct committees. It is easy

enough to point out the contradictions in the Goldwater platform:
e.g., the promise to cut federal spending and decrease the power
of national government coupled with the intent to build up still
further the armed forces toward possible adventure abroad. Such
contradictions are real enough, and no doubt there are a good
many Goldwater partisans who manage, through the magic of sheer
desire, to reconcile these perspectives in their minds. But in the
long run there can be no reconciling nostalgia for *laissez faire* with
lust for world domination.

Certain political commentators have been inclined to treat the
Goldwater movement primarily as an emotional reflex, a revulsion
from the complexities of the twentieth century. James Reston
writes, for example:

The more complicated life becomes, the more people are attracted to
simple solutions; the more irrational the world seems, the more they
long for rational answers; and the more diverse everything is, the
more they want it all reduced to identity.

Those who feel this way are undoubtedly attracted to Senator
Goldwater, and many part-political and part-ethical movements have
gone further on less. [*The New York Times,* July 21, 1964.]

Probably true, as far as it goes. A good part of the feeling
behind the Goldwater movement does stem from a nostalgia for
the days when Negroes knew their place, cities had not swamped
the landscape, income taxes were not so oppressive, and little
countries crossing the United States could be handled with gun-
boats. Part of the feeling behind the Goldwater movement also
rests upon a sense of national frustration: if the United States is
indeed as rich, powerful and good as it keeps telling itself, why
then do so many countries disobey it? and why, as we edge toward
omnipotence, can we not simply eradicate Communism with one
swoop of our strength?[1]

1. One trouble with this kind of motive-probing is that it explains either
too much or too little. Michael Walzer, writing from England, has a perti-
nent comment: "the theory of *ressentiment* has got to be stretched beyond
breaking point if it is going to include the frustrated, bankrupt, embittered

There is more to be said than this kind of impressionistic sociology allows. For what matters is not merely the inferred *motives* of the Goldwater supporters, but the visible *meaning* of the Goldwater movement. And here the kind of assuaging sentimentalism practiced by Reston and other moderate liberals is very annoying. For it is outrageous to be told again and again that Goldwater is sincere, nice, and good. I do not believe it. The man who voted against the Civil Rights Act is not a good man. The man who said that "because Joe McCarthy lived, we are a freer, safer, and more alert nation," is not a good man. The man who in his speech at the Republican convention stirred the bestialities of racism by his innuendoes about "bullies and marauders" in the streets is not a good man. And neither is the man who, when "asked by a European reporter to comment on his policies toward Europe and Germany," replied: "I think that Germany originated the modern concept of peace through strength." [*The New York Times,* August 13, 1964.]

Muddled nostalgia, homestead economics, daydream brinkmanship all enter the Goldwater complex. But there is also a hard ideology and a precise focus of interest. No one should have any trouble in identifying these: they animate a politics of reaction. This politics rests in part on the social selfishness of large segments among the upper middle class which consciously disdain the sentiments of "welfarism" and are prepared to let the poor and the ethnic minorities stew in silence or, if noisy, be slugged into submission. This politics rests on the desire of powerful men—Ralph Cordiner is not a Midwestern automobile salesman, George

---

types who voted for Hitler; the frightened, losing-status types who, we thought, supported McCarthy; and the triumphantly egotistical, prosperous types who seem to be behind Goldwater. Barry's men, or at least some of them, are even modern and urban: how are they to be accounted for by theories which have always emphasized that right-wing politics was the anxious response of pre-modern men to the cosmopolitan and contemporary world? Dallas may be a barbarous place, but it is absolutely up-to-date barbarism. Maybe, in his own way, Goldwater has something when he talks of moral malaise." [Author's note]

Humphrey not a malaise-smitten petty bourgeois, H. L. Hunt
not a bewildered storekeeper—to call a halt to social reform and
then slowly to push it back. And it is a politics that rests on the
dirty half-winks of racism, called euphemistically "the Southern
strategy."

To insist that there is a firm reactionary intent behind the
Goldwater movement is not, of course, to claim that the major centers of American big business are supporting it. Nor is it to assert
that the Goldwater movement is Fascist or neo-Fascist. A segment
of the business class is supporting Goldwater, and while not the
crucial segment, it is, in terms of resources and perhaps even numbers, big enough. (No right-wing movement ever *begins* with the
full support of big business.) And as for Fascism, obviously the
Goldwater movement, like all of our native right-wing movements, diverges crucially from the patterns of European Fascism.
But political phenomena must be seen not merely in their momentary appearance, but also in their potential. In and around the
Goldwater movement there reside the cadres of a Fascist group;
in its "culture" of social meanness, racist hostility, and chauvinist
mania they find sustenance. At the moment there is no serious possibility of an American Fascism on a mass scale; but given either
a depression or a group of major defeats in the Cold War, a
minority segment of the Goldwater movement could well transform
itself into pin-striped Fascists. That this potential simmers in
American society is significant enough.

FOR THE STUDENT

Rhetoric

1. *Howe's diction has a rather colloquial, salty quality (for
   example, the "housebroken" left, "slugged into submission"). Make a list of half a dozen of his more impressive
   colloquialisms.*

2. *How effective are the quotations from Goldwater in making Howe's case that he is "not a good man"?*

Discussion

1. *Who, in Howe's definition of him, would come close to being Goldwater's counterpart today?*
2. *How would you characterize some of your own campus groups: Left, Middle, or Right? What "kind and quantity" of pressure do the extremes put on the Middle?*

Writing

1. *In a paper, try to apply Howe's two "laws" to local or campus politics. If they don't work, speculate as to why.*
2. *Write a "political portrait" about someone in your student body, faculty, or administration. (Perhaps it would be discreet to omit names here.)*

FRANZ NEUMANN

Political Power

It is difficult, perhaps impossible, to add any new idea to a discussion of political power. To be sure, there are few books so named; but almost everything written in the field of the political sciences deals in one way or another with the subject. The purpose of this essay is not to develop a new theory of political power but rather to lay bare the approaches to its study, particularly for younger students.

I. Political Power and Psychology

Political power is an elusive concept. It embraces two radically different relations: control of nature, and control of man. Power over nature is mere intellectual power. It consists in man's understanding of the lawfulness of external nature for the ultimate purpose of subjecting external nature to man's needs. It is this accumulated knowledge which is the basis of the productivity of any given society. This power is powerless. It does not involve control of other men.

Political power is social power focused on the state. It involves control of other men for the purpose of influencing the behavior of the state, its legislative, administrative and judicial activities. Since political power is control of other men, political power (as contrasted with power over external nature) is always a two-sided relationship. Man is not simply a piece of external nature; he is an organism endowed with reason, although frequently not capable of, or prevented from, acting rationally. Consequently, those who wield political power are compelled to create emotional and rational responses in those whom they rule, inducing them to accept,

Reprinted with permission from the Political Science Quarterly, *LXV (June 1950), pp. 161–171.*

implicitly or explicitly, the commands of the rulers. Failure to evoke emotional or intellectual responses in the ruled compels the ruler to resort to simple violence, ultimately to liquidation.

The two-sided character of political power already marks political science off from natural science. It makes it impossible (even if it were desirable) to measure power relationships as one measures the behavior of external nature. The variations of the power relationships are numberless. One may classify and describe them, but one cannot measure them.

Political power is not comparable to the category of energy in physics. Nor is power the sole category of political science. Politics is not merely the art of getting something in a certain way regardless of the what and of the how. The trend to equate politics with power politics goes back to Machiavelli and appears to have become the predominant trait of American and, perhaps, of modern political science in general. Politics is viewed as a purely technical concern. "Values" (the term is used only provisionally) are then mere personal preferences; valid if they work, invalid if they fail. History is then quite meaningless. It is an indifferent repetition of the endless struggle of "in-groups" versus "out-groups." It is thus reduced to mere chronology, a file of illustrative materials for so-called hypotheses or, at best, is governed by what Machiavelli called Fortuna, the luck of the participants in the struggle.

The theoretical basis of this approach to politics and political science is usually psychological, as Machiavelli has already developed it. Men are the same throughout history. They have certain stable traits, and all, or almost all, are equipped with "power drive," an uncontrollable and irrational impulse for power. From this assertion are then derived such facile half-true generalizations as the famous statement of Lord Acton: "Power tends to corrupt, absolute power corrupts absolutely."

This is not to imply that the psychology of power has no place in political science. Its significance is great, but not decisive. Its contribution is twofold. First, it leads to the realization that the optimistic theories of human nature are one-sided and thus false.

Man, although endowed with reason, frequently knows not—or is not permitted to know—what his true interests are. This rediscovery of ancient truths is particularly the merit of the materialistic psychology of Freud. Secondly, psychological techniques permit us to describe in concrete and convincing terms the personality structures most capable of exerting or of suffering power. But psychology cannot go beyond concretization and description. It cannot supply a theory of political power. The action of each man is as much the result of the environment as it is the manifestation of a personality structure. Indeed, personality itself is historically conditioned. To the psychologist, the environment is a mere "stimulus" of the individual act. To the political scientist, it is one element in the total setting of political power.

The present orientation of psychology, besides, tends to make it simply a technique of rule, of maintaining and strengthening power relationships, an instrument of manipulation of the masses by the élite.

The rejection of the psychological approach involves in its positive aspect the view that politics (and thus history) is not simply a struggle of power groups for power, but an attempt to mold the world according to one's image, to impress one's view upon it. The historical process has a meaning. Provisionally, we may accept the traditional pre-positivistic formulation that politics is the struggle of ideas as well as of force.

II. Attitudes Toward Power

Consciously, or unconsciously, every student of politics has a specific attitude toward political power. It is this attitude which determines one's approach to all problems of political science. The valuative premises must be made clear so that objective analyses may be possible. The soul searching of the political scientist may be facilitated by a classification of the various attitudes exhibited in the history of political theory. The classification presented here is only suggested and is not meant to imply that there are no better and more convincing classifications.

1. For Plato and Aristotle, political power is more than a separate function of the organized community. It *is* the community. Political power is the total power of the community, distinguished from other relationships merely by its techniques. There is, in this view, no distinction between state and society, economics and politics, morals and politics, religion and politics, culture and politics. Man and citizen are equated. Every activity of the community and of its citizens is political. Only through political action can the citizen attain his fulfillment; only through politics does he become man.

2. To this, there is radically opposed what I shall call the Augustinian position. Politics is evil; political power is coercion, evil in origin and purpose. It is "unnatural" that man rule over man. Only at the end of history with the advent of the Kingdom of God can and will coercion be dispensed with. From this philosophy derive two radically different, and yet inherently related, attitudes: that of total conformism and that of total opposition to political power. If politics is evil, withdrawal is mandatory. Forms of government and objectives of political power become irrelevant. Salvation can be attained through faith, and the earthly life should be a mere preparation for it. Monasticism is the first consequence. By the same token, however, the demand for the immediate destruction of politics and the establishment of a Kingdom of God may equally be supported by the Augustinian premise. The Anabaptist movement was perhaps the most striking manifestation of the total rejection of society.

3. The radicalism of St. Augustine is, of course, "impractical." St. Thomas introduces what may be called a commonsense attitude toward political power. Power is not unnatural since hierarchic relationships already existed among the angels. Yet the attitude toward political power is not unambiguously positive. It is not only hedged in by many restraints but also, in some rather unclear

way, subordinated to spiritual power operating indirectly through various levels of law.

4. It is this climate which prepared the way for the liberal attitude. Its sole concern is the erection of fences around political power which is, allegedly, distrusted. Its aim is the dissolution of power into legal relationships, the elimination of the element of personal rule, and the substitution of the rule of law in which all relationships are to become purposive-rational, that is, predictable and calculable. In reality, of course, this is in large measure an ideology tending (often unintentionally) to prevent the search for the locus of political power and to render more secure its actual holders. Power cannot be dissolved in law.

5. Not to be confused with liberalism is the Epicurean attitude toward politics. In contrast to the Platonic-Aristotelian conception, politics is a separate business of society, clearly distinguished and distinguishable from all other activities. But it is a complete matter of indifference how it is organized, who exerts it, for what purposes it is used. Any power is justified which maintains that minimum external order of society which permits the individual to go on with his life.

6. In its psychological consequences, Epicureanism is sometimes closely related to the anarchistic approach. To the anarchist, political power is evil, society good; hence it is possible to organize a society without politics. As in Augustinism, conformism or putschism may follow. Conformism: one should not dirty one's hands by participation in politics; putschism: one can establish an associative society at any time that man wills it.

7. Marxism shares with anarchism and Augustinism the belief that political power is not a natural but an historical phenomenon. In contrast to anarchism, and with Augustinism, however, it believes it to be a necessary historical phenomenon, but the necessity is limited (in contrast to Augustinism) to one historical phase through which mankind must pass before the classless society (a society without politics) can be established. The remedy against political power (again against the anarchists) is more and highly

concentrated political power, skillfully used to smash political power (dictatorship of the proletariat). The Marxist thus has a positive approach to political power up to the establishment of a classless society.

8. Marx shares this positive approach with Rousseau. For the latter, political power is at once comprehensive and nonexistent. It is all-encompassing because the organized community (as in Plato and Aristotle) embraces all activities of man, economics, culture, religion; nonexistent because of the alleged identity of rulers and ruled in the general will. It is precisely this dual attitude toward political power which makes Robespierre's theory and actions understandable.

9. The liberal democrat shares with the total democrat a positive attitude toward political power which appears essentially as a rational instrument to be used for desired and desirable ends. Yet the fear of the liberal prevents him from accepting the total politicizing of life and causes him to insist on the separate character of political power. But the consistent liberal democrat is not, and cannot be, solely concerned with the erection of fences around political power. He is increasingly concerned with the potentialities of a rational use of political power.

This (or any other) typology of the attitudes toward political power enables us to discover contradictory statements often of a hypocritical or demagogic nature and to arrive at a consistent approach to the study of the power phenomenon. If a scholar or politician demands, in the same breath, the exclusion of dissenters from political participation and the inviolability of private property from governmental intrusion, we have before us a mixture of two attitudes: that of Plato-Rousseau, and that of liberalism.

The result is not a "new" attitude toward power but a propagandistic statement. Our typology of attitudes readily reveals that it contains contradictory positions. It is the duty of the critical student to remove such inconsistencies from his own thinking, to expose them when they appear in the statements of others, and to become aware of the premises of his own position.

III. Significance of Political Power

Once this self-examination is completed, the significance of political power should be squarely faced. No society in recorded history has ever been able to dispense with political power. This is as true of liberalism as of absolutism, as true of laissez faire as of an interventionist state. No greater disservice has been rendered to political science than the statement that the liberal state was a "weak" state. It was precisely as strong as it needed to be in the circumstances. It acquired substantial colonial empires, waged wars, held down internal disorders, and stabilized itself over long periods of time.

But the methods applied by those who wield power and the scope of its application vary, of course. And it is precisely this problem that is of major significance for the political scientist. Formally, the methods range from the marginal case of killing to the marginal case of education. Three basic methods are at the disposal of the power group: persuasion, material benefits, violence. Violence is probably most effective as a short range method, but little effective as the principal method of maintaining power over long periods since it compels the group (particularly under modern conditions) to intensify the methods of violence and to extend it to larger sections of the ruled. The most efficient (that is, cheapest form) is, of course, persuasion. Yet all three, persuasion, benefits, violence, are always present in all forms of government. And it is precisely the mixture of the three elements which constitutes another major problem for the political scientist. I shall attempt to clarify the meaning by the formulation of some sociological generalizations.

SOCIOLOGICAL GENERALIZATION I. The significance of persuasion grows with the growing complexity of society. It is, perhaps, legitimate to consider persuasion, as a rule, to be merely a form of violence, "violence committed against the soul" as the French historian of Catholic England under Henry VIII formulated it. Through persuasion, the rulers achieve a marked degree of habituation of the ruled so that their reactions assume an almost automatic character. The success of persuasion will, however, depend upon the scope and duration of the propaganda and the skills by which stereotypes are produced. There is little doubt that persuasion is a more efficient and cheaper exercise of political power than the employment of large police forces, armies and militias.

SOCIOLOGICAL GENERALIZATION 2. The increasing complexity of society requires that the rulers increasingly utilize arcane, secret techniques of rule. The struggle for power is a real struggle aiming at the control of the state machine. In any struggle, however, tactical decisions can be effectively made only in secret. Secrecy, in turn, can be preserved only by small numbers. It is this very fact that necessitates the rise of oligarchies within mass movements. Max Weber and Robert Michels (and probably many others) have drawn attention to this phenomenon, and Max Weber, besides, correctly stressed the superiority of small over large numbers because of the significance of secrecy for any rule designed to be more than temporary. It is precisely for this reason that the rule of the few becomes particularly marked in those mass organizations which, more than other movements, are essentially devoted to democracy: the trade unions and the social democratic (labor) parties. The reason is obvious. The opponents of these movements are usually numerically few, but individually powerful, subjects who are thus able to keep their strategic and tactical decisions secret. The mass organization, faced with such opposition, must, in turn, resort to the construction of forms of rule which also permit secrecy. Aristocratic rule thus becomes a sociologically necessary implementation of democratic movements. It is, therefore, no accident that the growth of oligarchies within mass movements was first studied in the example of the German Social Democratic party.

Lenin made a virtue of this necessity. His vanguard theory of leadership frankly replaces the traditional democratic conception of social democracy by an aristocratic one.

SOCIOLOGICAL GENERALIZATION 3. The higher the state of technological development, the greater the concentration of political power. The legal conception of ownership is quite irrelevant for an analysis of this phenomenon. It matters not who owns a technical unit: an individual, a corporation, a state, any other organized society. The social organization of large technical units may, of course, be a coöperative one. In every social group which is based on struggle, however, the organization will, of necessity, be hierarchic. The larger the size, the more hierarchic it becomes. Growing hierarchic trends lead to concentration of power at the top. . . .

SOCIOLOGICAL GENERALIZATION 4. With the growing complexity of society and its increasing industrialization, the significance of political power in the social process grows. Concentration of power (in the economy, in society, in culture) makes for more rigidity. A process of social petrifaction sets in and prevents the system from achieving a semiautomatic balance. The equilibrium, once disturbed, can be restored only through active intervention of the political power. Control of the state then becomes more precious than ever before.

SOCIOLOGICAL GENERALIZATION 5. The same trend also produces a greater separation of political power from social power —a phenomenon that shall concern us later.

Some or all of these generalizations are subject to challenge. They are not meant to be exhaustive, but merely point the direction to a proper study of political power. That they produce uneasiness is to be expected. At first sight it seems difficult to reconcile them with the theory of democracy. If by democracy is understood that mixture of diverse elements, of Locke and Rousseau, St. Augustine and St. Thomas, which is usually called "democratic theory," a reconciliation of those realistic trends with the doctrine is, indeed, impossible. We are not now concerned with the problem of democratic theory. For the present it suffices to say that an adequate democratic theory will have to deal with these problems. . . .

FOR THE STUDENT

Rhetoric

1. *Try to reduce the sense of this essay to a single thesis statement.*
2. *Make a list of ten words (plus their definitions) which you felt constrained to look up in your dictionary.*

Discussion

1. *What grain of truth is there in Machiavelli's theory about all men's lust for power? In Lord Acton's statement?*
2. *What light does Sociological Generalization 3 throw on the Goldwater movement?*

Writing

1. *There are ten major political thinkers cited in this essay. Write (or, for variety, give orally) a short report on the main features of the political thought of one of them.*
2. *Neumann mentions three main methods of applying political power: persuasion, material benefits, violence. Write a paper giving examples of each from American history.*

BARRY GOLDWATER

The Perils of Power

The New Deal, Dean Acheson wrote approvingly in a book called *A Democrat Looks At His Party,* "conceived of the federal government as the whole people organized to do what had to be done." A year later Mr. Larson wrote *A Republican Looks At His Party,* and made much the same claim in his book for Modern Republicans. The "underlying philosophy" of the New Republicanism, said Mr. Larson, is that "if a job has to be done to meet the needs of the people, and no one else can do it, then it is the proper function of the federal government."

Here we have, by prominent spokesmen of both political parties, an unqualified repudiation of the principle of limited government. There is no reference by either of them to the Constitution, or any attempt to define the legitimate functions of government. The government can do whatever *needs* to be done; note, too, the implicit but necessary assumption that it is the government itself that determines *what* needs to be done. We must not, I think, underrate the importance of these statements. They reflect the view of a majority of the leaders of one of our parties, and of a strong minority among the leaders of the other, and they propound the first principle of totalitarianism: that the State is competent to do all things and is limited in what it actually does only by the will of those who control the State.

It is clear that this view is in direct conflict with the Constitution which is an instrument, above all, for *limiting* the functions of government, and which is as binding today as when it was written. But we are advised to go a step further and ask why the Constitution's framers restricted the scope of government. Con-

From The Conscience of a Conservative, *by Barry Goldwater (1960). Reprinted by permission of Victor Publishing Co., Shepherdsville, Kentucky.*

servatives are often charged, and in a sense rightly so, with having an overly mechanistic view of the Constitution: "It is America's enabling document; we are American citizens; therefore," the Conservatives' theme runs, "we are morally and legally obliged to comply with the document." All true. But the Constitution has a broader claim on our loyalty than that. The founding fathers had a *reason* for endorsing the principle of limited government; and this reason recommends defense of the constitutional scheme even to those who take their citizenship obligations lightly. The reason is simple, and it lies at the heart of the Conservative philosophy.

Throughout history, government has proved to be the chief instrument for thwarting man's liberty. Government represents power in the hands of some men to control and regulate the lives of other men. And power, as Lord Acton said, *corrupts* men. "Absolute power," he added, "corrupts absolutely."

State power, considered in the abstract, need not restrict freedom: but absolute state power always does. The *legitimate* functions of government are actually conducive to freedom. Maintaining internal order, keeping foreign foes at bay, administering justice, removing obstacles to the free interchange of goods—the exercise of these powers makes it possible for men to follow their chosen pursuits with maximum freedom. But note that the very instrument by which these desirable ends are achieved *can* be the instrument for achieving undesirable ends—that government can, instead of extending freedom, restrict freedom. And note, secondly, that the "can" quickly becomes "will" the moment the holders of government power are left to their own devices. This is because of the corrupting influence of power, the natural tendency of men who possess *some* power to take unto themselves *more* power. The tendency leads eventually to the acquisition of *all* power—whether in the hands of one or many makes little difference to the freedom of those left on the outside.

Such, then, is history's lesson, which Messrs. Acheson and Larson evidently did not read: release the holders of state power from any restraints other than those they wish to impose upon themselves, and you are swinging down the well-travelled road to absolutism.

The framers of the Constitution had learned the lesson. They were not only students of history, but victims of it: they knew from vivid, personal experience that freedom depends on effective restraints against the accumulation of power in a single authority. And that is what the Constitution is: *a system of restraints against the natural tendency of government to expand in the direction of absolutism.* We all know the main components of the system. The first is the limitation of the federal government's authority to specific, delegated powers. The second, a corollary of the first, is the reservation to the States and the people of all power not delegated to the federal government. The third is a careful division of the federal government's power among three separate branches. The fourth is a prohibition against impetuous alteration of the system—namely, Article V's tortuous, but wise, amendment procedures.

Was it then a *Democracy* the framers created? Hardly. The system of restraints, on the face of it, was directed not only against individual tyrants, but also against a tyranny of the masses. The framers were well aware of the danger posed by self-seeking demagogues—that they might persuade a majority of the people to confer on government vast powers in return for deceptive promises of economic gain. And so they forbade such a transfer of power—first by declaring, in effect, that certain activities are outside the natural and legitimate scope of the public authority, and secondly by dispersing public authority among several levels and branches of government in the hope that each seat of authority, jealous of its own prerogatives, would have a natural incentive to resist aggression by the others.

But the framers were not visionaries. They knew that rules of government, however brilliantly calculated to cope with the imperfect nature of man, however carefully designed to avoid the pitfalls of power, would be no match for men who were determined to disregard them. In the last analysis their system of government would prosper only if the governed were sufficiently determined that it should. "What have you given us?" a woman asked Ben Franklin toward the close of the Constitutional Convention. "A Republic," he said, *"if you can keep it!"*

We have not kept it. The Achesons and Larsons have had their way. The system of restraints has fallen into disrepair. The federal government has moved into every field in which it believes its services are needed. The state governments are either excluded from their rightful functions by federal preemption, or they are allowed to act at the sufferance of the federal government. Inside the federal government both the executive and judicial branches have roamed far outside their constitutional boundary lines. And all of these things have come to pass without regard to the amendment procedures prescribed by Article V. The result is a Leviathan, a vast national authority out of touch with the people, and out of their control. This monolith of power is bounded only by the will of those who sit in high places.

There are a number of ways in which the power of government can be measured.

One is the size of its financial operations. Federal spending is now approaching a hundred billion dollars a year (compared with three and one-half billion less than three decades ago.)

Another is the scope of its activities. A study recently conducted by the *Chicago Tribune* showed that the federal government is now the "biggest land owner, property manager, renter, mover and hauler, medical clinician, lender, insurer, mortgage broker, employer, debtor, taxer and spender in all history."

Still another is the portion of the people's earnings government appropriates for its own use: nearly a third of earnings are taken every year in the form of taxes.

A fourth is the extent of government interference in the daily lives of individuals. The farmer is told how much wheat he can grow. The wage earner is at the mercy of national union leaders whose great power is a direct consequence of federal labor legislation. The businessman is hampered by a maze of government regulations, and often by direct government competition. The government takes six per cent of most payrolls in Social Security Taxes and thus compels millions of individuals to postpone until later years the enjoyment of wealth they might otherwise enjoy today. Increasingly, the federal government sets standards of education, health and safety.

How did it happen? How did our national government grow from a servant with sharply limited powers into a master with virtually unlimited power?

In part, we were swindled. There are occasions when we have elevated men and political parties to power that promised to restore limited government and then proceeded, after their election, to expand the activities of government. But let us be honest with ourselves. Broken promises are not the major causes of our trouble. *Kept* promises are. All too often we have put men in office who have suggested spending a little more on this, a little more on that, who have proposed a new welfare program, who have thought of another variety of "security." We have taken the bait, preferring to put off to another day the recapture of freedom and the restoration of our constitutional system. We have gone the way of many a democratic society that has lost its freedom by persuading itself that if "the people" rule, all is well.

The Frenchman, Alexis de Tocqueville, probably the most clairvoyant political observer of modern times, saw the danger when he visited this country in the 1830's. Even then he foresaw decay for a society that tended to put more emphasis on its democracy than on its republicanism. He predicted that America would produce, not tyrants but "guardians." And that the American people would "console themselves for being in tutelage by the reflection that they have chosen their own guardians. Every man allows himself to be put in lead-strings, because he sees that it is not a person nor a class of persons, but the people at large that hold the end of his chain."

Our tendency to concentrate power in the hands of a few men deeply concerns me. We can be conquered by bombs or by subversion; but we can also be conquered by neglect—by ignoring the Constitution and disregarding the principles of limited government. Our defenses against the accumulation of unlimited power in Washington are in poorer shape, I fear, than our defenses against the aggressive designs of Moscow. Like so many other nations before us, we may succumb through internal weakness rather than fall before a foreign foe.

I am convinced that most Americans now want to reverse the trend. I think that concern for our vanishing freedoms is genuine. I think that the people's uneasiness in the stifling omnipresence of government has turned into something approaching alarm. But bemoaning the evil will not drive it back, and accusing fingers will not shrink government.

The turn will come when we entrust the conduct of our affairs to men who understand that their first duty as public officials is to divest themselves of the power they have been given. It will come when Americans, in hundreds of communities throughout the nation, decide to put the man in office who is pledged to enforce the Constitution and restore the Republic. Who will proclaim in a campaign speech: "I have little interest in streamlining government or in making it more efficient, for I mean to reduce its size. I do not undertake to promote welfare, for I propose to extend freedom. My aim is not to pass laws, but to repeal them. It is not to inaugurate new programs, but to cancel old ones that do violence to the Constitution, or that have failed in their purpose, or that impose on the people an unwarranted financial burden. I will not attempt to discover whether legislation is 'needed' before I have first determined whether it is constitutionally permissible. And if I should later be attacked for neglecting my constituents' 'interests,' I shall reply that I was informed their main interest is liberty and that in that cause I am doing the very best I can."

FOR THE STUDENT

Rhetoric

1. *Notice the opening sentences of almost every paragraph in the second half of the essay. What generalizations can you make about Goldwater's style?*
2. *Study the transitions between paragraphs. Are they clear? Imaginative? Conventional? Mechanical?*

Discussion

1. *Goldwater shows a strong preference for the United States as a* republic *instead of a* democracy. *What distinction do you suppose he has in mind?*
2. *Goldwater endorses with approval Lord Acton's statement about power; Neumann classes the statement with "facile half-true generalizations." What evidence does either of them offer to support his opinion?*
3. *Of Neumann's nine classifications of attitudes toward power, does two or four seem to fit Goldwater better?*

Writing

1. *Thomas Jefferson argued that "every constitution and every law naturally expires" with each new generation, that the power of government belongs to the living, not the dead. How would Goldwater react to this view? Write a paper describing some of the consequences if it were employed.*
2. *Write an imaginary interview of Barry Goldwater by Irving Howe.*

8 Progress

Since the early nineteenth century, the term "progressive," at least in politics—and later in religion and education—has been associated with liberalism and the "Left." It served to identify those who quarreled with and would change the status quo in society. However, the term itself and the concept on which it was based (progress: change is inevitable and inevitably upward) became an assumed value of our culture. From this point of view, those who question the value—in whatever aspect—tend toward the "Left," while those who defend it as an absolute are the conservatives, the "Right."

The first selection in this section is by Carl Becker, an eminent American historian and writer on the philosophy of history. He analyzes the origin and development of the idea of progress and speculates about its present and future meanings. The Middle view is represented by W. R. Inge, onetime Dean of St. Paul's Cathedral in London. Diverging from Becker's position that progress is a mere fiction, Dean Inge sees no evidence that the world ever improves—individuals, perhaps, but society never. Will Durant, who has written voluminously in both philosophy and history, here defends the conservative view: "Step by step man has climbed from the savage to the scientist . . ." And, he asserts optimistically, this progress will continue into the future.

CARL BECKER

Progress

"Thought," says Pascal, "makes the greatness of man." The universe can destroy an individual by a mere breath; but even if the entire force of the universe were employed to destroy a single man, the man "would still be more noble than that which destroys him, since he is aware of his own death and of the advantage which the universe has over him: of all this the universe knows nothing." This awareness of himself and of the universe is no doubt what chiefly distinguishes man from all other forms of life. Man alone is conscious in the sense that he alone can stand outside of himself, as it were, and watch himself functioning for a brief span in the universe of which he is part. Man alone can coördinate memory of things past, perception of things present, anticipation of things to come, sufficiently so at least to know that he, like generations before him and after him, will live his brief span and will die. It is in virtue of this awareness, and somewhat in proportion to its intensity, that man alone asks the fundamental questions. Why and for what purpose this brief and precarious existence in a universe that endures? What is man's relation to the universe that is sometimes friendly, sometimes hostile, but in the end always fatal to him? How may he elude its hostility, win its favor, find compensations for the intolerable certainty of the death which it will inflict upon him? The answers which men have given to these questions are to be found in the various myths, religious doctrines, philosophical and ethical interpretations which they have accepted, and in those unconsciously held preconceptions which in every age so largely shape their thought and conduct. The modern idea of progress belongs in this category of answers to necessary but

Reprinted with permission of The Macmillan Company from Encyclopedia of the Social Sciences, *Vol. XII, (ed.) Seligman and Johnson. Copyright 1934, 1962 by The Macmillan Company.*

insoluble questions. Like the myths of primitive peoples and the religious and philosophical beliefs of more advanced societies, it springs from the nature of man as a conscious creature, who finds existence intolerable unless he can enlarge and enrich his otherwise futile activities by relating them to something more enduring and significant than himself.

Although grounded in the nature of man as a conscious creature, the idea of progress belongs historically to the European tradition, and its origin may be derived from two sources. One of these is the classical conception of history as an endless series of cycles; the other is the Hebraic-Christian doctrine of messianic intervention and salvation.

In Greek mythology the reign of Cronus was regarded as a golden age when men lived like gods free from toil and grief. The present appeared to be a period of degeneration, and improvement or progress could be conceived only in terms of regeneration—a return to the lost golden age. After the myth ceased to be believed, the Greeks continued to look back to the time of great lawgivers, such as Lycurgus and Solon, whose work they idealized, and forward to the time when other great lawgivers would appear and give them better laws again. "Until philosophers become kings . . . ," said Plato, "cities will not cease from ill." Yet however often restoration was accomplished by inspired lawgivers or philosopher-kings, fate and human frailty would again bring degeneration; so that, since "time is the enemy of man," most classical writers regarded human history as an endless series of cycles, a continual repetition of the familiar phenomena of recovery and degeneration. The rational mind, according to Marcus Aurelius, "stretches forth into the infinitude of Time, and comprehends the cyclical Regeneration of all things, and . . . discerns that our children will see nothing fresh, just as our fathers too never saw anything more than we" (*The Communings with Himself of Marcus Aurelius Antoninus,* tr. by C. R. Haines, Loeb Classical Library, London 1916, bk. XI, sect. I). To regenerate the Roman Empire was obviously less easy than to construct a constitution for a small city-state; and Marcus Aurelius, philosopher-king though he was, instead of giving new laws to society recommended that the individual cultivate resignation. The later centuries of the Roman Empire, when resignation became at once more necessary and more difficult, were therefore a suitable time for the hopeless classical doctrine of endless cycles to be replaced by the Hebraic-Christian doctrine of messianic intervention and salvation.

The Jews like the Greeks looked back to a golden age, but it was identified with the creation of the world and with the Garden of Eden, in which the first men lived in innocence. Like the Greeks the Jews regarded the present as a period of degeneration, but they attributed the "fall" to Adam's disobedience to God's commands. God was at once the omniscient creator of the world and the supreme lawgiver, so that regeneration was identified with the coming of a God-inspired king of the house of David. Multiplied reverses and the destruction of the Hebraic state gave to this doctrine a less political, a more mystical and transcendent character. The once actual but now vanished kingdom was replaced by an ideal Israel, symbolized as the "son of man"; and the idea of a God-inspired king was replaced by the idea of a messiah who would effect a catastrophic intervention in the affairs of men and pronounce a doomlike judgment on the world. The Christian myth was but an elaboration of these ideas. Jesus, son of man, son of God, was the Messiah. But the end was not yet. The death of Jesus was expiation for the sins of men, faith in Him the means of salvation. Jesus the man was dead, but Christ the Lord still lived and would come again; then the earthly city would be destroyed and all the faithful be gathered with God in the heavenly city, there to dwell in perfection forever.

The weakness of the classical version of degeneration and recovery was that it offered no ultimate hope; of the Jewish, that its promise was for the chosen people only. The strength of the Christian version was that, conceiving human history as a cosmic drama in which all men played their predestined part, it offered to all the hope of eternal life as a compensation for the frustrations of temporal existence: by transferring the golden age from the past to the future it substituted an optimistic for a disillusioned view of human destiny. It is easily to be understood that such a view won wide assent in the Roman Empire during the centuries (300–500) of declining prosperity and increasing oppression or that it served so well to make existence tolerable in the relatively anarchic, isolated and static society of western Europe from the dissolution of the Roman Empire to the Renaissance of classical learning. But it lost its hold on the imaginations of men as a result of profound changes in the outward conditions of life which occurred in western Europe from the fourteenth to the nineteenth century. Among these changes were the rise of ordered secular governments, the growth of towns and industry, the geographical discoveries and the extension of commerce which brought western Europe into direct contact with alien customs and ideas, and above all the rise of an educated middle class whose interests were hampered by a form of society in which both the power and the doctrines of the Christian church supported the autocracy of kings and the privileges of a landed aristocracy. It was in this time of revolt against ecclesiastical and secular authority that the Christian doctrine of salvation was gradually transformed into the modern idea of progress.

So long as Christian philosophy was little questioned, men could afford to ignore the factual experience of mankind since they were so well assured of its ultimate significance. But the declining influence of the church was accompanied by an increasing interest in the worldly activities of men in the past. Italian humanists turned to the study of classical writers; Protestant reformers appealed from current theologians to the beliefs and practices of the primitive church. Thus was born the modern historical approach to problems, and human life came increasingly to be regarded rather as a historical process than as a finished drama to be played out according to a divine plan. Seen in historical perspective, classical civilization emerged for the humanists as a resplendent epoch from which the middle period of ecclesiastical ascendancy was manifestly a degeneration. Until the seventeenth century secular thought and learning turned for inspiration to the past—to the golden ages of Pericles and Augustus; and classical writers were idealized as models to be imitated, to be equaled if possible but hardly to be surpassed. In all this there was nothing that could not be found in the Greek notion of history with its cycles of recovery and degeneration, and but for two general influences modern thought might have been no more than a return to the classical view of human destiny.

One of these influences was Christian philosophy itself. Although it was gradually discredited as an account of events historically verifiable, Christian philosophy had so thoroughly habituated men to the thought of an ultimate happy destiny that they could never be content with a pale imitation of Greek pessimism. The other influence was experimental science which, in proportion as it displaced the Christian notion of a utopian existence after death to be brought about by the miraculous intervention of God, opened up the engaging prospect of indefinite improvement in this life to be effected by the application of human reason to the mastery of the physical and social environment which determines men's lives for good or ill.

In the seventeenth century Galileo and Newton made possible a new attitude toward nature. Nature was now seen to be friendly to man since the universe behaved in a uniform way according to universal natural laws—a behavior capable of being observed and measured and subjected to the uses of men. God was still the supreme lawgiver, the author of the universe; but His will was revealed in the great book of nature which men were to study in order to interpret, and to interpret in order that their ideas and customs might attain an increasing perfection by being brought into greater harmony with the laws of nature and of nature's God. God's revelation to men was thus made not through an inspired book or a divinely established church but through His works, and man had been endowed with reason precisely that he might learn through the course of the centuries what that revelation was. It was therefore no longer so necessary to think of the golden age of Greece and Rome as unsurpassable. "Those whom we call the ancients were really those who lived in the youth of the world," said Pascal, and "as we have added the experience of the ages between us and them to what they knew, it is in ourselves that is to be found that antiquity which we venerate in others." In the ascription of antiquity to the race there is still the implication of degeneration; but if a continuously richer experience made the moderns wiser than the ancients, it was not difficult to hit upon the idea that future generations would, in virtue of the same advantages, surpass the moderns. "We have admired our ancestors less," said Chastellux, "but we have loved our contemporaries better, and have expected more of our descendants" (*De la félicité publique*, 2 vols., new ed. Paris 1822, vol. ii, p. 71). Thus in the eighteenth century the modern idea of progress was born. Under the pressure of social discontents the dream of perfection, that necessary compensation for the limitations of the present state, having long been identified with the golden age or the Garden of Eden or life eternal in the heavenly city of God, was at last projected into the temporal life of man on earth and identified with the desired and hoped for regeneration of society.

As formulated by the *philosophes* the doctrine of progress was but a modification, however important, of the Christian doctrine of redemption; what was new in it was faith in the goodness of man and the efficacy of conscious reason to create an earthly utopia. The French Revolution was the outward expression of this faith. In the nineteenth century the doctrine of progress still reigned and won even a wider popular support, but it was somewhat differently conceived. After the disillusionment occasioned by the revolution and the Napoleonic conquests the prevailing desire was for social stability and national independence. The rationalization of this desire was provided by the historians and jurists who formulated the notion of historical continuity and deprecated the attempt to transform institutions according to a rational plan. Change was considered necessary but was thought to be beneficial only when it issued spontaneously from national tradition; the concept of natural law was not abandoned, but it was regarded as implicit in historical evolution rather than as a conclusion from abstract reason. Law is not made by the legislator, said Savigny, any more than language is made by the grammarian. Ranke, who influenced three generations of historians, viewed progress as something to be discovered by tracing the history of each nation just as it had occurred and by noting the peculiar contribution which each nation at the appropriate moment had made to European civilization. Hegel formulated the point of view of early nineteenth century jurists and historians in his *Philosophie der Geschichte*. A reason of nature working over the heads of men, a transcendent *Vernunft* reconciling within its cloudy recesses innumerable and conflicting *Verstände,* progressively realized itself in the actual events of history.

After the middle of the century natural science invested the doctrine of progress with a more materialistic implication. Progress was still regarded as the result of a force external to man; but the force was to be found not above but inherent in the phenomenal world. This view found support in the Darwinian theory of struggle for existence and survival of the fittest and in Schopenhauer's doctrine of the will as an aspect of a universal blind force. Guided by these preconceptions, thinkers abandoned the effort to hasten progress by describing utopias and turned to the search for the inevitable law by which progress had been and would be achieved. Of the many efforts of this sort the most important were those of August Comte and Karl Marx. Comte looked upon history as the result of the instinctive effort of men to ameliorate their condition —an effort which could be observed to fall into three stages of culture, the theological, the metaphysical and the positive, or scientific. Marx, interpreting the historic process in terms of Hegel's famous dialectic, found the determining force in the economic class

conflict which, having substituted the nineteeth century capitalist
competitive society for the aristocratic landed society of the Middle
Ages and early modern times, would in turn replace the capitalist
competitive society of the nineteenth century by the proletarian
communist society of the future.

Of the many theories of progress formulated in the nineteenth
century the only one that had much influence on the thought of
common men was that of Marx. Yet the idea of progress, vaguely
conceived as a rapid improvement in general prosperity and happiness, became a living force. The chief reason for this was no doubt
the rapid changes in the outward conditions of life consequent
upon the technological revolution. The common man, before whose
eyes the marvels of science and invention were constantly displayed, noted the unprecedented increase in wealth, the growth of
cities, the new and improved methods of transportation and communication, the greater security from disease and death and all the
conveniences of domestic life unknown to previous generations,
and accepted the doctrine of progress without question: the world
was obviously better than it had been, obviously would be better
than it was. The precise objective toward which the world was
progressing remained, however, for the common man and for the
intellectual, somewhat vague.

Thus the nineteenth century doctrine of progress differed
somewhat from that of the eighteenth. The difference may be expressed, with some exaggeration in the contrast, by saying that
whereas the eighteenth century held that man can by taking thought
add a cubit to his stature, the nineteenth century held that a cubit
would be added to his stature whether he took thought or not.
This latter faith that the stars were carrying men on to better things
received a rude shock during the World War and subsequently;
and there may be noted two significant changes in the present
attitude toward the doctrine of progress. Certain thinkers, notably
Spengler, are returning to the Greek notion of cycles, now formulated in terms of the rise, flourishing and decline of "cultures."
Others are reverting to the eighteenth century idea that by delib-

erate purpose and the rational use of knowledge man can recon-
struct society according to a more just and intelligible design. To
this class belong those who have faith in communism, fascism and
the planned capitalist society.

The doctrine of progress is peculiarly suited to western society
in modern times; that is, a highly dynamic society capable of seeing its achievements against a long historical background. From
the practical and from the rational point of view there is no reason
to suppose that it will have a more enduring virtue than other
doctrines, which it has supplanted. If, as may well happen, the
possibilities of scientific discovery and of technological invention
should sometime be exhausted, the outward conditions of life
might become sufficiently stabilized so that the idea of progress
would cease to be relevant. Rationally considered, the idea of
progress is always at war with its premises. It rests upon the notion
of a universe in perpetual flux; yet the idea of progress has always
carried the implication of finality, for it seems to be meaningless
unless there is movement toward some ultimate objective. The
formal theories of progress are all vitiated by this radical inconsistency. In Hegel's scheme the objective was freedom, already
realized in the Prussian state. In Comte's theory the objective was
the final positive stage into which Europe had already entered.
Marx criticized Hegel for explaining history by a process which
would not explain the future, but he is himself open to the criticism
of having explained history in terms of a class conflict which would
end with the establishment of a classless society. It is easy to picture history as a process working toward an ultimate good if the
world is to come to an end when that good is attained; but if the
universe as presented by modern science is to be accepted—a universe in perpetual flux—then a law of history which at some de-
terminate time ceases to apply leaves much to be desired.

Thus the final good, absolute standards of value, are sought in
vain; there is merely a universe in which the ideas of things as well
as the things themselves arise out of temporary conditions and are
transformed with the modification of the conditions out of which

they arose. On this assumption we must dispense with the notion of finality, must suppose that the idea of progress and all of its special formulations are but temporary insights useful for the brief moment in which they flourish. "In escaping from the illusion of finality, is it legitimate to exempt that dogma itself? Must not it, too, submit to its own negation of finality? Will not that process of change for which Progress is the optimistic name, compel 'Progress' too to fall from the commanding position in which it is now, with apparent security, enthroned?" (Bury, J. B., *The Idea of Progress,* p. 352). The price we pay for escaping from the illusion of finality is the recognition that nothing, not even the belief that we have escaped that illusion, is likely to endure. All philosophies based upon the absolute and the unconditioned have their defects; but all philosophies based upon the universal relativity of things have their defects also, a minor one being that they must be prepared, at the appropriate moment, to commit hara-kiri in deference to the ceaseless change which they postulate.

Belief in progress as a fact depends upon the standards of value chosen for measuring it and upon the time perspective in which it is measured. If we look back a hundred years, it is obvious that there has been progress in the mastery of physical forces. If we look back two thousand years, it is uncertain whether there has been much if any progress in intelligence and the art of living. If we look back two hundred and fifty thousand years, it is apparent that there has been progress in all those aspects of life which civilized men regard as valuable. All these judgments are based on standards of value appreciable by the mind of civilized man. But if we take a still longer perspective and estimate the universe as a whole, as an omniscient intelligence indifferent to human values. might estimate it, in terms of cosmic energy, then progress and the very existence of man himself become negligible and meaningless. In such a perspective we should see the whole life of man on the earth as a mere momentary ripple on the surface of one of the minor planets in one of the minor stellar systems.

FOR THE STUDENT

Rhetoric

1. *Write a one-paragraph summary of this essay including only the* key *ideas.*
2. *Make a chronological list (from the Greeks to modern times) of the main contributors to the idea of progress.*
3. *What ideas of the opening paragraph are central to Becker's whole argument?*

Discussion

1. *An American electrical corporation advertises itself: "Progress is our most important product." Reread Becker's concluding paragraph and discuss what time perspective and standard of value the corporation would use to define* progress.
2. *Does Becker hold that progress is a mere fiction, like Santa Claus? Is it?*
3. *How many modern examples of progress can you think of which are not based on comfort, speed, or quantity?*

Writing

1. *Becker analyzes the* origin *and* historical development *of an abstract idea. In a short research paper, apply his method to some other abstract idea: for example, democracy, Christianity, university.*
2. *Scrutinize an appropriate number of TV commercials or magazine advertisements to find out how heavily they lean on "progress" and what criteria they assume to define it. Write a paper analyzing and generalizing upon your findings.*

DEAN W. R. INGE

The Idea of Progress

The racial life of the species to which we happen to belong is a brief episode even in the brief life of the planet. And what we call civilization or culture, though much older than we used to suppose, is a brief episode in the life of our race. For tens of thousands of years the changes in our habits must have been very slight, and chiefly those which were forced upon our rude ancestors by changes of climate. Then in certain districts man began, as Samuel Butler says, to wish to live beyond his income. This was the beginning of the vast series of inventions which have made our life so complex. And, we used to be told, the "law of all progress is the same, the evolution of the simple into the complex by successive differentiations." This is the gospel according to Herbert Spencer. As a universal law of nature, it is ludicrously untrue. Some species have survived by becoming more complex; others, like the whole tribe of parasites, by becoming more simple. On the whole, perhaps the parasites have had the best of it. The progressive species have in many cases flourished for a while and then paid the supreme penalty. The living dreadnoughts of the Saurian age have left us their bones, but no progeny. But the microbes, one of which had the honor of killing Alexander the Great at the age of thirty-two, and so changing the whole course of history, survive and flourish. The microbe illustrates the wisdom of the maxim, λάθε βιώσας.[1] It took thousands of years to find him out. Our own species, being rather poorly provided by nature for offense and defense, had to live by its wits, and so came to the top. It developed many new needs, and set itself many insoluble problems. Physiologists like Metchnikoff have shown how very ill-adapted our bodies are to the tasks which we

From Outspoken Essays, *by W. R. Inge (1922). Reprinted by permission of Longmans, Green & Co., Ltd.*

1. "Live obscurely."

[274]

impose upon them; and in spite of the Spencerian identification of complexity with progress, our surgeons try to simplify our structure by forcibly removing various organs which they assure us that we do not need. If we turn to history for a confirmation of the Spencerian doctrine, we find, on the contrary, that civilization is a disease which is almost invariably fatal, unless its course is checked in time. The Hindus and Chinese, after advancing to a certain point, were content to mark time; and they survive. But the Greeks and Romans are gone; and aristocracies everywhere die out. Do we not see today the complex organization of the ecclesiastic and college don succumbing before the simple squeezing and sucking apparatus of the profiteer and trade unionist? If so-called civilized nations show any protracted vitality, it is because they are only civilized at the top. Ancient civilizations were destroyed by imported barbarians; we breed our own.

It is also an unproved assumption that the domination of the planet by our own species is a desirable thing, which must give satisfaction to its Creator. We have devastated the loveliness of the world; we have exterminated several species more beautiful and less vicious than ourselves; we have enslaved the rest of the animal creation, and have treated our distant cousins in fur and feathers so badly that beyond doubt, if they were able to formulate a religion, they would depict the Devil in human form. If it is progress to turn the fields and woods of Essex into East and West Ham, we may be thankful that progress is a sporadic and transient phenomenon in history. It is a pity that our biologists, instead of singing paeans to Progress and thereby stultifying their own researches, have not preached us sermons on the sin of racial self-idolatry, a topic which really does arise out of their studies. *L'anthropolatrie, voila l'ennemi,* is the real ethical motto of biological science, and a valuable contribution to morals.

It was impossible that such shallow optimism as that of Herbert Spencer should not arouse protests from other scientific thinkers. Hartmann had already shown how a system of pessimism, resembling that of Schopenhauer, may be built upon the foundation of evolutionary science. And in this place we are not likely to forget the second Romanes Lecture, when Professor Huxley astonished his friends and opponents alike by throwing down the gauntlet in the face of nature, and bidding mankind to find salvation by accepting for itself the position which the early Christian writer Hippolytus gives as a definition of the Devil—"he who resists the cosmic process" (ὁ ἀντιτάττων τοῖς κοσμικοῖς). The revolt was not in reality so sudden as some of Huxley's hearers supposed. He had already realized that "so far from gradual progress forming any necessary part of the Darwinian creed, it appears to us that it is perfectly consistent with indefinite persistence in one state, or with a gradual retrogression. Suppose, e.g., a return of the glacial period or a spread of polar climatical conditions over the whole globe." The alliance between determinism and optimism was thus dissolved; and as time went on, Huxley began to see in the cosmic process something like a power of evil. The natural process, he told us in this place, has no tendency to bring about the good of mankind. Cosmic nature is no school of virtue, but the headquarters of the enemy of ethical nature. Nature is the realm of tiger rights; it has no morals and no ought-to-be; its only rights are brutal powers. Morality exists only in the "artificial" moral world: man is a glorious rebel, a Prometheus defying Zeus. This strange rebound into Manichaeism sounded like a blasphemy against all the gods whom the lecturer was believed to worship, and half-scandalized even the clerics in his audience. It was bound to raise the question whether this titanic revolt against the cosmic process has any chance of success. One recent thinker, who accepts Huxley's view that the nature of things is cruel and immoral, is willing to face the probability that we cannot resist it with any prospect of victory. Mr. Bertrand Russell, in his arresting essay, "A Free Man's Worship," shows us Prometheus again, but Prometheus chained to the rock and still hurling defiance against God. He proclaims the moral bankruptcy of naturalism, which he yet holds to be forced upon us:

That man is the product of causes which had no prevision of the end they were achieving; that his origin, his growth, his hopes and fears, his loves and his beliefs, are but the outcome of accidental collocations of atoms; that no fire, no heroism, no intensity of thought and feeling, can preserve an individual life beyond the grave; that all the labors of the ages, all the devotion, all the inspiration, all the noonday brightness of human genius, are destined to extinction in the vast death of the solar system, and that the whole temple of man's achievement must inevitably be buried beneath the debris of a universe in ruins—all these things, if not quite beyond dispute, are yet so nearly certain, that no philosophy which rejects them can hope to stand. Only within the scaffolding of these truths, only on the firm foundation of unyielding despair, can the soul's habitation henceforth be safely built.

Man belongs to "an alien and inhuman world," alone amid "hostile forces." What is man to do? The God who exists is evil; the God whom we can worship is the creation of our own conscience, and has no existence outside it. The "free man" will worship the latter; and, like John Stuart Mill, "to hell he will go."

If I wished to criticize this defiant pronouncement, which is not without a touch of bravado, I should say that so complete a separation of the real from the ideal is impossible, and that the choice which the writer offers us, of worshiping a Devil who exists or a God who does not, is no real choice, since we cannot worship either. But my object in quoting from this essay is to show how completely naturalism has severed its alliance with optimism and belief in progress. Professor Huxley and Mr. Russell have sung their palinode and smashed the old gods of their creed. No more proof is needed, I think, that the alleged law of progress has no scientific basis whatever.

But superstition has also invaded and vitiated our history, our political science, our philosophy, and our religion.

The historian is a natural snob; he sides with the gods against Cato, and approves the winning side. He lectures the vanquished for their willfulness and want of foresight, sometimes rather prematurely, as when Seeley, looking about for an example of perverse refusal to recognize facts, exclaims "Sedet, aeternumque sedebit unhappy Poland!" The nineteenth century historian was so loath to admit retrogession that he liked to fancy the river of progress flowing underground all through the Dark Ages, and endowed the German barbarians who overthrew Mediterranean civilization with all the manly virtues. If a nation, or a religion, or a school of art dies, the historian explains why it was not worthy to live.

In political science the corruption of the scientific spirit by the superstition of progress has been flagrant. It enables the disputant to overbear questions of right and wrong by confident prediction, a method which has the double advantage of being peculiarly irritating and incapable of refutation. On the theory of progress, what is "coming" must be right. Forms of government and modes of thought which for the time being are not in favor are assumed to have been permanently left behind. A student of history who believed in cyclical changes and long swings of the pendulum would take a very different and probably much sounder view of contemporary affairs. The votaries of progress mistake the flowing tide for the river of eternity, and when the tide turns they are likely to be left stranded like the corks and scraps of seaweed which mark the high-water line. This has already happened, though few realize it. The praises of liberty are mainly left to Conservatives, who couple it with property as something to be defended, and to conscientious objectors, who dissociate it from their country, which is not to be defended. Democracy—the magic ballot-box—has few worshipers any longer except in America, where men will still shout for about two hours—and indeed much longer—that she is "great." But our pundits will be slow to surrender the useful words "progressive" and "reactionary." The classification is, however, a little awkward. If a reactionary is anyone who will not float with the stream, and a progressive anyone who has the flowing tide with him, we must classify the Christian Fathers and the French Encyclopaedists as belonging to the same type, the progressive; while the Roman Stoics under the Empire and the Russian bureaucrats under Nicholas II will be placed together under the opposite title, as reactionaries. Or is the progressive not the supporter of the winning cause for the time being, but the man who thinks, with a distinguished head of a college who, as I remember, affirmed his principles in Convocation, that "any leap in the dark is better than standing still"; and is the reactionary the man whose constitutional timidity would deter him from performing this act of faith when caught by a mist on the Matterhorn? Machiavelli recognizes fixed types of human character, such as the cautious Fabius and the impetuous Julius II, and observes that these qualities lead sometimes to success and sometimes to failure. If a reactionary only means an adherent of political opinions which we happen to dislike, there is no reason why a bureaucrat should not call a republican a reactionary, as Maecenas may have applied the name to Brutus and Cassius. Such examples of evolution as that which turned the Roman Republic into a principate, and then into an empire of the Asiatic type, are inconvenient for those who say "It is coming," and think that they have vindicated the superiority of their own theories of government.

We have next to consider the influence of the superstition of progress on the philosophy of the last century. To attempt such a task in this place is a little rash, and to prove the charge in a few minutes would be impossible even for one much better equipped than I am. But something must be said. Hegel and Comte are often held to have been the chief advocates of the doctrine of progress among philosophers. Both of them give definitions of the word—a very necessary thing to do, and I have not yet attempted to do it. Hegel defines progress as spiritual freedom; Comte as true or positive social philosophy. The definitions are peculiar; and neither theory can be made to fit past history. . . . Hegel is perhaps more independent of facts; his predecessor Fichte professes to be entirely indifferent to them. "The philosopher," he says, "follows the *a priori* thread of the world plan which is clear to him without any history; and if he makes use of history, it is not to prove anything, since his theses are already proved independently of all history." Certainly, Hegel's dialectical process cannot easily be recognized in the course of European events; and, what is more fatal to the believers in a law of progress who appeal to him, he does not seem to have contemplated any further marked improvements upon the political system of Prussia in his own time, which he admired so much that his critics have accused him of teaching that the Absolute first attained full self-consciousness at Berlin in the nineteenth century. He undoubtedly believed that there has been progress in the past; but he does not, it appears, look forward to further changes; as a politician, at any rate, he gives us something like a closed system. Comte can only bring his famous "three stages" into history by arguing that the Catholic monotheism of the Middle Ages was an advance upon pagan antiquity. A Catholic might defend such a thesis with success; but for Comte the chief advantage seems to be that the change left the Olympians with only one neck, for Positive Philosophy to cut off. But Comte himself is what his system requires us to call a reactionary; he is back in the "theological stage"; he would like a theocracy, if he could have one without a God. The state is to be subordinate to the Positive Church, and he will allow "no unlimited freedom of thought." The connection of this philosophy with the doctrine of progress seems very slender. It is not so easy to answer the question in the case of Hegel, because his contentment with the Prussian government may be set down to idiosyncrasy or to prudence; but it is significant that some of his ablest disciples have discarded the belief. To say that "the world is as it ought to be" does not imply that it goes on getting better, though some would think it was not good if it was not getting better. It is hard to believe that a great thinker really supposed that the universe as a whole is progressing, a notion which Mr. Bradley has stigmatized as "nonsense, unmeaning or blasphemous." Mr. Bradley may perhaps be interpreting Hegel rightly when he says that for a philosopher "progress can never have any temporal sense," and explains that a perfect philosopher would see the whole world of appearance as a "progress," by which he seems to mean only a rearrangement in terms of ascending and descending value and reality. But it might be objected that to use "progress" in this sense is to lay a trap for the unwary. Mathematicians undoubtedly talk of progress, or rather of progression, without any implication of temporal sequence; but outside this science to speak of "progress without any temporal sense" is to use a phrase which some would call self-contradictory. Be that as it may, popularized Hegelianism has laid hold of the idea of a self-improving universe, of perpetual and universal progress, in a strictly temporal sense. The notion of an evolving and progressing cosmos, with a Creator who is either improving himself (though we do not put it quite so crudely) or who is gradually coming into his own, has taken strong hold of the popular imagination. The latter notion leads straight to ethical dualism of the Manichaean type. The theory of a single purpose in the universe seems to me untenable. Such a purpose, being infinite . . . could never be accomplished. The theory condemns both God and man to the doom of Tantalus. Mr. Bradley is quite right in finding this belief incompatible with Christianity.

It would not be possible, without transgressing the limits set for lecturers on this foundation, to show how the belief in a law of progress has prejudicially affected the religious beliefs of our time. I need only recall to you the discussions whether the perfect man could have lived in the first, and not in the nineteenth or twentieth century—although one would have thought that the ancient Greeks, to take one nation only, have produced many examples of hitherto unsurpassed genius; the secularization of religion by throwing its ideals into the near future—a new apocalyptism which is doing mischief enough in politics without the help of the clergy; and the unauthorized belief in future probation, which rests on the queer assumption that, if a man is given time enough, he must necessarily become perfect. In fact, the superstition which is the subject of this lecture has distorted Christianity almost beyond recognition. Only one great church, old in worldly wisdom, knows that human nature does not change, and acts on the knowledge. Accordingly, the papal syllabus of 1864 declares: "*Si quis dixerit:* Romanus pontifex potest ac debet cum progressu, cum liberalismo, et cum recenti civilitate sese reconciliare et componere, *anathema sit.*"[2]

Our optimists have not made it clear to themselves or others what they mean by progress, and we may suspect that the vagueness of the idea is one of its attractions. There has been no physical progress in our species for many thousands of years. The Cro-Magnon race, which lived perhaps twenty thousand years ago, was at least equal to any modern people in size and strength; the ancient Greeks were, I suppose, handsomer and better formed than we are; and some unprogressive races, such as the Zulus, Samoans, and Tahitians, are envied by Europeans for either strength or beauty. Although it seems not to be true that the sight and hearing of civilized people are inferior to those of savages, we have certainly lost our natural weapons, which from one point of view is a mark of degeneracy. Mentally, we are now told that the men of the Old Stone Age, ugly as most of them must have been, had as large brains as ours; and he would be a bold man who should claim that we are intellectually equal to the Athenians or superior to the Romans. The question of moral improvement is much more difficult. Until the Great War few would have disputed that civilized man had become much more humane, much more sensitive to the sufferings of others, and so more just, more self-controlled, and less brutal in his pleasures and in his resentments. The habitual honesty of the Western European might also have been contrasted with the rascality of inferior races in the past and present. It was often forgotten that, if progress means the improvement of human nature itself, the question to be asked is whether the modern civilized man behaves better in the same circumstances than his ancestor would have done. Absence of temptation may produce an appearance of improvement; but this is hardly what we mean by progress, and there is an old saying that the Devil has a clever trick of pretending to be dead. It seems to me very doubtful whether when we

2. "It shall be anathema for anyone to say that the head of the Roman Church either could or should reconcile himself with and make concessions to progress, liberalism, and recent political ideas." [Author's note]

are exposed to the same temptations we are more humane or more sympathetic or juster or less brutal than the ancients. Even before this war, the examples of the Congo and Putumayo, and American lynchings, proved that contact with barbarians reduces many white men to the moral condition of savages; and the outrages committed on the Chinese after the Boxer rebellion showed that even a civilized nation cannot rely on being decently treated by Europeans if its civilization is different from their own. During the Great War, even if some atrocities were magnified with the amiable object of rousing a good-natured people to violent hatred, it was the well-considered opinion of Lord Bryce's commission that no such cruelties had been committed for three hundred years as those which the Germans practiced in Belgium and France. It was startling to observe how easily the blood lust was excited in young men straight from the fields, the factory, and the counter, many of whom had never before killed anything larger than a wasp, and that in self-defense. As for the Turks, we must go back to Jenghiz Khan to find any parallel to their massacres in Armenia; and the Russian terrorists have reintroduced torture into Europe, with the help of Chinese experts in the art. With these examples before our eyes, it is difficult to feel any confidence that either the lapse of time or civilization has made the *bête humaine* less ferocious. On biological grounds there is no reason to expect it. No selection in favor of superior types is now going on; on the contrary, civilization tends now, as always, to an *Ausrottung der Besten*—a weeding-out of the best; and the new practice of subsidizing the unsuccessful by taxes extorted from the industrious is cacogenics erected into a principle. The best hope of stopping this progressive degeneration is in the science of eugenics. But this science is still too tentative to be made the basis of legislation, and we are not yet agreed what we should breed for. The two ideals, that of the perfect man and that of the perfectly organized state, would lead to very different principles of selection. Do we want a nation of beautiful and moderately efficient Greek gods, or do we want human mastiffs for policemen, human greyhounds for postmen, and so on? However, the opposition which eugenics has now to face is based on less respectable grounds, such as pure hedonism ("Would the superman be any happier?"); indifference to the future welfare of the race ("Posterity has done nothing for me; why should I do anything for posterity?"); and, in politics, the reflection that the unborn have no votes.

We have, then, been driven to the conclusion that neither science nor history gives us any warrant for believing that humanity has advanced, except by accumulating knowledge and experience and the instruments of living. The value of these accumulations is not beyond dispute. Attacks upon civilization have been frequent, from Crates, Pherecrates, Antisthenes, and Lucretius in antiquity to Rousseau, Walt Whitman, Thoreau, Ruskin, Morris, and Edward Carpenter in modern times. I cannot myself agree with these extremists. I believe that the accumulated experience of mankind, and his wonderful discoveries, are of great value. I only point out that they do not constitute real progress in human nature itself, and that in the absence of any real progress these gains are external, precarious, and liable to be turned to our destruction, as new discoveries in chemistry may easily be.

But it is possible to approach the whole question of progress from another side, and from this side the results will not be quite the same, and may be more encouraging. We have said that there can be no progress in the macrocosm, and no single purpose in a universe which has neither beginning nor end in time. But there may be an infinite number of finite purposes, some much greater and others much smaller than the span of an individual life; and within each of these some divine thought may be working itself out, bringing some life or series of lives, some nation or race or species, to that perfection which is natural to it—what the Greeks called its "nature." The Greeks saw no contradiction between this belief and the theory of cosmic cycles, and I do not think that there is any contradiction. It may be that there is an immanent teleology which is shaping the life of the human race toward some completed development which has not yet been reached. To advocate such a theory seems like going back from Darwin to Lamarck; but "vitalism," if it be a heresy, is a very vigorous and obstinate one; we can hardly dismiss it as unscientific. The possibility that such a development is going on is not disproved by the slowness of the change within the historical period. Progress in the recent millennia seems to us to have been external, precarious, and disappointing. But let this last adjective give us pause. By what standard do we pronounce it disappointing, and who gave us this standard? This disappointment has been a constant phenomenon, with a very few exceptions. What does it mean? Have those who reject the law of progress taken it into account? The philosophy of naturalism always makes the mistake of leaving human nature out. The climbing instinct of humanity, and our discontent with things as they are, are facts which have to be accounted for, no less than the stable instincts of nearly all other species. We all desire to make progress, and our ambitions are not limited to our own lives or our lifetimes. It is part of our nature to aspire and hope; even on biological grounds this instinct must be assumed to serve some function. The first Christian poet, Prudentius, quite in the spirit of Robert Browning, names hope as the distinguishing characteristic of mankind.

Nonne hominum et pecudum distantia separat una?
quod bona quadrupedum ante oculos sita sunt, ego contra spero.[3]

We must consider seriously what this instinct of hope means and implies in the scheme of things.

It is of course possible to dismiss it as a fraud. Perhaps this was the view most commonly held in antiquity. Hope was regarded as a gift of dubious value, an illusion which helps us to endure life, and a potent spur to action; but in the last resort an *ignis fatuus*. A Greek could write for his tombstone:

I've entered port. Fortune and Hope, adieu!
Make game of others, for I've done with you.

3. "Does not the distinction between man and beast lie in one fact alone? The beast seeks advantages in what is before his eyes, while I rely upon hope."

And Lord Brougham chose this epigram to adorn his villa at Cannes. So for Schopenhauer hope is the bait by which Nature gets her hook in our nose, and induces us to serve her purposes, which are not our own. This is pessimism, which, like optimism, is a mood, not a philosophy. Neither of them needs refutation, except for the adherent of the opposite mood; and these will never convince each other, for the same arguments are fatal to both. If our desires are clearly contrary to the nature of things, of which we are a part, it is our wisdom and our duty to correct our ambitions, and, like the Bostonian Margaret Fuller, to decide to "accept the universe." "Gad! she'd better," was Carlyle's comment on this declaration. The true inference from nature's law of vicarious sacrifice is not that life is a fraud, but that selfishness is unnatural. The pessimist cannot condemn the world except by a standard which he finds somewhere, if only in his own heart; in passing sentence upon it he affirms an optimism which he will not surrender to any appearances.

The ancients were not pessimists; but they distrusted hope. I will not follow those who say that they succumbed to the barbarians because they looked back instead of forward; I do not think it is true. If the Greeks and Romans had studied chemistry and metallurgy instead of art, rhetoric, and law, they might have discovered gunpowder and poison gas and kept the Germans north of the Alps. But St. Paul's deliberate verdict on pagan society, that it "had no hope," cannot be lightly set aside. No other religion, before Christianity, ever erected hope into a moral virtue. "We are saved by hope" was a new doctrine when it was pronounced. The later Neoplatonists borrowed St. Paul's triad, Faith, Hope, and Love, adding Truth as a fourth. Hopefulness may have been partly a legacy from Judaism; but it was much more a part of the intense spiritual vitality which was disseminated by the new faith. In an isolated but extremely interesting passage St. Paul extends his hope of "redemption into the glorious liberty of the children of God" to the "whole creation" generally. In the absence of any explanation or parallel passages it is difficult to say what vision of cosmic de-

liverance was in his mind. Students of early Christian thought must
be struck by the vigor of hope in the minds of men, combined with
great fluidity in the forms or molds into which it ran. After much
fluctuation, it tended to harden as belief in a supramundane future,
a compromise between Jewish and Platonic eschatology, since the
Jews set their hopes on a terrestrial future, the Platonists on a
supramundane present. Christian philosophers still inclined to the
Platonic faith, while popular belief retained the apocalyptic Jewish
ideas under the form of millenarianism. Religion has oscillated between these two types of belief ever since, and both have suffered
considerably by being vulgarized. In times of disorder and deca-
dence, the Platonic ideal world, materialized into a supra-terrestrial
physics and geography, has tended to prevail: in times of crass
prosperity and intellectual confidence the Jewish dream of a kingdom of the saints on earth has been coarsened into promises of
"a good time coming." At the time when we were inditing the
paeans to Progress which I quoted near the beginning of my lecture, we were evolving a Deuteronomic religion for ourselves even
more flattering than the combination of determinism with optimism which science was offering at the same period. We almost
persuaded ourselves that the words "the meek-spirited shall possess the earth" were a prophecy of the expansion of England.

It is easy to criticize the forms which hope has assumed. But
the hope which has generated them is a solid fact, and we have to
recognize its indomitable tenacity and power of taking new shapes.
The belief in a law of progress, which I have criticized so unmerci-
fully, is one of these forms; and if I am not mistaken, it is nearly
worn out. Disraeli in his detached way said, "The European talks
of progress because by the aid of a few scientific discoveries he has
established a society which has mistaken comfort for civilization."
It would not be easy to sum up better the achievements of the
nineteenth century, which will be always remembered as the century of accumulation and expansion. It was one of the great ages
of the world; and its greatness was bound up with that very idea
of progress which, in the crude forms which it usually assumed, we

have seen to be an illusion. It was a strenuous, not a self-indulgent age. The profits of industry were not squandered, but turned into new capital, providing new markets and employment for more labor. The nation, as an aggregate, increased in wealth, numbers, and power every day; and public opinion approved this increase, and the sacrifices which it involved. It was a great century; there were giants in the earth in those days; I have no patience with the pygmies who gird at them. But, as its greatest and most representative poet said: "God fulfills himself in many ways, Lest one good custom should corrupt the world." The mold in which the Victorian age cast its hope is broken. There is no law of progress; and the gains of that age now seem to some of us to have been purchased too high, or even to be themselves of doubtful value. In Clough's fine poem, beginning "Hope evermore and believe, O man," a poem in which the ethics of Puritanism find their perfect expression, the poet exhorts us:

> Go! say not in thine heart, And what then, were it accomplished,
> Were the wild impulse allayed, what were the use and the good?

But this question, which the blind Puritan asceticism resolutely thrust on one side, has begun to press for an answer. It had begun to press for an answer before the great cataclysm, which shattered the material symbols of the cult which for a century and a half had absorbed the chief energies of mankind. Whether our widespread discontent is mainly caused, as I sometimes think, by the unnatural conditions of life in large towns, or by the decay of the ideal itself, it is not easy to say. In any case, the gods of Queen Victoria's reign are no longer worshiped. And I believe that the dissatisfaction with things as they are is caused not only by the failure of nineteenth century civilization, but partly also by its success. We no longer wish to progress on those lines if we could. Our apocalyptic dream is vanishing into thin air. It may be that the industrial revolution which began in the reign of George III has produced most of its fruits, and has had its day. We may have to look forward to such a change as is imagined by Anatole France at the end of his *Isle of the Penguins,* when, after an orgy of revolution and destruction, we shall slide back into the quiet rural life of the early modern period. If so, the authors of the revolution will have cut their own throats, for there can be no great manufacturing towns in such a society. The race will have tried a great experiment, and will have rejected it as unsatisfying. We shall have added something to our experience. Fontenelle exclaimed, "How many foolish things we should say now, if the ancients had not said them all before us!" Fools are not so much afraid of plagiarism as this Frenchman supposed; but it is true that "Eventu rerum stolidi didicere magistro."[4]

There is much to support the belief that there is a struggle for existence among ideas, and that those tend to prevail which correspond with the changing needs of humanity. It does not necessarily follow that the ideas which prevail are better morally, or even truer to the law of nature, than those which fail. Life is so chaotic, and development so sporadic and one-sided, that a brief and brilliant success may carry with it the seeds of its own early ruin. The great triumphs of humanity have not come all at once. Architecture reached its climax in an age otherwise barbarous; Roman law was perfected in a dismal age of decline; and the nineteenth century, with its marvels of applied science, has produced the ugliest of all civilizations. There have been notable flowering times of the spirit of man—Ages of Pericles, Augustan Ages, Renaissances. The laws which determine these efflorescences are unknown. They may depend on undistinguished periods when force is being stored up. So in individual greatness, the wind bloweth where it listeth. Some of our greatest may have died unknown, "carent quia vate sacro."[5] Emerson indeed tells us that "One accent of the Holy Ghost The careless world has never lost." But I should like to know how Emerson obtained this information. The world has not always been "careless" about its inspired prophets; it has often, as Faust remarks, burned or crucified them,

4. Freely translated, "The stupid learn from no master but experience."
5. "Lacking anyone to herald their fame."

before they have delivered all their message. The activities of
the race spirit have been quite unaccountable. It has stumbled
along blindly, falling into every possible pitfall.

The laws of nature neither promise progress nor forbid it. We
could do much to determine our own future; but there has been
no consistency about our aspirations, and we have frequently followed false lights, and been disillusioned as much by success as by
failure. The well-known law that all institutions carry with them
the seeds of their own dissolution is not so much an illustration of
the law of cyclical revolution, as a proof that we have been carried
to and fro by every wind of doctrine. What we need is a fixed and
absolute standard of values, that we may know what we want to
get and whither we want to go. It is no answer to say that all
values are relative and ought to change. Some values are not relative but absolute. Spiritual progress must be within the sphere of a
reality which is not itself progressing, or for which, in Milton's
grand words, "progresses the dateless and irrevoluble circle of its
own perfection, joining inseparable hands with joy and bliss in
over-measure forever." Assuredly there must be advance in our
apprehension of the ideal, which can never be fully realized because it belongs to the eternal world. We count not ourselves to
have apprehended in aspiration any more than in practice. As
Nicholas of Cusa says: "To be able to know ever more and more
without end, this is our likeness to the eternal Wisdom. Man
always desires to know better what he knows, and to love more
what he loves; and the whole world is not sufficient for him, because it does not satisfy his craving for knowledge." But since our
object is to enter within the realm of unchanging perfection, finite
and relative progress cannot be our ultimate aim, and such progress,
like everything else most worth having, must not be aimed at too
directly. Our ultimate aim is to live in the knowledge and enjoyment of the absolute values, Truth, Goodness, and Beauty. If
the Platonists are right, we shall shape our surroundings more
effectively by this kind of idealism than by adopting the creed and
the methods of secularism. I have suggested that our disappoint-

ments have been very largely due to the unworthiness of our ideals, and to the confused manner in which we have set them before our minds. The best men and women do not seem to be subject to this confusion. So far as they can make their environment, it is a society immensely in advance of anything which has been realized among mankind generally.

If any social amelioration is to be hoped for, its main characteristic will probably be simplification rather than further complexity. This, however, is not a question which can be handled at the end of a lecture.

Plato says of his ideal state that it does not much matter whether it is ever realized on earth or not. The type is laid up in Heaven, and approximations to it will be made from time to time, since all living creatures are drawn upward toward the source of their being. It does not matter very much, if he was right in believing—as we too believe—in human immortality. And yet it does matter; for unless our communing with the eternal Ideas endows us with some creative virtue, some power which makes itself felt upon our immediate environment, it cannot be that we have made those Ideas in any sense our own. There is no alchemy by which we may get golden conduct out of leaden instincts—so Herbert Spencer told us very truly; but if our ideals are of gold, there is an alchemy which will transmute our external activities, so that our contributions to the spiritual temple may be no longer "wood, hay, and stubble," to be destroyed in the next conflagration, but precious and durable material.

For individuals, then, the path of progress is always open; but as Hesiod told us long before the Sermon on the Mount, it is a narrow path, steep and difficult, especially at first. There will never be a crowd gathered round this gate; "few there be that find it." For this reason, we must cut down our hopes for our nation, for Europe, and for humanity at large, to a very modest and humble aspiration. We have no millennium to look forward to; but neither need we fear any protracted or widespread retrogression. There will be new types of achievement which will enrich the experience

of the race; and from time to time, in the long vista which science
seems to promise us, there will be new flowering-times of genius
and virtue, not less glorious than the Age of Sophocles or the Age
of Shakespeare. They will not merely repeat the triumphs of the
past, but will add new varieties to the achievements of the human
mind.

Whether the human type itself is capable of further physical,
intellectual, or moral improvement, we do not know. It is safe to
predict that we shall go on hoping, though our recent hopes have
ended in disappointment. Our lower ambitions partly succeed and
partly fail, and never wholly satisfy us; of our more worthy visions
for our race we may perhaps cherish the faith that no pure hope
can ever wither, except that a purer may grow out of its roots.

FOR THE STUDENT

Rhetoric

1. *This essay falls into two clearly defined parts with a clear
   transition between them. Make a sentence outline.*
2. *There are many learned allusions (references to authors,
   historical events, and the like) in this essay. Ask your instructor to explain them.*
3. *See how specific you can be in describing the audience for
   whom this essay was intended.*

Discussion

1. *Dean Inge refers to "pessimism, which, like optimism, is a
   mood, not a philosophy." Which mood best fits him?
   Which fits some of the other authors he cites?*
2. *How successful a clergyman would American congrega-
   tions regard Dean Inge?*

3. *In his concluding paragraphs Inge refers to "golden" and "leaden" concepts. Give examples of each from the text and from your own wisdom.*

Writing

1. *Write a short comparison of the views of Inge and Becker on* progress.
2. *Write a three-page dialogue between a pessimist and an optimist.*

WILL DURANT

Is Progress a Delusion?

Let us try to see the problem of progress in a total view. It is unnecessary to refute the pessimist; it is only necessary to enclose his truth, if we can, in ours. When we look at history in the large we see it as a graph of rising and falling states—nations and cultures disappearing as on some gigantic film. But in that irregular movement of countries and that chaos of men, certain great moments stand out as the peaks and essence of human history, certain advances which, once made, were never lost. Step by step man has climbed from the savage to the scientist; and these are the stages of his growth.

First, *speech*. Think of it not as a sudden achievement, nor as a gift from the gods, but as the slow development of articulate expression, through centuries of effort, from the mate-calls of animals to the lyric flights of poetry. Without words, or common nouns, that might give to particular images the ability to represent a class, generalization would have stopped in its beginnings, and reason would have stayed where we find it in the brute. Without words, philosophy and poetry, history and prose, would have been impossible, and thought could never have reached the subtlety of Einstein or Anatole France. Without words man could not have become man, nor woman woman.

Second, *fire*. For fire made man independent of climate, gave him a greater compass on the earth, tempered his tools to hardness and durability, and offered him as food a thousand things inedible before. Not least of all it made him master of the night, and shed an animating brilliance over the hours of evening and dawn. Picture the dark before man conquered it; even now the terrors of that primitive abyss survive in our traditions and perhaps in our blood. Once every twilight was a tragedy, and man crept into his cave at sunset trembling with fear. Now we do not creep into our caves until sunrise; and though it is folly to miss the sun, how good it is to be liberated from our ancient fears! This overspreading of the night with a billion man-made stars has brightened the human spirit, and made for a vivacious jollity in modern life. We shall never be grateful enough for light.

Third, *the conquest of the animals*. Our memories are too forgetful, and our imagination too unimaginative, to let us realize the boon we have in our security from the larger and sub-human beasts of prey. Animals are now our playthings and our helpless food; but there was a time when man was hunted as well as hunter, when every step from cave or hut was an adventure, and the possession of the earth was still at stake. This war to make the planet human was surely the most vital in human history; by its side all other wars were but family quarrels, achieving nothing. That struggle between strength of body and power of mind was waged through long and unrecorded years; and when at last it was won, the fruit of man's triumph—his safety on the earth— was transmitted across a thousand generations, with a hundred other gifts from the past, to be part of our heritage at birth. What are all our temporary retrogressions against the background of such a conflict and such a victory?

Fourth, *agriculture*. Civilization was impossible in the hunting stage; it called for a permanent habitat, a settled way of life. It came with the home and the school; and these could not be till the products of the field replaced the animals of the forest or the herd as the food of man. The hunter found his quarry with increasing difficulty, while the woman whom he left at home tended an ever more fruitful soil. This patient husbandry by the wife threatened to make her independent of the male; and for his own lordship's sake he forced himself at last to the prose of tillage. No doubt it took centuries to make this greatest of all transitions in human history; but when at last it was made, civilization began.

Meredith said that women will be the last creature to be civilized by man. He was as wrong as it is possible to be in the limits of one sentence. For civilization came through two things chiefly: the home, which developed those social dispositions that form the psychological cement of society; and agriculture, which took man from his wandering life as hunter, herder and killer, and settled him long enough in one place to let him build homes, schools, churches, colleges, universities, civilization. But it was woman who gave man agriculture and the home; she domesticated man as she domesticated the sheep and the pig. Man is woman's last domestic animal; and perhaps he is the last creature that will be civilized by woman. The task is just begun: one look at our menus reveals us as still in the hunting stage.

Fifth, *social organization.* Here are two men disputing: one knocks the other down, kills him, and then concludes that he who is alive must have been right, and that he who is dead must have been wrong—a mode of demonstration still accepted in international disputes. Here are two other men disputing: one says to the other, "Let us not fight—we may both be killed; let us take our difference to some elder of the tribe, and submit to his decision." It was a crucial moment in human history! For if the answer was No, barbarism continued; if it was Yes, civilization planted another root in the memory of man: the replacement of chaos with order, of brutality with judgment, of violence with law. Here, too, is a gift unfelt, because we are born within the charmed circle of its protection, and never know its value till we wander into the disordered or solitary regions of the earth. God knows that our congresses and our parliaments are dubious inventions, the distilled mediocrity of the land; but despite them we manage to enjoy a security of life and property which we shall appreciate more warmly when civil war or revolution reduces us to primitive conditions. Compare the safety of travel today with the robber-infested highways of medieval Europe. Never before in history was there such order and liberty as exist in England today, —and may some day exist in America, when a way is found of opening municipal office to capable and honorable men. However, we must not excite ourselves too much about political corruption or democratic mismanagement; politics is not life, but only a graft upon life; under its vulgar melodrama the traditional order of society quietly persists, in the family, in the school, in the thousand devious influences that change our native lawlessness into some measure of cooperation and goodwill. Without consciousness of it, we partake in a luxurious patrimony of social order built up for us by a hundred generations of trial and error, accumulated knowledge, and transmitted wealth.

Sixth, *morality*. Here we touch the very heart of our problem —are men morally better than they were? So far as the intelligence is an element in morals, we have improved: the average of intelligence is higher, and there has been a great increase in the number of what we may vaguely call developed minds. So far as character is concerned, we have probably retrogressed; subtlety of thought has grown at the expense of stability of soul; in the presence of our fathers we intellectuals feel uncomfortably that though we surpass them in the number of ideas that we have crowded into our heads, and though we have liberated ourselves from delightful superstitions which still bring them aid and comfort, we are inferior to them in uncomplaining courage, fidelity to our tasks and purposes, and simple strength of personality.

But if morality implies the virtues exalted in the code of Christ, we have made some halting progress despite our mines and slums, our democratic corruption, and our urban addiction to lechery. We are a slightly gentler species than we were: capable of greater kindness, and of generosity even to alien or recently hostile peoples whom we have never seen. In one year (1928) the contributions of our country to private charity and philanthropy exceeded two billions of dollars—one half of all the money circulating in America. We still kill murderers if, as occasionally happens, we catch them and convict them; but we are a little uneasy about this ancient retributive justice of a life for a life, and the number of crimes for which we mete out the ultimate punishment has rapidly decreased. Two hundred years ago, in Merrie England, men might be hanged by law for stealing a shilling; and people are still severely punished if they do not steal a great deal. One hundred and forty years ago miners were hereditary serfs in Scotland, criminals were legally and publicly tortured to death in France, debtors were imprisoned for life in England, and respectable people raided the African coast for slaves. Fifty years ago our jails were dens of filth and horror, colleges for the graduation of minor criminals into major criminals; now our prisons are vacation resorts for tired murderers. We still exploit the lower strata of our working classes, but we soothe our consciences with "welfare work." Eugenics struggles to balance with artificial selection the interference of human kindliness and benevolence with that merciless elimination of the weak and the infirm which was once the mainspring of natural selection.

We think there is more violence in the world than before, but in truth there are only more newspapers; vast and powerful organizations scour the planet for crimes and scandals that will console their readers for stenography and monogamy; and all the villainy and politics of five continents are gathered upon one page for the encouragement of our breakfasts. We conclude that half the world is killing the other half, and that a large proportion of the remainder are committing suicide. But in the streets, in our homes, in public assemblies, in a thousand vehicles of transportation, we are astonished to find no murderers and no suicides, but rather a blunt democratic courtesy, and an unpretentious chivalry a hundred times more real than when men mouthed chivalric phrases, enslaved their women, and ensured the fidelity of their wives with irons while they fought for Christ in the Holy Land.

Our prevailing mode of marriage, chaotic and deliquescent as it is, represents a pleasant refinement on marriage by capture or purchase, and *le droit de seigneur*. There is less brutality between men and women, between parents and children, between teachers and pupils, than in any recorded generation of the past. The emancipation of woman, and her ascendancy over man, indicate an unprecedented gentility in the once murderous male. Love, which was unknown to primitive men, or was only a hunger of the flesh, has flowered into a magnificent garden of song and sentiment, in which the passion of a man for a maid, though vigorously rooted in physical need, rises like incense into the realm of living poetry. And youth, whose sins so disturb its tired elders, atones for its little vices with such intellectual eagerness and moral courage as may be invaluable when education resolves at last to come out into the open and cleanse our public life.

Seventh, *tools*. In the face of the romantics, the machine-wreckers of the intelligentsia, the pleaders for a return to the primitive (dirt, chores, snakes, cobwebs, bugs), we sing the song of the tools, the engines, the machines, that have enslaved and are liberating man. We need not be ashamed of our prosperity: it is good that comforts and opportunities once confined to barons and earls have been made by enterprise the prerogatives of all; it was necessary to spread leisure—even though at first misused—before a wide culture could come. These multiplying inventions are the new organs with which we control our environment; we do not need to grow them on our bodies, as animals must; we make them and use them, and lay them aside till we need them again. We grow gigantic arms that build in a month the pyramids that once consumed a million men; we make for ourselves great eyes that search out the invisible stars of the sky, and little eyes that peer into the invisible cells of life; we speak, if we wish, with quiet voices that reach across continents and seas; we move over the land and the air with the freedom of timeless gods. Granted that mere speed is worthless: it is as a symbol of human courage and persistent will that the airplane has its highest meaning for us; long chained, like Prometheus, to the earth, we have freed ourselves at last, and now we may look the eagle in the face.

No, these tools will not conquer us. Our present defeat by the machinery around us is a transient thing, a halt in our visible progress to a slaveless world. The menial labor that degraded both master and man is lifted from human shoulders and harnessed to the tireless muscles of iron and steel; soon every waterfall and every wind will pour its beneficent energy into factories and homes, and man will be freed for the tasks of the mind. It is not revolution but invention that will liberate the slave.

Eighth, *science*. In a large degree Buckle was right: we progress only in knowledge, and these other gifts are rooted in the slow enlightenment of the mind. Here in the untitled nobility of research, and the silent battles of the laboratory, is a story fit to balance the chicanery of politics and the futile barbarism of war. Here man is at his best, and through darkness and persecution mounts steadily towards the light. Behold him standing on a little planet, measuring, weighing, analyzing constellations that he cannot see; predicting the vicissitudes of earth and sun and moon; and witnessing the birth and death of worlds. Or here is a seemingly unpractical mathematician tracking new formulas through laborious labyrinths, clearing the way for an endless chain of inventions that will multiply the power of his race. Here is a bridge: a hundred thousand tons of iron suspended from four ropes of steel flung bravely from shore to shore, and bearing the passage of countless men; this is poetry as eloquent as Shakespeare ever wrote. Or consider this city-like building that mounts boldly into the sky, guarded against every strain by the courage of our calculations, and shining like diamond-studded granite in the night. Here in physics are new dimensions, new elements, new atoms, and new powers. Here in the rocks is the autobiography of life. Here in the laboratories biology prepares to transform the organic world as physics transformed matter. Everywhere you come upon them studying, these unpretentious, unrewarded men; you hardly understand where their devotion finds its source and nourishment; they will die before the trees they plant will bear fruit for mankind. But they go on.

Yes, it is true that this victory of man over matter has not yet been matched with any kindred victory of man over himself. The argument for progress falters here again. Psychology has hardly begun to comprehend, much less to control, human conduct and

desire; it is mingled with mysticism and metaphysics, with psychoanalysis, behaviorism, glandular mythology, and other diseases of
adolescence. Careful and modified statements are made only by
psychologists of whom no one ever hears; in our country the democratic passion for extreme statements turns every science into a
fad. But psychology will outlive these ills and storms; it will be
matured, like older sciences, by the responsibilities which it undertakes. If another Bacon should come to map out its territory,
clarify the proper methods and objectives of its attack, and point
out the "fruits and powers" to be won,—which of us, knowing the
surprises of history and the pertinacity of men, would dare set
limits to the achievements that may come from our growing knowledge of the mind? Already in our day man is turning round from
his remade environment, and beginning to remake himself.

Ninth, *education*. More and more completely we pass on to
the next generation the gathered experience of the past. It is almost
a contemporary innovation, this tremendous expenditure of wealth
and labor in the equipment of schools and the provision of instruction for all; perhaps it is the most significant feature of our time.
Once colleges were luxuries, designed for the male half of the
leisure class; today universities are so numerous that he who runs
may become a Ph.D. We have not excelled the selected geniuses of
antiquity, but we have raised the level and average of human
knowledge far beyond any age in history. Think now not of Plato
and Aristotle, but of the stupid, bigoted and brutal Athenian Assembly, of the unfranchised mob and its Orphic rites, of the se-
cluded and enslaved women who could acquire education only by
becoming courtesans.

None but a child would complain that the world has not yet
been totally remade by these spreading schools, these teeming
bisexual universities; in the perspective of history the great experiment of education is just begun. It has not had time to prove itself;
it cannot in a generation undo the ignorance and superstition of
ten thousand years; indeed, there is no telling but the high birth
rate of ignorance, and the determination of dogma by plebiscite,

may triumph over education in the end; this step in progress is not one of which we may yet say that it is a permanent achievement of mankind. But already beneficent results appear. Why is it that tolerance and freedom of the mind flourish more easily in the northern states than in the South, if not because the South has not yet won wealth enough to build sufficient schools? Who knows how much of our preference for mediocrity in office, and narrowness in leadership, is the result of a generation recruited from regions too oppressed with economic need and political exploitation to spare time for the ploughing and sowing of the mind? What will the full fruitage of education be when every one of us is schooled till twenty, and finds equal access to the intellectual treasures of the race? Consider again the instinct of parental love, the profound impulse of every normal parent to raise his children beyond himself: here is the biological leverage of human progress, a force more to be trusted than any legislation or any moral exhortation, because it is rooted in the very nature of man. Adolescence lengthens: we begin more helplessly, and we grow more completely towards that higher man who struggles to be born out of our darkened souls. We are the raw material of civilization.

We dislike education, because it was not presented to us in our youth for what it is. Consider it not as the painful accumulation of facts and dates, but as an ennobling intimacy with great men. Consider it not as the preparation of the individual to "make a living," but as the development of every potential capacity in him for the comprehension, control, and *appreciation* of his world. Above all, consider it, in its fullest definition, as the technique of transmitting as completely as possible, to as many as possible, that technological, intellectual, moral, and artistic heritage through which the race forms the growing individual and makes him human. Education is the reason why we behave like human beings. We are hardly born human; we are born ridiculous and malodorous animals! we *become* human, we have humanity thrust upon us through the hundred channels whereby the past pours down into the present that mental and cultural inheritance, whose preservation, accumulation and transmission place mankind today, with all its defectives and illiterates, on a higher plane than any generation has ever reached before.

Tenth and last, *writing and print*. Again our imagination is too weak-winged to lift us to a full perspective; we cannot vision or recall the long ages of ignorance, impotence and fear that preceded the coming of letters. Through those unrecorded centuries men could transmit their hard-won lore only by word of mouth from parent to child; if one generation forgot or misunderstood, the weary ladder of knowledge had to be climbed anew. Writing gave a new permanence to the achievements of the mind; it preserved for thousands of years, and through a millennium of poverty and superstition, the wisdom found by philosophy and the beauty carved out in drama and poetry. It bound the generations together with a common heritage; it created that Country of the Mind in which, because of writing, genius need not die.

And now, as writing united the generations, print, despite the thousand prostitutions of it, can bind the civilizations. It is not necessary any more that civilization should disappear before our planet passes away. It will change its habitat; doubtless the land in every nation will refuse at last to yield its fruit to improvident tillage and careless tenancy; inevitably new regions will lure with virgin soil the lustier strains of every race. But a civilization is not a material thing, inseparably bound, like an ancient serf, to a given spot of the earth; it is an accumulation of technical knowledge and cultural creation; if these can be passed on to the new seat of economic power the civilization does not die, it merely makes for itself another home. Nothing but beauty and wisdom deserve immortality. To a philosopher it is not indispensable that his native city should endure forever; he will be content if its achievements are handed down, to form some part of the possessions of mankind.

We need not fret, then, about the future. We are weary with too much war, and in our lassitude of mind we listen readily to a Spengler announcing the downfall of the Western world. But this

learned arrangement of the birth and death of civilizations in even
cycles is a trifle too precise; we may be sure that the future will
play wild pranks with this mathematical despair. There have been
wars before, and wars far worse than our "Great" one. Man and
civilization survived them; within fifteen years after Waterloo . . .
defeated France was producing so many geniuses that every attic
in Paris was occupied. Never was our heritage of civilization and
culture so secure, and never was it half so rich. We may do our
little share to augment it and transmit it, confident that time will
wear away chiefly the dross of it, and that what is finally fair and
worthy in it will be preserved, to illuminate many generations.

FOR THE STUDENT

Rhetoric

1. *Reorganize Durant's essay—some of his ten points overlap
   —and outline it under three or four main headings.*
2. *Notice how often Durant uses the* future tense *for his verbs.
   Why is this? Compare this usage with Inge's and Becker's.*
3. *Pick any long paragraph from each of the three essays on
   progress. Can you make any generalizations about the
   writers' vocabularies.*

Discussion

1. *In Shakespeare's time the word* progress *had nothing like
   its present meaning. Does this mean that progress didn't
   exist?*
2. *In the beginning of the seventh part, Durant attacks those
   who* romanticize *the past. Can he be accused of romanti-
   cizing the present and future?*
3. *Forty years ago Durant saw reason to be rather optimistic*

about the future. What events since that time might have tempered his optimism?

Writing

1. *Write your personal evaluation of Durant's essay.*
2. *Write an essay discussing progress from the point of view of a visitor from another planet. From the point of view of a cave man.*
3. *Compare and contrast Becker, Inge, and Durant on* progress.

9 Science and Literature

Literature has long been a traditional part of a liberal and classical education. Science, a Johnny-come-lately, had to fight for acceptance in the university curriculum and was admitted only in the late nineteenth century. Even then many remained uncertain whether science was a legitimate child of the universities. Today the situation is almost entirely reversed. Science and technology in the past one hundred and fifty years have made phenomenal changes in the physical and perhaps the spiritual world. In the scientific age of the mid-twentieth century, the layman stands in awe of science and frequently will not question anything labeled scientific, even his morning deodorant. Russia's Sputnik in 1957 caused the United States to demand additional emphasis on science in education. With today's emphasis upon facts as knowledge, literature as a form of knowledge is given a secondary, if not a tertiary, place in education. Those who still value literature as a form of knowledge emphasize the insights to be gained into the imponderables—like our many-faceted human nature, the ambiguity of personality, man's moral nature. It must be stated, however, that the best minds in either discipline see profound values in the other.

Determining who represents the Left and who the Right depends upon the point of view taken. Betrand Russell, English mathematician and philosopher, maintains that the discipline of science can train the mind (that is, provide culture in the good sense of the word) as well as literature does. In that he is thus rejecting the long-established and traditional view, he is on the Left. Marjorie Nicolson, an English professor with a lifelong interest in the relation between science and literature, finds much value in the two voices of science and literature. In her final question, "Which will triumph in our time?" she asserts her neutral position. Stephen Spender, an English poet, in responding to C. P. Snow's "The Two Cultures," shows his unwillingness to break with the traditional view. Literature speaks to what is most personal and most human in man.

On the other hand, if we think of liberalism as an ideal concerned with the sanctity of the individual and with individual freedom and rights, the positions of Russell and Spender must be reversed. Spender then falls on the Left because of his emphasis upon the individual and Russell on the Right because of his renunciation of individual desires and whatever is subjective to scientific truth.

STEPHEN SPENDER

Imagination Is Personal

The view has been put forward by C. P. Snow, in a famous and much debated essay, that there are today two cultures, a scientific and a literary. It is clear that what Sir Charles means in this context by "culture" is the ideas and *mores* of scientists, and those of writers. He is concerned with what is being discovered, and with what is being imagined. He reproaches scientists for their ignorance of literature and writers for their ignorance of science. He wants there to be bridges between the so-called two cultures. He tries to apportion blame equally to both sides in the alleged controversy, but it is evident that his sympathies are really with the scientists: he enters into their reasons for not appreciating the poets. He does not enter into the reasons of the poets for not appreciating the scientists. For he bases his whole case on the question of ignorance and knowledge. The scientists do not *know* literature and the men of letters do not *know* science. Put like this, obviously the writers are the more to blame, for science is knowledge, whereas literature is creating art from that which can be imagined. On grounds of knowledge, the scientists are not to be blamed for not knowing works of the imagination which from their point of view offer little to know. The members of the literary culture have, in his view, ignored a renaissance taking place in science; all that the scientists, on their side, appear to have ignored is the medieval ideas of antiprogressive men of letters.

As a thesis, a good deal of this seems open to dispute. I happen to know that the favourite reading of one of the most eminent physicists, J. D. Bernal, is *Finnegans Wake*. In itself this may not be statistically significant. Yet one can see why a physicist might be interested in Joyce, whose novels are just as much an invention of the modern mind as is a jet aircraft, whose technique has resemblances to work in the laboratory, and whose intelligence expresses a new kind of sensibility. It would be crude, surely, of scientists to think that novels, to be scientific, have to be about scientists, or about matters of social administration, and poems, about social progress. A scientist would surely agree that if literature is scientific it is nevertheless dealing with special kinds of material, and uses special techniques. An argument defending poetry on the ground that poets employ extremely subtle and complex techniques for expressing the psychology of individuals, has been put forward by I. A. Richards, and should rightly have been considered by C. P. Snow if he wished to avoid the charge that what he really meant was that literature should reflect scientific progress, and so earn the interest of scientists.

Sir Charles raises important points which have not, perhaps, so much to do with culture as with education. But he blurs the distinction between the world viewed by scientists and the world viewed by poets. Restricting even the distinction to the level of Sir Charles' argument (that the scientists are progressives, and the writers reactionaries), it is apparent that science is concerned with the extension of the resources of materials and power which can be put to general use; literature is concerned with the meaning which individual life has in the world in which these resources have been made available.

It may be true that certain modern writers—poets, especially —have shown too great antipathy to the progressive aspects of science. But the reason they have done so is because they are concerned not with science but with the world which is so largely the result of science. It is a world in which past values have been fragmented, in which the constructive powers of science are cancelled by its powers of destruction, in which the forces of human personality have broken down, and men and women have come to think of themselves as "social units." Of course, to blame scientists, in their disinterested pursuit of knowledge, for this world, would be as unwarranted as to blame writers for delivering their warnings against progress. On the whole, it would seem that it is right for the so-called literary culture to be critical of the so-called scientific. As Wilfred Owen, the most interesting poet of World War I, wrote in the Preface to his poems: "All a poet can do today is to warn."

The literary culture is essentially critical of the contemporary world which is the result of the scientific. This criticism may be expressed explicitly in critical works or imaginatively in poetic ones. It keeps alive the sense of the past as living thoughts and feelings crystallized, and in this way it judges present values by the values of past life.

Science is not, then, like literature because it is, as method, concerned with knowledge and truth and technology, not with aesthetic and moral judgements. Sir Charles Snow attacks the representatives of the "literary culture" (he means Ezra Pound and T. S. Eliot) for their hostility to progressive ideas, and he argues that to take sides against progress today means letting large numbers of people starve. But even while he is making it, the moral bias of this attack does not come out of the methods of science, which are conducive equally to killing large numbers of people as to feeding them. The idea of progress itself derives from the literary culture. It is one of those ideas with roots in primitive Christianity, humanism, and the French Revolution which are one aspect of a long debate that is an important part of Victorian and twentieth-century literature. Scientists who support progress do not belong to a special scientific culture, but to that of Dickens, Shaw, and Wells.

Progress produces material benefits but it is only through the alive intelligence of the imagination that these can be related to significant values. And although the great material needs of the world can and should be satisfied by progress, there is the great spiritual danger of judging individual lives as units in the progressive society: that is, as social units which ought to be statistically happier and to live statistically better lives because statistically they are better fed. But perhaps a parallel problem with undernourishment is that people are not automatically better or even happier as a result of social improvements. For example, it is notorious that in England the real benefits accomplished by the Welfare State have produced an unprecedented spiritual malaise. If there were any danger of progress being stopped as a result of the "reactionary" attitude towards it of T. S. Eliot, there might be justification for the charge that the supporters of the literary culture are in favour of taking potential bread out of the mouths of the starving. But since this is not the case, they are surely right in drawing attention to the spiritual crisis which results from beneficial materialism.

Though I do not agree with the formula of the Two Cultures, I think that within the "literary culture" itself, it may well be just to criticize poets for their ignorance of the great advances made by science. But this leads back to the problem of the imagination. For there are examples enough to show—the effect on Coleridge's poetry of his delvings into abstract philosophy is one —that the poetic imagination is harmed by absorbing more intellectual knowledge than it can digest. The poet can use no more knowledge than he can transform into his poetry, the novelist no more than he can make the behaviour and dialogue of realized action and characters.

What writers may fruitfully know is that which they can experience with their sensibility. And it is not so important that they should know the second law of thermodynamics as that they should perceive the subtle changes effected in the rhythm of language by the environment resulting from inventions, their influence on human behaviour, and modes of feeling. It is not scientific knowledge but its effects which become part of the experience of modern life. Joyce, Eliot, and Lawrence certainly reflect in their works the results of science. In his own novels even, C. P. Snow is creating a fiction about the results of science and power, not about scientific theories and abstract policies. And if one were to defend the two-dimensional characters in these novels, one might argue that these embodiments of ideas and petty ambitions are studies of the effect on human beings of working in laboratories, colleges, and corridors of power. It may be that, without knowing it, with his imagination Sir Charles creates a picture which is critical of progress, and that as an artist he agrees with the T. S. Eliot whom, as a critic, he dismisses as reactionary, that "we are the hollow men." In this case, a criticism of Snow the novelist would be that, like Galsworthy, he writes unconscious satire.

The position of the literary culture is that it is a different mode of interpreting experience from organizing, inventing, statistical procedure. The "literary intellectuals," unless they betray their task or are conscripted into doing so, cannot assume that because there is the knowledge and the technology to improve the situation of millions of people who are hungry, people will necessarily be better or even happier as the result of those means being used. They cannot accept the concept of social man as a unit among many units who will improve because his material conditions improve. They think that human life is made up of individuals, and that the present situation of the life that has taken up its habitation in the bodies of the living (as it previously did the bodies of the dead) is reflected in the minds of the most aware, most fully conscious, and most able to compare the condition of life in the present with that of the past. "Belonging to a tradition" means simply living spiritually on a chart where you are aware that your physical existence is but a small point in the whole of the life that has reached us from the past, and being able to have a realization of the equal intensity of past living with present existence, so that you can measure present life against the lives of the dead. Unless the sense that flesh and blood are just the outposts of a continuity of living is maintained, there is a considerable chance that material improvements, however beneficial and welcome, will lead to a loss of consciousness of the whole significance of life. To be as aware as the most aware minds were at other times is surely an indisputable aim, a responsibility, of being alive. To measure genius in our time against its achievements in the past is therefore also a way of seeing whether our ways of living are not weakening the consciousness which can be thought of as timeless, carried on for a moment within eternity, by ourselves.

If the literary intellectuals seem sceptical of the benefits produced by science, one reason may be that so many scientific advances seem to result in a deadening of consciousness. I mean by this, they destroy life-memory, which is not mechanical memory, but is memory of the kind that can retain significant experiences—can cultivate awareness of consciousness before our day. Such judging and comparing and savouring memory is the essential quality of full and complex consciousness. Instead of our living in an extremely complex present moment, packed as it were with experiences of the past related to immediate ones, technology enables more and more people to live in a single-strand moment, receiving the latest sensation, which obliterates previous impressions. The literary intellectuals are, it is hoped, those who have attained the greatest degree of that subjective or self-awareness which is also awareness of the potentiality of such mental and spiritual living in others, so that in being most individual it is most representative of human consciousness.

The poets and creators are as it were separate witnesses, each reflecting his world, and in an interrelationship in which each corrects the vision of the whole. Without them we might have a great deal of information about people's analysable capacities and needs, and broad pictures, based on statistics, describing their material and perhaps also their psychological condition. But we would not have those voices which express the subjective and spiritual reactions of the most perceptive recording instruments in a civilization.

The responsibilty of saying "this is how I see things," and "this is how they happen to me," is entirely different from the responsibility of scientists. Their responsibility is to make their minds the instruments through which objective truths add to the sum of disinterested knowledge, and inventions advance according to the logic of preceding processes.

Technology can of course be put to beneficial ends, and is being so. But it can also be put to totally destructive ones. And "Science," as such, is that system of truth and discovery which is indifferent to the results. If there is any morality of the scientist injected into science, if there is any "spirit of science," it is expressed in the phrase "the truth at any price and without regard to the results."

The man of literary culture is, in a very complicated way, responsible for the effects of his work. Thus it is arguable that some of the writings of Nietzsche were in some way responsible for that demonstration of the vision of the superman which was Nazi Germany. The poet infuses into the pattern which he makes from his experience his view of life, for which he is responsible. But the last person who is responsible for his own inventions is the scientist. If the world were all but destroyed by atomic war, it would be possible—according to our present way of thinking— to blame philosophy, politics, religion, poetry, which could all be seen as leading to this result. The one person who would not be to blame would be the scientist who invented the bomb, because he is regarded as the mental instrument which invented the physical instrument. If blame ever were attached to science it would be on account of this very lack of responsibility to anything except objective truth and technological performance. But for the scientist to be held responsible for his science would require a revolution in our thinking.

The different responsibilities of the "scientific" and the "literary culture" can be demonstrated, I think, by considering a passage in an essay by Snow which appeared some years before *The Two Cultures*. It is from the volume of essays by various hands, called *The Baldwin Age,* and is on Rutherford and Cavendish:

The scientists were themselves part of the deepest revolution in human affairs since the discovery of agriculture. They could accept what was happening, while other intellectuals shrank away. They not only accepted it, they rejoiced in it. It was difficult to find a scientist who did not believe that the scientific-technical-industrial revolution, accelerating under his eyes, was not doing incomparably more good than harm.

This was the characteristic optimism of scientists in the 'twenties and 'thirties. It still is. In some ways it was too easy an optimism, but the counter-attitude of the non-scientific intellectuals was too easy a pessimism. Between Rutherford and Blackett on the one hand, and, say, Wyndham Lewis and Ezra Pound on the other, who are on the side of their fellow beings? The only people who would have any doubt about the answer are those who dislike the human race.

We are told here that the scientists made revolutionary discoveries, and this is doubtless true. We are told that they rejoiced in the discoveries, and it is quite natural that they should have done so. "Other intellectuals," we are told, "shrank away." By them is meant the writers, and two writers, certainly unrepresentative in their views, are mentioned, in order to emphasize the burden of implicit complaint against the literary culture for not rejoicing in the scientific revolution.

Next we are told that Rutherford and Blackett were confident that their "scientific-technical-industrial revolution" was doing "incomparably more good than harm." But everything we know about the development of technology in the scientific age warns us that this subjective reaction of theirs has no connection with the actual results of their revolutionary theories or discoveries.

Belief in progress simply reflects an optimistic view of human nature: that on the whole, perhaps as the result of the pressures of various conflicting self-interests, the means put at the disposal of the politicians and managers of the world by science will be used for good rather than bad ends.

So progress is nothing more than a general hope which has been attached to the certainty that knowledge and invention will advance. It is a mistranslation of the concept of material advancement into the concept of human improvement.

One thing we cannot escape from is the qualities of the human beings who use the knowledge and forces put at their disposal by science. If the scientists can be regarded as simple midwives of technological progress, the political leaders, the managerial class, the bureaucrats, cannot. They are in a directive position in which the complexity of their nature counts; and in a technological society in which the endeavours of the inventors are directed to alleviating the condition of the people, and the demand is made that all the writers and artists should share in the enthusiasm for the technological revolution, and in which those who express reactionary views can be silenced: in such a society, where no poet is allowed to say he is unhappy in case his doing so hinders the great processes of amelioration, a Stalin is liable to assume control. And although, as decent human beings, the scientists may be dismayed at the emergence at the top of society of such a miscalculation, where all their mechanical calculations have been so exact, there is nothing in their culture of objectivity to prevent a Stalin, who, after all, in his way, is the direct result, in a given set of circumstances, of the scientific culture. Defending the study of literature, Matthew Arnold observed in his Rede lecture on *Literature and Science:* "At present it seems to me, that those who are for giving to natural knowledge, as they call it, the chief place in the education of the majority of mankind, leave one important thing out of their account: the constitution of human nature."

To the reader of Matthew Arnold's lecture, as to that of Peacock's *The Four Ages of Poetry,* it may seem that the controversy started by Snow is familiar. It is like a volcano, supposed to have become extinct a century ago, suddenly erupting in the mid-twentieth century.

The reasons for the excitement are several. Firstly, there is a real debate going on all over the world today about technological education. In the conflict between East and West, Soviet successes in rocketry have produced a panicky feeling that we must train more and more scientists.

But deeper than this, the proposition suggested perhaps even more by the title than by the content of Snow's lecture, that there are two cultures, and that the one of knowing and technology is on the defensive against the other of imagining and creating, stirs up fears which reach to the subconscious. Indeed one way of restating the argument might be to say "there is a responsible culture of the conscious, and an irresponsible culture of the subconscious. The subconscious is ignorant and reactionary, and does not appreciate the great public benefits being achieved by science. The subconscious must learn the lessons of progress."

We should have learned by now that it is dangerous to attack the subconscious on grounds of public morals and public works. Moreover we are today uncomfortably aware of the existence of a vast threatening world not of the unconscious, but of reason and logic, whose inventions we fear—despite the optimism of the members of the "scientific culture"—may destroy our civilization. And we know that somewhere the destructive-constructive powers are after all not just works of pure reason to be used in purely beneficial ways by officials who are not appreciated by reactionary poets: we know that they are the terrifying expressions of alternatives of good or ill, now realized externally on a colossal scale, of human nature.

The author of *The Two Cultures,* with his dislike of the literary culture, and his simple trust in optimistic scientists, does not understand this. We are driven to the conclusion that it requires imagination to do so.

Here we are brought back to Shelley, and to that time when the Romantic imagination became released from the enlightened views of the rationalist eighteenth century: released, because it was cut loose, and was left with no view of the world outside its own power of continual subjective interpretation to which it could remain attached. The old systems had ceased to explain the terrible forces brought into the world.

Shelley had an idea, which was perhaps wrong, that poetry had a task, which was to imagine the world of concrete realizations by abstract processes. It is easy enough to see that the moment you have named a task—of imagining that which we know—you call upon poets to write out of intellect and conscious will—just that which is impossible. At the same time, the nightmare remains,

that without such imaginative comprehension of the powers released by the "sorcerer's apprentice" we are at the mercy of those
powers.

Two types of procedure have been discussed here as "cultures,"
and although one may not be happy with the word, one can see
what is meant. The people who know and the people who imagine
are in their opposite ways both interpreters of contemporary
reality. The behaviour of scientists or writers—what sociologists
would call their cultural pattern—is indeed only a red herring
drawn across the controversy. What is really the matter of debate
is that research, specialization, analysis, statistics, are supposed to
be "progressive," whereas the imagining, picture-making faculty
of communicating in visions the understanding by individual internal life, the spiritual condition of our time, our life, in relation
to past times and past life, is held to be anachronistic, negative,
reactionary.

Science, as it is understood by most people, and certainly by
Sir Charles Snow, is, as I have explained, the realization of objective processes of theory and invention that transform the material environment, and multiply immensely man's power over
nature. We are told that the second law of thermodynamics is
"beautiful." This means that the operation of natural laws is in
itself beautiful and that their exposition and demonstration by a
human mind is also beautiful.

Part of the beauty of this, however, is that the human mind
does not "interfere" in the demonstration. When one is talking
about the beauty of a poem, one means something quite different
from the beauty of the second law of thermodynamics.

For the beauty of the poem consists of the fact that when the
poet operates upon the subject of his experience to make the poem,
the poem is penetrated with the subjective qualities of his being.
When we say that Keats' "Ode to a Nightingale" is beautiful we
do not mean that it is a beautiful demonstration of a particular
nightingale, we mean that in treating of the object of his ex-

perience, which was (perhaps) listening to the nightingale, Keats revealed qualities of his sensibility which we intensely admire.

Precisely what is beautiful about the scientific law is that if another scientist had discovered it, it would have been the same law. It is objective truth. Precisely what is beautiful about the poem is that if another poet had written about the same subject, it would have been entirely different.

The "literary culture"—if one can admit such a term—is a culture because it cultivates the object with the qualities of human personality. There is no such thing as a "scientific culture" (apart from, perhaps, the group behaviour of scientists) because science does not, as such, cultivate objective reality with subjective states of mind which are the results of a long history of civilization. Science simply realizes the true nature of the object, it releases into the stream of life discoveries and inventions which, although they may be chosen for utility or destructive purposes, in themselves incorporate no subjective vision of the individual who discovered or invented them.

FOR THE STUDENT

Rhetoric

1. *In the first seven paragraphs study the rhetorical devices used to establish the dichotomy between the scientific and the literary cultures.*
2. *Demonstrate the effectiveness of the analogy of the controversy to the volcano. How does it help to clarify meaning?*
3. *Explain the allusion to the "sorcerer's apprentice."*
4. *In the closing six paragraphs, Spender refines Snow's definition of culture. What is Spender's definition of the term?*

5. *Cite examples of Spender's pique toward Snow and Snow's analysis of the two cultures.*

Discussion

1. *What does Spender conceive to be the special function and duty of the "poets and creators" in our society?*
2. *Do you agree that the scientist is so little morally responsible as Spender suggests? If you disagree, in what ways should the scientist exercise his moral responsibility?*

Writing

1. *Spender speaks frequently of the world which is largely the result of science. Derive your own thesis from Spender's idea and develop it carefully in a paper of about five paragraphs.*
2. *Theme topic: The beauty of the law of gravity (or any other scientific law) and the beauty of a poem (or short story, play, or novel).*

MARJORIE HOPE NICOLSON

Two Voices: Science and Literature

I have taken my title from the opening phrase of one of
Wordsworth's sonnets on liberty:

> Two voices are there; one is of the sea,
> One of the mountains; each a mighty voice.

Yet I confess that I had in mind not only the original sonnet
but also the wickedly brilliant parody in which James Stephen
heard two voices in Wordsworth, one a mighty voice, the other
that

> of an old half-witted sheep
> Which bleats articulate monotony,
> And indicates that two and one are three,
> That grass is green, lakes damp, and mountains steep. . . .

You will see why the parody came into my mind, I think, as I
try to awaken for you echoes of two voices that were raised in
the early days of our modern era, when the sciences, as we
know them today, either emerged or became so changed that
they seem just to have been born; when astrology became astronomy, alchemy chemistry; when the microscope transformed
botany, zoology, and medicine, and geology gradually emerged
from the shadow of Genesis, which delayed its development
longer than the other sciences. The voices will sometimes be
those of scientists, sometimes those of laymen, particularly
poets. One group responded to the "New Philosophy" (they did

Originally published in The Rockefeller University Review, *Vol. I,
no. 3 (June, 1963). Published in the present form in* American
Scientist, *Vol. 51 (December, 1963). Reprinted by permission of
The Rockefeller University Press,* American Scientist, *and the author.*

[323]

not yet generally use our word "science" in its modern sense) with enthusiasm, acclaim, even rapture. The other drew back in fear or doubt, or took refuge in satire, parody, laughter, not very different from that of James Stephen.

Melancholy, and the End of the World

The seventeenth century has been called "The Century of Revolutions" and "The Century of Genius," both titles well deserved. There were revolutions in politics, in religion, in society, in economics. But a century that has left a roster of such names as those of Harvey, Kepler, Galileo, Boyle, Newton, as Bruno, Bacon, Hobbes, Spinoza, Leibniz, Locke, was, even more, a century of genius. Yet in England as the sixteenth century gave way to the next, we are conscious of a cloud of melancholy, reflected in much literature of the changing years. To be sure, some of this is only "white melancholy," a literary fad, rather than the "black melancholy" the word implies. When Shakespeare's Antonio opens *The Merchant of Venice* by saying, "In sooth, I know not why I am so sad," he is using literary patter, since there was nothing in the world to make him sad. Although "Monsieur Melancholy," Jaques in *As You Like It,* "can suck melancholy out of a song as a weasel sucks eggs," we need not fear for his mental health. Milton's "divinest Melancholy" is robed in black, but her spirit is white. Antonio, Jaques, Il Penseroso were in no danger of committing suicide. But Shakespeare also wrote *Hamlet*; and Donne his *Anniversaries,* the most somber poems in our language, not long after he had written a tract on suicide. In 1621 Robert Burton published the first edition of *The Anatomy of Melancholy,* that extraordinary series of case histories of white, black, and shaded melancholy, in which he was as conscious of the prevalence and danger of melancholy as any modern psychiatrist could have been. There was profoundly serious "black melancholy" in this period which not only might lead to individual suicide but, as Burton and Bacon both realized, was holding back a generation from advancement in its ways of thinking. "'Tis too late to be ambitious," Sir Thomas Browne wrote in his *Hydriotaphia*. "The great mutations of the world are acted, or time may be too short for our designs. [Our] generations are ordained in the setting part of time."

It would take far too long to answer the question: why were our ancestors of the seventeenth century so melancholy? Burton understood, better than many modern historians, the complexities in the political, economic, and social scene that were leading to despondency and inanition. Of the preconceptions and presuppositions the age took for granted, I shall stop over only one, in many ways the most basic of all, which lay behind Sir Thomas Browne's feeling that it was too late to be ambitious. Our forefathers believed implicitly in Biblical prophecy. Accepting Genesis reverently, they knew the date of the creation of the world, and they also knew the date of its end. By the kind of analogical thinking prevalent in the period, since the world had been created in six days, it would remain for six millennia. Created approximately 4000 B.C., it must end no later than 2000 A.D.—as still seems tragically possible. The great teachers of the Reformation, particularly Martin Luther, constantly warned that, if evil continued, God would not permit the world to run its course, but might destroy it at any moment. . . .

Optimism, and the "New Philosophy"

The century that began under a pall of gloom ended in a great burst of optimism. While there were many reasons for the remarkable change, there is little doubt that the greatest single stimulus to optimism came about through the "New Philosophy," as it continued to be called throughout the century. The temper of the later period was largely determined by the work of one man, Francis Bacon. Historians differ sharply in their estimate of Bacon's importance in the history of either science or philosophy. There can be little disagreement about the part he played in making an age "science conscious," as no age until our own has been. In the *Novum Organum,* published in 1620, a year before the first edition of Burton's *Anatomy,* Bacon, like Burton, though in a different idiom, analyzed many reasons for despondency and found the most serious in the fact that "men despair and *think things impossible.*" Across the lethargy he describes, we hear the clarion call of optimism in the great passage beginning, "I am now to speak concerning Hope." And speak he did. In his hands, "the thing became a trumpet."

When I am teaching Bacon, I urge my students to read Marlowe's *Doctor Faustus* just before they read Bacon's *New Atlantis* to see the popular interpretation in literature of science and scientists. . . .

Marlowe's *Doctor Faustus* was played in London in 1592. Bacon's first philosophical work, *The Advancement of Learning,* was published in 1605, his last work, the *New Atlantis,* was written in 1626, the year of his death. Thirteen years between *Doctor Faustus* and the first, only thirty-four between the drama and Bacon's last work. It happened as quickly as that: a complete transformation of the popular conception of both science and scientist.

Bacon never did a wiser thing than to write that last work, the epitome of all his philosophical and scientific thinking, in fictional form. Here is a story anyone could read and understand. Like most Renaissance utopias, it is a tale of travel to a new land —really an old land, since the new Atlantis proves to be the "lost Atlantis" of Platonic myth. The new Atlantis is a monarchy, but from the beginning we are aware that the real center of the kingdom is not the throne but "Salomon's House," a foundation, somewhat in our sense of the word. Bacon has gone a step farther than Plato with his "philosopher-kings." In Bacon's imaginary world, scientists are kings. When I visualize "Salomon's House," I find myself thinking of the campuses of certain modern American universities: this campus of The Rockefeller Institute, for example, or those of the Massachusetts and the California Institutes of Technology. On such campuses today, Bacon would find his dream come true, his suppressed desires abundantly fulfilled. "Salomon's House" had its campus, buildings in which experimentation was carried on, as well as other kinds of laboratories: deep caves and lakes, real or artificial, in which men were working on problems of refrigeration and preservation; high towers, something like observatories; museums of natural history (unknown in Bacon's time), orchards, gardens, in all of which experimentation went on.

Bacon's scientists are no lonely alchemists, working secretly for their own gain. They are groups of men ranging in a hierarchy down from "top-secret" heads through various ranks to many laboratory assistants. They work according to a scientific method, pooling their knowledge and their findings. They have various instruments for "weighing, measuring, verifying." They have discovered and invented many things we take for granted today: flying machines, for example, submarines, instruments "for hearing at a distance," prophesying our telephones, telegraphs, radios. They make synthetic medicines, even synthetic perfumes. All their labors are devoted to the end Bacon reiterated throughout his works: "the benefit and use of man, the relief of man's estate." Like Faustus, Bacon took all knowledge to be his province, but his road to knowledge was very different.

Lewis Mumford in his *Story of Utopias* dismisses the *New Atlantis* with some contempt in comparison with More's *Utopia,* because Bacon's ideal world was still a monarchy and he did not suggest a political, social, or economic revolution as a clue to the future. Thomas More foresaw a world in which socialism, perhaps communism, would rule. Bacon believed that that nation would be most powerful in which science had made the greatest strides. We who live today on this side of an iron curtain behind which communism prevails, in an Atomic Age made by science, and dominated at the moment by Russian and American competition, may look back to both our far-sighted Renaissance utopian ancestors as prophets of the future. Which of them guessed most truly, time has not as yet finally told.

Plus Ultra

From the *New Atlantis* England caught fire, even more than from Bacon's philosophical works. Under its influence men gathered strength and went on, as Bacon had hoped, to discover new "intellectual worlds" as their grandfathers had discovered new geographical worlds. Under its influence, at least in large part, the Royal Society of London was chartered in 1661, to begin its distinguished career, celebrated in 1961, as the only academy in the world which has had an unbroken history of three hundred years. . . . Throughout the Restoration period the prevailing tone of the "Bacon-faced" generation was one of optimism. The motto of his followers was *Plus Ultra.* . . . .

The Voice of Doubt

For a number of years after I first began exploring the relationships between literature and science, I thought that the voice of Scientia in this period was universally optimistic, that all scientists, within or without the Royal Society, believed, as did Bacon, that the effects of science would be entirely benign, only "for the benefit and use of man." Then I heard another note, even in science. Bacon's "Fathers of Salomon's House" had invented flying machines, among other things. In 1670 many men throughout Europe believed that the principle of flight had been discovered by an Italian scientist, Francesco Lana, who, whether his own invention was successful or not, may well be considered the real father of aerostatics, in that his little model laid the basis for the balloon, the first flying machine in which animals, then men, rose perilously from the ground and ascended into the air. In his *Prodromo,* Lana

insisted that the basic problems of weight and gravity were readily
soluble and that in a short time sizable flying machines could be
developed in which men might fly, even to the moon. But then he
wrote—and remember, this is a scientist speaking—"Other difficulties I do not foresee that could prevail against this invention, *save
one only, which seems to me the greatest of all, and that is, that
God would surely never allow such a machine to be successful.*"
Consider, he said, what might follow: airships could be steered
over public squares, over navies lying at anchor in a harbor. Iron
weights could be dropped, fireballs and bombs thrown down. So
the first important inventor in aviation prophesied in 1670 what
we have lived to see: the destruction of ships and cities from the
air. "God would surely never allow such a machine to be successful."

The Vast and the Minute

Two voices were there, even among scientists. What of
literary voices in this first great age of invention and discovery?
The first science to make an immediate appeal to laymen was
astronomy. Throughout Europe excitement was aroused by
Galileo's spectacular discoveries through his fifth telescope, announced in 1610 in the *Sidereus Nuncius,* a starry messenger and
message to man. Almost overnight Galileo had discovered not only
a new world but a new universe. His observations had proved the
truth of the Copernican hypothesis, establishing the sun rather than
the earth as the center of our system. He had discovered many
other things as well: stars innumerable, never before seen; the
phases of Venus; the true nature of the Milky Way; the fact that
the moon was a world, topographically much like our own; and—
for a time, he thought—four new planets, which later proved to be
the satellites of Mars. Astrology was doomed that night, and astronomy was born. All these discoveries passed quickly into literature.

The development of the microscope, following inevitably upon the invention of the telescope, opened to human imagination another new universe—that of the small, stretching perhaps to infinity, as did the new universe of the vast. Antony van Leeuwenhoek and other microbiologists discovered a new world of life in stagnant water, in saliva, in blood and urine, life infinitesimal, but still life. Was there any point, asked an amazed and astounded generation, at which life ceased? . . .

The Voice of Scorn

But there was still another literary voice, of a different sort. Anyone who has read Restoration literature will realize that the "Restoration Wits" were not likely to share the exuberance and lack of restraint of these early Romanticists. We begin to hear the voice of satire most clearly shortly after the invention of the microscope. Until the development of the compound microscope, the enthusiasm of scientists and laymen alike was as simple and childlike as that of youngsters when they first discover magnification. Samuel Pepys, always avid for novelty, bought himself a microscope and he and Mistress Pepys spent an evening with it, sharing the experience of many students in "Freshman Biology." At first they could see nothing, and when they saw something they did not know what they were seeing until Pepys wisely bought a book that told him. Scientists, gentlemen and ladies alike—ladies proved as important a new "buying public" for glass grinders as they have proved for cigarette manufacturers in our own time—were fascinated by seeing through their lenses simple, ordinary, homely things they had always known but never really seen. Bacon had warned his followers not to avoid "mean and even filthy things." He would have been delighted to watch his descendants—scientists and laymen alike—engrossed with the magnified flea and louse. There grew up what I like to call a "literature of vermin," expatiating on fleas, lice, maggots, ants, tadpoles, worms, and even rats' testicles. Inevitably the Restoration satirists had their fun with such childlike enthusiasm. Part of the great popularity of *Hudibras* was the result of Butler's many satiric passages on science and scientists. He turned his light artillery upon Virtuosi who spent hours upon such problems as

> How many different specieses
> Of maggots breed in rotten cheeses,

and pilloried a distinguished member of the Royal Society

> whose task was to determine
> And solve the appearances of vermin,
> Who had made profound discoveries
> In frogs, and toads, and rats, and lice.

The most familiar lines on the flea have been quoted and misquoted ever since they were written by Jonathan Swift:

> So naturalists observe, a flea
> Has smaller fleas that on him prey,
> And these have smaller still to bite 'em,
> And so proceed *ad infinitum*.

Only a few weeks ago I was delighted to discover in the Huntington Library two works which I was sure must have been written but which I had never seen: two mock epics, one called *The Louseiad*, the other *The Fleaiad*.

Yet light satire may be a more deadly weapon than more serious literature. So it proved in the Restoration period. Today many people are concerned with the effect modern science may have upon literature, particularly poetry. In this early period the tables were turned. There was a time when literature almost put an end to an important chapter in the advancement of science. If one reads Sprat's *History of the Royal Society* carefully, it becomes clear that Sprat was commissioned to write it by members of the Society, greatly concerned with the public attitude toward their scientific work. They were clearly less worried about the attitude of men of religion than they were about the "Restoration Wits." . . .

On the surface, Charles II, who had chartered the Society, remained its patron, but behind the scenes his attitude was different. Pepys tells of an evening when the King attended an aristocratic party and spent an hour and a half laughing at the Virtuosi. Why? Because, said His Majesty, those silly men had spent their time, ever since their foundation, in "weighing the air," and doing nothing else. Weighing the air, indeed. It sounds as absurd to the layman today as it must have to the aristocrats that evening. As it happens, the experiments at which the King was laughing were largely those of Robert Boyle, who was laying down some of the premises upon which modern physics still rests. But the King's jibe passed from mouth to mouth, as some of Butler's satiric verses seem to have passed from hand to hand before they were published. On the stage too were sly digs at the absurdities of the new science, culminating a few years later in the comedy of Shadwell's *Virtuoso,* the most extensive, drastic, and amusing stage criticism of the Royal Society in which the name character, Sir Nicholas Gimcrack, epitomizes all that seemed absurd in science. He not only weighed the air, but bottled it up and kept it in his wine cellar, like fine champagne, to open in his chamber when he desired a change of climate. Each of Gimcrack's discoveries and experiments had its source in a real experiment or discovery by a member of the Royal Society, as the audience well knew. As Shadwell satirized them, they sound as silly as Boyle's weighing the air did to the King and his courtiers. . . .

Antiphonal Music

During the many years I have spent in trying to recapture these various voices of the past, as they echoed in science and literature, I have heard them as a sort of antiphonal music, one voice replying to the other, one strain now dominant, then another. A few weeks ago I was surprised and delighted to learn that my "Voices" have actually been set to music by Ross Lee Finney,

Composer in Residence at the University of Michigan, once my colleague at Smith College. He sent me the score of a choral composition, *Still Are New Worlds,* which is to be performed for the first time at the May Festival in Ann Arbor. When I asked if I might describe it to you, he replied with characteristic generosity, "I wrote the music; you wrote the words." The words are mine only to the extent that they have largely been taken from passages I have collected and quoted in books and articles dealing with the impact of science upon literary imagination. Mr. Finney has added another dimension to my studies: to science and literature, he has added music. Then, too, at the end of the composition, he uses electronic tape, suggesting a way in which modern science is affecting music, and affording still another medium of communication in the arts. . . .

It is significant, I think, that Mr. Finney sought a long time in modern science and modern poetry for the language he needed to express emotions many of us share in this Atomic Age. Only in *Paradise Lost* could he find the language he was seeking. He has deliberately wrenched the words out of Milton's context, and, to my mind, has made the great rhetoric even more profound than it was originally. The first lines from Milton were used by the poet to describe "the Almighty Power," God, casting out the rebel Satan from Heaven. In Mr. Finney's score, "the Almighty Power" has become, not God, but nuclear physics:

> He with ambitious aim
> . . . . the Almighty Power
> Hurled headlong flaming from the ethereal sky
> With hideous ruin and combustion down
> To bottomless perdition . . .
> Who durst defy the Omnipotent.

As the full power of the music echoes that fearful sound some human beings heard in reality, but all of us have heard in nightmare imagination, it seems that, as in the Book of Revelation, there should be silence in Heaven for the space of half an hour.

Only Milton, long before it happened, described the desolation of a
devastated city caused by the atomic bomb:

> The dismal . . . waste
> On all sides round . . .
> As one great furnace flamed . . .
> No light, but rather darkness visible,
> Regions of sorrow . . . where peace
> Can never dwell, hope never comes.

As the words are used, they are no longer what they were—a
description of the Hell God made for Satan—but a description of
the Hell man made for man.

Lines from Milton serve, too, for the conclusion of *Still Are
New Worlds*. The words from the Prologue to *Paradise Lost* have
again been deliberately removed from their original context. Milton
wrote of God,

> Thou from the first
> Wast present, and with mighty wings outspread,
> Dove-like satst brooding on the vast abyss
> And madst it pregnant.

It is no longer God who, brooding upon an abyss, brought order
out of chaos to create a world. The source of power in the great
abyss is something man has discovered which may destroy a world.

Still Are New Worlds concludes with the familiar words that
conclude the General Prologue to *Paradise Lost*. As Milton wrote
them, they said,

> That so I may assert Eternal Providence
> And justify the ways of God to men.

I do not pretend to know how Mr. Finney interprets them, but
read against the history which I have been tracing, the familiar
words echo in my ears with a melancholy far more profound than
that against which science dawned. To me they say something which
I can express only by changing both order and meaning. Milton
ended with an affirmation. He believed that man could assert

Eternal Providence. We end with a question: May we assert
Eternal Providence? Milton could and did justify the ways of God
to men. I read the line today as a profoundly ironic query: Can
we justify *the ways of men to God?* Two voices are there. Which
will triumph in our time?

FOR THE STUDENT

Rhetoric

1. *The first paragraph does much to show why Miss Nicolson
   thought of Stephen's parody in choosing her title. Explain
   the two voices of the parody in the development of the
   paragraph.*
2. *What function is served by the two-paragraph discussion of
   melancholy? How is this idea related to the rest of the
   essay?*
3. *Study Miss Nicolson's comments on the Finney choral
   composition to determine how her comments upon the
   music and the words become a device for bringing together
   the two voices.*

Discussion

1. *In the section entitled "Optimism, and the 'New Philosophy,'" what attitude toward science dominates the discussion? What is the querulous note introduced in the last
   paragraph of this section? What further statement is this
   note given?*
2. *Miss Nicolson speaks of the two voices of both science and
   literature. Define them. How do they relate to the two
   voices of Wordsworth's sonnet and of Stephen's parody?*

3. *What are the two voices of which Miss Nicolson speaks at the end of the essay?*

Writing

1. *Write a paper in which you show the Voice of Doubt or the Voice of Scorn expressing a concern about a contemporary problem. You should focus on one specific point.*
2. *Theme topics: "Sir Nicholas Gimcrack evaluates modern science"; "The Almighty Power: God or nuclear physics."*

BERTRAND RUSSELL

Science as an Element in Culture

I

Science, to the ordinary reader of newspapers, is represented by a varying selection of sensational triumphs, such as wireless telegraphy and aeroplanes, radio-activity and the marvels of modern alchemy. It is not of this aspect of science that I wish to speak. Science, in this aspect, consists of detached up-to-date fragments, interesting only until they are replaced by something newer and more up-to-date, displaying nothing of the systems of patiently constructed knowledge out of which, almost as a casual incident, have come the practically useful results which interest the man in the street. The increased command over the forces of nature which is derived from science is undoubtedly an amply sufficient reason for encouraging scientific research, but this reason has been so often urged and is so easily appreciated that other reasons, to my mind quite as important, are apt to be overlooked. It is with these other reasons, especially with the intrinsic value of a scientific habit of mind in forming our outlook on the world, that I shall be concerned in what follows.

The instance of wireless telegraphy will serve to illustrate the difference between the two points of view. Almost all the serious intellectual labour required for the possibility of this invention is due to three men—Faraday, Maxwell, and Hertz. In alternating layers of experiment and theory these three men built up the modern theory of electromagnetism, and demonstrated the identity of light with electromagnetic waves. The system which they discovered is one of profound intellectual interest, bringing together and unifying an endless variety of apparently detached phenomena,

From The New Statesman, *May 24 and May 31, 1913. Reprinted by permission.*

and displaying a cumulative mental power which cannot but afford delight to every generous spirit. The mechanical details which remained to be adjusted in order to utilise their discoveries for a practical system of telegraphy demanded, no doubt, very considerable ingenuity, but had not that broad sweep and that universality which could give them intrinsic interest as an object of disinterested contemplation.

From the point of view of training the mind, of giving that well-informed, impersonal outlook which constitutes culture in the good sense of this much-misused word, it seems to be generally held indisputable that a literary education is superior to one based on science. Even the warmest advocates of science are apt to rest their claims on the contention that culture ought to be sacrificed to utility. Those men of science who respect culture, when they associate with men learned in the classics, are apt to admit, not merely politely, but sincerely, a certain inferiority on their side, compensated doubtless by the services which science renders to humanity, but none the less real. And so long as this attitude exists among men of science, it tends to verify itself: the intrinsically valuable aspects of science tend to be sacrificed to the merely useful, and little attempt is made to preserve that leisurely, systematic survey by which the finer quality of mind is formed and nourished.

But even if there be, in present fact, any such inferiority as is supposed in the educational value of science, this is, I believe, not the fault of science itself, but the fault of the spirit in which science is taught. If its full possibilities were realised by those who teach it, I believe that its capacity of producing those habits of mind which constitute the highest mental excellence would be at least as great as that of literature, and more particularly of Greek and Latin literature. In saying this I have no wish whatever to disparage a classical education. I have not myself enjoyed its benefits, and my knowledge of Greek and Latin authors is derived almost wholly from translations. But I am firmly persuaded that the Greeks fully deserve all the admiration that is bestowed upon them, and that it is a very great and serious loss to be unacquainted with

their writings. It is not by attacking them, but by drawing attention
to neglected excellences in science, that I wish to conduct my
argument.

   One defect, however, does seem inherent in a purely classical
education—namely, a too exclusive emphasis on the past. By the
study of what is absolutely ended and can never be renewed a
habit of criticism towards the present and the future is engendered.
The qualities in which the present excels are qualities to which the
study of the past does not direct attention, and to which, therefore,
the student of Greek civilisation may easily become blind. In what
is new and growing there is apt to be something crude, insolent,
even a little vulgar, which is shocking to the man of sensitive taste;
quivering from the rough contact, he retires to the trim gardens of
a polished past, forgetting that they were reclaimed from the wilderness by men as rough and earth-soiled as those from whom he
shrinks in his own day. The habit of being unable to recognise
merit until it is dead is too apt to be the result of a purely bookish
life, and a culture based wholly on the past will seldom be able to
pierce through everyday surroundings to the essential splendour of
contemporary things, or to the hope of still greater splendour in
the future.

> My eyes saw not the men of old;
> And now their age away has rolled.
> I weep—to think I shall not see
> The heroes of posterity.

So says the Chinese poet; but such impartiality is rare in the more
pugnacious atmosphere of the West, where the champions of past
and future fight a never-ending battle, instead of combining to seek
out the merits of both. . . .

II

   Two opposite and at first sight conflicting merits belong to
science as against literature and art. The one, which is not in-

herently necessary, but is certainly true at the present day, is hopefulness as to the future of human achievement, and in particular as to the useful work that may be accomplished by any intelligent student. This merit and the cheerful outlook which it engenders prevent what might otherwise be the depressing effect of another aspect of science, to my mind also a merit, and perhaps its greatest merit—I mean the irrelevance of human passions and of the whole subjective apparatus where scientific truth is concerned. Each of these reasons for preferring the study of science requires some amplification. Let us begin with the first.

In the study of literature or art our attention is perpetually riveted upon the past: the men of Greece or of the Rensaissance did better than any men do now; the triumphs of former ages, so far from facilitating fresh triumphs in our own age, actually increase the difficulty of fresh triumphs by rendering originality harder of attainment; not only is artistic achievement not cumulative, but it seems even to depend upon a certain freshness and *naiveté* of impulse and vision which civilisation tends to destroy. Hence comes, to those who have been nourished on the literary and artistic productions of former ages, a certain peevishness and undue fastidiousness towards the present, from which there seems no escape except into the deliberate vandalism which ignores tradition and in the search after originality achieves only the eccentric. But in such vandalism there is none of the simplicity and spontaneity out of which great art springs: theory is still the canker in its core, and insincerity destroys the advantages of a merely pretended ignorance.

The despair thus arising from an education which suggests no pre-eminent mental activity except that of artistic creation is wholly absent from an education which gives the knowledge of scientific method. The discovery of scientific method, except in pure mathematics, is a thing of yesterday; speaking broadly, we may say that it dates from Galileo. Yet already it has transformed the world, and its success proceeds with ever-accelerating velocity.

In science men have discovered an activity of the very highest value in which they are no longer, as in art, dependent for progress upon the appearance of continually greater genius, for in science the successors stand upon the shoulders of their predecessors; where one man of supreme genius has invented a method, a thousand lesser men can apply it. No transcendent ability is required in order to make useful discoveries in science; the edifice of science needs its masons, bricklayers, and common labourers as well as its foremen, master-builders, and architects. In art nothing worth doing can be done without genius; in science even a very moderate capacity can contribute to a supreme achievement.

In science the man of real genius is the man who invents a new method. The notable discoveries are often made by his successors, who can apply the method with fresh vigour, unimpaired by the previous labour of perfecting it; but the mental calibre of the thought required for their work, however brilliant, is not so great as that required by the first inventor of the method. There are in science immense numbers of different methods, appropriate to different classes of problems; but over and above them all, there is something not easily definable, which may be called *the* method of science. It was formerly customary to identify this with the inductive method, and to associate it with the name of Bacon. But the true inductive method was not discovered by Bacon, and the true method of science is something which includes deduction as much as induction, logic and mathematics as much as botany and geology. I shall not attempt the difficult task of stating what the scientific method is, but I will try to indicate the temper of mind out of which the scientific method grows, which is the second of the two merits that were mentioned above as belonging to a scientific education.

The kernel of the scientific outlook is a thing so simple, so obvious, so seemingly trivial, that the mention of it may almost excite derision. The kernel of the scientific outlook is the refusal to regard our own desires, tastes, and interests as affording a key to

the understanding of the world. Stated thus baldly, this may seem
no more than a trite truism. But to remember it consistently in
matters arousing our passionate partisanship is by no means easy,
especially where the available evidence is uncertain and inconclu-
sive. A few illustrations will make this clear.

Aristotle, I understand, considered that the stars must move in
circles because the circle is the most perfect curve. In the absence
of evidence to the contrary, he allowed himself to decide a question of fact by an appeal to aesthetico-moral considerations. In
such a case it is at once obvious to us that this appeal was un-
justifiable. We know now how to ascertain as a fact the way in
which the heavenly bodies move, and we know that they do not
move in circles, or even in accurate ellipses, or in any other kind
of simply describable curve. This may be painful to a certain hank-
ering after simplicity of pattern in the universe, but we know that
in astronomy such feelings are irrelevant. Easy as this knowledge
seems now, we owe it to the courage and insight of the first inventors of scientific method, and more especially of Galileo.

We may take as another illustration Malthus's doctrine of
population. This illustration is all the better for the fact that his
actual doctrine is now known to be largely erroneous. It is not his
conclusions that are valuable, but the temper and method of his
inquiry. As everyone knows, it was to him that Darwin owed an
essential part of his theory of natural selection, and this was only
possible because Malthus's outlook was truly scientific. His great
merit lies in considering man not as the object of praise or blame,
but as a part of nature, a thing with a certain characteristic behaviour from which certain consequences must follow. If the behaviour is not quite what Malthus supposed, if the consequences
are not quite what he inferred, that may falsify his conclusions, but
does not impair the value of his method. The objections which
were made when his doctrine was new—that it was horrible and
depressing, that people ought not to act as he said they did, and so
on—were all such as implied an unscientific attitude of mind; as

against all of them, his calm determination to treat man as a
natural phenomenon marks an important advance over the reformers of the eighteenth century and the Revolution.

Under the influence of Darwinism the scientific attitude
towards man has now become fairly common, and is to some people quite natural, though to most it is still a difficult and artificial
intellectual contortion. There is, however, one study which is as yet
almost wholly untouched by the scientific spirit—I mean the study
of philosophy. Philosophers and the public imagine that the scientific spirit must pervade pages that bristle with allusions to ions,
germ-plasms and the eyes of shell-fish. But as the devil can quote
Scripture, so the philosopher can quote science. The scientific
spirit is not an affair of quotation, of externally acquired information, any more than manners are an affair of the etiquette-book.
The scientific attitude of mind involves a sweeping away of all
other desires in the interests of the desire to know—it involves
suppression of hopes and fears, loves and hates, and the whole
subjective emotional life, until we become subdued to the material,
able to see it frankly, without preconceptions, without bias, without
any wish except to see it as it is, and without any belief that what
it is must be determined by some relation, positive or negative, to
what we should like it to be, or to what we can easily imagine it to
be.

Now in philosophy this attitude of mind has not as yet been
achieved. A certain self-absorption, not personal, but human, has
marked almost all attempts to conceive the universe as a whole.
Mind, or some aspect of it—thought or will or sentience—has
been regarded as the pattern after which the universe is to be conceived, for no better reason, at bottom, than that such a universe
would not seem strange, and would give us the cosy feeling that
every place is like home. To conceive the universe as essentially
progressive or essentially deteriorating, for example, is to give
to our hopes and fears a cosmic importance which *may,* of course,
be justified, but which we have as yet no reason to suppose justi-

fied. Until we have learnt to think of it in ethically neutral terms, we have not arrived at a scientific attitude in philosophy; and until we have arrived at such an attitude, it is hardly to be hoped that philosophy will achieve any solid results.

Human beings cannot, of course, wholly transcend human nature; something subjective, if only the interest that determines the direction of our attention, must remain in all our thought. But science comes nearer to objectivity than any other human pursuit, and gives us, therefore, the closest contact and the most intimate relation with the outer world that it is possible to achieve. To the primitive mind everything is either friendly or hostile; but experience has shown that friendliness and hostility are not the conceptions by which the world is to be understood. Science thus represents, though as yet only in a nascent condition, a higher stage of evolution than any pre-scientific thought or imagination, and, like every approach to self-transcendence, it brings with it a rich reward in increase of scope and breadth and comprehension. I have spoken so far largely of the negative aspect of the scientific spirit, but it is from the positive aspect that its value is derived. The instinct of constructiveness, which is one of the chief incentives to artistic creation, can find in scientific systems a satisfaction more massive than any epic poem. Disinterested curiosity, which is the source of almost all intellectual effort, finds with astonished delight that science can unveil secrets which might well have seemed for ever undiscoverable. The desire for a larger life and wider interests, for an escape from private circumstances, and even from the whole recurring human cycle of birth and death, is fulfilled by the impersonal cosmic outlook of science as by nothing else. To all these must be added, as contributing to the happiness of the man of science, the admiration of splendid achievement, and the consciousness of inestimable utility to the human race. A life devoted to science is therefore a happy life, and its happiness is derived from the very best sources that are open to dwellers on this troubled and passionate planet.

FOR THE STUDENT

Rhetoric

1. *Analyze the development of the first paragraph to see how Russell limits and defines his subject.*
2. *Russell's style is known for its clarity and precision. Analyze several of his longer sentences in order to study their rhetorical structure.*
3. *Russell frequently uses examples, analogies, concrete details. Cite instances of each and show how they help to clarify ideas.*
4. *Make a topic outline of the essay and state the thesis in one sentence.*

Discussion

1. *Compare Russell's views on the conflict between a scientific and a literary (or classical) education with those of Nicolson and Spender.*
2. *Russell wrote this essay in 1913. Might this fact partially explain the optimism of the first merit he attributes to science?*
3. *Russell emphasizes the necessity for objectivity in the scientific outlook by using the examples of Aristotle and Malthus. Would such an example as that of Francesco Lana (see Nicolson) have added any dimension to Russell's discussion?*
4. *Does Russell, in your opinion, give sufficient attention to the subjectivity of man's nature?*

Writing

1. *Show that Russell should or should not give more consideration to Miss Nicolson's two voices in his discussion of science as an element in culture.*

2. *Theme topic: "The happy life of the scientist on 'this troubled and passionate planet.'"*

10 Religion

The subject of religion virtually demands speculation (*what it* is, *what it* ought to be), *and it lends itself to widely, sometimes violently divergent, views: witness
the various "holy wars" and "reformations" which have characterized the histories of the great religions. But religion-in-
general, though it is dealt with ably by great modern theologians like Niebuhr and Tillich, is much too comprehensive a
subject for a book of this sort or for its intended audience. It
seems best, therefore, to delimit the subject and to present a
fan or spectrum of opinions dealing, almost exclusively, with
Christianity.*

The first selection is a symposium from Commonweal, *one
of the more liberal American Catholic journals. The participants, all products of Catholic families and education, speak
with varying degrees of disaffection toward the Church. They
may be said to represent the "New Left." The next selection
is by C. E. M. Joad, a British philosopher, who may be called
moderate in this sense: that he opposes those modern rationalists who would discount the need for religion (and most
of their arguments are directed toward Christianity) by dis-
crediting its origins. However Joad, in his insistence that religion is continually evolving, is not so conservative as C. S.
Lewis, the author of the third selection. Lewis is perhaps the
foremost modern apologist for historical Christianity: hell,
heaven, the devil, the redemption, and the sacraments.*

The Cool Generation and the Church

The following symposium features six students from Catholic college backgrounds, brought together in New York by Commonweal *for an exchange of views among themselves in a taping session with the Editors.*

Frank Carling was graduated last June from Fordham College, where he was president of the student government. He is now studying international law at Yale.

John J. Burke Jr., a Jesuit seminarian, studied at both Holy Cross and Boston Colleges. He recently began graduate work in English at Northwestern.

William T. Wilson is an undergraduate at La Salle College in Philadelphia.

Mary Frances Campion, a graduate student in Temple University's school of education, is an alumna of Rosary College, River Forest, Ill.

Martha Ann Brazier is a junior in the school of education at Boston College.

Kathleen A. McHale, a 1963 graduate of Newton College of the Sacred Heart, in Massachusetts, has done work toward a master's degree at Stanford.

Most of the students have been associated with student community and activist organizations, notably in the area of peace and civil rights.

EDITOR   We might begin from where some of the participants in our earlier symposium on the woman intellectual in the Church ended their discussion. Rosemary Ruether said that among students she knew there definitely is no interest in any doctrine about the supernatural. The interest is in human values. And Mary Daly said that many students won't even read Catholic theologians anymore. They feel they only get the party line, with some

From Commonweal, *Vol. 86 (October 6, 1967). Reprinted by permission.*

liberal ideas thrown in. Do you think they catch the flavor of the contemporary Catholic student?

CARLING   There is not so much rejection of the supernatural as there is rejection of the idea that there's a great difference between supernatural and human values. Students today are trying to find some way of fusing the two.

BURKE   The type of thing Rosemary Ruether is describing has been occurring in Catholic schools for a long time, but I think it a bit inaccurate to say people are uninterested in reading Catholic theologians. Look at how Teilhard de Chardin is read. I do admit, though, that in many respects Catholic theology is sterile, and I'm not particularly convinced by anybody on the contemporary scene that it is balanced.

WILSON   The reason I don't read Catholic theologians is because I find it hard to read with my eyes closed; I fall asleep when I read Catholic theologians. Young people I know are interested in living, about how tomorrow's going to get on, about whether you're going to be here tomorrow. We're interested in having fun. And we're not such bad people either; we're not killing people. But we're not obeying sex laws either.

CAMPION   It's bad to generalize and say students aren't reading Catholic theologians. I think people are more drawn to what is relevant to what is happening to them now. It's perhaps true that more Protestant than Catholic theologians are producing materials to satisfy this interest. But again, a great many people are reading Teilhard, and he happens to be Catholic.

BRAZIER   But you've also got to remember that the people who are reading Teilhard and other theologians, Catholic and Protestant, are maybe 15 percent of the Catholic population. That means 85 percent are not doing the reading, yet at the same time remain interested Catholics. I think these people are more interested in what some call secular theology. They find greater relevance in helping somebody put up his storm windows than in reading Teilhard.

MCHALE   Let me speak first of interest in the supernatural: many people my age—25—grew up in a religious, intellectual tradition which purported to establish a vertical relationship between yourself and God. And that meant that one's religious experience was somehow direct, although it was unclear exactly what it was. But there were enough people around who supposedly knew God and loved Him; and if you didn't know Him it bothered you a great deal. There are people my age who have had enormous difficulty dealing with that problem of vertical relationships. They have an attraction to the cultural, imaginative and symbolic traditions of the Church, which are based on vertical relationships; also, there's a kind of obsession, a kind of taste for the Divine, which is very hard to give up. In that sense many people my age *are* still interested in supernatural values.

That same tradition likewise tried to establish religious values which would protect you from social and political corruption, so that if you were holy in the valid sense—you went to Mass; you prayed; you did Catholic Charities' work—you wouldn't be corrupted by the fact that you had a lot of money. I went to school with a lot of girls with a lot of money. I began to discover when I got out that we were being corrupted by the society. I suppose I became a kind of environmentalist and that helped me to change my attitude toward the vertical relationship with God. It also helped me to become very cynical about older religious values.

As for reading Catholic theologians, I do read them. But I have great difficulty doing so. They are dull. Besides that, there's a language problem. I was asked recently to read some ecumenical documents and I started with one by Pope John. I was so offended that I had to put him down. The language of the Church is really offensive. It's not very direct. There's a restraint even in the most modern theologians, because they are trying to talk to the older Church. This is a restraint which is not easy for me to adjust to. Rage operates much more freely in my mind than a desire to communicate.

BURKE   You identify marvelously why Catholic theology is
sterile: language. It *is* offensive. Take the papal encyclicals. Even
a particularly brilliant, forward-looking encyclical like *Populorum
Progressio* makes you irritated. The noble "we" is used so often
that it makes the encyclical sound almost arrogant—though the
encyclical actually carries an intense compassion for the misery of
the human race.

A lot of this language problem goes back to the roots of Catholic theology, which are in Thomism. Why, one teacher I had was
hopping up and down with delight because Karl Rahner had "discovered" quasi-formal causality. These people are talking a language that nobody understands and that nobody wants to understand.

BRAZIER   There is a hypocrisy here and it has existed for
centuries. Churchmen speak in noble terms and noble language,
but their acts are far from noble. Everybody indicts the Nazis for
the slaughter of the Jews. But where was the Pope and where were
the Catholic spokesmen then? Indeed, where are the spokesmen,
the bishops of America, when it comes to the war in Vietnam? We
young people are extremely idealistic and we expect this old and
very ancient institution, the Church, to be just as idealistic as we
are. Instead it chooses to be "realistic." Naturally young people
get frustrated. Some stay with the Church, but many just ignore
it and pretend it doesn't exist. Look at Pope Paul. After John he
is such a letdown, almost a Hamlet. He seems to see so many sides
to every question.

CHAMPION   The problem we're getting at is the deeper one of
honesty. Young people who are involved in the contemporary
world are very much put off by people who seem to be compro-
mising, who hedge around problems, who do not come to grips
with things honestly. This accounts for part of the sterility in a lot
of Catholic theology. Many theologians have a valid point to
make, but they ensconce it in verbal compromise so that it won't be
too offensive to the powers that be. Students are very aware of this

tactic; they can spot this kind of phoniness a mile away. It creates an immediate communication barrier.

EDITOR   Do you think that the younger generation is as honest with itself as it would like the older generation to be honest with itself? For instance, before we started to tape, one of the speakers was talking about wanting to stay out of the draft and to stay out of jail at the same time. Are you facing up to your problems?

BURKE   Certainly many of the younger generation are failing to maintain the type of integrity that they demand of others. Look at the amount of cheating that goes on in college. It seems hypocritical to me for persons in this kind of situation to accuse the older generation of dishonesty. They've made themselves dishonest in the context of their own world. It's very easy to accuse someone else of compromise when you're making compromises yourself.

WILSON   Let me interrupt. I'm honest with myself. I know that I'm in college to avoid the draft. And I'm not criticizing the older generation, because I gave up on that generation. No one's going to change it. It's lost, right? . . . And about the papal encyclicals; they're terrible; they stink; they don't say anything. What I'm waiting for, instead of papal encyclicals, is a new Bob Dylan album. Now there is somebody saying something that pertains to me. He inspires me.

CARLING   I think we can get a little perspective by thinking for a minute about which students we are talking. I go to a Catholic college, Fordham. I find—and I suppose this is true of most Catholic and non-Catholic colleges—that a very small percentage of students is active, either socially or religiously or politically. Most students are primarily interested in what they are studying and their careers. Generally, it is the students who read theology, whether Catholic or non-Catholic, who are interested in problems involving the relevance of the religious point of view. So you have students who are primarily interested in careers, and you have students who are interested in the social order and who feel religion has something to say in this area. Now one of the marks of this latter group is that it is hard-pressed for time. Accordingly, it reads the theology that touches most closely on the problems it is working with. This means that these students are reading little Catholic theology. Whatever one may think of Father Rahner and his quasi-formal causality, they don't exactly tell you what you want to know about Vietnam and the civil rights movement.

So it is not so much a matter of turning against Catholicism as such. If Harvey Cox had been a Catholic, his *Secular City* book would have been read. Rather it is the failure of Catholic theologians to discuss the kind of problems that students are most concerned about.

EDITOR   What violence does disenchantment with Catholic theology and with the system do to belief in the supernatural among young people?

MCHALE   A kind of violence. Still, there is a logic in what we're saying and the way we're living. (We are very much Americans and therefore some of the things that we say about ourselves as Catholics can be said about young Americans generally.) It seems to me that we begin with the problem of identity. This is a problem quite different for us than it was for our parents, partly because some of the options available to them for identity purposes are meaningless now. For example, making a great deal of money: for those of us raised in an affluent society, this is a pointless identity value. So we seek other means of identity. They call us ahistorical perhaps, and say we're not interested in the magisterium. Really what it is is that we don't know where we start and it ends, and so we prefer not to deal with it at all. Until we come to a much deeper understanding of identity, I think we are always going to be like that.

CARLING   One of the problems of our generation is that in some ways it expects too much. We wish that President Johnson would lie less, but at the same time we know a political figure must present his case in the best light possible; and that often borders on duplicity of some kind or another. But in the religious sphere, we expect no equivocating. So when you have Pope Paul saying that the Church is not significantly divided on birth control, or not divided to the point where the issue is in doubt, we get turned off. His is an obvious lie. You see, we expect religious issues not to be treated the same as political issues; we expect the supernatural not to be pleaded the same way a dubious political cause might be. If the man who is the official pronouncer, guardian and proclaimer of the supernatural finds it necessary to lie or to tamper with supernatural truths, it is understandable that students should regard the values they are intended to reflect as irrelevant.

BRAZIER   I agree that on birth control Pope Paul has proclaimed what seems to us an obvious lie. On the other hand, we young people have to develop a tolerance of the other person's opinion and have got to learn to see the other side of the questions. On birth control, Pope Paul has to remain silent. Think of the thousands of people who have 10, 11, 12, 13 children, because they lived the Catholic faith as it existed four or five years ago. How many of those people would be disillusioned and alienated if the Pope abruptly changed the teaching on birth control? Young people can't become dogmatic, as the Church itself has been for so long. We've got to guard against one-sidedness and one-perspectiveness. We can't just walk in and say "folk Masses are great, abortion is good, there is no just war concept," and be mindless of other people. This is the problem of youth: impatience. I agree with every single one here that the older generation isn't honest; we want more honesty. But we ourselves must have more tolerance and patience.

BURKE   I am sick and tired of being told to be patient. The old guard says, "Be patient, be patient; things will change." At the same time we are taught that silence means consent. Well, I don't think we should be expected to be silent on ideals that are spelled out in the Gospels. The Church is our Church; it is not somebody else's Church; it is the whole people of God. And we have clearly founded principles as to what we can expect from the

people who are in authority. We have every right, almost a duty,
to demand from them that people in authority live up to the
principles they are proclaiming. And that means *all* the principles;
that means honesty, mercy, justice, charity—not just sexual ethics.

MCHALE   When you talk about the Church speaking in a forth-
right way and being honest, you're talking about its taking a
critical position with respect to the society. When you do that,
and talk at the same time about freedom and involvement and the
people of God, you are speaking about a variety of pressures,
about conflicts of interest and all those lovely theories in American
history courses. Which means that the social institution you're
imagining has to have some kind of intimate relationship with the
society, and that its critical position is deeply endangered by this
intimacy.

In a way our Church is deeply involved in social society. It's
pervaded by American values—values which we've been rejecting.
We're trying to establish some kind of critical distance from those
values, and do it on a religious basis. At the same time, we can't;
for if we get too far away, we have no relevance to the society.
It's a problem which has to be worked out systematically and
intellectually, as well as in the light of experience. And I don't
know anything about how it is to be done.

The problem of patience is the same thing. We're told to be
patient; we know we should be. But patience is a liberal value.
Fifty-year-old guys like Michael Harrington are really upset because we're not patient. [Harrington was born in 1928.—Ed.]
We're saying, "Patience is not the problem, old man; it's your
method!" The New Deal is dead, and so is Marxism. We're talking about a qualitative, profoundly different approach to the same
old problems. There are plenty of people in the New Left as well
as the Church who will say, "I'll work all my life; I'll be very
patient; but I want to take it from a different standpoint."

WILSON   I really don't give a damn what the Church has to
say. It's speaking to its own line of people, in their own different
world. The Church, as far as I'm concerned, is lost. It's on the

way out. We started a new world; oh, maybe it's not new but it's different, and we're happy. Leave us alone and we'll leave Church people alone to follow their foolish practices, their superstitions, their Masses. We have a world that has relevance to the way we live. We get up in the morning, we feel good; we go to bed and we feel good. In the Church they go to bed wondering how they feel.

CAMPION The issue is deeper than that. Take the liberal movement in the Church the last few years. Much of the liberal vision has become part of the structure, yet a lot of liberals are just as dissatisfied as before. They have not found the fulfillment that they were seeking, even though structures changed. I think we will find that people who today totally reject structures and envision the day that we'll be rid of them won't be satisfied either. To me it is not as much a question of the structures or the externals of the thing, as the attitude involved. I think what young people are searching for is an inner thing, a sense of value that goes way beyond the existing structure. And so getting rid of the structures, or changing structures, or rejecting the Church, or rejecting the government—these really are not avenues to fulfillment.

CARLING There's been a most interesting development with our generation. In the past one's religious life was so wrought up with the religious institution that they were pretty much the same thing. The choice was between the Church and becoming completely secularized, or whatever the current phrase is—or was. In our generation the option has changed dramatically. Students have developed their own kind of religious life outside the institution. This is another way of jumping ship, but it doesn't have the same effect as it used to have. Now the only options aren't "I'll stay a Roman Catholic or I'll be an atheist." Now students are saying, "Well, I've developed a kind of religious life of my own that I find infinitely more valuable and valid than the one I had in the Church. Therefore I don't have to accept the institution. I don't need the Church to give a kind of religious side to my life."

EDITOR   Is there a faithfulness to certain minimal requirements or is this a total cutting off?

CARLING   If by minimal requirements you mean liturgical requirements, then there is not a total cutting off. But because of the freedom that is taken in the liturgy, a lot of what goes on is underground. Yet through it many students who are quite out of the institutional structure of the Church, are able to maintain their sacramental life. This was utterly impossible before.

EDITOR   I take it for granted that what the Pope has to say, his worries and concerns, don't make the least bit of difference.

CARLING   Even on liturgical matters, I don't think anybody any longer cares what the Pope says. Young people especially feel that the Pope doesn't have a right to tell them that they can't have a special kind of liturgy. It's understandable. Priests who participate in new, radical liturgies nearly always say that it's the most stirring liturgical event of their lives. Others say, "It's the first Mass I've ever been to that is really a Mass." These people are not diverted when the Pope says this is all quite dangerous and you must secure permission (which in the New York archdiocese is virtually impossible). People say, "Well, this is a completely fulfilling liturgical experience and you simply do not have the right to tell us that we cannot participate in it. Your religious fiat does not extend that far."

MCHALE   I live in San Francisco and spend a lot of time among Hippies. I live, I suppose, like a middle-class Hippie. If you identify three kinds of groups—the Hippies, New Leftists with their parallel institutions, and radical Catholics my age who are attempting to develop community, either in houses or unions—you find a great deal in common among all. In a way all have dropped out. All have stopped worrying about how you get the archbishop or the President, or the mayor, or anybody, to see your point of view. You just act; as the Hippies say, you do your thing. I do not think it's a case simply of saying we are what we are and this is the way we are going to do things. It's also that we've been affected by what's been happening in this country. In a way we're exhibiting what you might call withdrawal symptoms, as the result of the effect of the Vietnam war on us; the floundering state of the civil rights movement, and the confusion that now exists among the most advanced student movements. Still we know that we want to be related to other people, that we want to develop community. That's hard but we're beginning to solve real problems along those lines, problems which our institutional friends haven't even begun to imagine. In a sense we're still connected with the institution, but we are withdrawing from the structures—not only because they are totally irrelevant to the problems we see as valid, but also because they seem impervious to change. And we have no power.

Another point: it is true that whatever the Pope says is, especially to New Leftists and to radical Catholics, just a joke. He really doesn't have very much effect on what I think or don't think, except as a kind of visceral reaction. I recall a Wilfred Sheed article in *Commonweal* about growing up in the '30s. One comment of his really impressed me. It was that he suddenly realized (and other people his age did too) that he was going along thinking, "oh well, the Church around me is terrible but that's not the real Church"; then it occurred to him that he had to take responsibility for the Church. I would say that the same is happening to me and, in a peculiar way, to my friends. I feel some very deep need, an obligation, to take responsibility for the Church, for all of its evil, all of its monstrosities, all of its wild, bizarre rococo. It's not only in my blood and in my viscera; it's in my mind. I have to take a responsibility for history, if I'm going to be honest. I can't pretend that I'm different from other Catholics. I am a Catholic. I am also an American.

This brings me back to the problem of dealing with institutions. In a way I think that Hippies, New Leftists and radical Catholics, even if they don't talk about taking responsibility, will sooner or later move out of their withdrawal symptoms and come to terms with the institutions. What they're all interested in is producing change, in, as the Hippies would say, making love. That means making love with everybody. So that means you have to talk to

people. It's not so much that you want to make your parents
understand and change them. It's that you want to make everybody
live decently, honestly, lovingly.

BRAZIER   I agree to an extent that young people are having
withdrawal symptoms, and I say this is a good thing. But so far
as the institutional Church is concerned, these people are actually
going back to what we had in the beginning—the twelve apostles,
and Antioch, and small communities.

But as you say, we are an American people; we're an American Church. We're not an Italian Church, and this is why we're
throwing away the Pope. We resent having an Italian sitting over
there telling us how to run our Church in America. Not only that,
we resent having a bishop of a large city telling us in a small town
how we should worship God. We prefer to get together in a community with people of like mind and worship God in the way we
feel we should.

EDITOR   As you withdraw into your small communities, do
you see yourselves as part of a universal Church or as isolated
communities of Christians?

BRAZIER   As a universal Church, yes. But not with everything
set up and decisions made on certain levels. Each community
should have power within itself.

EDITOR   What is the source of the unity?

BRAZIER   Faith itself; not institution. The question then is,
where does the institutional Church stand in the future Church?
Will it go; will it stay? I have reached the conclusion that it has
got to go—at least as it exists today. I think just about everybody
here agrees on that.

BURKE   It is a mistake to say our generation is withdrawing.
I agree that there are withdrawal symptoms, but the matter is
centripetal as well as centrifugal. I go to bed at night haunted by
the misery of what people suffer in South America and India. It's
hard to describe the compassion that burns in my heart for these
people. I'm haunted, too, by what American society has done to
the Negroes, how it has defeated them, squashed them, just com-

pletely eroded their self-respect. McLuhan and the electronic technology have cultivated this reaction. We all feel guilty. . . . We feel guilty for what the Church has done, for what American society has done. But we cannot withdraw, because this is the milieu we live in.

CARLING   What we are viewing in fact is the evolution of the idea of what an institution is. There are a number of reasons why this had to occur. The most obvious, it seems, is the breakdown of the parish structure. Parishes are geographical. Those of us in urban environments do not live in geographical units any longer; our primary community is no longer our neighborhood. Those of us on campuses lose all ties with the parish by being away from it for four years. We develop a new kind of community, a community of interest and not of location; a community with its own liturgy, its own priests and, more often than not, its own set of doctrines. Now this movement, which can never be turned back, has led to the realization, first, that the institutional Church is not the same thing as the hierarchy. People in this movement might have left the Church 20 years ago, or remained in it, frustrated; now they feel themselves very much a part of the Church but not as members of a parish of a particular archdiocese. A group like this pretty much removes itself from chancery and diocese. But still not completely. It was such a group that picketed the New York chancery last year after it made a defensive gesture and sent a priest away (we feel, at least, it had a large part in sending the priest away), and told two others to shut up and to stop associating with particular students. We took to the streets, caused a lot of trouble, and embarrassed the chancery. The point is obvious; we cannot entirely break our connection with the hierarchy since the hierarchy, in fact, still holds the power.

Now many of the problems we are talking about—the papacy credibility gap and that sort of thing—are connected with the spread of these communities, because these communities have their own kind of rules; they are self-sustaining; generally they're academic, and therefore very sure of themselves and of the kind of beliefs they are evolving. They resent very much the intrusion of anyone from the outside, and especially from above, telling them what to believe, or how to worship, or where to be and when.

But we have to watch very closely where this movement is going. There are dangers in it. The most obvious is that these groups tend to turn in upon themselves. We talk a lot about this. It's not so much a matter of alienation in the classic sense; it's a matter of being so self-sufficient, so self-sustaining that it's hard to be part of the institution at large any more. The problem then is, what kind of unity do you maintain? I don't know. I see every day groups I associate with getting farther and farther away from the institution, and people in them rejecting the idea of real membership in the institution. The Church is a funny kind of club anyway. It doesn't have any membership card or membership lists; there are no dues. And this is probably the thing. You wonder after a while what it means to be a member, to be a Catholic, I don't know how to answer. I'm not sure it's a relevant question. Am I or am I not a Catholic? I'm not even certain it's an either-or proposition.

Thus we begin to inhabit a kind of twilight zone between the world and the Church. This is good, I think, and necessary. But at the same time we find ourselves becoming inverted, quite rigid in some ways and dogmatic in others; we're very much too sure of ourselves. Still the movement as a whole is only not good but necessary, because the alternative for so many of us who cannot function within the structure as it exists would be to leave it altogether.

WILSON I'd like to make an observation about the Church. When you read the Gospel concept of Jesus Christ, he seems to be, pardon the expression, hip, cool, with it. Right? But the Church today is so different from what Christ had in mind; it just doesn't jive. Someone said youth groups resemble the early Church. That's a good observation. We're starting all over again. Christ would have fit right in at a pot party.

BRAZIER   What you're saying is that Christ was a man of his time, which I don't think anybody will deny.

EDITOR   Where does the motivation come from for social, political and interpersonal good if you diminish the institution and papacy? You don't look to the state. Where do you look? Back to the Gospels? To Christ? Or to a secular humanism?

CARLING   One reason a dichotomy grew between our social and religious consciousness *vis à vis* the institution was the discovery—whether from being brought up in the slums, as I was, or through other means—that our social consciousness didn't come from the institution. Consequently there seemed little point in reading encyclicals or pronouncements to try to find there justification or motivation for what we already felt most deeply.

I think that social consciousness can be heightened by reading the Gospel, and ought to be; ideally, it should be seen in the context not only of the Gospel and Christianity, but of our whole religious tradition. However, having developed itself independently, I don't think that social consciousness will ever be seen merely as a part of our religious tradition, our Catholicity, our Christianity, or anything else. It is essentially part of ourselves as persons and as humans.

The fact that truths we hold most dear have evolved this way inevitably influences our idea of what real truths are and where they ought to be found. We have a tendency to seek religious and other kinds of truths in the same way we found social consciousness. Hence, we look to the Church less and less for any kind of inspiration.

EDITOR   Where specifically do you find this inspiration or the motivation?

CARLING   Right out on the streets.

MCHALE   There are people I have read that I could point to and say "I've gotten a lot of my values from them; they articulate my needs." But it still remains true that the reason I go to these people, and the reason all of us go to the streets, is that they offer something that we already feel, something that we need. We are just looking for new sources. But in a way what produced our needs is simply the logic of history. That may be impossible to discuss but there are certain facts. History develops. There is a kind of evolution and it produces changes in consciousness, if not in love, as McLuhan points out so horribly. There is a kind of change in epistemology taking place, simply because we're alive and we live in the culture. We may reject values that institutions now articulate, but actually we haven't rejected the culture. We're products of it. We're just trying to find more relevant and, I hate this word, meaningful ways of expressing needs that history has produced in us.

This leads to a point on the question of liturgy. It's not so much liturgy, it's a style of life that we're looking for. Michael Novak once talked about the difference between the Christian and the atheist being one of symbolic content. Others talk that way, too. If you take that to be your language for the moment, and say it is symbolic content which makes me different from the atheist or which makes me what I am, then you have to find rituals and language and styles which are symbolic and which express your content, so to speak. They have to be related to the society. You look at this country and you think what have I got in common with it; America, I don't know you or like you. So you go off with your own friends and you stumble around and try to find rituals and language and symbols which you have in common.

EDITOR   Many of my generation came out of the radical Catholic movements. We denied that the older people represented the real Church, because we recognized the Church in something like the *Catholic Worker*. We were intent on changing the Church, insisting that the *Catholic Worker* represented the *real* Church. Do you see yourselves as working to change the conception of the Church or are you just sort of "out"?

CARLING   The fact is that increasingly the most articulate young Catholics are Catholics who have gone through our type of experience. Within a period of generations this has simply got to change the Church, even if we can't tell exactly how. I think, on the other hand, we should be less dogmatic about wanting to change the Church consciously. The institution has its rules; it functions on the kind of principles that it considers relevant and that's perfectly fine. But I have ceased worrying about trying to convert Cardinal Spellman to my point of view. I simply would rather that he didn't try to stop me from living my own way or take the priests away from me who are trying to help me live that way.

CAMPION   I think our motivation and inspiration come from person, in the deepest sense of that word. Young people today are so much more aware of the ultimate value of person.

BURKE   With regard to motivation, we respond as we do socially because of the way we have been trained within Catholicism. We see the Church as being a miserable flop. But nevertheless it is the Church that gave us birth, that created us, that had us read the Gospel, that made us sensitive and responsive to particular types of values. At the same time, ours is an electronic milieu. The viewer sees; he reacts. He rages at Cardinal Spellman or other members in the Church who don't respond to values they have supposedly committed themselves to. Then occurs the process of alienation by which the person moves outside the institution.

MCHALE   The same thing is happening to people who have not been raised in religious institutions. Mario Savio, in an article just after the free speech movement was more or less dead, said something which expresses a very interesting quality among young people who are not religiously affected. He said it should be enough just to point to an evil. It's there and it's wrong. Mario Savio took quite literally all the baloney about democracy that we were taught in civics class. For some peculiar reason, we tend to take our culture quite literally.

BURKE   But why does Savio or anyone else even talk about evil? He talks about evil because of the process of Christofication that has occurred over 20 centuries. I think that we have so absorbed the Christian evangelical morality into our sensibilities, into our way of perceiving the world, that we even talk in those terms, whether specifically we have been religiously trained or not. I think this is one of the reasons why things like compassion and being in love really mean so much to us.

MCHALE   I disagree with you. What you're engaging in is an act of appropriation. Michael Novak does the same damn thing. It's an act of appropriation to say Christianity has given all these values to Western civilization. That's really not true.

CARLING   It's very interesting that our Jesuit friend here is one who has made the most harsh pronouncements about the Church. He's the only one who's come out and said the Church has flopped, that its approach sometimes makes him nauseous. This is illustrative of the greatest single failure of the Church: so many of us don't care any more. We lose less and less sleep about the distance between the hierarchical Church and the real world. We have so little time, we want to spend it working in the real world and just don't worry about the Church. It is those men who are committed professionally to the Church, as I presume a Jesuit seminarian would be, who have to live day after day with this distance in a way we're all lucky enough not to have to. The fact that the Church fails to inspire rage in us is more indicative than anything else of the extent to which it has failed to touch our generation.

CAMPION   I agree. Students now are not much concerned with trying to reconcile the historical Church with their view of reality. They're much more concerned with living valid lives, and being in the world in as personal and as efficacious a way as possible. When more people begin to live valid lives themselves as individuals, perhaps with person as ultimate value, then the structures will begin to express themselves validly.

MCHALE   Maybe because I'm a few years older I differ on this point. But still it's not just me, or I wouldn't bother to say it. There are other people my age who feel the same. What it amounts to is this. We are, as you say, trying to live decent, valid lives and trying to figure out how to relate to this society. We simply don't worry what the Church has to offer in the way of guidelines and morals. It has failed. In that sense we are like you.

But in another sense none of us is capable of really being indifferent. In other words, I still get enraged, and so do many of my friends who are at least as radical as I am. They don't much bother about what you should do about archbishops. They debate it theoretically; it is a technical problem. But it's also a visceral problem. I can't justify my relationship with the Church on intellectual grounds. I mean it. I'm stuck with it and so are others my age. We're in it and it's in our blood. There's no way out. When Archbishop McGucken says something absolutely asinine, my stomach gets all upset. I can't ignore him, even though the man has never said anything that I could possibly consider worthwhile.

CAMPION What I meant is that on a theoretical, intellectual level, I don't think people are concerned anymore about trying to reconcile the Church. On an existential-experiential level, it's quite a different thing. The Church does cause rage; it does cause frustration. We realize that we're a part of it, and that it's part of our cultural heritage.

CARLING I think it's the other way around. I have great intellectual interest in the Church. What convinces me more every day that the Church is failing is that I can no longer react viscerally to the Church. That's more frightening, because the intellectual interest will always be there—though it may not be very compelling.

WILSON This feeling that you are stuck with the Church . . . if you don't like the Church you should get out. The way I did; the way my friends did. As far as we're concerned, God may or not be dead, but the Church is certainly long gone. The services have already been held.

BRAZIER No, you can't get out. If you don't believe in Christ, okay, get out of the Catholic Church, get out of Christianity. If you don't believe in democracy, get out of America. But because you deny the right of the Catholic Church as an institution to dictate your acts, you should not just drop out. I don't altogether believe that you should work within its confines. Perhaps ignore some of the more stringent rules, if you feel you can't work with them. But you've got to work within the establishment that you've got, and try and take it to an end, to some goal. You don't throw it away. You become a nihilist if you throw it away.

BURKE   You people have not explained why you care.

MCHALE   I care because I was born Kathy McHale, an Irish-Catholic.

BURKE   That's my point about Teilhard and Christofication. I'm talking about an evolution that has occurred within the human race in terms of revelation, in terms of a theology—and I don't mean Rahnerian theology. We *do* care about living decent valid lives and the fact that we care is what is significant. It is indicative of the extent to which we have absorbed the Gospels or the data of revelation. It is a reason why you have to make a careful distinction between the Church as church and the Church as institution. I think we are perhaps past the point of the Church as an institution, at least as we know it today. But that doesn't mean we are beyond the Church in the sense of revelation.

CARLING   I hardly think that we absorb our idea of valid living from the Gospel or any other source. It's there. It hits you every time you look at it. The validity of life leaps out at you.

BURKE   Then why not just go out, get a job, earn money, have a nice life, get yourself a couple of swimming pools and things like that? Why do we care about something in life more than that?

CARLING   The reason we care more is because we have found that life is not just that. I don't deny that our tradition, our upbringing and all the rest have a profound effect on this type of consciousness. I don't know whether I could have developed a sensitivity of this sort had I not been raised the way I was and even been exposed to the Christian Catholic tradition. At the same time I'm convinced that the sensitivity itself and the kind of consciousness it produces in me are not a result in any sense of that upbringing. They're a result of my contact, always a surprising one, with life itself. When you undergo such a process you automatically think back to your tradition. Our minds are continually correlating what we are doing with what we have read and learned. I'm certain that there are two distinct sources here. The source of my basic sensitivity is experience itself and any kind of correlation I make between that and my tradition is something I do after the fact.

BURKE   I think you're denying experience of the psyche. This is learning psychology in general.

MCHALE   I would only subscribe to what you are saying if you were willing to admit that theology follows sociology. I have been wanting to know for a long time how many Catholics or ex-Catholics there are in the New Left. I asked a friend of mine who knows a great many New Leftists and she said half. I can't get any figures, but if I ever do! There is a connection. It may be religious, but if theology is what is making us care, it's because theology is coming to terms with society, with cultural facts, cultural traditions—which theology hasn't been doing since the nineteenth century. That's what I mean when I say theology follows sociology.

BURKE   When I use the word theology, though, I'm not talking about academic theology. I'm talking about a theological event that occurred in history. I don't want to associate myself with Rahner, Küng or any of those people whatsoever. I don't think they have done anything.

MCHALE   I would carry it farther. I would say that I'm not sure what Christ did either. That's what I'm saying.

EDITOR   Most of you seem to go or have gone to Catholic colleges. Are you glad or sorry?

MCHALE   I went to a Catholic college and in the four years since I have spent an undue amount of time examining that education, on the assumption that if I didn't find out what it did to me, I wouldn't know who I was. I developed a lot of very abstract theories, most of which were violently antagonistic about the system, which is one of the most subtle, the most Machiavellian that anyone could be exposed to. I went back to that college recently. I found that what I take to be the epistemology changes in America and the world are going on even there. One can't say I hated my Catholic education, although I would prefer to have gone elsewhere. All I can say is that I am what I am and that the Catholic Church and the Irish tradition have made me that way. And so has America. So has Camus. I would never pay a dime if I were rich to a Catholic school, to create one, but I would support a place where people are studying religious traditions and talking about religious matters, and thinking about God and Christ. I'm not willing to say there should be no religious academic institutions. I believe in academic professionalism, to some degree. That means scholars working on theology. That means someone paying them, too. But I would never support a Catholic school, especially one that had nothing but girls. And nothing but girls from an upper economic income, being taught by nothing but women, and sorry, sorry academic has-beens, and a few intellectuals. I'm not attacking the entire faculty of any Catholic college. Catholic schools have a lot of really brilliant intellectuals. But the whole idea of a Catholic college is really bad; it can't work.

CAMPION   I think that most of us who have run the gamut of Catholic education are more sorry about the provincialism inherent in the system than we are with Christian attitudes it seeks to communicate. There's such a lack of integration with the whole of reality.

BRAZIER   I have never gone to an institution—they're all been Catholic by the way—of which I can honestly say I'm proud. I've always had a feeling of shame, a need to apologize. This is my fault as well as the institutions'. I shouldn't feel as though I have to apologize. At the same time, however, my classmates have felt the same way. Catholic schools have a reputation of being provincial, of being one-minded, of being dogmatic.

CARLING   Fordham is different from any other Catholic college, so it's hard for me to generalize. It has its weaknesses; but not in terms of its Catholicity. That is a great compliment that I can pay Fordham. I think of Fordham as an educational institution and the criticisms that automatically crop up in my mind are educational criticisms. There are certain weaknesses that are directly attributable to the school's religious orientation; for example, weaknesses in the philosophy department. But other weaknesses have been erased so quickly that three years from now, I probably wouldn't be able to make that criticism at all. So while I think that Fordham has weaknesses, many of which derive from its history as a Catholic institution, its weaknesses today are not attributable to its Catholicity. I'm not altogether pleased about the education I received there, but I certainly can't condemn it as a ghetto or Catholic enclave. The religious influence at Fordham —and this may shock some people—is nil. You can go through four years there and have one, two, three priests as teachers, perhaps none. You can also have 20. Generally you have only one or two. There are no religious requirements at all, except that Catholic students take theology. There are no compulsory religious services. You go for months at a time and never see a priest, and never hear God mentioned. From the point of view of some people that may be bad. I thought it was terrific. I had the freedom to look for what I wanted to find and to avoid what I wished to avoid.

WILSON   Two good points have been overlooked about going to a Catholic institution. The first is that if you're the type that looks to revolt against stuffed shirts, Catholic institutions give you an excellent opportunity because there are so many of them there. Good point two: most of the students I know at the Catholic college I have been attending have lost their faith.

BRAZIER   Catholic education on the whole has failed. The schools are inferior to secular institutions. They cannot attract the faculty, and they have neither the money nor the facilities to compete educationally with secular institutions. They do not even fulfill the goal of keeping people in the faith or converting people to Catholicism.

BURKE   When I graduated from high school I was in a position to go to just about any college or university that I wanted. I was offered a scholarship to Harvard and I refused; I said I would go to a Catholic school and no other. I have changed my opinion considerably since that moment of my life. Why? This is a complicated question and distinctions have to be made.

There is what I call Chinese brainwashing at its best that occurs in the Catholic school system, and I resent that bitterly. On the other hand, I am grateful to Catholic education, because with it I have developed a sensibility, a type of perception which involves compassion and sensitivity (I have the uncomfortable feeling at times, however, that I developed this in spite of what I had been through).

Over-all, though, I feel shortchanged—for several reasons. I have come as an older and wiser person to realize that most of our Catholic schools on the university level are third-rate at best, and to recognize that dialogue and communication are severely hampered between the intellectual who is a product of the Catholic school system and American society as a whole. I also feel shortchanged that I could never really develop myself as a person. At Holy Cross, my college, I associated only with Catholics, and Catholics of a certain type—what *Time* very wittily termed "wall to wall Irish." I never had any significant dealings with people who are Jewish, who are Negro, who are Protestant, who are atheists. I feel deprived as a person because of this.

I feel shortchanged, finally, because of the quality of the education I have received. You can graduate from a Catholic college at the top of your class, yet the very best schools in a secular society —Stanford, Harvard, Yale, the University of Chicago—will still be very reluctant to accept you for graduate work.

EDITOR   There has been much talk about changes going on in Catholic education, and all of you are from schools that are often cited as places where exciting things are happening. Is yours a reflection of the true situation? Does the brainwashing still go on despite all the changes?

CAMPION   Of late, Catholic institutions have felt compelled to offer at least some part of the other side of questions. My big complaint is that, although they do this, they don't take the questions

seriously. Not until they do will they really begin to open up intellectually.

EDITOR   Is there a complacency on the Catholic college campus? How representative are your misgivings of those of students
generally?

BURKE   Representative of the articulate few. Communications
media create the illusion that the Left—the draft card burners, the
Hippies and all those people—are taking over. But the facts are
different. There are fewer people, for instance, dodging the draft
today than there were ten years ago. Many people on the college
level are preoccupied with the same questions the generation of
the '50s was—the generation that was accused of being the apathetic, of being concerned with security, nothing else. That type person is still around. There is a significant vocal minority, but it's
not everyone nor everywhere.

CARLING   Also, there is a difference between the level of
activism at Catholic universities and secular universities. At a
place like Fordham there are perhaps two percent who are active;
at Columbia, there may be eight percent. The point is that the vast
majority of college students in this country at whatever institution you name (with a few exceptions like Antioch and Berkeley)
are primarily concerned with the life they're going to lead, the
professions they're going to enter, the money they're going to
make. I don't want to disparage that too much; at least those
students are spared a lot of the anguish that some of us undergo
occasionally.

MCHALE   It is inaccurate to make a strict dichotomy between
activitists and the apathetic types because of the change of epistemology going on in this country. A lot of young people who are
not activists, who are still apathetic, are interested more and more
in finding out who they are, and that's the beginning.

When I gave my talk on the New Left at the college I attended,
the students didn't ask questions, so I directed questions at them. I
said, "What do you think of Newton?" One of them, very sweetly,

just like a good Catholic girl, said, "I am very grateful to Newton; it's a wonderful testing place for frustration. I'm grateful to Newton for teaching me how to overcome disappointment in all the people I thought I was going to admire."

There are lots of people like her, who are really Americans more than they are Catholics. They talk to the dean and say they want to read more; that they don't want to go to lecture classes. Well, that happens in Berkeley. The students are changing and the institutions have to change. I would never say that the Catholic schools are going through any kind of logical evolutionary process. But, because they have students who are American as well as Catholic, they have no choice but to change. I don't know whether I'm interested any more in whether they do change. Education has a lot more pressing problems than whether Catholic schools should or should not exist.

EDITOR   I notice a great emphasis on the note American. What America do you identify with? Do you identify with majority America, minority America? Is it Johnson's America, or Humphrey's? Whose?

MCHALE   I'm an American who's 25, and that means there's a lot of Johnson in me. There's a lot in me which is attracted to practical politics, to compromise, to making a new deal with the system, to cooperating. There's a lot of me which is electronic. I can't learn in linear fashion anymore. What I learn is much more cobwebby than neat little lines. Part of that is happening to everyone—except maybe Johnson. It's happening to people my age, Catholic or whatever. I also identify with Americans who are Irish-Catholics, but American Irish-Catholic.

EDITOR   What I'm asking is, are you as discontented in any comparable way with America as you are with the Church?

MCHALE   Yes, we're disgusted with this country—it's sick, it's wild, it's surreal. It's not just the Church; the whole country is mad.

EDITOR   Are there radicals of the right on the campuses you're in touch with?

WILSON   Most definitely; for instance, our ROTC people. They had an exhibit in which they claimed that a certain piece of artillery was famous for the fact that it killed more people in war than any other machine. They were really proud of the fact. And this is at a Catholic college! I can't understand it. It certainly doesn't jibe with what you'd expect to be Christian interests. And there are conservatives, and young Bill Buckleys and young Barry Goldwaters around. They're not all locked up.

CARLING   Nor should they be.

EDITOR   How about student discontent with the war in Vietnam? Does it spring from a genuine idealism or moral view, or is it that the students just want to get on with their jobs and their careers and don't want to be disturbed?

CARLING   There are some of the latter, certainly. There are any number of people who oppose the war in Vietnam because they don't want to go there. But it would be a mistake to attribute the mass of student dissent to that factor. Many students are pragmatic politically. They're the kind of Schlesinger liberal, who say I'm anti-Communist; or the Kennan liberal, who say Communism must be stopped, but this is not the right way to do it. While their discontent is very narrow, it is expanding—as it has to. Where this discontent is going to lead, I'm not quite sure. But it is going to go somewhere. This professionally-oriented, measuredly liberal student group is going to grow very rapidly.

MCHALE   Something has happened to us in the process of being against the war. In the beginning I used to think that people who yelled about Vietnam peasants and babies being murdered were hysterical, but now that killing haunts my imagination. Somebody said to me, "Well, the moral rationale for killing those people has collapsed." That may be true, but I think there is another explanation. It is that I'm learning by what you might call total experience. All of us are more and more affected by our imaginations. We go to dances where there are light shows and sounds; we become absorbed in them. We don't think in distinctions anymore. The Vietnam war becomes an imaginative experience. It's true we've never been there; it's true we are idealistic. But we can imagine much better than our parents can, because of the way we're learning these days. That has to do with what McLuhan talks about.

BURKE   I have interpreted the bulk of the dissent against the war, especially the type of dissent practiced by Martin Luther King, as inspired by moral, religious values. I am wholeheartedly in favor of this type of dissent. I think that killing in war is wrong, and the killing in Vietnam gives me nightmares. On the other hand, I haven't been convinced yet about the reality of American aggression there. I haven't seen anything that would convince me that the policies that Johnson is following are wrong in terms of the reality of the situation. I know they're wrong from an ideal point of view. There's no question in my mind about that. The war is horrible. If you have one grain of compassion in you, you can't sit down in front of your television set watching those marines and those planes bombing and shooting and killing people without becoming terribly upset. I think it's the television that feeds the dissent.

I judge my government in terms of how well it is fulfilling its obligations in terms of our Constitution. I don't think it's doing a terribly bad job; in many respects I think Johnson is a very brilliant President. Some of the things he has done on civil rights are fantastic. On the international question—you know, is this the way to fight Communism or not?—this is more complex and subtle and I don't know what to think.

BRAZIER   It seems to me you're saying the Sermon on the Mount is a good and efficacious code but when you bring it down to earth it doesn't apply.

BURKE   I can't judge President Johnson and the people who are dealing with the realities of a small country in Southeast Asia. I hear stories about the kind of things the Viet Cong do. I know that over a million people fled North Vietnam when Ho Chi Minh took over. These are realities that those who are arguing against war don't take account of. Their clever selectivity of facts upsets me. In any case I don't feel competent to judge in that area. But when it comes to the Constitution and government in our society, to civil rights and equal opportunities for Negroes, then things are clear to me and I will judge my President and my Congress in those terms.

When I'm dealing in the Church, I develop my criteria from a completely different angle and am more ruthless in pursuing those criteria. But I can't say to President Johnson, you're committed to the Sermon on the Mount, therefore you can't do this.

CAMPION   Don't you think you're making an artificial distinction? I don't find it quite so easy to differentiate between the Church and society, between Christian and political values. The two overlap and I can't maintain a double standard of morality and judge on two different levels.

BURKE   I see what you mean. I'm just incapable of articulating it any better than I did.

MCHALE   I don't think there's much point in arguing with you now about whether or not the war in Vietnam is right, but you express very vividly what a lot of us have already gone through —in precisely the same kind of language and with precisely the same distinctions. At the risk of offending you, I would be willing to bet that in two years you'll change. And I don't mean that to be arrogant. I really don't. I'm saying that the logic of your thought processes will continue along the same lines and you will begin to find it more and more difficult to draw your political-religious distinctions.

FOR THE STUDENT

Rhetoric

1. *Analyze the* style *of any one of the speakers: consider vocabulary, logic, metaphors, tone, and the like.*
2. *If you have ever listened to group conversations, you know that they are never as well-ordered as this one. What measures must the editors of* Commonweal *have taken to prepare this symposium for print?*

Discussion

1. *Are the objections these students raise applicable to your own church?*
2. *Which attitude toward religion—indifference or rage— comes closest to your own? Or do you have a quite different attitude?*
3. *Which, if any, of the speakers would you like to talk further with?*
4. *Burke is a Jesuit seminarian. What sort of priest do you think he will make?*

Writing

1. *Isolate the opinions of any one speaker. Organize them into a formal essay of, say, five hundred words. You might wish to present this, as it were, in the speaker's own voice.*
2. *Write a personality sketch or profile of any of the speakers; for example, Wilson, McHale. Include from the text— or invent—as much biography as seems appropriate.*

C. E. M. JOAD

The Origin and Evolution of Religion

In discussing the need for religion, I use the words "origin and nature" deliberately, because the conjunction of these two words seems to me to mask a fallacy which it is important to bring to light. The fallacy is to assume that to lay bare the origins of a thing is tantamount to describing its present nature.

That this is very far from being the case, I shall try to show; yet we more often assume that it is, especially if we are of a scientific turn, than we are commonly aware, and the assumption is nowhere more prevalent than in regard to religion. By most of us, indeed, it is not even realized that an assumption is involved. We take it for granted that to demonstrate that religion began as witchcraft, totemism, or exogamy is to prove that it is in essence no more than witchcraft, totemism, and exogamy now, although we should never dream of asserting that the fact that the savage can only count on the fingers of one hand, coupled with the demonstration that arithmetic began with and developed from such counting, invalidates the multiplication table. To show how a belief arises is not to describe, still less to discredit it, and, unless we are to deny to religion the kind of growth which we are prepared to concede to other expressions of the human spirit, it is obvious that there must be more in the religious consciousness today than in the savage fears and flatteries from which it may be shown to have arisen. And, if there is, it will be for just that "more" that an account of religion in terms of its origin and history will fail to make provision. The point is of importance because the interpretation of religion in terms of its origin is often used to prove that religion

From C. E. M. Joad, The Present and Future of Religion (*1930*). *Reprinted by permission of Ernest Benn, Ltd., London, England.*

is not a permanent and necessary need of the human spirit; savage in inception, it will, it is urged, disappear when we have finally left our savagery behind us. Religion, it is often said, belongs to the childhood of the race, and will one day be outgrown, together with war and other savage habits, such as the habit of imprisoning men for punishment and animals for show, or the habit of decking the bodies of women with fragments of stone, lumps of metal, and portions of dead birds.

For myself, I do not hold this view, and I shall try to show the fallacy latent in the mode of reasoning upon which it rests. For the present, let us see what the explanations of religions in terms of origin involve.

They are advanced chiefly by anthropologists, who visit remote Melanesian islands for the purpose of observing the religious practices of the natives. Recording them, they conclude that primitive religion is the offspring of human fear and human conceit; it springs from the desire to propitiate the alien forces of nature, to invest human life with significance in face of the vast indifference of the universe, and to secure the support of an immensely powerful and ferocious personage for the individual, the tribe, or the nation. This general attitude to religion, by ascribing it to a subjective need of human nature, robs it of objective validity. Religion, if this account is correct, is not a revelation of reality, but a symptom of a state of mind; it is an expression of what man is like. To say that there is God is not to say anything more than that we need to think that there is, and the need is in no sense a guarantee of the existence of that which satisfies it. Thus the great religions of the world are not theology, but psychology; witnesses, not to the attributes of God, but to the inventive faculty of man. God is not a real being; He is the image of man, projected, enlarged, upon the empty canvas of the universe.

This view of religion as subjective expresses itself in different forms, according to the nature of the primitive feelings upon which it lays stress. I will take three as examples.

(1) The argument from man's feeling of loneliness and in-

security may be summarized as follows: Human life is immensely insignificant. It is an accidental development of matter, the chance product of forces, an accident unplanned and unforeseen in the history of the planet. A casual and unwanted passenger, it struggles across a fundamentally alien and hostile environment, in which the material and the brutal on all sides condition and determine the spiritual and the vital. One day it will finish its pointless journey with as little noise and significance as, in the person of the amoeba, it began it. Until this consummation occurs, man will fare naked and forlorn through an indifferent universe, a puppet twitched into love and war by an indifferent showman who pulls the strings. His destiny is swayed by an inescapable fate; his fortunes are at the mercy of an irresponsible chance. He is a mere target for the shafts of doom.

These things we know; yet the knowledge is intolerable to us. We cannot bear to be without significance in the universe; we long to feel that we count, that somehow and to something we matter. And so we invent an immensely powerful and important personage called God, to whom we matter enormously.

By making ourselves important to a person who is Himself so enormously important, we achieve the desired significance, and the more powerful God is conceived to be, the more significant do we, His chief concern, become. So tremendously does He care about us that He has made the material universe for our benefit, this world rightly regarded being merely a school for human nature, in which it is trained and educated for life elsewhere; while by making Him in our own image we secure His special interest in the human race. The creation of the brute beasts to sustain our bodies and obey our orders is a token of that interest.

Interested as He is in the human species as a whole, He is quite specially interested in the particular race, nation, or tribe to which we happen to belong; so that, whatever the quarrel upon which the nation or tribe may happen to be engaged, it may rest assured of His support, since He is guaranteed to take the same view of the rights and wrongs of it as we do ourselves.

Among polytheistic peoples this concept causes no difficulty; each has its own deity or set of deities, and the strongest gods win. But where there is one God, and only one, who sustains the worship and is the repository of the prayers of opposed nations, the zeal of His adherents tends to place the Almighty in a dilemma.

> To God the embattled nations sing and shout,
>   "God strafe England" and "God save the King,"
>   God this, that, and God the other thing.
> "Good God!" said God, "I've got my work cut out."

But it is easy to provide for God's solution of the difficulty by invoking His omnipotence.

Interested in the nation or tribe to which we happen to belong, He is quite specially interested in ourselves; interested in and favorable toward, assisting us against those who seek to humiliate us, and generally discomfiting our enemies. This is a world in which the good man is notoriously oppressed, while the wicked flourish like a green bay tree. The arrangement offends our sense of justice, and, what is more, since we are good men ourselves, it is unfair to us personally. Very well, then, we invent another world in which the good man flourishes eternally and the bad one is eternally punished. Thus the fundamental rightness of things is vindicated, and we incidentally benefit in the process.

But in order that the system may work, it is necessary that the good man and the bad man should be under continual observation, that neither the unrequited goodness of the one nor the unchastised badness of the other may go unregistered. This function is admirably performed by the vertical or upstairs God. Thoughtfully accommodated with an abode in the skies, a position admirably adapted for purposes of espionage, He keeps a dossier of each individual, recognizing in us the worth that others unaccountably fail to recognize, and observing the wickedness and hypocrisy of those whom the world equally unaccountably exalts. These things are carefully noted, and in the next world all is made right. Immensely important, admired and envied—for are we not the favored children of Omnipotence?—we live happily ever afterward; scorned and hated, our enemies are convincingly humiliated. Assuredly an admirable arrangement! It is difficult to see how it could be improved upon. But God is essential to its proper working, and God flourishes accordingly.

God, then, on this view, is at once the product of human terror and the prop of human pride. He comforts our wretchedness, calms our fears, gives us an assurance of justice, and makes us feel important. "Religious ideas," says Freud, "have sprung from the same need as all the other achievements of culture; from the necessity for defending oneself against the crushing supremacy of nature."

(2) But though Freud recognizes one of the sources of religion in man's subjection to the forces of nature, he finds its chief root in his relationship to society. Hence his main account of the origin of religion is rather different from that just summarized.

This account will be found in Freud's book, *The Future of an Illusion,* which appeared in 1928. It is not very original, but it is typical of a certain attitude to religion, and may be taken as fairly representative of the view of many educated people, especially psychological and scientific workers today. Freud proceeds upon the basis of what is, in effect, a social contract theory of the origin of society. This theory is admirably stated early in the second book of Plato's *Republic.* Essential to it is the conception of primitive man as a completely non-moral animal; as such his natural inclination is to get his own way at all costs, without thought of the consequences to his neighbors. If his neighbor's wife attracts him, he makes off with her; if his neighbor annoys him, he knocks him on the head. Thus every man has, as Glaucon puts it in the *Republic,* a *natural* tendency to do injustice to his fellows. Admirable in theory, this system, or lack of system, has one serious drawback in practice; the right of every man to do injustice to his neighbors carries with it a corresponding right on the part of his neighbors to do injustice to him. He is one, but his neighbors are many, with the result that, where his hand is against every man and every man's hand is against him, he tends to get the worst of the bargain. His existence is intolerably insecure, he must be perpetually on his guard, and he has no secure enjoyment of his possessions. In the days before society was formed man's life, as the philosopher Hobbes puts it, was "nasty, brutish, and short." Finding the situation intolerable, men ended it by making a compact known as the social contract.

The compact was to form society. Consenting to live in society, man surrendered his natural right to do what he pleased to his fellows, on condition that they made a similar concession as regards himself. Social relations were regulated by public opinion, which later crystallized into law, and man for the future restrained his natural instincts lest he incur the social displeasure of his fellows. Thus was society formed, and from its formation springs the system of inhibitions and restraints which men call morality. To act morally is the reverse of acting naturally and implies a victory over the "natural man"; we obey the law, and keep our hands off our neighbor's wife and property, not because we are by nature moral, but in fear of the penalties with which society has prescribed actions which violate the contract upon which it was formed. In other words, we do right only through fear of the consequences of doing wrong. Remove this fear of consequences, as, for example, by endowing the individual with the gift of invisibility at will, and the social man would immediately relapse into the natural man, with the result that no property would be safe, no wife inviolable. The conclusion is that morality, which is simply the habit of acting in a manner of which other people approve, is not natural to man; on the contrary, it runs counter to his natural interests, frustrates his natural desires, and requires him to surrender his natural rights.

Now, man is not born social. He only becomes so at the cost of suffering and repression. Every child is born "natural," endowed with an egotism that bids him tyrannize over his world. Seeking to impose his imperious will upon his environment, he is suprised when his environment fails to respond, pained when it begins to resent. For a creature who starts with this "natural" endowment the business of growing up into a social adult who knows the lawful limits that must be set upon his desires is, it is obvious, a formidable one—so formidable that, according to Freud, it is seldom more than partially achieved, and never achieved without suffering and injury. To assist him in the difficult process of social adjustment the individual invokes the aid of religion. Hence the essence of religion, according to Freud, is compensation. It is compensation for man's loneliness in face of the vast indifference of the universe; it is also, and more importantly, compensation for the renunciations which he must undertake at the bidding of society.

Wherein (asks Freud) lies the peculiar virtue of religious ideas? We have spoken of the hostility to culture produced by the pressure it exercises and the instinctual renunciations that it demands. If one imagined its prohibitions removed, then one could choose any woman who took one's fancy as one's sexual object, one could kill without hesitation one's rival or whoever interfered with one in any other way, and one could seize what one wanted of another man's goods without asking his leave: how splendid, what a succession of delights life would be!

Forgo these delights, we must, if we are to achieve civilization. And, forgoing them we demand that the gods shall reward us for our sacrifice. Hence religion is the force that reconciles man to the burden of civilization. It is the most important of the compensations that civilization offers to its citizens; so important that only by offering it does civilization become possible. When we have learned as by second nature to refrain from incest, murder, torture, and arson, when we "pass right along the car, please," adjust our dress before leaving, and take our places at the end of the queue, without thinking whether we want to do these things or not, the external restrictions which society imposes have become instinctive habits, the primitive child has become the civilized adult, and social adjustment has been achieved. But achieved only by the aid of religion. Had we no God to whom to turn for comfort and consolation, to whom to tell the unfulfilled wishes and thwarted ambitions, to whom to pray for fortitude to suffer and strength to forbear, the task would be too great for us.

With the very dawn of consciousness, the need for a father confessor makes itself felt.

Thus little by little I became conscious where I was, and to have a wish to express my wishes to those who could content them; and I could not; for the wishes were within me and they without; nor could they, by any sense of theirs, enter within my spirit.

Thus St. Augustine, who proceeds to tell how he sought and found in God the confidant whom the world denied.

Nor is it only from others that we need a refuge. There is the riot of our desires, there are the prickings of our consciences; there is the sting of remorse. For, though manhood is achieved, the adjustment to society is not yet complete; still, though with decreasing vigor as the individual grows older and society more civilized, the natural man raises his head and rebels. When the rebellion comes into the open, when we refuse to pass down the car, take the head of the queue, or insist upon our inalienable privilege of driving upon the right-hand side of the road, society has little difficulty in quelling us. There are policemen, there are law courts, there are prisons, there are even scaffolds. But sometimes the rebellion stays underground, or, though it comes to the surface, goes undetected.

Against these hidden revolts society must protect itself, and evolves accordingly a system of espionage. There is a spy within the individual citadel itself, a spy in the service of society. This is our old Victorian acquaintance, the conscience, the policeman of society, stationed within the individual to see that social interests are duly observed. Directly we go wrong—directly, that is to say, we cease to act in a way of which society approves—conscience begins to nag. Like a dog that does not stop us from passing, but that we cannot prevent from barking, conscience voices the disapproval of society. The voice of conscience is an unpleasant one, causing us grave discomfort, and in extreme cases driving us to madness. Some refuge from the stings of conscience we must find, and we duly find it—in religion. Stricken by remorse, we demand that our sins be forgiven us. Who can forgive sin but God? Fouled by sour sins of wrong-doing, we demand to be made clean. How can we be cleansed save by bathing in the blood of Jesus? And so we come to a new function of religion, a new use for God. Again religion takes the form of an insurance. We deny ourselves the minor luxuries, abstain from the grosser forms of vice, and submit to a little boredom on Sunday, and in return we are guaranteed against discomfort from the stings of conscience in the present and possible discomfort at the hands of the Almighty in the hereafter.

In all these ways and in many others religion seeks to compensate us for the strain and stress of living in society.

Freud traces the gradual evolution of religion to perform this function and the success with which it has, in fact, performed it. He distinguishes various stages in the growth of religion, determined by the nature of the need which at each successive stage it has been chiefly invoked to satisfy. Initially, the chief use of the gods is to protect man from the capriciousness of nature; but, as man progressed, the discoveries of science introduced order into disorder, and substituted law for caprice. At the same time, the growing complexity of civilization increases the strain of social adjustment. Less needed in the physical world, God becomes an indispensable refuge for the harassed soul of man. Thus history records a decline in the physical and a growth in the moral attributes of the gods.

In the course of time the first observations of law and order in natural phenomena are made, and therewith the forces of nature lose their human traits. But men's helplessness remains, and with it their father-longing and the gods. . . . And the more autonomous nature becomes and the more the gods withdraw from her, the more earnestly are all expectations concentrated on the third task assigned to them and the more does morality become their real domain. It now becomes the business of the gods to adjust the defects and evils of culture, to attend to the sufferings that men inflict on each other in their communal life, and to see that the laws of culture, which men obey so ill, are carried out. The laws of culture themselves are claimed to be of divine origin, they are elevated to a position above human society, and they are extended over nature and the universe.

Thus Freud records the progress of religion, and summarizes the different functions which it performs. Nor is his account singular. On the contrary, it is one to which, with minor modifications, most psychologists and anthropologists would subscribe. The more we learn about our mental, the more we learn about our bodily natures, the more, it is said, do we lay bare the roots of religion in the fundamental needs of our natures. Psychologists derive the doctrine of original sin from the sense of man's impotence in the face of chance and destiny; physiologists from the transgressions of his passionate body against the taboos of society. From our infancy we walk between a fear and a fear, between ruthless nature and restricting culture, like Bunyan's Pilgrim, "What shall I do to be saved?" And demanding salvation at all costs, we create God to save us.

Thus religion is the consolation of mankind, and as such its appeal is universal.

(3) But we now come to a more limited, but scarcely less important, function which religion has played in the history of man. To its successful performance of this function its growth and vigor in more modern times is mainly attributable.

There are evils which are the common heritage of all men; they are death, disease, the ingratitude of man to man, the malevolence of destiny. These are no respecters of persons, and bear with impartial severity upon us all. But there are others which do not belong to the essential conditions of human life, but are incidental to the way in which man has chosen collectively to organize his life. For men, equal in the eyes of God, are far from equal in the eyes of society. There are, and always have been, rulers and ruled, oppressors and oppressed, rich and poor; according to many authorities, there always will be. Society, moreover, is based upon force, which its rulers employ to maintain and perpetuate the inequalities on which they thrive. To make their task easier they invoke the assistance of religion. For religion is not only a means of reconciling the individual to society; it is also, and more particularly, a device for inducing the poor and oppressed to tolerate the particular order of society which impoverishes and oppresses them. Thus religion becomes the instrument of the rich and the bridle of the poor. How is the oracle worked?

It is significant, in the first place, that most religions extol the virtues appropriate to slaves—namely, meekness, humility, unselfishness, and contentment—and censure as the vices of pride and presumption the virtues of courage, originality, and independence, and that passionate resentment at injustice and wrong which are characteristic of those who aspire to rise above their servitude. The Christian religion goes further, and makes a virtue of poverty. It is only, we are assured, with the greatest difficulty that the rich man shall enter the Kingdom of Heaven, which opens its gates to the humble and needy. Poverty and insignificance are not, therefore, as they appear to be, and as the world insists on regarding them, disabilities to be avoided at all costs; they are passports to celestial bliss. . . .

As it has pleased Him to call ninety-nine out of every hundred of us to an extremely lowly state, religion, in so far as it is taken seriously, assists in keeping us where we are. Assists whom? Those who benefit by our remaining where we are—namely, our rulers. For the governing classes have been quick to seize the chance religion has offered them of not only subduing their inferiors, but of representing their subjection as a positive asset to their subjects. Ever since an early governing-class realist slipped the parable about Lazarus into the text of the Gospel of St. Luke, the priest and the parson, seeking to persuade the poor that it was only by remaining poor that they would go to Heaven, have been able to produce good scriptural backing for their propaganda. The poor, on the whole, have been only too ready to agree, and have gladly embraced the promise of celestial bliss in the next world as a compensation for the champagne and cigars they were missing in this one. Since the celestial bliss was known to be of indefinite continuance, while the champagne and cigars could not last at most for more than a beggarly fifty years (as a matter of fact, they often lasted less, God having from time to time seen fit to punish the excesses of the worldly by dulling their palates and depriving them of their appetites in the present as an earnest of His intentions for the future; more recently, of course, He has added cancer to the list of penalties), the poor—it is obvious—have the best of the bargain. If it has ever occurred to them to wonder why the rich and powerful should recklessly jeopardize the chances which they have so freely proffered and warmly recommended to their poorer brethren, they may possibly have comforted themsleves with the reflection that *quem deus vult perdere prius dementit*.[1] Possibly, but not probably, for, on the whole, the poor and oppressed have been too much engaged with their poverty and oppression to reflect upon the motives of their betters.

Religion, from this point of view, is a gigantic social hoax, a hoax which has been, on the whole, remarkably successful; so much so, indeed, that from time to time one or another of the rulers of mankind, franker or more secure than the rest, has not scrupled to show how the trick was worked. Thus Napoleon, a notorious skeptic, taxed with the protection which he afforded to a religion in which he did not believe, and stoutly refusing to be drawn into anti-Christian or anti-clerical legislation:

"What is it," he asked his critics, "that makes the poor man think it quite natural that there are fires in my palace while he is dying of cold? that I have ten coats in my wardrobe while he goes naked? that at each of my meals enough is served to feed his family for a week? It is simply religion, which tells him that in another life I shall be only his equal, and that he actually has more chance of being happy there than I. Yes, we must see to it that the doors of the churches are open to all, and that it does not cost the poor man much to have prayers said on his tomb."

Napoleon was right. The poor have a need for religion which the rich do not feel, and it is not surprising, therefore, to find that, while skepticism and atheism have on occasion flourished among

1. "Whom the gods would destroy, they first make mad."

the rich, religion has uniformly been embraced with eagerness by the poor. The growth of disbelief in governing-class circles, while it may have evoked the censure of society—the rich have always thought it prudent to keep up religious observances—has rarely called down the penalties of the law. Thus governing-class writers of the eighteenth century, Gibbon, Voltaire, or the Encyclopaedists, for example, who were notoriously irreligious or hostile to religion, went comparatively scathless. Naturally, since they wrote for the educated upper, not for the ignorant lower, classes. Most of the early rationalists, again, were academic people whose books were too difficult or too dull to command a popular circulation. Excepting Woolston, they escaped unpunished. But Peter Annett, a schoolmaster who tried to popularize free thought and held forth on the village green, was sentenced to the pillory and hard labor in 1763. "If we take the cases in which the civil authorities have intervened to repress the publication of unorthodox opinions during the last two centuries," says Professor Bury, "we find that the object has always been to prevent the spread of free thought among the masses." . . .

In the nineteenth century, as the danger to society from the new proletariat first made itself felt, the beliefs of the governing classes, it is interesting to note, become more pronounced as their religious example becomes more edifying. It was most important that the wage slaves of the industrial revolution should learn to know God, and in knowing Him to respect their betters. Their betters, then, should show them the way. This they proceeded to do. . . .

That the position remains radically unaltered is shown by the following dialogue between Cusins and Undershaft from Shaw's *Major Barbara,* a dialogue which has become a classic.

CUSINS (*in a white fury*) Do I understand you to imply that you can buy Barbara?

UNDERSHAFT No; but I can buy the Salvation Army.

CUSINS Quite impossible.

UNDERSHAFT   You shall see. All religious organizations exist by selling themselves to the rich.

CUSINS   Not the Army. That is the church of the poor.

UNDERSHAFT   All the more reason for buying it.

CUSINS   I don't think you quite know what the Army does for the poor.

UNDERSHAFT   Oh yes, I do. It draws their teeth: that is enough for me—as a man of business—

CUSINS   Nonsense! It make them sober—

UNDERSHAFT   I prefer sober workmen. The profits are larger.

CUSINS   —honest—

UNDERSHAFT   Honest workmen are the most economical.

CUSINS   —attached to their homes—

UNDERSHAFT   So much the better: they will put up with anything sooner than change their shop.

CUSINS   —happy—

UNDERSHAFT   An invaluable safeguard against revolution.

CUSINS   —unselfish—

UNDERSHAFT   Indifferent to their own interests, which suits me exactly.

CUSINS   —with their thoughts on heavenly things—

UNDERSHAFT (*rising*)   And not on trade unionism nor socialism. Excellent.

CUSINS (*revolted*)   You really are an infernal old rascal.

Summing up, we may note that this conception of the special function of religion as the instrument of the rich and the bridle of the poor follows logically from its main social function considered above. I have already summarized Freud's account of religion as man's compensation for the renunciations which society demands of him. This may be described as the general social function of religion. It is the part which religion has been called upon to play in the lives of tribal and civilized men, because they live in tribes and societies. But in addition to the general there is a special social function of religion, which is to render the inequalities of society tolerable to the masses. Civilization, requiring of the many poor far greater instinctive renunciations than it demands of the rich, has given them far fewer material compensations. It is essential, therefore, if they are to acquiesce in a state of society which on the material side demands so much while giving so little, that they should receive some compensation of the spirit, a compensation which brings comfort in the present and gives hope for the future. Such compensation is afforded by an ingeniously devised and richly satisfying religious system, which, while making a virtue of humility, feeds the fires of self-esteem, lest, revolting against their insignificance, the poor and the many should turn against society and destroy it. This, then, is one of the functions which religion, and especially the Christian religion, has performed in civilized societies; it has taken the revolutionary sting from poverty and blunted the edge of present discontent with promises of future well-being. Performing this function, religion has been sedulously exploited and used by the rich as an instrument of class domination. God, it has been found, is cheaper than a living wage. Very well, then, let us invest in Him! Religion is a show to keep the poor amused. Very well, then, let us build churches in the slums! For this reason socialists have tended to be hostile to religion, and the Bolshevik government veers between reluctant toleration and covert persecution.

I have endeavored briefly to summarize a number of different accounts of the origin, the growth, and the function of religion. These accounts dominate the modern psychological and sociological treatment of the subject, which is, on the whole, markedly hostile to religion. There are, admittedly, differences on points of detail, and different writers put the emphasis differently according to the purposes which their account is intended to serve and the aspect of religion with which it is chiefly concerned. But all the accounts which I have summarized are in fundamental agreement in interpreting religion on subjectivist lines.

On this one fundamental point they concur. When faced with the question, "Why is there religion?" they answered unanimously, "Because man wants it." When asked, "Whence does religion rise?"

their reply is, "From the needs of man's nature." Pressed for an explanation of its authority and appeal, they represent it as a "rationalization of his instinctive wishes." Thus all these accounts are in their different ways subjectivist. They affirm that religion enables man to accommodate himself to this world, that it expresses a human need, and that it is, therefore, pleasant and consoling; they do not say that it represents an objective fact, that it points forward to a different world, and that it is therefore true. With most of what they assert I am largely, if not entirely, in agreement. I think that the interpretations they give of the origin of religion in terms of the needs which it fulfills, and of the ground of its appeal in terms of the wishes that it rationalizes, are in the main true. But I do not think that they are complete. They are, that is to say, interpretations in terms of origin only, and they take no account of the conception of end or purpose. They ask how religion began and why it flourished; they do not ask what it may become. Both conceptions are, I am convinced, necessary to an adequate description of the status of religion in the present, and a reasoned estimate of its chance of survival in the future.

Now, I shall consider the reasons for including in our survey an account of religion in terms of what it may become.

If a thing's nature is exhibited only in its complete development, a complete account of its nature can be given only in terms of that development. Thus, to describe its nature *as it is now,* we must seek to estimate its future; so only can we hope to understand the tentative beginnings and premonitory stirrings that foreshadow it. A thing reflects its past, no doubt, and to understand it we must know its past; but it also foreshadows its future, and to understand it we must seek to forecast its future; and we must do this not only as a disinterested exercise in prophecy, but because the future in part determines and renders intelligible the present. It follows that, adequately to understand a growing and developing thing, we must take into account not only the origins from which it sprang, but the goal which it may be seeking to achieve. We must think of it not only as determined from behind by its past, but determined from in front by its future. We must, in a word, introduce the notion of purpose.

Our conclusion is in accordance with, indeed it is demanded by, the teaching of evolution. Life, we are agreed, changes; it evolves. If the changes which evolution implies are real changes—and if they are not, everything that exists must have existed always, and time and growth and movement are illusions—then at any given stage in the growth of a living organism the organism must be different from what it was at the preceding stages. But it not only changes; it develops, and in saying that it develops we are implying that at each stage it is not only different from but also more than it was before. Consider, for example, the case of the growing human body. The matter of which a living body is composed, beginning as a microscopic speck of protoplasm, ends as a many-millioned colony of cells. These cells are highly organized, and specialized for the performance of different functions. Some are marshaled to carry on the work of the nervous system; others to form the engines we call muscles; others, again, serve the comparatively lowly purpose of bone-levers. Instruments of incredible delicacy, the eye and the ear, are evolved; yet the whole complex mechanism of a living human body is developed from a particle of living matter smaller than the finest pinhead. Now, either these complex cells and organs were present in the pinhead to begin with or they were not. If they were not, then they are literally new; there was, that is to say, a time when they were not, and we are entitled to say that there is more in the present state of the body than there was in its origin.

What is true of the life of the body is true also of that of the mind. Knowledge which is literally new comes into the world. An engineer knows how to build a bridge, a mathematician understands the differential calculus. Either this knowledge and this understanding are new in the sense that there was a time when no mind possessed them, or they are not. If they are not, then they existed in some form when the earth was populated by amoebas. A similar argument may be applied to any other planet upon which life has appeared, the conclusion being that there is nothing new under the sun. Thus change is unreal, since whatever is always has been, and evolution is an illusion. If they are new, then there was a time when the universe knew them not; in other words, they have appeared from nowhere, since there is nowhere outside the universe, and evolved out of nothing. Granted, then, that the fact of growth implies the coming into being of new elements, that there may be more in a thing's present state than there was in its ingredients or its origin; granted further that this is true of the human mind or spirit, why should we deny its application to expressions of the human spirit, to art, for example, to science or to religion? To art and to science, indeed, we apply it readily enough; but of religion? Why should we arbitrarily exclude religion from the operation of the laws of growth and development? For it is high time to apply these considerations to the subject of this article. Applying them, we assert that religion can no more receive an adequate interpretation in terms of its origin alone than can any other growing and developing thing. This is not to say that the interpretation in terms of origin is inappropriate, but merely that it is not complete; it is not complete because the religious consciousness is more than the ingredients from which it has emerged.

It is also more than the psychological machinery which is involved in its emergence. Psychoanalysts are fond of pointing out that religion is sublimated emotion. Primitive lusts, social maladjustments and misfits, and unacknowledged desires are mixed together in an unholy brew of which the religious consciousness is the distilled essence. The ingredients exposed, it is somehow implied that their outcome is discredited. Erroneously, for to lay bare the assorted and possibly disreputable elements of which the religious consciousness may have been compounded is not to show that they *are* that consciousness; the theory of sublimation, if it means anything at all, means, in fact, that they are not.

I assert that an account of the origin, the history, and the psychology of religion, interesting as it is to the anthropologist, the historian, and the psychologist, is not an account of religion, and that arguments derived from it cannot, therefore, be used to discredit or to dispose of religion. Were it not for the fears of the savage and the social maladjustments of the citizen, religion admittedly would be very different from what it is. But, originating in the stress of human need and flowering on the dunghill of human emotions, the religious consciousness rises above its origins and transcends its machinery. The mechanism, I repeat, is other than its product.

In its account of religion, and not of religion alone, psychoanalysis makes the mistake of identifying, and therefore confusing, the unconscious trends of our nature with their conscious outcrop. Unmasking the malevolence of our unconscious wishes, analysts exhibit the ingenuity with which they are sublimated to appear honorable; they succeed; but they also exhibit the efficiency with which they are sublimated so that they are indeed honorable. One day, no doubt, psychoanalysts will succeed, if they have not done so already, in reducing the sense of duty to something else, probably to something discreditable, but this would not explain away the sense of duty any more than the successful reduction of matter to electricity explains away matter, or of religion to the needs and desires of which it can be shown to be a sublimation explains away religion.

For this reason criticisms of religion urged by psychoanalysts, valid up to a point, are valueless beyond it. It is not that they are not true, but that they are incomplete.

If religion does, in fact, derive from the sources previously mentioned, if it has fulfilled the needs and served the purposes enumerated, then it still fulfills those needs and serves those purposes now. If it is the product of human fear, and the projection of human vanity, then it will still reassure man's nervousness and flatter his egotism. But while it still sustains the rôle which it has sustained through the ages, it will no longer sustain that rôle alone. It will both do more and be more, and the "more" that it does and is will receive adequate interpretation, in so far as it can be interpreted at all, not in terms of the origin and history of religion, but in terms appropriate to its future and its goal. Admittedly, we do not know its future and we can only dimly guess its goal. But of this at least we may be sure: that in the confused complex of tendencies—social and individual, inherited and acquired, instinctive and intellectual—in the vaguely felt aspirations and the scarce acknowledged faith, the sense of the spiritual loneliness and the need of spiritual communion, that go to make up what is called religion today, there will always be present an element to which the Freudian, or the anthropological, or the social, or any similar account of the appeal and functions of religion will not only not apply, but which it will completely falsify. I say an element, but there is no need to limit my assertion to one. Religion in the past has been a rope of many strands; it is not likely to grow simple and single in the future. Let us, then, say provisionally that there are two or, perhaps, three aspects or phases of the religious consciousness which none of the subjectivist explanations in terms of the origin and past of religion can explain, and which can be understood only in terms of what religion may become. These aspects we must try to separate from the rest, and, having separated, use as the point of departure for our account of the religion of the future.

To answer the question whether religion is a permanent and necessary growth of the human spirit, and whether as such it will have a future, it is sufficient to point out that there are such aspects. Requiring interpretation in terms of the future rather than the past, it is clear that, as man advances in the path of evolution, they will become more prominent and definite than they are today. Religion, therefore, in so far as it contains them, will not die out . . . .

In conclusion, let us summarize the results at which we have arrived. When we have to deal with growing and developing things, with living organisms, with the institutions in which they are organized, and the activities in which they find expression, the explanation of their present state in terms of their origin is inadequate. This statement is true both of morals and of religion.

To say that the moral consciousness arose because it promoted tribal efficiency, or that the religious consciousness arose because it promoted cosmic comfort, tells us something but not everything about the moral or the religious consciousness now. To understand them as they are now we must judge them not only by their roots but by their fruits, looking not only to what they have been, but to what they may become. The mind, in short, is Janus-like; it looks forward as well as backward, bearing upon it at any given moment traces not only of what it has been, but what it may become. . . .

The conclusion is that there is more in a complex product like the religious consciousness than can be adequately explained by a reference to its origin. This "more" will be a pointer to the future, and we must try, therefore, to disentangle it from the rest, in order to estimate the prospects of religion in the future.

FOR THE STUDENT

Rhetoric

1. *This is an unusually well-organized essay, with a clearly stated thesis, distinct transitions, and a summary before the conclusion. It lends itself admirably to* outlining.
2. *Summarize briefly (one sentence) each of the three theories Joad discounts.*

Discussion

1. *What problems, unknown in primitive societies where religions had their origin, must be confronted by religions of today and of the future?*
2. *Will the religions of the future be* contemplative *(like the*

Oriental religions) or activist, *as the Cool Generation seems to demand?*

3. *Many rationalists assert that civilized man has outgrown his need for religion. Would the Cool Generation agree? Would you?*

4. *What would you guess to be the religious background of Freud? of G. B. Shaw? of Joad?*

Writing

1. *Apply Joad's thesis—that* origins *do not explain the present nature of a thing—to, say, "democracy" or "chivalry" or what you will.*

2. *Describe imaginatively the morals and ritual of the religion of 3000* A.D. *Or of 50,000* B.C.

C. S. LEWIS

What Christians Believe

1. The Rival Conceptions of God

I have been asked to tell you what Christians believe, and I am going to begin by telling you one thing that Christians do not need to believe. If you are a Christian you do not have to believe that all the other religions are simply wrong all through. If you are an atheist you do have to believe that the main point in all the religions of the whole world is simply one huge mistake. If you are a Christian, you are free to think that all these religions, even the queerest ones, contain at least some hint of the truth. When I was an atheist I had to try to persuade myself that most of the human race have always been wrong about the question that mattered to them most; when I became a Christian I was able to take a more liberal view. But, of course, being a Christian does mean thinking that where Christianity differs from other religions, Christianity is right and they are wrong. As in arithmetic—there is only one right answer to a sum, and all other answers are wrong: but some of the wrong answers are much nearer being right than others.

The first big division of humanity is into the majority, who believe in some kind of God or gods, and the minority who do not. On this point, Christianity lines up with the majority—lines up with ancient Greeks and Romans, modern savages, Stoics, Platonists, Hindus, Mohammedans, etc., against the modern Western European materialist.

Now I go on to the next big division. People who all believe in God can be divided according to the sort of God they believe in. There are two very different ideas on this subject. One of them is the idea that He is beyond good and evil. We humans call one thing good and another thing bad. But according to some people that is merely our human point of view. These people would say that the wiser you become the less you would want to call anything good or bad, and the more clearly you would see that everything is good in one way and bad in another, and that nothing could have been different. Consequently, these people think that long before you got anywhere near the divine point of view the distinction would have disappeared altogether. We call a cancer bad, they would say, because it kills a man; but you might just as well call a successful surgeon bad because he kills a cancer. It all depends on the point of view. The other and opposite idea is that God is quite definitely "good" or "righteous," a God who takes sides, who loves love and hates hatred, who wants us to behave in one way and not in another. The first of these views—the one that thinks God beyond good and evil—is called Pantheism. It was held by the great Prussian philosopher Hegel and, as far as I can understand them, by the Hindus. The other view is held by Jews, Mohammedans and Christians.

And with this big difference between Pantheism and the Christian idea of God, there usually goes another. Pantheists usually believe that God, so to speak, animates the universe as you animate your body: that the universe almost *is* God, so that if it did not exist He would not exist either, and anything you find in the universe is a part of God. The Christian idea is quite different. They think God invented and made the universe—like a man making a picture or composing a tune. A painter is not a picture, and he does not die if his picture is destroyed. You may say, "He's put a lot of himself into it," but you only mean that all its beauty and interest has come out of his head. His skill is not in the picture in the same way that it is in his head, or even in his hands. I expect you see how this difference between Pantheists and Christians hangs together with the other one. If you do not take the distinction between good and bad very seriously, then it is easy to say that anything you find in this world is a part of God. But, of course, if you think some things really bad, and God really good, then you cannot talk like that. You must believe that God is separate from the world and that some of the things we see in it are contrary to His will. Confronted with a cancer or a slum the Pantheist can say, "If you could only see it from the divine point of view, you would realise that this also is God." The Christian replies, "Don't talk damned nonsense."[1] For Christianity is a fighting religion. It thinks God made the world—that space and time, heat and cold, and all the colours and tastes, and all the animals and vegetables, are things that God "made up out of His head" as a man makes up a story. But it also thinks that a great many things have gone wrong with the world that God made and that God insists, and insists very loudly, on our putting them right again.

And, of course, that raises a very big question. If a good God made the world why has it gone wrong? And for many years I simply refused to listen to the Christian answers to this question, because I kept on feeling "whatever you say, and however clever your arguments are, isn't it much simpler and easier to say that the world was not made by any intelligent power? Aren't all your arguments simply a complicated attempt to avoid the obvious?" But then that threw me back into another difficulty.

My argument against God was that the universe seemed so cruel and unjust. But how had I got this idea of *just* and *unjust?* A man does not call a line crooked unless he has some idea of a straight line. What was I comparing this universe with when I called it unjust? If the whole show was bad and senseless from A to Z, so to speak, why did I, who was supposed to be part of the show, find myself in such violent reaction against it? A man feels wet when he falls into water, because man is not a water animal: a fish would not feel wet. Of course I could have given up my idea of justice by saying it was nothing but a private idea of my own.

1. One listener complained of the word *damned* as frivolous swearing. But I mean exactly what I say—nonsense that is *damned* is under God's curse, and will (apart from God's grace) lead those who believe it to eternal death. [Author's note]

But if I did that, then my argument against God collapsed too—for the argument depended on saying that the world was really unjust, not simply that it did not happen to please my private fancies. Thus in the very act of trying to prove that God did not exist—in other words, that the whole of reality was senseless—I found I was forced to assume that one part of reality—namely my idea of justice—was full of sense. Consequently atheism turns out to be too simple. If the whole universe has no meaning, we should never have found out that it has no meaning: just as, if there were no light in the universe and therefore no creatures with eyes, we should never know it was dark. *Dark* would be without meaning.

2. The Invasion

Very well then, atheism is too simple. And I will tell you another view that is also too simple. It is the view I call Christianity-and-water, the view which simply says there is a good God in Heaven and everything is all right—leaving out all the difficult and terrible doctrines about sin and hell and the devil, and the redemption. Both these are boys' philosophies.

It is no good asking for a simple religion. After all, real things are not simple. They look simple, but they are not. The table I am sitting at looks simple: but ask a scientist to tell you what it is really made of—all about the atoms and how the light waves rebound from them and hit my eye and what they do to the optic nerve and what it does to my brain—and, of course, you find that what we call "seeing a table" lands you in mysteries and complications which you can hardly get to the end of. A child saying a child's prayer looks simple. And if you are content to stop there, well and good. But if you are not—and the modern world usually is not—if you want to go and ask what is really happening—then you must be prepared for something difficult. If we ask for something more than simplicity, it is silly then to complain that the something more is not simple.

Very often, however, this silly procedure is adopted by people

who are not silly, but who, consciously or unconsciously, want to
destroy Christianity. Such people put up a version of Christianity
suitable for a child of six and make that the object of their attack.
When you try to explain the Christian doctrine as it is really held
by an instructed adult, they then complain that you are making
their heads turn round and that it is all too complicated and that
if there really were a God they are sure He would have made "religion" simple, because simplicity is so beautiful, etc. You must
be on your guard against these people for they will change their
ground every minute and only waste your time. Notice, too, their
idea of God "making religion simple"; as if "religion" were something God invented, and not His statement to us of certain quite
unalterable facts about His own nature.

Besides being complicated, reality, in my experience, is usually
odd. It is not neat, not obvious, not what you expect. For instance,
when you have grasped that the earth and the other planets all go
round the sun, you would naturally expect that all the planets
were made to match—all at equal distances from each other, say,
or distances that regularly increased, or all the same size, or else
getting bigger or smaller as you go farther from the sun. In fact,
you find no rhyme or reason (that we can see) about either the
sizes or the distances: and some of them have one moon, one has
four, one has two, some have none, and one has a ring.

Reality, in fact, is usually something you could not have
guessed. That is one of the reasons I believe Christianity. It is a
religion you could not have guessed. If it offered us just the kind
of universe we had always expected, I should feel we were making
it up. But, in fact, it is not the sort of thing anyone would have
made up. It has just that queer twist about it that real things have.
So let us leave behind all these boys' philosophies—these over-
simple answers. The problem is not simple and the answer is not
going to be simpler either.

What is the problem? A universe that contains much that is
obviously bad and apparently meaningless, but containing creatures like ourselves who know that it is bad and meaningless.

There are only two views that face all the facts. One is the Christian view that this is a good world that has gone wrong, but still retains the memory of what it ought to have been. The other is the view called Dualism. Dualism means the belief that there are two equal and independent powers at the back of everything, one of them good and the other bad, and that this universe is the battlefield in which they fight out an endless war. I personally think that next to Christianity Dualism is the manliest and most sensible creed on the market. But it has a catch in it.

The two powers, or spirits, or gods—the good one and the bad one—are supposed to be quite independent. They both existed from all eternity. Neither of them made the other, neither of them has any more right than the other to call itself God. Each presumably thinks it is good and thinks the other bad. One of them likes hatred and cruelty, the other likes love and mercy, and each backs its own view. Now what do we mean when we call one of them the Good Power and the other the Bad Power? Either we are merely saying that we happen to prefer the one to the other—like preferring beer to cider—or else we are saying that, whatever the two powers think about it, and whichever we humans, at the moment, happen to like, one of them is actually wrong, actually mistaken, in regarding itself as good. Now if we mean merely that we happen to prefer the first, then we must give up talking about good and evil at all. For good means what you ought to prefer quite regardless of what you happen to like at any given moment. If "being good" meant simply joining the side you happened to fancy, for no real reason, then good would not deserve to be called good. So we must mean that one of the two powers is actually wrong and the other actually right.

But the moment you say that, you are putting into the universe a third thing in addition to the two Powers: some law or standard or rule of good which one of the powers conforms to and the other fails to conform to. But since the two powers are judged by this standard, then this standard, or the Being who made this standard, is farther back and higher up than either of them, and He will be the real God. In fact, what we meant by calling them good and bad turns out to be that one of them is in a right relation to the real ultimate God and the other in a wrong relation to Him.

The same point can be made in a different way. If Dualism is true, then the bad Power must be a being who likes badness for its own sake. But in reality we have no experience of anyone liking badness just because it is bad. The nearest we can get to it is in cruelty. But in real life people are cruel for one of two reasons— either because they are sadists, that is, because they have a sexual perversion which makes cruelty a cause of sensual pleasure to them, or else for the sake of something they are going to get out of it—money, or power, or safety. But pleasure, money, power, and safety are all, as far as they go, good things. The badness consists in pursuing them by the wrong method, or in the wrong way, or too much. I do not mean, of course, that the people who do this are not desperately wicked. I do mean that wickedness, when you examine it, turns out to be the pursuit of some good in the wrong way. You can be good for the mere sake of goodness: you cannot be bad for the mere sake of badness. You can do a kind action when you are not feeling kind and when it gives you no pleasure, simply because kindness is right; but no one ever did a cruel action simply because cruelty is wrong—only because cruelty was pleasant or useful to him. In other words badness cannot succeed even in being bad in the same way in which goodness is good. Goodness is, so to speak, itself: badness is only spoiled goodness. And there must be something good first before it can be spoiled. We called sadism a sexual perversion; but you must first have the idea of a normal sexuality before you can talk of its being perverted; and you can see which is the perversion, because you can explain the perverted from the normal, and cannot explain the normal from the perverted. It follows that this Bad Power, who is supposed to be on an equal footing with the Good Power, and to love badness in the same way as the Good Power loves goodness, is a mere bogy. In order to be bad he must have good things to want and then to pursue in the wrong way: he must have impulses which were originally good in order to be able to pervert them. But if he is bad he cannot supply himself either with good things to desire or with good impulses to pervert. He must be getting both from the Good Power. And if so, then he is not independent. He is part of the Good Power's world: he was made either by the Good Power or by some power above them both.

Put it more simply still. To be bad, he must exist and have intelligence and will. But existence, intelligence and will are in themselves good. Therefore he must be getting them from the Good Power; even to be bad he must borrow or steal from his opponent. And do you now begin to see why Christianity has always said that the devil is a fallen angel? That is not a mere story for the children. It is a real recognition of the fact that evil is a parasite, not an original thing. The powers which enable evil to carry on are powers given it by goodness. All the things which enable a bad man to be effectively bad are in themselves good things—resolution, cleverness, good looks, existence itself. That is why Dualism, in a strict sense, will not work.

But I freely admit that real Christianity (as distinct from Christianity-and-water) goes much nearer to Dualism than people think. One of the things that surprised me when I first read the New Testament seriously was that it talked so much about a Dark Power in the universe—a mighty evil spirit who was held to be the Power behind death and disease, and sin. That difference is that Christianity thinks this Dark Power was created by God, and was good when he was created, and went wrong. Christianity agrees with Dualism that this universe is at war. But it does not think this is a war between independent powers. It thinks it is a civil war, a rebellion, and that we are living in a part of the universe occupied by the rebel.

Enemy-occupied territory—that is what this world is. Christianity is the story of how the rightful king has landed, you might say landed in disguise, and is calling us all to take part in a great campaign of sabotage. When you go to church you are really listening in to the secret wireless from our friends; that is why the enemy is so anxious to prevent us from going. He does it by playing on our conceit and laziness and intellectual snobbery. I know someone will ask me, "Do you really mean, at this time of day, to re-introduce our friend the devil—hoofs and horns and all?" Well, what the time of day has to do with it I do not know. And I am not particular about the hoofs and horns. But in other respects my answer is "Yes, I do." I do not claim to know anything about his personal appearance. If anybody really wants to know him better I would say to that person, "Don't worry. If you really want to, you will. Whether you'll like it when you do is another question."

3. The Shocking Alternative

Christians, then, believe that an evil power has made himself for the present the Prince of this World. And, of course, that raises problems. Is this state of affairs in accordance with God's will or not? If it is, He is a strange God, you will say; and if it is not, how can anything happen contrary to the will of a being with absolute power?

But anyone who has been in authority knows how a thing can be in accordance with your will in one way and not in another. It may be quite sensible for a mother to say to the children, "I'm not going to go and make you tidy the schoolroom every night. You've got to learn to keep it tidy on your own." Then she goes up one night and finds the Teddy bear and the ink and the French Grammar all lying in the grate. That is against her will. She would prefer the children to be tidy. But on the other hand, it is her will which has left the children free to be untidy. The same thing arises in any regiment, or trade union, or school. You make a thing voluntary and then half the people do not do it. That is not what you willed, but your will has made it possible.

It is probably the same in the universe. God created things

which had free will. That means creatures which can go either wrong or right. Some people think they can imagine a creature which was free but had no possibility of going wrong; I cannot. If a thing is free to be good it is also free to be bad. And free will is what has made evil possible. Why, then, did God give them free will? Because free will, though it makes evil possible, is also the only thing that makes possible any love or goodness or joy worth having. A world of automata—of creatures that worked like machines—would hardly be worth creating. The happiness which God designs for His higher creatures is the happiness of being freely, voluntarily united to Him and to each other in an ecstasy of love and delight compared with which the most rapturous love between a man and a woman on this earth is mere milk and water. And for that they must be free.

Of course God knew what would happen if they used their freedom the wrong way; apparently He thought it worth the risk. Perhaps we feel inclined to disagree with Him. But there is a difficulty about disagreeing with God. He is the source from which all your reasoning power comes; you could not be right and He wrong any more than a stream can rise higher than its own source. When you are arguing against Him you are arguing against the very power that makes you able to argue at all; it is like cutting off the branch you are sitting on. If God thinks this state of war in the universe a price worth paying for free will—that is, for making a live world in which creatures can do real good or harm and something of real importance can happen, instead of a toy world which only moves when He pulls the strings—then we may take it it is worth paying.

When we have understood about free will, we shall see how silly it is to ask, as somebody once asked me: "Why did God make a creature of such rotten stuff that it went wrong?" The better stuff a creature is made of—the cleverer and stronger and freer it is—then the better it will be if it goes right, but also the worse it will be if it goes wrong. A cow cannot be very good or very bad; a dog can be both better and worse; a child better and worse still; an ordinary man, still more so; a man of genius, still more so; a superhuman spirit best—or worst—of all.

How did the Dark Power go wrong? Here, no doubt, we ask a question to which human beings cannot give an answer with any certainty. A reasonable (and traditional) guess, based on our own experiences of going wrong, can, however, be offered. The moment you have a self at all, there is a possibility of putting yourself first—wanting to be the centre—wanting to be God, in fact. That was the sin of Satan; and that was the sin he taught the human race. Some people think the fall of man had something to do with sex, but that is a mistake. (The story in the Book of Genesis rather suggests that some corruption in our sexual nature followed the fall and was its result, not its cause.) What Satan put into the heads of our remote ancestors was the idea that they could "be like gods"—could set up on their own as if they had created themselves—be their own masters—invent some sort of happiness for themselves outside God, apart from God. And out of that hopeless attempt has come nearly all that we call human history—money, poverty, ambition, war, prostitution, classes, empires, slavery—the long terrible story of man trying to find something other than God which will make him happy.

The reason why it can never succeed is this: God made us, invented us as a man invents an engine. A car is made to run on gasoline, and it would not run properly on anything else. Now God designed the human machine to run on Himself. He Himself is the fuel our spirits were designed to burn, or the food our spirits were designed to feed on. There is no other. That is why it is just no good asking God to make us happy in our own way without bothering about religion. God cannot give us a happiness and peace apart from Himself, because it is not there. There is no such thing.

That is the key to history. Terrific energy is expended—civilisations are built up—excellent institutions devised; but each time

something goes wrong. Some fatal flaw always brings the selfish
and cruel people to the top and it all slides back into misery and
ruin. In fact, the machine conks. It seems to start up all right and
runs a few yards, and then it breaks down. They are trying to run
it on the wrong juice. That is what Satan has done to us humans.

And what did God do? First of all He left us conscience, the
sense of right and wrong; and all through history there have been
people trying (some of them very hard) to obey it. None of them
ever quite succeeded. Secondly, He sent the human race what I
call good dreams; I mean those queer stories scattered all through
the heathen religions about a god who dies and comes to life
again and, by his death, has somehow given new life to men.
Thirdly, He selected one particular people and spent several
centuries hammering into their heads the sort of God He was
—that there was only one of Him and that He cared about right
conduct. Those people were the Jews, and the Old Testament
gives an account of the hammering process.

Then comes the real shock. Among these Jews there suddenly
turns up a man who goes about talking as if He was God. He
claims to forgive sins. He says He has always existed. He says
He is coming to judge the world at the end of time. Now let us
get this clear. Among Pantheists, like the Indians, anyone might
say that he was a part of God, or one with God; there would be
nothing very odd about it. But this man, since He was a Jew,
could not mean that kind of God. God, in their language, meant
the Being outside the world Who had made it and was infinitely
different from anything else. And when you have grasped that,
you will see that what this man said was, quite simply, the most
shocking thing that has ever been uttered by human lips.

One part of the claim tends to slip past as unnoticed because we
have heard it so often that we no longer see what it amounts to.
I mean the claim to forgive sins; any sins. Now unless the speaker
is God, this is really so preposterous as to be comic. We can all
understand how a man forgives offences against himself. You
tread on my toe and I forgive you, you steal my money and I

forgive you. But what should we make of a man, himself unrobbed and untrodden on, who announced that he forgave you for treading on other men's toes and stealing other men's money? Asinine fatuity is the kindest description we should give of his conduct. Yet this is what Jesus did. He told people that their sins were forgiven, and never waited to consult all the other people whom their sins had undoubtedly injured. He unhesitatingly behaved as if He was the party chiefly concerned, the person chiefly offended in all offences. This makes sense only if He really was the God whose laws are broken and whose love is wounded in every sin. In the mouth of any speaker who is not God, these words would imply what I can only regard as a silliness and conceit unrivalled by any other character in history.

Yet (and this is the strange, significant thing) even His enemies, when they read the Gospels, do not usually get the impression of silliness and conceit. Still less do unprejudiced readers. Christ says that He is "humble and meek" and we believe Him; not noticing that, if He were merely a man, humility and meekness are the very last characteristics we could attribute to some of His sayings.

I am trying here to prevent anyone saying the really foolish thing that people often say about Him: "I'm ready to accept Jesus as a great moral teacher, but I don't accept His claim to be God." That is the one thing we must not say. A man who was merely a man and said the sort of things Jesus said would not be a great moral teacher. He would either be a lunatic—on a level with the man who says he is a poached egg—or else he would be the Devil of Hell. You must make your choice. Either this man was, and is, the Son of God; or else a madman or something worse. You can shut Him up for a fool, you can spit at Him and kill Him as a demon; or you can fall at His feet and call Him Lord and God. But let us not come with any patronising nonsense about His being a great human teacher. He has not left that open to us. He did not intend to.

4. The Perfect Penitent

We are faced, then, with a frightening alternative. This man we are talking about either was (and is) just what He said or else a lunatic, or something worse. Now it seems to me obvious that He was neither a lunatic nor a fiend; and consequently, however strange or terrifying or unlikely it may seem, I have to accept the view that He was and is God. God has landed on this enemy-occupied world in human form.

And now, what was the purpose of it all? What did He come to do? Well, to teach, of course; but as soon as you look into the New Testament or any other Christian writing you will find they are constantly talking about something different—about His death and His coming to life again. It is obvious that Christians think the chief point of the story lies here. They think the main thing He came to earth to do was to suffer and be killed.

Now before I became a Christian I was under the impression that the first thing Christians had to believe was one particular theory as to what the point of this dying was. According to that theory God wanted to punish men for having deserted and joined the Great Rebel, but Christ volunteered to be punished instead, and so God let us off. Now I admit that even this theory does not seem to me quite so immoral and so silly as it used to; but that is not the point I want to make. What I came to see later on was that neither this theory nor any other is Christianity. The central Christian belief is that Christ's death has somehow put us right with God and given us a fresh start. Theories as to how it did this are another matter. A good many different theories have been held as to how it works; what all Christians are agreed on is that it does work. I will tell you what I think it is like. All sensible people know that if you are tired and hungry a meal will do you good. But the modern theory of nourishment—all about the vitamins and proteins—is a different thing. People ate their dinners and felt better long before the theory of vitamins was ever heard of; and if the theory of vitamins is some day abandoned they will go on eating their dinners just the same. Theories about Christ's death are not Christianity; they are explanations about how it works. Christians would not all agree as to how important these theories are. My own church—the Church of England—does not lay down any one of them as the right one. The Church of Rome goes a bit further. But I think they will all agree that the thing itself is infinitely more important than any explanations that theologians have produced. I think they would probably admit that no explanation will ever be quite adequate to the reality. But as I said in the preface to this book, I am only a layman, and at this point we are getting into deep water. I can only tell you, for what it is worth, how I, personally, look at the matter.

On my view the theories are not themselves the thing you are asked to accept. Many of you no doubt have read Jeans or Eddington. What they do when they want to explain the atom, or something of that sort, is to give you a description out of which you can make a mental picture. But then they warn you that this picture is not what the scientists actually believe. What the scientists believe is a mathematical formula. The pictures are there only to help you to understand the formula. They are not really true in the way the formula is; they do not give you the real thing but only something more or less like it. They are only meant to help, and if they do not help you can drop them. The thing itself cannot be pictured, it can only be expressed mathematically. We are in the same boat here. We believe that the death of Christ is just that point in history at which something absolutely unimaginable from outside shows through into our own world. And if we cannot picture even the atoms of which our own world is built, of course we are not going to be able to picture this. Indeed, if we found that we could fully understand it, that very fact would show it was not what it professes to be—the inconceivable, the uncreated, the thing from beyond nature, striking down into nature like lightning. You may ask what good will it be to us if we do not understand it. But that is easily answered. A man can eat his dinner without understanding exactly how food nourishes him. A man can accept what Christ has done without knowing how it works; indeed, he certainly would not know how it works until he has accepted it.

We are told that Christ was killed for us, that His death has washed out our sins, and that by dying He disabled death itself. That is the formula. That is Christianity. That is what has to be believed. Any theories we build up as to how Christ's death did all this are, in my view, quite secondary; mere plans or diagrams to be left alone if they do not help us, and, even if they do help us, not to be confused with the thing itself. All the same, some of these theories are worth looking at.

The one most people have heard is the one I mentioned before —the one about our being let off because Christ had volunteered to bear a punishment instead of us. Now on the face of it that is a very silly theory. If God was prepared to let us off, why on earth did He not do so? And what possible point could there be in punishing an innocent person instead? None at all that I can see, if you are thinking of punishment in the police-court sense. On the other hand, if you think of a debt, there is plenty of point in a person who has some assets paying it on behalf of someone who has not. Or if you take "paying the penalty," not in the sense of being punished, but in the more general sense of "standing the racket" or "footing the bill," then, of course, it is a matter of common experience that, when one person has got himself into a hole, the trouble of getting him out usually falls on a kind friend.

Now what was the sort of "hole" man had got himself into? He had tried to set up on his own, to behave as if he belonged to himself. In other words, fallen man is not simply an imperfect creature who needs improvement; he is a rebel who must lay down his arms. Laying down your arms, surrendering, saying you are sorry, realising that you have been on the wrong track and getting ready to start life over again from the ground floor—that is the only way out of a "hole." This process of surrender—this movement full speed astern—is what Christians call repentance. Now repentance is no fun at all. It is something much harder than merely eating humble pie. It means unlearning all the self-conceit and self-will that we have been training ourselves into for thousands of years. It means killing part of yourself, undergoing a kind of death. In fact, it needs a good man to repent. And here comes the catch. Only a bad person needs to repent; only a good person can repent perfectly. The worse you are the more you need it and the less you can do it. The only person who could do it perfectly would be a perfect person—and he would not need it.

Remember, this repentance, this willing submission to humiliation and a kind of death, is not something God demands of you before He will take you back and which He could let you off if He chose; it is simply a description of what going back to Him is like. If you ask God to take you back without it, you are really asking Him to let you go back without going back. It cannot happen. Very well, then, we must go through with it. But the same badness which makes us need it, makes us unable to do it. Can we do it if God helps us? Yes, but what do we mean when we talk of God helping us? We mean God putting into us a bit of Himself, so to speak. He lends us a little of His reasoning powers and that is how we think: He puts a little of His love into us and that is how we love one another. When you teach a child writing, you hold its hand while it forms the letters; that is, it forms the letters because you are forming them. We love and reason because God loves and reasons and holds our hand while we do it. Now if we had not fallen, that would be all plain sailing. But unfortunately we now need God's help in order to do something which God, in His own nature, never does at all—to surrender, to suffer, to submit, to die. Nothing in God's nature corresponds to this process at all. So that the one road for which we now need God's leadership most of all is a road God, in His own nature, has never walked. God can share only what He has; this thing, in His own nature, He has not.

But supposing God became a man—suppose our human nature which can suffer and die was amalgamated with God's nature in one person—then that person could help us. He could surrender

His will, and suffer and die, because He was man; and He could do it perfectly because He was God. You and I can go through this process only if God does it in us; but God can do it only if He becomes man. Our attempts at this dying will succeed only if we men share in God's dying, just as our thinking can succeed only because it is a drop out of the ocean of His intelligence; but we cannot share God's dying unless God dies; and He cannot die except by being a man. That is the sense in which He pays our debt, and suffers for us what He Himself need not suffer at all.

I have heard some people complain that if Jesus was God as well as man, then His sufferings and death lose all value in their eyes, "because it must have been so easy for him." Others may (very rightly) rebuke the ingratitude and ungraciousness of this objection; what staggers me is the misunderstanding it betrays. In one sense, of course, those who make it are right. They have even understated their own case. The perfect submission, the perfect suffering, the perfect death were not only easier to Jesus because He was God, but were possible only because He was God. But surely that is a very odd reason for not accepting them? The teacher is able to form the letters for the child because the teacher is grown-up and knows how to write. That, of course, makes it easier for the teacher; and only because it is easier for him can he help the child. If it rejected him because "it's easy for grown-ups" and waited to learn writing from another child who could not write itself (and so had no "unfair" advantage), it would not get on very quickly. If I am drowning in a rapid river, a man who still has one foot on the bank may give me a hand which saves my life. Ought I to shout back (between my gasps) "no, it's not fair! You have an advantage! You're keeping one foot on the bank"? That advantage—call it "unfair" if you like—is the only reason why he can be of any use to me. To what will you look for help if you will not look to that which is stronger than yourself?

Such is my own way of looking at what Christians call the Atonement. But remember this is only one more picture. Do not mistake it for the thing itself; and if it does not help you, drop it.

5. The Practical Conclusion

The perfect surrender and humiliation were undergone by Christ: perfect because He was God, surrender and humiliation because He was man. Now the Christian belief is that if we somehow share the humility and suffering of Christ we shall also share in His conquest for death and find a new life after we have died and in it become perfect, and perfectly happy, creatures. This means something much more than our trying to follow His teaching. People often ask when the next step in evolution—the step to something beyond man—will happen. But on the Christian view, it has happened already. In Christ a new kind of man appeared; and the new kind of life which began in Him is to be put into us.

How is this to be done? Now, please remember how we acquired the old, ordinary kind of life. We derived it from others, from our father and mother and all our ancestors, without our consent—and by a very curious process, involving pleasure, pain, and danger. A process you would never have guessed. Most of us spend a good many years in childhood trying to guess it: and some children, when they are first told, do not believe it—and I am not sure that I blame them, for it is very odd. Now the God who arranged that process is the same God who arranges how the new kind of life—the Christ life—is to be spread. We must be prepared for it being odd too. He did not consult us when He invented sex: He has not consulted us either when He invented this.

There are three things that spread the Christ life to us: baptism, belief, and that mysterious action which different Christians call by different names—Holy Communion, the Mass, the Lord's Supper. At least, those are the three ordinary methods. I am not saying there may be special cases where it is spread without one or more of these. I have not time to go into special cases, and I do not know enough. If you are trying in a few minutes to tell a man how to get to Edinburgh you will tell him the trains: he can, it is true, get there by boat or by a plane, but you will hardly bring that in. And I am not saying anything about which of these three things is the most essential. My Methodist friend would like me to say more about belief and less (in proportion) about the other two. But I am not going into that. Anyone who professes to teach you Christian doctrine will, in fact, tell you to use all three, and that is enough for our present purpose.

I cannot myself see why these things should be the conductors of the new kind of life. But then, if one did not happen to know, I should never have seen any connection between a particular physical pleasure and the appearance of a new human being in the world. We have to take reality as it comes to us; there is no good jabbering about what it ought to be like or what we should have expected it to be like. But though I cannot see why it should be so, I can tell you why I believe it is so. I have explained why I have to believe that Jesus was (and is) God. And it seems plain as a matter of history that He taught His followers that the new life was communicated in this way. In other words, I believe it on His authority. Do not be scared by the word authority. Believing things on authority only means believing them because you have been told them by someone you think trustworthy. Ninety-nine per cent of the things you believe are believed on authority. I believe there is such a place as New York. I have not seen it myself. I could not prove by abstract reasoning that there must be such a place. I believe it because reliable people have told me so. The ordinary man believes in the Solar System, atoms, evolution, and the circulation of the blood on authority—because the scientists say so. Every historical statement in the world is believed on authority. None of us has seen the Norman Conquest or the defeat of the Armada. None of us could prove them by pure logic as you prove a thing in mathematics. We believe them simply because people who did see them have left writings that tell us about them; in fact, on authority. A man who jibbed at authority in other things as some people do in religion would have to be content to know nothing all his life.

Do not think I am setting up baptism and belief and the Holy Communion as things that will do instead of your own attempts to copy Christ. Your natural life is derived from your parents; that does not mean it will stay there if you do nothing about it. You can lose it by neglect, or you can drive it away by committing suicide. You have to feed it and look after it; but always remember you are not making it, you are only keeping up a life you got from someone else. In the same way a Christian can lose the Christ life which has been put into him, and he has to make efforts to keep it. But even the best Christian that ever lived is not acting on his own steam—he is only nourishing or protecting a life he could never have acquired by his own efforts. And that has practical consequences. As long as the natural life is in your body, it will do a lot towards repairing that body. Cut it, and up to a point it will heal, as a dead body would not. A live body is not one that never gets hurt, but one that can to some extent repair itself. In the same way a Christian is not a man who never goes wrong, but a man who is enabled to repent and pick himself up and begin over again after each stumble—because the Christ-life is inside him, repairing him all the time, enabling him to repeat (in some degree) the kind of voluntary death which Christ Himself carried out.

That is why the Christian is in a different position from other people who are trying to be good. They hope, by being good, to please God if there is one; or—if they think there is not—at least they hope to deserve approval from good men. But the Christian thinks any good he does comes from the Christ-life inside him. He does not think God will love us because we are good, but that God will make us good because He loves us; just as the roof of a greenhouse does not attract the sun because it is bright, but becomes bright because the sun shines on it.

And let me make it quite clear that when Christians say the Christ-life is in them, they do not mean simply something mental or moral. When they speak of being "in Christ" or of Christ being "in them," this is not simply a way of saying that they are thinking about Christ or copying Him. They mean that Christ is actually operating through them; that the whole mass of Christians are the physical organism through which Christ acts—that we are His fingers and muscles, the cells of His body. And perhaps that explains one or two things. It explains why this new life is spread not only by purely mental acts like belief, but by bodily acts like baptism and Holy Communion. It is not merely the spreading of an idea; it is more like evolution—a biological or super-biological fact. There is no good trying to be more spiritual than God. God never meant man to be a purely spiritual creature. That is why He uses material things like bread and wine to put the new life into us. We may think this rather crude and unspiritual. God does not: He invented eating. He likes matter. He invented it.

Here is another thing that used to puzzle me. Is it not frightfully unfair that this new life should be confined to people who have heard of Christ and been able to believe in Him? But the truth is God has not told us what His arrangements about the other people are. We do know that no man can be saved except through Christ; we do not know that only those who know Him can be saved through Him. But in the meantime, if you are worried about the people outside, the most unreasonable thing you can do is to remain outside yourself. Christians are Christ's body, the organism through which He works. Every addition to that body enables Him to do more. If you want to help those outside you must add your own little cell to the body of Christ who alone can help them. Cutting off a man's fingers would be an odd way of getting him to do more work.

Another possible objection is this. Why is God landing in this enemy-occupied world in disguise and starting a sort of secret society to undermine the devil? Why is He not landing in force, invading it? Is it that He is not strong enough? Well, Christians think He is going to land in force; we do not know when. But we can guess why He is delaying. He wants to give us the chance of joining His side freely. I do not suppose you and I would have thought much of a Frenchman who waited till the Allies were marching into Germany and then announced he was on our side. God will invade. But I wonder whether people who ask God to interfere openly and directly in our world quite realise what it will be like when He does. When that happens, it is the end of the world. When the author walks on to the stage the play is over. God is going to invade, all right: but what is the good of saying you are on His side then, when you see the whole natural universe melting away like a dream and something else—something it never entered your head to conceive—comes crashing in; something so beautiful to some of us and so terrible to others that none of us will have any choice left? For this time it will be God without disguise; something so overwhelming that it will strike either irresistible love or irresistible horror into every creature. It will be too late then to choose your side. There is no use saying you choose to lie down when it has become impossible to stand up. That will not be the time for choosing: it will be the time when we discover which side we really have chosen, whether we realised it before or not. Now, today, this moment, is our chance to choose the right side. God is holding back to give us that chance. It will not last for ever. We must take it or leave it.

FOR THE STUDENT

Rhetoric

1. *Lewis thinks of himself as trying to write in a "middle style"—about halfway between the heavy, pedantic style of theologians and the emotionalism of the revivalists. Analyze his diction and sentence structure to see if he achieves his aim. Compare a paragraph of his with one from Joad or Dean Inge.*

2. *Lewis is famous for his analogies (for example, "the drowning man" at the end of the fourth part). Pick out three or four other examples and evaluate them.*

Discussion

1. *Which features of Lewis' creed could be explained by the theories of* origins *in the Joad essay? Would the theories account for evil? For baptism? For atonement?*
2. *The Cool Generation once believed all of what Lewis affirms and were relatively satisfied with their beliefs. What happened? Are there any parts of Lewis' creed which any of them still seem to support?*

Writing

1. *Compare Lewis' explanation of the atonement or free will or the fall with the explanation from some other source, for example,* The Catholic Encyclopaedia, The Encyclopaedia of Religion and Ethics.
2. *Compose an imaginary letter from C. S. Lewis to the Cool Generation or to Sigmund Freud.*

11 Technology

Will our technology lead us to the earthly paradise or to a totalitarian nightmare? Will the developments in science and technology bring into existence a new world in which all men can satisfy the physical necessities of life—and even more—and at the same time achieve the best of which man is capable in the spiritual realm? Or, will our scientists and technologists, by the very things they choose to bring into existence, be the new dictators, making the politician impotent, the moralist and humanist obsolete, and man himself a mere automaton responding properly to induced stimuli? The first is the age-old dream of man which he has described variously in his literature in every age. The second is the twentieth-century nightmare which pictures a technology beyond man's control, a world in which machines and techniques dominate man through the artificial environment which he has created and in which he has chosen to live.

The proponents of these two extremes, as well as all those who fall between the extremes, do not differ so much in their views of man the human being and the individual as in the means to assist man in achieving his fullest potential. The scientists add to man's knowledge, the technologists translate the scientists' theories into practice, and man's environment undergoes another modification. The humanists ask how many technical modifications man can tolerate in his environment before it is too artificial and restrictive for him. The problem is not satisfactorily resolved by suggesting that man must make the choices that best satisfy his needs, physical and spiritual, as man. There is much disagreement about the ends and especially the means to the ends.

The following essays present a diversity of views on

twentieth-century technology and where it may be taking us. (*A word of caution on point of view is necessary before we examine these essays. Although Ellul on the Left is pessimistic and Slichter on the Right is optimistic, one must not identify pessimism with the Left nor optimism with the Right, though these views may be more characteristic on this subject than they are on some other subjects.*) Jacques Ellul, professor of law at the University of Bordeaux, has been called the philosopher of the technological society. While he freely admits that technology can make valuable contributions to man and his world, his central concern is that man be granted the privilege of remaining a human being and an individual instead of being turned into an automaton dependent upon an artificial environment. Max Lerner, author, editor, columnist, and professor of social science and government, shares some of Ellul's concern about the possibilities of the technological society, but states firmly that man can and must make the choice where technology will lead him. He shares some of the enthusiasm of Slichter on the possibilities of technology. Sumner H. Slichter, a professor of economics, maintains that technology has almost limitless possibilities for "making the good life and the good things of life available to everyone." He virtually becomes a spokesman for the business community —traditionally conservative—and its doctrine of progress. Ellul, and even Lerner, might ask him to be more precise as to what constitutes the "good life." The debate on the subject shows no signs of diminishing; in fact, it will probably be intensified as we approach the year 2000 and our technological paradise or technological nightmare.

JACQUES ELLUL

A Look at the Future

We have completed our examination of the monolithic technical world that is coming to be. It is vanity to pretend it can be checked or guided. Indeed, the human race is beginning confusedly to understand at last that it is living in a new and unfamiliar universe. The new order was meant to be a buffer between man and nature. Unfortunately, it has evolved autonomously in such a way that man has lost all contact with his natural framework and has to do only with the organized technical intermediary which sustains relations both with the world of life and with the world of brute matter. Enclosed within his artificial creation, man finds that there is "no exit"; that he cannot pierce the shell of technology to find again the ancient milieu to which he was adapted for hundreds of thousands of years.

The new milieu has its own specific laws which are now the laws of organic or inorganic matter. Man is still ignorant of these laws. It nevertheless begins to appear with crushing finality that a new necessity is taking over from the old. It is easy to boast of victory over ancient oppression, but what if victory has been gained at the price of an even greater subjection to the forces of the artificial necessity of the technical society which has come to dominate our lives?

In our cities there is no more day or night or heat or cold. But there is overpopulation, thraldom to press and television, total absence of purpose. All men are constrained by means external to them to ends equally external. The further the technical mechanism develops which allows us to escape natural necessity, the more we are subjected to artificial technical necessities. (I have analyzed human victory over hunger in this vein.) The artificial necessity

From Jacques Ellul, The Technological Society. *Copyright 1967. Reprinted by permission of Alfred A. Knopf, Inc.*

of technique* is not less harsh and implacable for being much less obviously menacing than natural necessity. When the Communists claim that they place the development of the technical society in a historical framework that automatically leads to freedom through the medium of the dialectical process; when Humanists such as Bergson, or Catholics such as Mounier, assert that man must regain control over the technical "means" by an additional quantity of soul, all of them alike show both their ignorance of the technical phenomenon and an impenitent idealism that unfortunately bears no relation to truth or reality.

Alongside these parades of mere verbalisms, there has been a real effort, on the part of the technicians themselves, to control the future of technical evolution. The principle here is the old one we have so often encountered: "A technical problem demands a technical solution." At present, there are two kinds of new techniques which the technicians propose as solutions.

The first solution hinges on the creation of new technical instruments able to mediate between man and his new technical milieu. Robert Jungk, for example, in connection with the fact that man is not completely adaptable to the demands of the technical age, writes that "it is impossible to create interstellar man out of the existing prime matter; auxiliary technical instruments and apparatus must compensate for his insufficiencies." The best and most striking example of such subsidiary instruments is furnished by the complex of so-called "thinking machines," which certainly belong to a very different category of techniques than those that have been applied up to now. But the whole ensemble of means designed to permit human mastery of what were means and have now become milieu are techniques of the second degree, and nothing more. Pierre de Latil, in his *La Pensée artificielle,* gives an ex-

---

*John Wilkinson, translator of The Technological Society, *in his introduction quotes Harold Lasswell's definition of technique as being closest to Ellul's conception: "The ensemble of practices by which one uses available resources to achieve values." [Editor's note]*

cellent characterization of some of these machines of the second degree.

"In the machine, the notion of finality makes its appearance, a notion sometimes attributed in living beings to some intelligence inherent in the species, innate to life itself. Finality is artificially built into the machine and regulates it, an effect requiring that some factor be modified or reinforced so that the effect itself does not disturb the equilibrium . . . Errors are corrected without human analysis, or knowledge, without even being suspected. The error itself corrects the error. A deviation from the prescribed track itself enables the automatic pilot to rectify the deviation . . . For the machine, as for animals, error is fruitful; it conditions the correct path."

The second solution revolves about the effort to discover (or rediscover) a new end for human society in the technical age. The aims of technology, which were clear enough a century and a half ago, have gradually disappeared from view. Humanity seems to have forgotten the wherefore of all its travail, as though its goals had been translated into an abstraction or had become implicit; or as though its ends rested in an unforeseeable future of undetermined date, as in the case of Communist society. Everything today seems to happen as though ends disappear, as a result of the magnitude of the very means at our disposal.

Comprehending that the proliferation of means brings about the disappearance of the ends, we have become preoccupied with rediscovering a purpose or a goal. Some optimists of good will assert that they have rediscovered a Humanism to which the technical movement is subordinated. The orientation of this Humanism may be Communist or non-Communist, but it hardly makes any difference. In both cases it is merely a pious hope with no chance whatsoever of influencing technical evolution. The further we advance, the more the purpose of our techniques fades out of sight. Even things which not long ago seemed to be immediate objectives —rising living standards, hygiene, comfort—no longer seem to have that character, possibly because man finds the endless adaptation to new circumstances disagreeable. In many cases, indeed, a higher technique obliges him to sacrifice comfort and hygienic amenities to the evolving technology which possesses a monopoly of the instruments necessary to satisfy them. Extreme examples are furnished by the scientists isolated at Los Alamos in the middle of the desert because of the danger of their experiments; or by the would-be astronauts who are forced to live in the discomfort of experimental camps in the manner so graphically described by Jungk.

But the optimistic technician is not a man to lose heart. If ends and goals are required, he will find them in a finality which can be imposed on technical evolution precisely because this finality can be technically established and calculated. It seems clear that there must be some common measure between the means and the ends subordinated to it. The required solution, then, must be a technical inquiry into ends, and this alone can bring about a systematization of ends and means. The problem becomes that of analyzing individual and social requirements technically, of establishing, numerically and mechanistically, the constancy of human needs. It follows that a complete knowledge of ends is requisite for mastery of means. But, as Jacques Aventur has demonstrated, such knowledge can only be technical knowledge. Alas, the panacea of merely theoretical humanism is as vain as any other.[1]

"Man, in his biological reality, must remain the sole possible reference point for classifying needs," writes Aventur. Aventur's dictum must be extended to include man's psychology and sociology, since these have also been reduced to mathematical calculation. Technology cannot put up with intuitions and "literature." It must necessarily don mathematical vestments. Everything in

1. It must be clear that the ends sought cannot be determined by moral science. The dubiousness of ethical judgments, and the differences between systems, make moral science unfit for establishing these ends. But, above all, its subjectivity is a fatal blemish. It depends essentially on the refinement of the individual moral conscience. An average morality is ceaselessly confronted with excessive demands with which it cannot comply. Technical modalities cannot tolerate subjectivity. [Author's note]

human life that does not lend itself to mathematical treatment must be excluded—because it is not a possible end for technique—and left to the sphere of dreams.

Who is too blind to see that a profound mutation is being advocated here? A new dismembering and a complete reconstitution of the human being so that he can at last become the objective (and also the total object) of techniques. Excluding all but the mathematical element, he is indeed a fit end for the means he has constructed. He is also completely despoiled of everything that traditionally constituted his essence. Man becomes a pure appearance, a kaleidoscope of external shapes, an abstraction in a milieu that is frighteningly concrete—an abstraction armed with all the sovereign signs of Jupiter the Thunderer.

A Look at the Year 2000. In 1960 the weekly *l'Express* of Paris published a series of extracts from texts by American and Russian scientists concerning society in the year 2000. As long as such visions were purely a literary concern of science-fiction writers and sensational journalists, it was possible to smile at them.[2] Now we have like works from Nobel Prize winners, members of the Academy of Sciences of Moscow, and other scientific notables whose qualifications are beyond dispute. The visions of these gentlemen put science fiction in the shade. By the year 2000, voyages to the moon will be commonplace; so will inhabited artificial satellites. All food will be completely synthetic. The world's population will have increased fourfold but will have been stabilized. Sea water and ordinary rocks will yield all the necessary metals. Disease, as well as famine, will have been eliminated; and there will be universal hygienic inspection and control. The problems of energy production will have been completely resolved. Serious scientists, it must be repeated, are the source of these predictions, which hitherto were found only in philosophic utopias.

The most remarkable predictions concern the transformation of educational methods and the problem of human reproduction.

2. Some excellent works, such as Robert Jungk's *Le Futur a déjà commencé,* were included in this classification. [Author's note]

Knowledge will be accumulated in "electronic banks" and transmitted directly to the human nervous system by means of coded
electronic messages. There will no longer be any need of reading
or learning mountains of useless information; everything will be
received and registered according to the needs of the moment.
There will be no need of attention or effort. What is needed will
pass directly from the machine to the brain without going through
consciousness.

In the domain of genetics, natural reproduction will be forbidden. A stable population will be necessary, and it will consist of
the highest human types. Artificial insemination will be employed.
This, according to Muller, will "permit the introduction into a
carrier uterus of an ovum fertilized *in vitro,* ovum and sperm . . .
having been taken from persons representing the masculine ideal
and the feminine ideal, respectively. The reproductive cells in question will preferably be those of persons dead long enough that a
true perspective of their lives and works, free of all personal
prejudice, can be seen. Such cells will be taken from cell banks and
will represent the most precious genetic heritage of humanity.
. . . The method will have to be applied universally. If the people of a single country were to apply it intelligently and inten-
sively . . . they would quickly attain a practically invincible level
of superiority. . . ." Here is a future Huxley never dreamed of.

Perhaps, instead of marveling or being shocked, we ought to
reflect a little. A question no one ever asks when confronted with
the scientific wonders of the future concerns the interim period.
Consider, for example, the problems of automation, which will
become acute in a very short time. How, socially, politically, morally, and humanly, shall we contrive to get there? How are the
prodigious economic problems, for example, of unemployment, to
be solved? And, in Muller's more distant utopia, how shall we
force humanity to refrain from bearing children naturally? How
shall we force them to submit to constant and rigorous hygienic
controls? How shall man be persuaded to accept a radical transformation of his traditional modes of nutrition? How and where

shall we relocate a billion and a half persons who today make their livings from agriculture and who, in the promised ultrarapid conversion of the next forty years, will become completely useless as cultivators of the soil? How shall we distribute such numbers of people equably over the surface of the earth, particularly if the promised fourfold increase in population materializes? How will we handle the control and occupation of outer space in order to provide a stable *modus vivendi?* How shall national boundaries be made to disappear? (One of the last two would be a necessity.) There are many other "hows," but they are conveniently left unformulated. When we reflect on the serious although relatively minor problems that were provoked by the industrial exploitation of coal and electricity, when we reflect that after a hundred and fifty years these problems are still not satisfactorily resolved, we are entitled to ask whether there are any solutions to the infinitely more complex "hows" of the next forty years. In fact, there is one and only one means to their solution, a world-wide totalitarian dictatorship which will allow technique its full scope and at the same time resolve the concomitant difficulties. It is not difficult to understand why the scientists and worshippers of technology prefer not to dwell on this solution, but rather to leap nimbly across the dull and uninteresting intermediary period and land squarely in the golden age. We might indeed ask ourselves if we will succeed in getting through the transition period at all, or if the blood and the suffering required are not perhaps too high a price to pay for this golden age.

If we take a hard, unromantic look at the golden age itself, we are struck with the incredible naïveté of these scientists. They say, for example, that they will be able to shape and reshape at will human emotions, desires, and thoughts and arrive scientifically at certain efficient, pre-established collective decisions. They claim they will be in a position to develop certain collective desires, to constitute certain homogeneous social units out of aggregates of individuals, to forbid men to raise their children, and even to persuade them to renounce having any. At the same time, they speak of assuring the triumph of freedom and of the necessity of avoiding dictatorship at any price.[3] They seem incapable of grasping the contradiction involved, or of understanding that what they are proposing, even after the intermediary period, is in fact the harshest of dictatorships. In comparison, Hitler's was a trifling affair. That it is to be a dictatorship of test tubes rather than of hobnailed boots will not make it any less a dictatorship.

When our savants characterize their golden age in any but scientific terms, they emit a quantity of down-at-the-heel platitudes that would gladden the heart of the pettiest politician. Let's take a few samples. "To render human nature nobler, more beautiful, and more harmonious." What on earth can this mean? What criteria, what content, do they propose? Not many, I fear, would be able to reply. "To assure the triumph of peace, liberty, and reason." Fine words with no substance behind them. "To eliminate cultural lag." What culture? And would the culture they have in mind be able to subsist in this harsh social organization?" "To conquer outer space." For what purpose? The conquest of space seems to be an end in itself, which dispenses with any need for reflection.

We are forced to conclude that our scientists are incapable of any but the emptiest platitudes when they stray from their specialties. It makes one think back on the collection of mediocrities accumulated by Einstein when he spoke of God, the state, peace, and the meaning of life. It is clear that Einstein, extraordinary mathematical genius that he was, was no Pascal; he knew nothing of political or human reality, or, in fact, anything at all outside his mathematical reach. The banality of Einstein's remarks in matters outside his specialty is as astonishing as his genius within it. It seems as though the specialized application of all one's faculties in a particular area inhibits the consideration of things in general. Even J. Robert Oppenheimer, who seems receptive to a general culture, is not outside this judgment. His political and social dec-

3. The material here and below is cited from actual texts. [Author's note]

larations, for example, scarcely go beyond the level of those of the man in the street. And the opinions of the scientists quoted by *l'Express* are not even on the level of Einstein or Oppenheimer. Their pomposities, in fact, do not rise to the level of the average. They are vague generalities inherited from the nineteenth century, and the fact that they represent the furthest limits of thought of our scientific worthies must be symptomatic of arrested development or of a mental block. Particularly disquieting is the gap between the enormous power they wield and their critical ability, which must be estimated as null. To wield power well entails a certain faculty of criticism, discrimination, judgment, and option. It is impossible to have confidence in men who apparently lack these faculties. Yet it is apparently our fate to be facing a "golden age" in the power of sorcerers who are totally blind to the meaning of the human adventure. When they speak of preserving the seed of outstanding men, whom, pray, do they mean to be the judges. It is clear, alas, that they propose to sit in judgment themselves. It is hardly likely that they will deem a Rimbaud or a Nietszche worthy of posterity. When they announce that they will conserve the genetic mutations which appear to them most favorable, and that they propose to modify the very germ cells in order to produce such and such traits; and when we consider the mediocrity of the scientists themselves outside the confines of their specialties, we can only shudder at the thought of what they will esteem most "favorable."

None of our wise men ever pose the question of the end of all their marvels. The "wherefore" is resolutely passed by. The response which would occur to our contemporaries is: for the sake of happiness. Unfortunately, there is no longer any question of that. One of our best-known specialists in diseases of the nervous system writes: "We will be able to modify man's emotions, desires and thoughts, as we have already done in a rudimentary way with tranquillizers." It will be possible, says our specialist, to produce a conviction or an impression of happiness without any real basis for it. Our man of the golden age, therefore, will be capable of "happiness" amid the worst privations. Why, then, promise us extraordinary comforts, hygiene, knowledge, and nourishment if, by simply manipulating our nervous systems, we can be happy without them? The last meager motive we could possibly ascribe to the technical adventure thus vanishes into thin air through the very existence of technique itself.

But what good is it to pose questions of motives? of Why? All that must be the work of some miserable intellectual who balks at technical progress. The attitude of the scientists, at any rate, is clear. Technique exists because it is technique. The golden age will be because it will be. Any other answer is superfluous.

FOR THE STUDENT

Rhetoric

1. *Define Ellul's terms "natural necessity" and "artificial necessity."*
2. *The first part of the essay is difficult and at times, because of the nature of the subject, abstract. Consult your dictionary frequently and try to provide some illustrations to aid your understanding.*
3. *The first section discusses means and ends generally. How does the second section make the first more meaningful?*
4. *Explain the phrase "dictatorship of test tubes."*
5. *Examine Ellul's analysis of the scientists' platitudes. Is his analysis valid?*

Discussion

1. *Why does Ellul find the scientists' picture of the world in 2000 a frightening one? Do you?*

2. *Have we begun to pass through the interim period to the year 2000? Substantiate your answer.*
3. *If Ellul's analysis of scientists' critical ability is even approximately correct, is there cause for alarm? Is his pessimism understandable?*
4. *Would you be satisfied to be given the kind of happiness described in the next-to-last paragraph?*
5. *How deeply concerned do you think Ellul is with the individual and his right to individualism?*

Writing

1. *Answer Ellul on a specific point with which you disagree. Support your answer well.*
2. *Write a science-fiction description of some technical advance that is about to become a reality. Point out the possible psychological and sociological significance of this advance.*

MAX LERNER

The Culture of Machine Living

Any principle that comes to dominate a culture can do so only by making itself part of the life processes of the people. This has happened in the case of America, and it is one of the reasons we can speak seriously, and not as a literary flourish, of the culture of machine living. Siegfried Giedion points out that the machine has mechanized such fundamentals as the soil (mechanized agriculture), bread (mechanized milling), death (assembly-line slaughtering pens and the use of by-products by the big meat packers), and the household (the kitchen revolution, the household-appliance revolution, mechanized laundering, and the mechanized bathroom). The analysis can be carried further. Mechanization has extended to transport (boats, trains, autos, busses, trucks, subways, planes), to living outside the home (hotels, motels, sleeping cars, "automats"), and to the basic phases of communications revolution (newsprint, book publishing, magazines, telephone, telegraph, movies, radio, TV).

Aside from these arterial forms of American living there is also the interminable gadgetry. From the automatic vending machines to the automatic gas stations, from the gadgeted car to the gadgeted bed, America has taken on the aspect of a civilization cluttered with artifacts and filled with the mechanized bric-a-brac of machine living. The Big Technology of the mass-production industries is supplemented by the Little Technology of everyday living.

One could draw a gloomy picture of machine living in America and depict it as the Moloch swallowing the youth and resilience of American manhood. From Butler's *Erewhon* to Capek's *R.U.R.*,

European thinkers have seized on the machine as the cancer of modern living. Some have even suggested that there is a daimon in Western man, and especially in the American, that is driving him to the monstrous destruction of his instinctual life and indeed of his whole civilization.

Part of the confusion flows from the failure to distinguish at least three phases of the machine culture. One is what I have just described: *machine living* as such, the use of machinery in work and in leisure and in the constant accompaniments of the day. The second is cultural *standardization,* aside from the machine, but a standardization that flows from machine production. The third is *conformism* in thought, attitude, and action. All three are parts of the empire of the machine but at varying removes and with different degrees of danger for the human spirit.

The danger in machine living itself is chiefly the danger of man's arrogance in exulting over the seemingly easy triumphs over Nature which he calls "progress," so that he cuts himself off increasingly from the organic processes of life itself. Thus with the soil: the erosion of the American earth is not, as some seem to believe, the result of the mechanization of agriculture; a farmer can use science and farm technology to the full, and he need not exhaust or destroy his soil but can replenish it, as has been shown in the TVA, which is itself a triumph of technology. But the machines have been accompanied by a greed for quick results and an irreverence for the soil which are responsible for destroying the balance between man and the environment. What is true of the soil is true of the household: the mechanized household appliances have not destroyed the home or undermined family life; rural electrification has made the farmer's wife less a drudge, and the mass production of suburban houses has given the white-collar family a better chance than it had for sun and living space. What threatens family life is not the "kitchen revolution" or the "housing revolution" but the restless malaise of the spirit, of which the machine is more product than creator.

Even in a society remarkable for its self-criticism the major American writers have not succumbed to the temptation of making the machine into a Devil. Most of the novelists have amply expressed the frustrations of American life, and some (Dreiser, Dos Passos, Farrell and Algren come to mind) have mirrored in their style the pulse beats of an urban mechanized civilization. But except for a few isolated works, like Elmer Rice's *Adding Machine* and Eugene O'Neill's *Dynamo,* the writers have refrained from the pathetic fallacy of ascribing the ills of the spirit to the diabolism of the machine. The greatest American work on technology and its consequences—Lewis Mumford's massive four-volume work starting with *Man and Technics* and ending with *The Conduct of Life*—makes the crucial distinction between what is due to the machine itself and what is due to the human institutions that guide it and determine its uses.

It is here, moving from machine living to cultural standardization, that the picture becomes bleaker. Henry Miller's phrase for its American form is "the air-conditioned nightmare." Someone with a satiric intent could do a withering take-off on the rituals of American standardization.

Most American babies (he might say) are born in standardized hospitals, with a standardized tag put around them to keep them from getting confused with other standardized products of the hospital. Many of them grow up either in uniform rows of tenements or of small-town or suburban houses. They are wheeled about in standard perambulators, shiny or shabby as may be, fed from standardized bottles with standardized nipples according to standardized formulas, and tied up with standardized diapers. In childhood they are fed standardized breakfast foods out of standardized boxes with pictures of standardized heroes on them. They are sent to monotonously similar schoolhouses, where almost uniformly standardized teachers ladle out to them standardized information out of standardized textbooks. They pick up the routine wisdom of the streets in standard slang and learn the routine terms which constrict the range of their language within dishearteningly narrow limits. They wear out standardized shoes playing standardized games, or as passive observers they follow through standardized newspaper accounts or standardized radio and TV programs the highly ritualized antics of grown-up professionals playing the same games. They devour in millions of uniform pulp comic books the prowess of standardized supermen.

As they grow older they dance to canned music from canned juke boxes, millions of them putting standard coins into standard slots to get standardized tunes sung by voices with standardized inflections of emotion. They date with standardized girls in standardized cars. They see automatons thrown on millions of the same movie and TV screens, watching stereotyped love scenes adapted from made-to-order stories in standardized magazines.

They spend the days of their years with monotonous regularity in factory, office, and shop, performing routinized operations at regular intervals. They take time out for standardized "coffee breaks" and later a quick standardized lunch, come home at night to eat processed or canned food, and read syndicated columns and comic strips. Dressed in standardized clothes they attend standardized club meetings, church services, and socials. They have standardized fun at standardized big-city conventions. They are drafted into standardized armies, and if they escape the death of mechanized warfare they die of highly uniform diseases, and to the accompaniment of routine platitudes they are buried in standardized graves and celebrated by standardized obituary notices.

Caricature? Yes, perhaps a crude one, but with a core of frightening validity in it. Every society has its routines and rituals, the primitive groups being sometimes more tyrannously restricted by convention than the industrial societies. The difference is that where the primitive is bound by the rituals of tradition and group life, the American is bound by the rituals of the machine, its products, and their distribution and consumption.

The role of the machine in this standardized living must be made clear. The machine mechanizes life, and since mass production is part of Big Technology, the machine also makes uniformity of life possible. But it does not compel such uniformity. The American who shaves with an electric razor and his wife who buys a standardized "home permanent" for her hair do not thereby have to wear a uniformly vacuous expression through the day. A newspaper that uses the press association wire stories and prints from a highly mechanized set of presses does not thereby have to take the same view of the world that every other paper takes. A novelist who uses a typewriter instead of a quill pen does not have to turn out machine-made historical romances.

The answer is that some do and some don't. What the machine and the mass-produced commodities have done has been to make conformism easier. To buy and use what everyone else does, and live and think as everyone else does, becomes a short cut involving no need for one's own thinking. Those Americans have been captured by conformist living who have been capturable by it.

Cultural stereotypes are an inherent part of all group living, and they become sharper with mass living. There have always been unthinking people leading formless, atomized lives. What has happened in America is that the economics of mass production has put a premium on uniformity, so that America produces more units of more commodities (although sometimes of fewer models) than other cultures. American salesmanship has sought out every potential buyer of a product, so that standardization makes its way by the force of the distributive mechanism into every life. Yet for the person who has a personality pattern and style of his own, standardization need not mean anything more than a set of conveniences which leave a larger margin of leisure and greater scope for creative living. "That we may be enamored by the negation brought by the machine," as Frank Lloyd Wright has put it, "may be inevitable for a time. But I like to imagine this novel negation to be only a platform underfoot to enable a greater splendor of life to be ours than any known to Greek or Roman, Goth or Moor.

We should know a life beside which the life they knew would seem not only limited in scale and narrow in range but pale in richness of the color of imagination and integrity of spirit."

Which is to say that technology is the shell of American life, but a shell that need not hamper or stultify the modes of living and thinking. The real dangers of the American mode of life are not in the machine or even in standardization as much as they are in conformism. The dangers do not flow from the contrivances that men have fashioned to lighten their burdens, or from the material abundance which, if anything, should make a richer cultural life possible. They flow rather from the mimesis of the dominant and successful by the weak and mediocre, from the intolerance of diversity, and from the fear of being thought different from one's fellows. This is the essence of conformism.

It would be hard to make the connection between technology and conformism, unless one argues that men fashion their minds in the image of their surroundings, and that in a society of automatism, human beings themselves will become automatons. But this is simply not so. What relation there is between technology and conformism is far more subtle and less mystical. It is a double relation. On the one hand, as Jefferson foresaw, the simpler society of small-scale manufacture did not involve concentration of power in a small group, was not vulnerable to breakdown, and did not need drastic governmental controls; a society of big-scale industry has shown that it does. In that sense the big machines carry with them an imperative toward the directed society, which in turn—whether in war or peace—encourages conformism. On the second score, as De Tocqueville saw, a society in which there is no recognized elite group to serve as the arbiter of morals, thought, and style is bound to be a formless one in which the ordinary person seeks to heal his insecurity by attuning himself to the "tyranny of opinion"—to what others do and say and what they think of him. He is ruled by imitation and prestige rather than a sense of his own worth.

These are dangerous trends, but all of social living is dangerous. The notable fact is that in spite of its machines and standardization America has proved on balance less conformist than some other civilizations where the new technology has played less of a role. One thinks of the totalitarian experience of Italy, of Spain and Portugal, of Germany, of Russia and the East European countries, of Japan, of China. Some, like the Germans, the Japanese, and the Russian and Chinese Communists have been seized with an admiration for the machine; the others have had clerical and feudal traditions, and have lagged in industrial development. The totalitarian spirit can come to reside in a culture no matter what the shell of its technology is. There is no unvarying relation between machines and rigidity of living and thinking.

Americans have, it is true, an idolatry of production and consumption as they have an idolatry of success. But they have not idolized authority or submitted unquestioningly to human or supernatural oracles. They have had their cranks, eccentrics, and anarchists, and they still cling to individualism, even when it is being battered hard. It will take them some time before they can become "man in equipoise," balancing what science and the machine can do as against the demands of the life processes. But where they have failed, the failure has been less that of the machines they have wrought than of the very human fears, greeds, and competitive drives that have accompanied the building of a powerful culture.

It has been suggested that the American, like the Faustian, made a bargain with the Big Technology: a bargain to transform his ways of life and thought in the image of the machine, in return for the range of power and riches the machine would bring within his reach. It is a fine allegory. But truer than the Faustian bargain, with its connotations of the sale of one's soul to the Devil, is the image of Prometheus stealing fire from the gods in order to light a path of progress for men. The path is not yet clear, nor the meaning of progress, nor where it is leading: but the bold intent, the irreverence, and the secular daring have all become part of the American experience.

FOR THE STUDENT

Rhetoric

1. *Study for their rhetorical effectiveness the three paragraphs describing our cultural standardization. What adjectives add variety, yet nevertheless suggest standardization? Do these paragraphs illustrate Henry Miller's "air-conditioned nightmare"?*
2. *Study the organization of the essay and explain the logic underlying the order that Lerner gives his three most important points.*
3. *How do the allusions to Faust and Prometheus in the final paragraph help to clinch Lerner's chief point?*

Discussion

1. *What distinctions does Lerner wish to make between the "arterial forms of American living" and the "interminable gadgetry"?*
2. *Contrast the views of Ellul and Lerner on three or four specific points. Try to find sentences that state these contrasting views.*
3. *Would you say that Lerner is pessimistic, optimistic, or neutral in his views on technology? Cite evidence to support your conclusion.*
4. *According to Lerner, what relationship exists between technology and conformism? Is conformism an inevitable product of technology?*

Writing

1. *Take a topic of your choice, or one suggested by your instructor, and imitate Lerner's rhetorical tour de force in the section on cultural standardization. See if you can introduce some variety as Lerner did.*
2. *Write a critical or satirical paper on the standardized education you are receiving in your standardized college.*

SUMNER H. SLICHTER

Technology and the
Great American Experiment

I

The cultural history of America needs to be rewritten to take proper account of the impact of technology upon life and thought in the United States, especially upon social and political philosophy. Technology is a major influence in molding thought in the modern world, but its influence is in the main indirect. Karl Marx, whose inquiry into the effects of technology is still the most famous of all such studies, thought that the principal influence of technology would be to sharpen the class struggle. As technological change increased the capital needed per worker, the savings of the community would be less and less sufficient to provide the jobs needed by the growing labor force, unemployment would increase, and deepening misery would eventually produce revolution and the introduction of socialism. Marx misjudged the effects of technology mainly for two reasons—he failed to see that changing technology would increase the demand for skilled labor, and he failed to see that rising productivity would raise wages. Hence, Marx failed to see that technological change, instead of increasing the spread between the haves and the have-nots would greatly expand the middle class.

Thorstein Veblen has made the most ambitious attempt by an American scholar to examine the effects of technology upon thought. He believed that the habits of thought engendered by the technological disciplines undermined respect for property and other

Reprinted by permission of the publishers from John T. Dunlop (editor), Potentials of the American Economy: Selected Essays of Sumner H. Slichter. *Cambridge, Mass.: Harvard University Press, Copyright 1961 by the President and Fellows of Harvard College.*

[448]

traditional rights and thus created a demand for changes in the control of industry. He also believed that technology tended to create the kind of industrial system that could be properly run only by engineers. He hinted strongly that sooner or later the engineers would displace the businessmen as directors of industry. But Veblen eventually saw that he was wrong. In his last book, *The Engineers and the Price System,* he abandoned his earlier view that people who work closely with technology lose their respect for various traditional rights, and he conceded that engineers as a group are a rather conservative lot and have no desire to seize control of industry from the businessmen.

The failures of Marx and Veblen warn us that the effects of technology upon society are easily misjudged. It can be shown, however, that technology today is a principal influence (probably the most powerful single influence) keeping strong and vigorous the philosophy of democracy that has led the United States to embark upon one of the most magnificent experiments in human history. The American experiment is the attempt to make available to all members of the community (not simply to a privileged few limited by birth or wealth) the opportunity to lead the good life and to acquire the physical comforts of life. It is this bold and magnificent democratic philosophy which insists that all can and should have the good life that makes the American experiment something truly new in the history of mankind. The objective of the American experiment, as I have noted, has been twofold—to give people the opportunity to develop themselves and also the opportunity to acquire goods—but America has not sought to advance one of these objectives at the expense of the other.

Closely related to the American experiment and influenced by it has been the social and political revolution that has been going on in Europe for the last two hundred years. The two movements, however, are more or less distinct. Both the American experiment and the European revolution have the same basic philosophy—making the good life and the good things of life available to everyone. But the European movement has been occurring in old societies in which institutions of privilege were well established, in which resources were limited, and in which many people doubted the feasibility of opening the good life to all members of the community. Hence, the European movement has had to be revolutionary and it has, quite naturally, been accompanied by much philosophizing aimed at justifying the destruction of old institutions.

The great American experiment, developing among the settlers of a vacant continent, has had to do only limited tearing down of institutions of privilege. The American experiment had its beginning among the earliest settlers in New England, who sought opportunity to lead the good life, as they saw it, not by overthrowing institutions, but by escaping from them. The earliest settlers in New England were definitely seeking the good life, not the good things of life. The experiment developed as the natural response to conditions under which men in this country lived—not as the result of a carefully reasoned philosophy, though some philosophers and political theorists have affected American ideals. The rise of the democratic philosophy was accelerated by the Revolution. The fact that the people had to fight for their rights increased their self-assertiveness, and the large exodus of British loyalists at the end of the Revolution facilitated the replacement of institutions of privilege that had grown up in some colonies with institutions of democracy. But the most important condition that has produced and kept alive the kind of thinking that characterizes the American experiment is abundance of opportunity. Never in the world's history had men known opportunity in such abundance, and they came from Europe in millions to seize this great chance. Some sought primarily freedom from the restrictions and disabilities of stratified societies; others were mainly interested in the chance to make a living.

It is not surprising that men who were enjoying unprecedented abundance of opportunity should develop a more or less distinctive philosophy of life. No single great document fully expresses the philosophy of the American experiment, though the Declaration of Independence and the Bill of Rights contain much of it, and no philosopher has provided a comprehensive statement of the philosophy, though much of it is found in Emerson and John Dewey. Conditions of life in the United States have produced pretty general agreement among Americans, at least in the north, on three crucial propositions. One proposition is that economic, political, or social privileges are bad and should be prevented from arising and eliminated where they exist. At present the country is trying rather halfheartedly to apply this philosophy to the multitude of economic, political, and social discriminations against Negroes. A second proposition is that steps should be taken to make opportunity even more abundant. The best manifestation of this belief is the development of tax-supported free or almost-free public education, extending through the college and graduate school level. Even as early as 1860 the country had seventeen state universities. It has always been somewhat of a struggle to implement the idea of free public education, and it is still a struggle today when many question the wisdom of investing heavily in our young people. But slowly the idea of free public education is making progress. A third proposition is acceptance of the idea that it is practicable as well as right that *all* members of the community, not merely a privileged few, should have the opportunity to develop themselves and to live well—that attainment of this ideal is not beyond our resources.

What role has modern technology played in the American experiment? Its influence has been indirect, but nevertheless of great importance. The abundance of opportunity that has been the most important single influence in producing the philosophy is usually explained by the rapid settlement of the vacant continent. Undoubtedly, occupation of the continent had much to do with creating opportunity—particularly until the Civil War and a little after. But historians have paid too much attention to growth of population and to geographical expansion and too little to the development of technology. During the last hundred years technological progress has surpassed geographical expansion as a creator of opportunity and social fluidity.

It is easy to demonstrate the great influence of technology upon the kind of thinking that is producing the great American experiment. When the geographical frontier closed, more than two generations ago, many people thought that opportunity would diminish, that class lines would become sharper and class conflict more bitter, and that America would lose its buoyant faith in the future that had always stimulated its expansion. In short, it was feared the United States would gradually take on the characteristics of the stratified European societies. But nothing of the sort has happened. Opportunity has remained abundant, society has become even more fluid, and confidence in the future has remained strong. Indeed, instead of America's becoming more like Europe, Europe, which is also under the influence of modern technology, is slowly becoming more like the United States.

The reason that the passing of the frontier turned out to be a far less momentous event than might have been expected is that technological change rather than geographical expansion has been the principal source of opportunity. An examination of the process by which opportunity has been created makes plain the superior influence of technology. Rapid occupation of the vacant continent, it is true, helped people who were already on the ground to rise in the economic and social scale. But growing opportunity for the community as a whole—a chance for *all* members of the community to live better-rounded lives, to obtain a better education and more leisure than their fathers had, and to live better than their fathers lived—requires gains in average per capita incomes and, therefore, in productivity.

Mere filling up the vacant continent does not necessarily bring about much increase in productivity—it does so in the main only to the extent that new resources are richer than old ones. The increase in productivity that kept opportunity abundant and growing has been principally the result of technological change. As the rate of technological change has increased, the gain in per capita incomes has accelerated. This gain was about twice as large in the second half of the nineteenth century as in the first half, and it has been faster in recent years than in any previous years.

But the effect of technology upon opportunity is not adequately described by showing in a general way that gains in productivity are the principal source of opportunity. Technological change *might* have diverted the gains of productivity to the property owners and *might* have produced abundant opportunities for property owners but not for workers. But that has not happened. Perhaps the course of technological development has been pretty much a happy accident—though I do not think so. At any rate, technological change has channeled most of the gains of productivity into the hands of workers rather than into the hands of property owners, so that the share of property owners in the national product today is far less than it was a hundred years ago. This has happened in large part because technological change has limited the need for unskilled workers and has increased the need for skilled and professional workers. The number of common laborers in the country today is considerably less than it was forty-five years ago, and the number of skilled and professional jobs has been growing far faster than the labor force. Indeed, today the shortages of skilled and professional workers are greater than ever.

Not only has technological development created opportunity by increasing productivity, but it has also increased opportunity by preventing the successful from entrenching themselves in positions of power and privilege. Technology has done this by bringing into existence one new industry after another. Many of these new industries have grown in large measure at the expense of old industries. Thus profits have not been allowed to flow year after year through the same channels into the hands of a given group of lucky investors. As the pattern of industry has changed, the flow of profits has shifted, and many well-yielding securities of yesterday (the securities of the turnpike companies of a century and a half ago, the canal companies, many railroads, many street railway lines, interurban lines, bus lines, coastwise steamship lines, some locomotive manufacturers, New England textile mills, Pennsylvania hosiery mills, Connecticut hat factories, many automobile manufacturers, automotive parts manufacturers, and many movie houses) have become the cats and dogs of today.

II

That modern technology has been much more than a provider of goods, that it has been a powerful influence upon thought and upon the values and the social organizations that determine the quality of thinking in the community is clearly seen by the critics of technology who fear its effects upon our civilization. Let us look at a few of the principal problems that critics of technology believe it imposes upon society.

The oldest charge against technology, that it degrades the workers by robbing them of skill and responsibility, is heard far less frequently today than it was heard a generation or more ago. The reason is that this charge is now pretty generally recognized to be false. There are, of course, many instances in which technology does reduce the need for skill and responsibility, but a look at the jobs in industry shows that the usual effect of technology is to increase the demands on the worker. The work of the common laborer, which could formerly be done by managing a few simple tools and bits of apparatus (picks, shovels, wheelbarrows), is now largely done by power-driven apparatus. As apparatus is made more and more automatic, the number of machine-tending jobs diminishes and the number of maintenance and repair jobs increases. Modern apparatus also increases the need for planning and scheduling jobs. Finally, and most important, the fact that technology is in a state of flux increases the need of a whole range of nonroutine jobs. The early views of the effect of technology upon men have turned out to be wide of the mark.

A recent charge against technology is the assertion that technology, by giving us more and more leisure and income, is weakening higher education by creating a strong and insistent demand for college work by persons not capable of doing it. Now it is clear that technology is indirectly responsible for the rapidly growing demand for higher education, and it is also clear that some students are capable of doing much better work than others. Naturally, a rapid influx of students with widely differing abilities creates difficult problems for colleges and universities. But I do not think that the facts state a problem for the community as a whole. Certainly we are not going back to a nondemocratic philosophy of higher education—to regarding it as something suitable for only a few prospective clergymen, lawyers, doctors, and persons of leisure. It is a good thing, not a bad thing, that a growing proportion of the population wishes to continue in school until past the age of twenty. The growing demand for college work is more of an opportunity for educators than it is a problem, and professors and others who see it only as a problem are lacking in vision and in a proper philosophy of education.

Quite contradictory to the notion that technology is creating an excessive demand for higher education is the charge by Edward Heimann, Reinhold Niebuhr, and others that technology is ruining our standards of value and our taste by producing an excessive interest in *things* at the expense of interest in personal development and human welfare.[1] This result is said to follow from the extraordinary productivity of industry.

The essence of Heimann's and Niebuhr's argument is that the cultural interests of man are too narrow and his altruistic impulses too weak to enable him to make proper use of the flood of goods produced by modern technology. Lacking adequate desire to improve themselves and lacking proper standards of generosity, men are led by the ever-growing flood of goods to attach undue importance merely to living well or better—to acquiring the comforts and conveniences of life. And in a society in which many men have very limited ambitions with respect to developing themselves and limited concern for the plight of others (especially

1. Edward Heimann, "The Economy of Abundance," *Social Action* (January 1957), pp. 6–11, especially pp. 8–9. [Author's note]

foreigners), the easiest way to sell goods in large quantities, it is said, is to build up bad standards of value and taste. In order to sell the "orgy" of goods turned out by modern technology, salesmanship and advertising must exploit all manner of mean and ignoble motives. In the words of Reinhold Niebuhr, our culture is the first in the world's history to become "captive to its economy." Unless we buy without regard to moral and esthetic qualities, he says, the industrial system will break down.[2]

Certainly, Heimann, Niebuhr, and others are right that abundance of goods as well as scarcity can create problems, and that ours is the first *major* civilization at least that must wrestle with the problems of abundance. Abundance creates the danger that men will become interested merely in living better rather than in living better lives. Nor can there be doubt that the excesses of salesmanship and advertising are among the more unlovely products of our civilization and that modern technology is responsible at least for the scale of salesmanship and advertising.

But the indictment by Heimann and Niebuhr goes much too far. There is an enormous interest in self-improvement and self-development, rather than in the mere acquisition of goods, as is made plain by the complaint that too many people seek to go to college. And when one looks at the kind of goods that people are acquiring, one's fear that the country is building up false standards of value takes a considerable drop. One notes an enormous increase in admirable uses of income—the purchase of millions of owner-occupied homes, a rapidly climbing demand for education, sharply growing outlays for medical care and for insurance of various kinds, fast-growing expenditures on vacation and travel, and a sensational expansion in spending on drudgery-reducing household appliances. Nor is bringing news and entertainment into the home a bad idea.

Related to the criticism of Heimann and Niebuhr is the charge

2. See his comment on Heimann's article in *Social Action* (January 1957), pp. 12–14, especially p. 12. [Author's note]

made by many artists that technology is debasing taste by making it far more profitable for artists of various kinds to cater to the uneducated many rather than to the cultured few. The charge that modern methods of communication stack the rewards in favor of products intended for the mass markets is undoubtedly correct. But this is only part of the story. Technology, by giving the artist command of new media, has created new forms of art and has invigorated old forms. Furthermore, while technology, by raising per capita incomes in the community and increasing leisure, makes immense rewards available to those who cater to the mass markets, it also enables the serious artist to make a better living than he could have gained in a poorer society. Indeed, modern technology, for all of the stimulus it has given to production for mass markets, has not prevented a great growth of art and writing that are often drastically introspective and subjective, and intended only for the initiated.

A bit of reflection will produce the conclusion, I think, that the charge that modern technology stacks the rewards in favor of the commonplace states a challenge as much as a problem—a challenge to every artist, every writer, every educator. Here is a new kind of society—a society in which leisure is broadly distributed in the form of a short work week rather than concentrated in a small class of the very rich; in which literally millions of people have gone to college and possess incomes that permit them to buy pictures and books in modest amounts and to travel. It is a society in which, thanks to technology, leisure, education, and incomes are growing. Here obviously are the makings of a cultural revolution, if artists can create broad interest in serious work. The opportunity is theirs, such opportunity as artists have never had. If they fail to produce the cultural revolution, perhaps the fault will be with the artists. One observation may be safely made. If serious art is to play a significant role in a society with such powerful democratic traditions as ours, where cultural developments and public policies alike are made by the whole community rather than by a small aristocracy or ruling class, artists must address themselves not solely to a small audience of the initiated; they must touch in a significant way the lives of the many.

An oft-repeated charge against modern technology is that it converts men into conformists and robs them of their individuality. It is said to do this because it exposes us to enormous pressures from media of mass communication—newspapers, magazines, billboards, radio, and television in which we are said to see or hear the same ideas or slogans endlessly repeated—and because it requires us to make our living as members of groups or teams in which our individualities are more or less suppressed.

These charges leave me unimpressed. Modern methods of communication are a good way of acquainting people with a multitude of conflicting points of view. How can conformity be encouraged if one is at a loss what to conform to? And if organizations suppress individuality, they do it quite inefficiently. Every organization that I have had a chance to observe has been full of strong-willed individuals, and the problem of the organization is to get a reasonable amount of teamwork.

All history has been a sort of struggle between man and his institutions. Organizations of various sorts, mainly governments and churches, have attempted to regiment their members—to suppress their individualities, to make them conformists. The most complete control of the group over the individual is found in primitive societies. Sometimes the conflict between individuals and institutions swings in favor of the individuals and sometimes in favor of the institutions, but the trend through the centuries shows individuals winning release from institutions. Certainly modern man in western Europe and America is more individualistic and more disposed to challenge authority than was medieval man.

The great enemies of conformity and the great sources of individualism have always been communication, travel, and educacation. Modern technology is steadily strengthening each of these sources of individualism. Education, especially higher education, is the strongest influence in our culture for individualism because it encourages the habit, dreaded by all regimenters, of thinking for oneself. The fight to keep institutions and organizations in their place and to build a community of strong, inquisitive, and independent individuals is far from won, but technology, through helping men afford travel and education and by bringing them better instruments of communication, is helping to win the day for individualism.

An outstanding contribution of technology, and of science as well, to the values that guide our lives is their influence upon the sense of social responsibility. Strangely enough, this effect has escaped the attention of the moralists who worry about the effects of technology upon our ethical standards. Before the rise of modern science and technology, man lived in an environment which was pretty much beyond his control. When he had tough problems, he could do little about them. But as science and technology have given him insights into his environment, this feeling of helplessness has been slowly disappearing. Today, we realize that even if we cannot solve a problem completely, we can at least do something about it. The result is a growing sense of social responsibility—a growing disposition to make planned attacks on our problems. No longer can we ignore human suffering or misery by taking refuge in the comfortable excuse that conditions are beyond our control, and that all we can do is to provide charity. Thus, by giving us new powers, science and technology also give us new responsibilities and foster a new willingness to act on those responsibilities. In this way science and technology contribute to the advancement of morals.

III

Technology will play an even greater role in our lives than it has played up to now. The reason is that each advance in science and technology increases man's capacity to make additional discoveries. Hence, the great American experiment will receive ever-growing support from science and technology. The outlook for the experiment looks bright.

In spite of this favorable outlook, however, the time has come to provide the American experiment with a comprehensive and well-considered statement of its objectives and its significance. To produce such a statement would require the work of men with great insight in the fields of history, philosophy, politics, and social institutions. Too long our great experiment has been merely the product of conditions without the stimulus and guidance that can be provided only by a well-expressed philosophy. We shall accomplish more effectively what we are trying to do if we have a greater awareness of our objectives. Furthermore, a well-expressed and well-understood philosophy will help us to see more clearly the deficiencies in our accomplishments. It will force us to consider whether we are giving too much attention to acquiring things and too little attention to developing men. It will give us tests by which to appraise institutions and policies. It will help overcome selfish obstacles to the experiment. Most important of all, it will enhance the significance of the lives of each and every one of us by giving us a sense of the magnificence of the great enterprise in which we are participating and of the worthwhileness of the goals for which we are striving.

FOR THE STUDENT

Rhetoric

1. *What is the function of paragraphs four and five, which discuss the American experiment and the social and political revolution in Europe?*
2. *What is Slichter's principle of organization and development in the second section?*
3. *In partial answer to Heimann's and Niebuhr's charge about*

false standards of value, Slichter states, "Nor is bringing news and entertainment into the home a bad idea." Why is this reply deficient?

Discussion

1. *Compare the charges against technology that Slichter answers in the second part with Ellul's criticisms of technology. What are some of the important differences between the views of the two men?*
2. *What is the nature of Slichter's answer to Heimann's and Niebuhr's charge? How well or how poorly does he answer that charge?*
3. *Compare and contrast Lerner and Slichter on the relationship between technology and conformism.*
4. *Evaluate the education you are now receiving as a force that "encourages the habit . . . of thinking for oneself."*

Writing

1. *Write a dialogue between Ellul and Slichter in which they discuss two or three of the criticisms of technology.*
2. *In a paper of 600–800 words, show which of the three men—Ellul, Lerner, Slichter—gives the best support to his argument. Use as much objective evidence as you can in your analysis.*

12 Poverty

The statement of Jesus that the poor will always be with you is often interpreted as a final statement of man's inability to eradicate poverty rather than as a description of a contemporaneous social situation. Those who quote this statement to uphold their opposition to a program intended to alleviate poverty may have forgotten the counsel in Deuteronomy to open wide the hand to the poor.

The problem of poverty, we all know, is as old as the history of man. Modern industry and technology, however, permit us to make a new approach to the problem in the last decades of the twentieth century. Many authorities now believe it possible to so organize our society and our economy within the framework of a democratic government as to effect the virtual elimination of poverty. When President Kennedy planned and President Johnson announced the war on poverty, they were taking the first steps of a very long journey toward a society which would permit a better life for all citizens. American industrial might can provide fully for the needs of all citizens, not just the middle and upper economic classes. The problems to be solved are numerous; the entire program is extremely complex; yet many believe man capable of solving the problems and establishing an effective program.

Opposition to the program arises for two basic reasons. At the bottom of our society, one group argues, are people who will never be profitably employed because they are too lazy and indolent to work. These form one part of the poor who will always be with us. A second group maintains that the middle and upper classes will be forced to support the lower economic class by being compelled to give up what they *have earned through incentive and hard work. This might be called the Robin Hood view. According to some students of poverty, however, the middle class actively desires that poverty not be eliminated, for the middle class sees its status threatened if poverty should no longer exist. There would be no lower class except that the middle class would then occupy that position.*

It is virtually impossible today to find any responsible thinker willing to put into print an argument opposing the elimination of poverty. Herbert Spencer, the English sociologist, argued in Social Statics *(1850) that man is unable to eliminate poverty and, further, that poverty has a purifying effect upon the race. His arguments were supported by men like Andrew Carnegie, but they are largely discarded now except as folk myths. Today we have representative statements like those of Michael Harrington in* The Other America, *which sparked President Kennedy's interest in a poverty program. Harrington maintains that the government can and should carry out a comprehensive program to eliminate poverty. Milton Friedman, a conservative economist, suggests the negative income tax as a more sufficient means than private charity and a more economical and effective one than our welfare program. Adam Walinsky, an attorney in Washington, D.C., has summed up the lower middle-class views opposing the elimination of poverty. The arguments are not his but are those sometimes made against any kind of poverty program.*

MICHAEL HARRINGTON

The Culture of Poverty

The millions who are poor in the United States tend to become increasingly invisible. Here is a great mass of people, yet it takes an effort of the intellect and will even to see them.

I discovered this personally in a curious way. After I wrote my first article on poverty in America, I had all the statistics down on paper. I had proved to my satisfaction that there were around 50,000,000 poor in this country. Yet, I realized I did not believe my own figures. The poor existed in the Government reports; they were percentages and numbers in long, close columns, but they were not part of my experience. I could prove that the other America existed, but I had never been there.

My response was not accidental. It was typical of what is happening to an entire society, and it reflects profound social changes in this nation. The other America, the America of poverty, is hidden today in a way that it never was before. Its millions are socially invisible to the rest of us. No wonder that so many misinterpreted Galbraith's title and assumed that "the affluent society" meant that everyone had a decent standard of life. The misinterpretation was true as far as the actual day-to-day lives of two-thirds of the nation were concerned. Thus, one must begin a description of the other America by understanding why we do not see it.

There are perennial reasons that make the other America an invisible land.

Poverty is often off the beaten track. It always has been. The ordinary tourist never left the main highway, and today he rides interstate turnpikes. He does not go into the valleys of Pennsylvania where the towns look like movie sets of Wales in the thirties. He does not see the company houses in rows, the rutted roads (the poor always have bad roads whether they live in the city, in towns, or on farms), and everything is black and dirty. And even if he were to pass through such a place by accident, the tourist would not meet the unemployed men in the bar or the women coming home from a runaway sweatshop.

Then, too, beauty and myths are perennial masks of poverty. The traveler comes to the Appalachians in the lovely season. He sees the hills, the streams, the foliage—but not the poor. Or perhaps he looks at a run-down mountain house and, remembering Rousseau rather than seeing with his eyes, decides that "those people" are truly fortunate to be living the way they are and that they are lucky to be exempt from the strains and tensions of the middle class. The only problem is that "those people," the quaint inhabitants of those hills, are undereducated, underprivileged, lack medical care, and are in the process of being forced from the land into a life in the cities, where they are misfits.

These are normal and obvious causes of the invisibility of the poor. They operated a generation ago; they will be functioning a generation hence. It is more important to understand that the very development of American society is creating a new kind of blindness about poverty. The poor are increasingly slipping out of the very experience and consciousness of the nation.

If the middle class never did like ugliness and poverty, it was at least aware of them. "Across the tracks" was not a very long way to go. There were forays into the slums at Christmas time; there were charitable organizations that brought contact with the poor. Occasionally, almost everyone passed through the Negro ghetto or the blocks of tenements, if only to get downtown to work or to entertainment.

Now the American city has been transformed. The poor still inhabit the miserable housing in the central area, but they are increasingly isolated from contact with, or sight of, anybody else. Middle-class women coming in from Suburbia on a rare trip may catch the merest glimpse of the other America on the way to an evening at the theater, but their children are segregated in suburban schools. The business or professional man may drive along the fringes of slums in a car or bus, but it is not an important experience to him. The failures, the unskilled, the disabled, the aged, and the minorities are right there, across the tracks, where they have always been. But hardly anyone else is.

In short, the very development of the American city has removed poverty from the living, emotional experience of millions upon millions of middle-class Americans. Living out in the suburbs, it is easy to assume that ours is, indeed, an affluent society.

This new segregation of poverty is compounded by a well-meaning ignorance. A good many concerned and sympathetic Americans are aware that there is much discussion of urban renewal. Suddenly, driving through the city, they notice that a familiar slum has been torn down and that there are towering, modern buildings where once there had been tenements or hovels. There is a warm feeling of satisfaction, of pride in the way things are working out: the poor, it is obvious, are being taken care of.

The irony in this . . . is that the truth is nearly the exact opposite to the impression. The total impact of the various housing programs in postwar America has been to squeeze more and more people into existing slums. More often than not, the modern apartment in a towering building rents at $40 a room or more. For, during the past decade and a half, there has been more subsidization of middle- and upper-income housing than there has been of housing for the poor.

Clothes make the poor invisible too: America has the best-dressed poverty the world has ever known. For a variety of reasons, the benefits of mass production have been spread much more evenly in this area than in many others. It is much easier in the United States to be decently dressed than it is to be decently housed, fed, or doctored. Even people with terribly depressed incomes can look prosperous.

This is an extremely important factor in defining our emotional and existential ignorance of poverty. In Detroit the existence of social classes became much more difficult to discern the day the companies put lockers in the plants. From that moment on, one did not see men in work clothes on the way to the factory, but citizens in slacks and white shirts. This process has been magnified with the poor throughout the country. There are tens of thousands of Americans in the big cities who are wearing shoes, perhaps even a stylishly cut suit or dress, and yet are hungry. It is not a matter of planning, though it almost seems as if the affluent society had given out costumes to the poor so that they would not offend the rest of society with the sight of rags.

Then, many of the poor are the wrong age to be seen. A good number of them (over 8,000,000) are sixty-five years of age or better; an even larger number are under eighteen. The aged members of the other America are often sick, and they cannot move. Another group of them live out their lives in loneliness and frustration: they sit in rented rooms, or else they stay close to a house in a neighborhood that has completely changed from the old days. Indeed, one of the worst aspects of poverty among the aged is that these people are out of sight and out of mind, and alone.

The young are somewhat more visible, yet they too stay close to their neighborhoods. Sometimes they advertise their poverty through a lurid tabloid story about a gang killing. But generally they do not disturb the quiet streets of the middle class.

And finally, the poor are politically invisible. It is one of the cruelest ironies of social life in advanced countries that the dispossessed at the bottom of society are unable to speak for themselves. The people of the other America do not, by far and large, belong to unions, to fraternal organizations, or to political parties. They are without lobbies of their own; they put forward no legislative program. As a group, they are atomized. They have no face; they have no voice.

Thus, there is not even a cynical political motive for caring about the poor, as in the old days. Because the slums are no longer centers of powerful political organizations, the politicians need not really care about their inhabitants. The slums are no longer visible to the middle class, so much of the idealistic urge to fight for those who need help is gone. Only the social agencies have a really direct involvement with the other America, and they are without any great political power.

To the extent that the poor have a spokesman in American life, that role is played by the labor movement. The unions have their own particular idealism, an ideology of concern. More than that, they realize that the existence of a reservoir of cheap, unorganized labor is a menace to wages and working conditions throughout the entire economy. Thus, many union legislative proposals—to extend the coverage of minimum wage and social security, to organize migrant farm laborers—articulate the needs of the poor.

That the poor are invisible is one of the most important things about them. They are not simply neglected and forgotten as in the old rhetoric of reform; what is much worse, they are not seen.

. . .

There are mighty historical and economic forces that keep the poor down; and there are human beings who help out in this grim business, many of them unwittingly. There are sociological and political reasons why poverty is not seen; and there are misconceptions and prejudices that literally blind the eyes. The latter must be understood if anyone is to make the necessary act of intellect and will so that the poor can be noticed.

Here is the most familiar version of social blindness: "The poor are that way because they are afraid of work. And anyway they all have big cars. If they were like me (or my father or my grandfather), they could pay their own way. But they prefer to live on the dole and cheat the taxpayers."

This theory, usually thought of as a virtuous and moral statement, is one of the means of making it impossible for the poor ever to pay their way. There are, one must assume, citizens of the other America who choose impoverishment out of fear of work (though, writing it down, I really do not believe it). But the real explanation of why the poor are where they are is that they made the mistake of being born to the wrong parents, in the wrong section of the country, in the wrong industry, or in the wrong racial or ethnic group. Once that mistake has been made, they could have been paragons of will and morality, but most of them would never even have had a chance to get out of the other America.

There are two important ways of saying this: The poor are caught in a vicious circle; or, The poor live in a culture of poverty.

In a sense, one might define the contemporary poor in the United States as those who, for reasons beyond their control, cannot help themselves. All the most decisive factors making for opportunity and advance are against them. They are born going downward, and most of them stay down. They are victims whose lives are endlessly blown round and round the other America.

Here is one of the most familiar forms of the vicious circle of poverty. The poor get sick more than anyone else in the society. That is because they live in slums, jammed together under unhygienic conditions; they have inadequate diets, and cannot get decent medical care. When they become sick, they are sick longer than any other group in the society. Because they are sick more often and longer than anyone else, they lose wages and work, and find it difficult to hold a steady job. And because of this, they cannot pay for good housing, for a nutritious diet, for doctors. At any given point in the circle, particularly when there is a major illness, their prospect is to move to an even lower level and to begin the cycle, round and round, toward even more suffering.

This is only one example of the vicious circle. Each group in the other America has its own particular version of the experience, and these will be detailed throughout this book. But the pattern, whatever its variations, is basic to the other America.

The individual cannot usually break out of this vicious circle. Neither can the group, for it lacks the social energy and political strength to turn its misery into a cause. Only the larger society, with its help and resources, can really make it possible for these people to help themselves. Yet those who could make the difference too often refuse to act because of their ignorant, smug moralisms. They view the effects of poverty—above all, the warping of the will and spirit that is a consequence of being poor—as choices. Understanding the vicious circle is an important step in breaking down this prejudice.

There is an even richer way of describing this same, general idea: Poverty in the United States is a culture, an institution, a way of life.

There is a famous anecdote about Ernest Hemingway and F. Scott Fitzgerald. Fitzgerald is reported to have remarked to Hemingway, "The rich are different." And Hemingway replied, "Yes, they have money." Fitzgerald had much the better of the exchange. He understood that being rich was not a simple fact, like a large bank account, but a way of looking at reality, a series of attitudes, a special type of life. If this is true of the rich, it is ten times truer of the poor. Everything about them, from the condition of their teeth to the way in which they love, is suffused and permeated by the fact of their poverty. And this is sometimes a hard idea for a Hemingway-like middle-class America to comprehend.

The family structure of the poor, for instance, is different from that of the rest of the society. There are more homes without a father, there is less marriage, more early pregnancy and, if Kinsey's statistical findings can be used, markedly different attitudes toward sex. As a result of this, to take but one consequence of the fact, hundreds of thousands, and perhaps millions, of children in the other America never know stability and "normal" affection.

Or perhaps the policeman is an even better example. For the middle class, the police protect property, give directions, and help old ladies. For the urban poor, the police are those who arrest you. In almost any slum there is a vast conspiracy against the forces of law and order. If someone approaches asking for a person, no one there will have heard of him, even if he lives next door. The outsider is "cop," bill collector, investigator (and, in the Negro ghetto, most dramatically, he is "the Man").

While writing this book, I was arrested for participation in a civil-rights demonstration. A brief experience of a night in a cell made an abstraction personal and immediate: the city jail is one of the basic institutions of the other America. Almost everyone whom I encountered in the "tank" was poor: skid-row whites, Negroes, Puerto Ricans. Their poverty was an incitement to arrest in the first place. (A policeman will be much more careful with a well-dressed, obviously educated man who might have political connections than he will with someone who is poor.) They did not have money for bail or for lawyers. And, perhaps most important, they waited their arraignment with stolidity, in a mood of passive acceptance. They expected the worst, and they probably got it.

There is, in short, a language of the poor, a psychology of the poor, a world view of the poor. To be impoverished is to be an internal alien, to grow up in a culture that is radically different from the one that dominates the society. The poor can be described statistically; they can be analyzed as a group. But they need a novelist as well as a sociologist if we are to see them. They need an American Dickens to record the smell and texture and quality of their lives. The cycles and trends, the massive forces, must be seen as affecting persons who talk and think differently.

I am not that novelist. Yet . . . I have attempted to describe the faces behind the statistics, to tell a little of the "thickness" of personal life in the other America. Of necessity, I have begun with large groups: the dispossessed workers, the minorities, the farm poor, and the aged. Then, there are three cases of less massive types of poverty, including the only single humorous component in the other America. And finally, there are the slums, and the psychology of the poor.

Throughout, I work on an assumption that cannot be proved by Government figures or even documented by impressions of the other America. It is an ethical proposition, and it can be simply

stated: In a nation with a technology that could provide every
citizen with a decent life, it is an outrage and a scandal that there
should be such social misery. Only if one begins with this assumption is it possible to pierce through the invisibility of 40,000,000
to 50,000,000 human beings and to see the other America. We
must perceive passionately, if this blindness is to be lifted from us.
A fact can be rationalized and explained away; an indignity cannot.

What shall we tell the American poor, once we have seen them?
Shall we say to them that they are better off than the Indian poor,
the Italian poor, the Russian poor? That is one answer, but it is
heartless. I should put it another way. I want to tell every well-fed
and optimistic American that it is intolerable that so many millions
should be maimed in body and in spirit when it is not necessary
that they should be. My standard of comparison is not how much
worse things used to be. It is how much better they could be if
only we were stirred.

.   .   .

Perhaps the most important analytic point to have emerged in
this description of the other America is the fact that poverty in
America forms a culture, a way of life and feeling, that it makes
a whole. It is crucial to generalize this idea, for it profoundly affects how one moves to destroy poverty.

The most obvious aspect of this interrelatedness is in the way
in which the various subcultures of the other America feed into
one another. This is clearest with the aged. There the poverty of
the declining years is, for some millions of human beings, a function of the poverty of the earlier years. If there were adequate
medical care for everyone in the United States, there would be less
misery for old people. It is as simple as that. Or there is the relation between the poor farmers and the unskilled workers. When
a man is driven off the land because of the impoverishment worked
by technological progress, he leaves one part of the culture of
poverty and joins another. If something were done about the low-
income farmer, that would immediately tell in the statistics of
urban unemployment and the economic underworld. The same is

true of the Negroes. Any gain for America's minorities will immediately be translated into an advance for all the unskilled workers. One cannot raise the bottom of a society without benefiting everyone above.

Indeed, there is a curious advantage in the wholeness of poverty. Since the other America forms a distinct system within the United States, effective action at any one decisive point will have a "multiplier" effect; it will ramify through the entire culture of misery and ultimately through the entire society.

Then, poverty is a culture in the sense that the mechanism of impoverishment is fundamentally the same in every part of the system. The vicious circle is a basic pattern. It takes different forms for the unskilled workers, for the aged, for the Negroes, for the agricultural workers, but in each case the principle is the same. There are people in the affluent society who are poor because they are poor; and who stay poor because they are poor.

To realize this is to see that there are some tens of millions of Americans who are beyond the welfare state. Some of them are simply not covered by social legislation: they are omitted from Social Security and from minimum wage. Others are covered, but since they are so poor they do not know how to take advantage of the opportunities, or else their coverage is so inadequate as not to make a difference.

The welfare state was designed during that great burst of social creativity that took place in the 1930's. . . . Its structure corresponds to the needs of those who played the most important role in building it: the middle third, the organized workers, the forces of urban liberalism, and so on. At the worst, there is "socialism for the rich and free enterprise for the poor," as when the huge corporation farms are the main beneficiaries of the farm program while the poor farmers get practically nothing; or when public funds are directed to aid in the construction of luxury housing while the slums are left to themselves (or become more dense as space is created for the well-off).

So there is the fundamental paradox of the welfare state: that it is not built for the desperate, but for those who are already capable of helping themselves. As long as the illusion persists that the poor are merrily freeloading on the public dole, so long will the other America continue unthreatened. The truth, it must be understood, is the exact opposite. The poor get less out of the welfare state than any group in America.

This is, of course, related to the most distinguishing mark of the other America: its common sense of hopelessness. For even when there are programs designed to help the other Americans, the poor are held back by their own pessimism.

On one level this fact has been described in this book as a matter of "aspiration." Like the Asian peasant, the impoverished American tends to see life as a fate, an endless cycle from which there is no deliverance. Lacking hope (and he is realistic to feel this way in many cases), that famous solution to all problems— let us educate the poor—becomes less and less meaningful. A person has to feel that education will do something for him if he is to gain from it. Placing a magnificent school with a fine faculty in the middle of a slum is, I suppose, better than having a rundown building staffed by incompetents. But it will not really make a difference so long as the environment of the tenement, the family, and the street counsels the children to leave as soon as they can to disregard schooling.

On another level, the emotions of the other America are even more profoundly disturbed. Here it is not lack of aspiration and of hope; it is a matter of personal chaos. The drunkenness, the unstable marriages, the violence of the other America are not simply facts about individuals. They are the description of an entire group in the society who react this way because of the conditions under which they live.

In short, being poor is not one aspect of a person's life in this country, it is his life. Taken as a whole, poverty is a culture. Taken on the family level, it has the same quality. These are people who lack education and skill, who have bad health, poor housing, low levels of aspiration and high levels of mental distress. They are, in the language of sociology, "multiproblem" families. Each disability is the more intense because it exists within a web of disabilities. And if one problem is solved, and the others are left constant, there is little gain.

One might translate these facts into the moralistic language so dear to those who would condemn the poor for their faults. The other Americans are those who live at a level of life beneath moral choice, who are so submerged in their poverty that one cannot begin to talk about free choice. The point is not to make them wards of the state. Rather, society must help them before they can help themselves.

FOR THE STUDENT

Rhetoric

1. *List the reasons why, according to Harrington, the poor are invisible. Then summarize his example for each reason and tell why it is effective.*
2. *Notice the short dialogue credited to Fitzgerald and Hemingway. The original source refers to "the very rich," and the reply goes, "Yes, they have more money." Why does Harrington omit two key words from his anecdote, and how would their inclusion affect the case he is making?*

Discussion

1. *Have you found the poor as invisible as Harrington suggests in the first section of his essay? Explain why or why not.*
2. *Explain what Harrington means by the culture of poverty.*
3. *How would you characterize Harrington's attitude toward*

the poor? Give evidence from the essay to support your view.

Writing

1. *Theme topic: "The invisible poor in my city." (Do not use this topic unless you have had firsthand experience.)*
2. *Attempt to be an American Dickens and record the smell, texture, and quality of the lives of the poor.*

MILTON FRIEDMAN

The Alleviation of Poverty

The extraordinary economic growth experienced by Western countries during the past two centuries and the wide distribution of the benefits of free enterprise have enormously reduced the extent of poverty in any absolute sense in the capitalistic countries of the West. But poverty is in part a relative matter, and even in these countries, there are clearly many people living under conditions that the rest of us label as poverty.

One recourse, and in many ways the most desirable, is private charity. It is noteworthy that the heyday of laissez-faire, the middle and late nineteenth century in Britain and the United States, saw an extraordinary proliferation of private eleemosynary organizations and institutions. One of the major costs of the extension of governmental welfare activities has been the corresponding decline in private charitable activities.

It can be argued that private charity is insufficient because the benefits from it accrue to people other than those who make the gifts—again, a neighborhood effect. I am distressed by the sight of poverty; I am benefited by its alleviation; but I am benefited equally whether I or someone else pays for its alleviation; the benefits of other people's charity therefore partly accrue to me. To put it differently, we might all of us be willing to contribute to the relief of poverty, *provided* everyone else did. We might not be willing to contribute the same amount without such assurance. In small communities, public pressure can suffice to realize the proviso even with private charity. In the large impersonal communities that are increasingly coming to dominate our society, it is much more difficult for it to do so.

Suppose one accepts, as I do, this line of reasoning as justifying governmental action to alleviate poverty; to set, as it were, a floor under the standard of life of every person in the community. There remain the questions, how much and how. I see no way of deciding "how much" except in terms of the amount of taxes we —by which I mean the great bulk of us—are willing to impose on ourselves for the purpose. The question, "how," affords more room for speculation.

Two things seem clear. First, if the objective is to alleviate poverty, we should have a program directed at helping the poor. There is every reason to help the poor man who happens to be a farmer, not because he is a farmer but because he is poor. The program, that is, should be designed to help people as people not as members of particular occupational groups or age groups or wage-rate groups or labor organizations or industries. This is a defect of farm programs, general old-age benefits, minimum-wage laws, pro-union legislation, tariffs, licensing provisions of crafts or professions, and so on in seemingly endless profusion. Second, so far as possible the program should, while operating through the market, not distort the market or impede its functioning. This is a defect of price supports, minimum-wage laws, tariffs and the like.

The arrangement that recommends itself on purely mechanical grounds is a negative income tax. We now have an exemption of $600 per person under the federal income tax (plus a minimum 10 per cent flat deduction). If an individual receives $100 taxable income, i.e., an income of $100 in excess of the exemption and deductions, he pays tax. Under the proposal, if his taxable income minus $100, i.e., $100 less than the exemption plus deductions, he would pay a negative tax, i.e., receive a subsidy. If the rate of subsidy were, say, 50 per cent, he would receive $50. If he had no income at all, and, for simplicity, no deductions, and the rate were constant, he would receive $300. He might receive more than this if he had deductions, for example, for medical expenses, so that his income, less deductions, was negative even before subtracting the exemption. The rates of subsidy could, of course, be graduated just as the rates of tax above the exemption are. In this way, it would be possible to set a floor below which no man's net income (defined now to include the subsidy) could fall—in the simple example $300 per person. The precise floor set would depend on what the community could afford.

The advantages of this arrangement are clear. It is directed specifically at the problem of poverty. It gives help in the form most useful to the individual, namely, cash. It is general and could be substituted for the host of special measures now in effect. It makes explicit the cost borne by society. It operates outside the market. Like any other measures to alleviate poverty, it reduces the incentives of those helped to help themselves, but it does not eliminate that incentive entirely, as a system of supplementing incomes up to some fixed minimum would. An extra dollar earned always means more money available for expenditure.

No doubt there would be problems of administration, but these seem to me a minor disadvantage, if they be a disadvantage at all. The system would fit directly into our current income tax system and could be administered along with it. The present tax system covers the bulk of income recipients and the necessity of covering all would have the by-product of improving the operation of the present income tax. More important, if enacted as a substitute for the present rag bag of measures directed at the same end, the total administrative burden would surely be reduced.

A few brief calculations suggest also that this proposal could be far less costly in money, let alone in the degree of governmental intervention involved, than our present collection of welfare measures. Alternatively, these calculations can be regarded as showing how wasteful our present measures are, judged as measures for helping the poor.

In 1961, government amounted to something like $33 billion (federal, state, and local) on direct welfare payments and programs of all kinds: old age assistance, social security benefit payments, aid to dependent children, general assistance, farm price support programs, public housing, etc.[1] I have excluded veterans' benefits in making this calculation. I have also made no allowance for the direct and indirect costs of such measures as minimum-wage laws, tariffs, licensing provisions, and so on, or for the costs of public health activities, state and local expenditures on hospitals, mental institutions, and the like.

There are approximately 57 million consumer units (unattached individuals and families) in the United States. The 1961 expenditures of $33 billion would have financed outright cash grants of nearly $6,000 per consumer unit to the 10 per cent with the lowest incomes. Such grants would have raised their incomes above the average for all units in the United States. Alternatively, these expenditures would have financed grants of nearly $3,000 per consumer unit to the 20 per cent with the lowest incomes. Even if one went so far as that one-third whom New Dealers were fond of calling ill-fed, ill-housed, and ill-clothed, 1961 expenditures would have financed grants of nearly $2,000 per consumer unit, roughly the sum which, after allowing for the change in the level of prices, was the income which separated the lower one-third in the middle 1930's from the upper two-thirds. Today, fewer than one-eighth of consumer units have an income, adjusted for the change in the level of prices, as low as that of the lowest third in the middle 1930's.

Clearly, these are all far more extravagant programs than can be justified to "alleviate poverty" even by a rather generous interpretation of that term. A program which *supplemented* the in-

1. This figure is equal to government transfer payments ($31.1 billion) less veterans' benefits ($4.8 billion), both from the Department of Commerce national income accounts, plus federal expenditures on the agricultural program ($5.5 billion) plus federal expenditures on public housing and other aids to housing ($0.5 billion), both for year ending June 30, 1961 from Treasury accounts, plus a rough allowance of $0.7 billion to raise it to even billions and to allow for administrative costs of federal programs, omitted state and local programs, and miscellaneous items. My guess is that this figure is a substantial underestimate. [Author's note]

comes of the 20 per cent of the consumer units with the lowest incomes so as to raise them to the lowest income of the rest would cost less than half of what we are now spending.

The major disadvantage of the proposed negative income tax is its political implications. It establishes a system under which taxes are imposed on some to pay subsidies to others. And presumably, these others have a vote. There is always the danger that instead of being an arrangement under which the great majority tax themselves willingly to help an unfortunate minority, it will be converted into one under which a majority imposes taxes for its own benefit on an unwilling minority. Because this proposal makes the process so explicit, the danger is perhaps greater than with other measures. I see no solution to this problem except to rely on the self-restraint and good will of the electorate.

Writing about a corresponding problem—British old-age pensions—in 1914, Dicey said, "Surely a sensible and a benevolent man may well ask himself whether England as a whole will gain by enacting that the receipt of poor relief, in the shape of a pension, shall be consistent with the pensioner's retaining the right to join in the election of a Member of Parliament."[2]

The verdict of experience in Britain on Dicey's question must as yet be regarded as mixed. England did move to universal suffrage without the disfranchisement of either pensioners or other recipients of state aid. And there has been an enormous expansion of taxation of some for the benefit of others, which must surely be regarded as having retarded Britain's growth, and so may not even have benefited most of those who regard themselves as on the receiving end. But these measures have not destroyed, at least as yet, Britain's liberties or its predominantly capitalistic system. And, more important, there have been some signs of a turning of the tide and of the exercise of self-restraint on the part of the electorate.

2. A. V. Dicey, *Law and Public Opinion in England*, (2d ed., London: Macmillan, 1914), p. xxxv. [Author's note]

Liberalism and Egalitarianism

The heart of the liberal philosophy is a belief in the dignity of the individual, in his freedom to make the most of his capacities and opportunities according to his own lights, subject only to the proviso that he not interfere with the freedom of other individuals to do the same. This implies a belief in the equality of men in one sense; in their inequality in another. Each man has an equal right to freedom. This is an important and fundamental right precisely because men are different, because one man will want to do different things with his freedom than another, and in the process can contribute more than another to the general culture of the society in which many men live.

The liberal will therefore distinguish sharply between equality of rights and equality of opportunity, on the one hand, and material equality or equality of outcome on the other. He may welcome the fact that a free society in fact tends toward greater material equality than any other yet tried. But he will regard this as a desirable by-product of a free society, not its major justification. He will welcome measures that promote both freedom and equality—such as measures to eliminate monopoly power and to improve the operation of the market. He will regard private charity directed at helping the less fortunate as an example of the proper use of freedom. And he may approve state action toward ameliorating poverty as a more effective way in which the great bulk of the community can achieve a common objective. He will do so with regret, however, at having to substitute compulsory for voluntary action.

The egalitarian will go this far, too. But he will want to go further. He will defend taking from some to give to others, not as a more effective means whereby the "some" can achieve an objective they want to achieve, but on grounds of "justice." At this point, equality comes sharply into conflict with freedom; one must choose. One cannot be both an egalitarian, in this sense, and a liberal.

FOR THE STUDENT

Rhetoric

1. *What effect do the phrases "in any absolute sense" and "in part a relative matter" give to Friedman's opening paragraph?*
2. *Outline the steps of Friedman's argument for the negative income tax. Do you find his order of arrangement effective? Why?*
3. *Examine several paragraphs to see if Friedman uses topic sentences at the beginning of most of his paragraphs.*

Discussion

1. *What is Friedman's argument to prove the insufficiency of private charity in our society?*
2. *What are Friedman's objections to programs designed to help particular groups?*
3. *In what sense does the heart of the liberal philosophy imply a belief in the equality of men? In their inequality?*
4. *Explain Friedman's closing statement.*
5. *Why do you suppose that an economist who is generally considered a conservative would propose a negative income tax as one of the most effective ways to alleviate poverty?*

Writing

1. *Theme topics: "Why I (do, do not) give to private charities"; "The poor are poor because they are inferior."*
2. *Write a paper in which you explain how the liberal David Spitz and the conservative Clinton Rossiter might react to the negative income tax. (See "Liberal Versus Conservative.")*

ADAM WALINSKY

Keeping the Poor
in Their Place:
Notes on the Importance
of Being One-Up

No significant shade of political opinion, from I. F. Stone to
Time magazine, can be found to oppose outright the War on
Poverty; the Great Society has thus far been received as an elec-
tion-year counterpart of the Big Rock Candy Mountain. And yet
most of us assume that Congress will not establish the giant public
works program for which Gunnar Myrdal calls. Nor will it lower
the work week to thirty hours, as Herbert Gans has suggested, nor
follow the suggestion of the Ad Hoc Committee on the Triple
Revolution and guarantee incomes to all regardless of the work
they do. The reasons for Congressional reluctance are familiar;
the poor are, by definition, without economic power; except for
the Negroes, they are without effective leaders; they are only one
fifth of a nation, and the rest of the country is roughly satisfied
with things as they are.

The liberals who argue that larger programs are necessary
admit readily that the critical barrier is the apathetic or even
hostile attitude of the middle-class majority—for present purposes,
whites who are not poor—which has been victimized by "myths":
that a balanced budget is desirable; that the government economy
should be run like a household budget; that free enterprise is inherently superior to government activity; that big government is a
bad thing; that tax cuts stimulate economic activity more than

government spending; that expeditures result not in a bigger pie, but only a smaller slice for solid taxpayers. If the public is educated in the truth about economics, one hears, these "myths" will disappear.

But the interesting question about a myth is not whether people believe it, but why. Myths are not capricious inventions of storytellers, but ways of organizing and rationalizing group-behavior patterns. They serve real needs; they are less affected by argument than by changes in the conditions to which they are responsive. Viewing these myths as a screen behind which tangible aims are pursued would require a second hypothesis: that the middle-class majority *does not want* to improve significantly the lot of the poor, or—a further step—that the middle-class actively desires to keep the poor where they are.

In present-day America, the middle class is defined largely by the fact that the poor exist. Doctors are middle class, but so are bookkeepers; factory workers vacation with lawyers, drive bigger cars than teachers, live next door to store-owners, and send their children to school with the children of bank tellers. In a middle class so diffuse, with almost no characteristic common to all, middle-class income, education, and housing are what the poor do not have. If the present poor should become middle class, no meaning would remain to that phrase; either it would be a euphemism for the lower part of a bipartite division, or it would cease to apply to those who now boast of their "middle" status. The middle class knows that the economists are right when they say that poverty can be eliminated if we only will it; they simply do not will it.

Such an explanation, of course, seems in direct conflict with American ideals of equality of opportunity and social justice— ideals on which the middle classes themselves insist. But the creed of equal opportunity is a very complex thing. Opportunity to better oneself is usually regarded as self-explanatory, a recognition of the basic human right to fully utilize one's talents and labor. And in part it is recognized as a refusal to admit that others are better than oneself, or (a variant of the last) that others' children are better than one's own. But it has other facets. Virtually everyone who has reached his final life-station must and does believe and say that choice, or more commonly "the breaks," or "the system," prevented him from rising higher. But this same man must and does believe and say that his own abilities are primarily responsible for how far he has risen above others. People above oneself are regarded as no better than equal; people below oneself are regarded as inferior.

It is of course necessary to tinker with the system occasionally. Not only is reform commanded by the ethic; but as long as they pose no threat of basic change, improvements in the opportunity-structure at once reaffirm the existence of the depressed who need help, and serve as further "proof" that their inferior position is the result of inherent inferiority. But since people will not and cannot admit to themselves that the inferior position of others is entirely, or even primarily, caused by an inherently unequal system, they do not support measures that could possibly eliminate all or even most of the inequalities. The result is tokenism.

I suspect that the tension between adherence to democratic ideals and a natural desire to preserve one's relative gains by denying them to others has been heightened by a general loss of middle-class security. One possible reason for such a loss of security is enlargement in the size of the middle class itself; by the social and economic elevation of production and service workers; by the slackening of immigration, which has produced an America 95 per cent native-born and thus eliminated much "native" prestige; by the spread of education, high school and now college; by the general availability of inexpensive goods (especially clothing) virtually identical to those used by the well-to-do. For the old middle class, this has meant a dilution of status, which they have attempted to recapture by shifting the criteria of middle-class membership from income ("mere money") to sophistication of various sorts— education, community service, culture. For the new middle class, the gain in status is precarious; they attempt to reinforce it by appropriating the symbols of the old middle class, especially suburban housing and education for the children. For both old and new middle classes, the problem of preserving status becomes more acute in direct proportion to the technical ease with which poverty can be eliminated from the country.

"Variety of Dingbats"

But the central factor in the loss of security is a general decline in the significance of work. Observers have noted this loss in many different places: among the unemployed and underemployed: among factory hands whose labor is ever more routinized and uncertain; among paper-work employees of great corporations whose only function is the creation of artificial differences between what Pegler called "an ingenious variety of dingbats for the immature"; among craftsmen whose only means of delaying obsolescence is in Luddite strikes, and who are reminded of their uselessness at every well-publicized contract negotiation. Indeed, the meaninglessness of work has become one the dominant themes of popular culture. But any decline thus far observed in the importance of work is but the start of a potential toboggan run. The impact of automation on the assembly line is increasingly clear. But white-collar workers are also being replaced by machines; and Donald N. Michael predicts that middle management, whose relatively unsophisticated job is being brought within computer capabilities, is the next threatened class. If present trends in the automation of factory and office continue, there will be fewer jobs, and most of them will be routine.

Understanding the full import of that development requires recognition of the function work has performed in the past. Work everywhere serves the obvious function of enabling men to eat and survive. But work in America has also been the primary source of status in the society. Men have marked out their relation to others through work. The rewards of the society—income, women, power, respect—have gone to men roughly in proportion to their market utility. (Divergences—such as great inherited wealth—have been

remarkable chiefly for their tendency to gravitate toward the norm
—as in the upper classes' compulsion to enter and subsidize public
affairs.) But work has been the organizing principle of American
society in more than an economic sense; it has in large part displaced and substituted for ancestry, social class, tradition, and family as bench-marks for men's knowledge of self and their relation
to others. Reliance on work as the primary social ethic has been
intimately bound up with the growth of a democratic, egalitarian
society. For work is alone among our status-givers in its diversity
and attendant uniqueness. No man can master all occupations; indeed, few can master more than one. No matter how brilliant a professor may be, he must still call the plumber when his water-pipes
freeze, or a mechanic when his car's transmission slips, a butcher
when he wants meat, and a laborer when he wants a drain dug. In
a diversified economy, so long as a man has a trade or skill, he has
something for which people in the community must turn to him—
some claim of importance which is recognized by others. It is not
even necessary that the job be itself intrinsically difficult to learn
or perform, so long as it is important to other people and would not
be done except for the labor of those doing it; thus Michael Harrington reports a striking pride of *metier* among many migrant
fruit-pickers in California. It is the status conferred by work that
allows people to live in reasonable contentment with themselves
and others.

The alienation of factory operatives from their work is a story
as old as the assembly line. But technological development continues the spiral. Automation removes workers from direct contact
with the line, and most from the factory itself; fewer workers remain to do more highly skilled jobs. "Service industries" are to
take up the employment slack of automation, in theory, but re-
pairmen, for instance, are little more than salesclerks for replacement parts; consumer goods are built to be sold cheaply and discarded, not repaired when they fail. Printed electrical circuits, for
example, are not, like their more expensive wired predecessors,
repairable by the normal electrician. Other "service" workers—

domestics, waiters, salesclerks, hospital orderlies—are menials easily replaced by anyone from the growing refuse-heap of the society.

But if work loses its diversity, and hence its importance, for a significant proportion of the society, we lose our only means for apportioning status on a roughly equal basis. Other status-givers can confer meaningful prestige only on those who have *more* than others.

Significance of Housing

The consequences of a decline in the prime importance of work are easily deduced. One is a rise in the status-importance of consumption, and of all consumption expenditures, housing has the greatest personal and financial importance; the one-family house with a plot of ground has always been the ideal American home. Its possession and quality have always been marks of social status. By excluding groups of people, communities have appropriated for themselves a mark of class superiority. In Washington, D.C., as in many other cities, houses in communities which exclude Jews (or Negroes) bring higher prices than equivalent houses in otherwise equal areas; the monetary value of such small differences in neighborhood quality should alert us to the fact that housing status is essentially predicated on success in excluding social "inferiors." The use of housing as a symbol of superior status has been increasing. Income-segregation, abetted by public-housing projects in which no member of the middle class will live, is well underway. Trends reported by the New York Metropolitan Region Study are being duplicated elsewhere: luxury apartments will soon house most older people who can afford them; the exodus of white couples with children from the large cities will continue, indeed will probably accelerate as fewer remain. Fair-housing ordinances will be passed in some cities, perhaps even some states; but the trend will, in general, be toward maintenance of racial segregation. (Surely it is significant that California will probably repeal this year, by popular referendum, its established fair-housing law, and that cities like Seattle and Berkeley have voted down fair-housing ordinances.) In the Philadelphia suburb of Folcroft, a few months ago, residents rioted for weeks to prevent a Negro family from moving in; there is no reason to think that community unique.

Education is a second major heir to the status-giving function once dominated by work. The late ebbing of the Sputnik mentality arises only in part from our missile successes. In large part, it is a way of raising a new standard of status—"liberal" education pursued for its own sake, which is particularly appropriate as a means of preserving present status-boundaries. First, it is an overexpensive luxury for the lower classes. Thus, Dr. Conant suggests that education for the poor should be vocational training suited to the jobs they can "reasonably" expect to get; a liberal education cannot be cheapened by too-wide distribution. Moreover, stressing the importance of liberal education insures the future position of the present middle class; its children will, by definition, score better on the class-biased tests which are used to determine their eligibility for such education. Lastly, the poor sense the futility of education in an economy where work (especially the kind for which they are trained) is declining, and shun and deprecate it; this phenomenon in turn serves as proof that opportunity is there, but is not taken advantage of by the poor.

A third critical status factor is income, which is important both in itself and as it affects access to other status-givers. In itself, income has been closely connected with work, often measuring the social worth of the work done; when inherited, it also reflects social class. But as work loses significance, income becomes most important as a determinant of consumption and education. To preserve status in these areas, income differentials will probably be preserved—as by making the tax structure more regressive, and keeping doles well below minimum-wage levels. People whose work is meaningless except as it allows them, by earning money, to differentiate themselves from the poor will continue to oppose large-scale employment projects. Instead, they will support transfer payments at a level too low to allow the recipients to compete for status in housing or education.

Two recent proposals, usually thought of as diametric opposites—the President's Poverty program and the Report of the Ad Hoc Committee on the Triple Revolution—are examples of programs which lend themselves to reinforcement of the social hierarchy.

The Kennedy-Johnson program does some excellent things. It attempts to train workers for jobs; to establish community-service programs for unoccupied youth; and to subsidize employment by special loans to municipalities and private employers. It directly will affect about half a million people. Christopher Jencks has stated its essential premise. . . .[1] The problems of poverty, he noted, will be solved by remedying imperfections in the opportunity-structure—education and jobs (with a side glance at motivation); the measures so far advanced, at any rate, are directed at these imperfections. A rationale advanced for the program's present modest size is that the tax cut will provide more jobs for the economy as a whole; some suggest the program will reach its full growth only after arms expenditures are cut as a result of lowered world tensions. It appears from his recent statements that the President plans to expand the government's domestic activities considerably; a program of rebuilding all our cities and countryside would itself be a major step toward the poverty war's expressed goals.

But if my earlier speculations are correct, expansion of the poverty war, or any government activity which tends to lessen class distinctions, will encounter resistance which increases in direct proportion to its size and probable effectiveness. Indeed, I would argue that the program thus far advanced has been received quietly because its fundamentally middle-class principles can be used by the middle class to prevent more significant action. Thus its concentration on opening up the opportunity-structure could be used

1. Jencks, Christopher, "Johnson vs. Poverty," *The New Republic*, March 28, 1964, pp. 15–18. [Author's note]

to justify inaction on government employment programs tailored to large numbers of the un- and underemployed. Similarly, the emphasis on job training could be used to justify class segregation in education à la Dr. Conant and reliance for job expansion on the tax cut could justify regressive taxation as an economic policy to aid the poor.

Guaranteed Incomes

But for all the long-range political dangers of the poverty program's initial direction, it is on far firmer ground than that of the Ad Hoc Committee on the Triple Revolution. Starting from the premise that further increases in worker productivity will make a scarcity-based economy irrelevant, the Ad Hoc Committee sees the vital function of the economy shifted from production to consumption. If machines can produce everything that is within our capacity to consume, and work is available to only a small fraction of the society, then consumption should be separated from labor; manifestly, it is as pointless to deny the products of the automatic machines to those without work as it would be to deny them air or sunlight. Income, therefore, should be guaranteed and paid by the government, regardless of work done in exchange.

In fact, this report is more a projection of the economy in fifty years' time than it is a blueprint for today; in this respect, it is an admirable effort at advanced social planning. But its advanced liberal tone should not blind us to its danger. Of all the devices that have been invented to keep the status-poor in their place, putting them on a dole is by far the most effective. The size of the dole can be controlled so as to keep them always in comparative poverty, and thus unable to compete for higher status in the society; indeed, the fact of being on the dole itself leads to lessened aspiration and pride. Most of the present unemployed continue to covet work because the society's ethic commands it; to make the dole legitimate is to lessen significantly the pressure for reform from below.

The dole, of course, would be extended gradually, in the form of increasing present welfare payments and extending their coverage. The gradual change would start with the present poor; and since the middle class would still have jobs when the dole was extended, a substantial differentiation would be maintained between dole-income and prevailing middle-class wage rates. This differential would then serve as a method for preserving housing and educational segregation and quality differentials. As more of the middle class lose traditional work, however, they would not slip onto the dole and into the ranks of the status-poor. Instead in all probability, they would become social-service workers of an advanced sort—tending, of course, to the needs of the poor. Or they might find large-scale employment overseas, as in a "Management Corps" to aid administration in the poor nations. Means will be found to preserve their status vis-à-vis the poor simply because the middle class is larger and has higher cards.

These developments are not inevitable; they can, and should, be arrested and reversed. But the programs so far suggested, even the most radical, treat symptoms—the poor—and not the illness, which is a loss of meaningful work for most of the society. So long as they treat symptoms which are directed primarily at poverty, they will be restricted by the majority to glorified pilot projects; the existence of these limited projects will salve the conscience and the egos of the middle class.

It cannot be said too often that we are faced with a problem of time, that the resistance of the middle class to change will increase as their own assurance decreases and the lower classes (particularly Negroes) assert themselves more strongly. But neither can it be stressed too much that to castigate the midlle class for their resistance to change is both useless and irresponsible. That resistance is based on sound fears that an effective drive on poverty will narrow status-differentials between them and the present poor. Those who criticize middle-class ignorance usually do so from privileged sanctuaries: a Harvard education, a house in an all-white suburb, and a firm position in the academic-political-foundation hierarchy guarantee status which will not be jeopardized no matter what improvement is made in the lot of the poor. But the increasingly useless middle class is being asked to surrender its claims to any superiority of status; even where jobs are insecure and meaningless, simply having one gives status superior to those who cannot support their families without public assistance. The middle class sense this perfectly, and no amount of talk about side effects on consumption and employment will convince them otherwise. A serious program must offer the middle class a new life style in return for the raise in status it would give to the poor; it must deal not only (or even primarily) with pockets of economic poverty, but with the poverty of satisfaction, purpose, and dignity that afflicts us all.

FOR THE STUDENT

Rhetoric

1. *What figure of speech appears in the first sentence? Explain its effectiveness.*
2. *In paragraph two, why is "myths" enclosed in quotation marks?*
3. *Look up* Luddite *in your dictionary in order to explain the phrase "Luddite strikes."*
4. *What would you make the major topics in an outline of this essay?*

Discussion

1. *Define the nature of the argument set forth to prove that the middle class does not wish to have poverty eliminated.*
2. *What connection exists between the general decline in the significance of work and the elimination of poverty?*

3. *Are you pursuing a college education for some of the snob values appreciated by the middle class?*

4. *Show that each major argument in the essay demonstrates the need to eliminate spiritual poverty in order to eliminate economic poverty.*

5. *Spencer argued, again in* Social Statics, *that poverty purifies society; hence, any attempt to eliminate poverty is morally wrong. Does Walinsky suggest that the middle class in any way makes a connection between poverty and morality?*

Writing

1. *Since the poverty issue is highly controversial, you may wish to reply to one of Walinsky's specific points. Remember that generalities based on narrow experience provide very shaky proof at best. Do not use this suggestion unless you have sufficient facts and details to support your contention.*

2. *Develop by means of illustration the statement: "People above oneself are regarded as no better than equal; people below oneself are regarded as inferior."*

3. *Theme topic: "Work as a status symbol."*